THE REVOLUTION OF '28

THE REVOLUTION
OF '28

AL SMITH, AMERICAN PROGRESSIVISM,
AND THE COMING OF THE NEW DEAL

ROBERT CHILES

CORNELL UNIVERSITY PRESS
Ithaca and London

First published 2018 by Cornell University Press
Printed in the United States of America

Library of Congress Cataloging-in-Publication Data

Names: Chiles, Robert Elliot, 1982– author.
Title: The revolution of '28 : Al Smith, American
    progressivism, and the coming of the New Deal /
    Robert Chiles.
Description: Ithaca : Cornell University Press, 2018. |
    Includes bibliographical references and index.
Identifiers: LCCN 2017028412 (print) | LCCN 2017028881
    (ebook) | ISBN 9781501714191 (pdf) | ISBN
    9781501714184 (epub/mobi) | ISBN 9781501705502
    (cloth : alk. paper)
Subjects: LCSH: Progressivism (United States politics)—
    History. | United States—Politics and govern-
    ment—1919–1933.
Classification: LCC E784 (ebook) | LCC E784 .C45 2018
    (print) | DDC 324.2732/7—dc23
LC record available at https://lccn.loc.gov/2017028412

Cornell University Press strives to use environmentally responsible suppliers and materials to the fullest extent possible in the publishing of its books. Such materials include vegetable-based, low-VOC inks and acid-free papers that are recycled, totally chlorine-free, or partly composed of nonwood fibers. For further information, visit our website at cornellpress.cornell.edu.

Cloth printing   10 9 8 7 6 5 4 3 2 1

*To Leslie
and Sarah
with love*

CONTENTS

ACKNOWLEDGMENTS

I am profoundly thankful for the support provided by Cornell University Press. First and foremost, I am grateful to Michael McGandy, who believed in this project from its earliest stages and provided both the vigorous advocacy and the constructive critiques necessary to transform my sprawling manuscript into a streamlined monograph. I am also particularly thankful to Bethany Wasik, Martyn Beeny, and Karen Hwa from Cornell Press, who all cheerfully helped me navigate the production process at various stages, as well as to Kristen Bettcher and Barbara Goodhouse of Westchester Publishing Services, who assiduously copyedited the manuscript and patiently collaborated with me to produce what I hope will prove a pleasantly readable ultimate product. Finally, I am greatly obliged to the two anonymous peer reviewers, whose critical insights helped me sharpen my argument and articulate my findings with further precision.

At the University of Maryland, David Sicilia consistently pressed me to be ambitious in both conceptualization and execution, while offering steadfast support from day one. Robyn Muncy also exhibited unwavering enthusiasm for this project, providing invaluable feedback grounded in her own mastery of overlapping themes. Whit Ridgway, Julie Greene, David Karol, James Henretta, Sonya Michel, James Gilbert, Lisa Mar, Keith Olson, Kate Keane, and Tom Zeller all provided helpful insights on diverse portions of this work at various stages of development.

Beyond College Park, many scholars contributed to this book's creation. William Leuchtenburg, dean of New Deal historians, provided both critical insights and kind guidance from very early in the research process. Oscar and Lilian Handlin both read portions of my output and were incredibly generous in discussing my work and counseling me more broadly on the vicissitudes of academic life. Richard Hamm, Lauren Kozakiewicz, Daniel Georgianna, and a host of others offered helpful commentary on sundry portions of the work. My colleague at Loyola University Maryland, Tom Pegram, was especially generous—reading the complete manuscript and providing key insights at crucial stages of the revision process. I am especially grateful for the thorough consideration of John Buenker, the leading historian of urban liberalism, who read several iterations of this manuscript in their entirety and offered valuable advice on my work and warm mentorship in my scholarly development.

During the research process I enjoyed support from too many archivists and librarians to name; the staffs at the New York State Library and the New York State Archives in Albany were especially helpful. I was also aided with material support. I am grateful for monetary awards from the New York State Library Cunningham Research Residency and the New York State Archives Partnership Trust Hackman Research Residency. The University of Maryland Department of History provided research and travel funds at various stages, and I am grateful to the chair, Phil Soergel, for his sustained generosity. Of even greater value was the childcare provided by a number of friends and family, especially my mother, Bonnie Chiles.

Most of all I want to thank my wife, Leslie, and my daughter, Sarah. The challenges of raising a child and caring for a family while teaching five or more courses per semester and composing and revising a historical monograph at times proved overwhelming; yet for any difficulties this may have presented, my daughter Sarah, who is now almost nine, is also deserving of thanks. Unconsciously, she compelled from me a level of self-discipline that strengthened my scholarship; naturally, she provided love and adventure and fun that kept me moored to humanity in the most challenging phases of my work. Indeed, nothing about this project was undertaken alone, and along with Sarah, my wife, Leslie, is deserving of the most thanks of all. Patiently enduring frustrations with me and cheering my small triumphs along the way, Leslie created with her unconditional love and support a world imperturbably secure from the worst uncertainties of scholarly life. Simultaneously, she has remained uniquely steadfast in her belief that I would succeed. It was Leslie who first convinced me to pursue the academic life (a fact of which I remind her regularly), and it has been her love and her faith in my endeavors that have inspired me occasionally to believe along with her.

THE REVOLUTION OF '28

Introduction
The Happy Warrior

> The campaign now beginning will prove memorable for many reasons. . . . It is destined to be marked by a breaking up of old political lines and the formation of new ones.
>
> —Senator Joseph T. Robinson (D-AR), August 31, 1928

It was a crisp New England autumn morning as the Democratic "Victory Special" steamed eastward into Massachusetts from upstate New York. On October 24, 1928, the temperature in Boston had dropped from an unseasonable 75 degrees the previous afternoon into the mid-fifties. By 3:30 p.m., when the locomotive arrived at South Station, the city had settled into "one of Boston's cloudy Fall days, considerably cooler than yesterday."[1] The anticipatory autumnal chill resulting from this atmospheric dynamism presaged with a sort of meteorological poetry the wave of energy and upheaval that would sweep from the Berkshires down to Massachusetts Bay in the wake of the Albany-born train. On board was the Democratic nominee for the presidency—the governor of New York, noted progressive crusader, champion of the urban working class, unashamed Catholic, and proponent of pluralist tolerance and liberal economic reform, Alfred E. Smith.

The train slowed first at Pittsfield in the west, greeted by 10,000 supporters; then "goodly numbers" cheered at Westfield, followed by about 30,000 at Springfield, where a band hailed the visitor with his familiar theme, "The Sidewalks of New York." There, Massachusetts senator David Ignatius Walsh, an Irish-Catholic Democrat from Fitchburg and a noted friend of labor, extended greetings on behalf of the New Yorker, who, on instructions of his physician, was saving his voice for the evening. Onward to Worcester, where another crowd of 30,000 filled Washington Square before that city's station and, less

1

concerned over its own vocal endurance, "yelled itself hoarse." Platforms at Framingham, Natick, and Newton all "jammed with cheering, flag-waving crowds." Finally, Boston. On Boston Common, Smith was greeted by 150,000. At Boston Arena, only 15,000 were able to enter out of the 50,000 who sought admittance, while avid mobs numbering in the hundreds of thousands radiated outward for blocks, enthralled by reports of events within proclaimed by an army of radios—all this as two other capacious auditoriums, Mechanics Hall and Symphony Hall, remained packed to the brim with ardent listeners after the nominee's brief greetings to those "delirious" overflow meetings. A reporter from New York found "the passion of the people . . . appalling in its intensity, more like what might be seen at a monster religious revival than at a political gathering." All told, police estimated that 750,000 people flooded the streets of Boston to greet the governor of New York—a gathering 2,000 greater than the city's population at the time of the 1920 census.[2]

Why had they come? What did they hear? How did they respond? In microcosm, these are the essential questions of this work; and the answers promise to enhance our understanding of American political development in the interwar period. Smith's national prominence as a gubernatorial champion of social welfare and of the laboring masses and his ambition to implement and expand that particular progressivism at the federal level, blended with his biographical appeal to a growing cohort of newer voters as a representative of the urban ethnic working classes, inspired these boisterous receptions in many of the nation's heterogeneous industrial cities—most especially but not exclusively in New England. In each case these crowds not only obliterated local attendance records but also received detailed explications of the Democrat's progressive vision for the United States, affirming his well-earned reputation for "getting at the heart of things and popularizing very abstruse questions so that the average fellow could understand them" and fulfilling his pledge to maintain "direct contact with the people . . . in this campaign."[3] The response produced the revolutionary early stages of a national political reshuffling that would help spur the onset of modern American liberalism.

Thus, the candidate's utterances mattered profoundly. American politics— like American life—moved briskly by the late 1920s. Three decades of maturation by increasingly organized, well-funded national parties begat a dynamic continental politics; well-established press agencies and wire services allowed campaign updates (and propaganda) to proliferate swiftly to a news-hungry public through a zealously competitive and often fiercely partisan local press; while the radio, a much more recent innovation, transmitted major and minor campaign personalities into the living rooms of millions of prospective voters nightly. Within the frenzied milieu of the Roaring Twenties, monitored by an unrestrained press and a diverse electorate, political campaigns were a frenetic rush of promises and polemics that—despite some leading politicians' reputations for reticence—demanded programmatic candor before a skeptical public and perpetual cultivation of an enthusiastic base.

The stakes for the Boston address were especially high. No serious contender for the presidency could allow the toxic charge of socialism to be associated with his national ambitions—and such was Smith's challenge beginning two days before his arrival in Boston, when his opponent, Herbert Hoover, alerted a crowd at New York's Madison Square Garden that their governor had offered "a series of proposals which, if adopted, would be a long step toward the abandonment of our American system and a surrender to the destructive operation of governmental conduct of commercial business"—that Smith had "abandon[ed] the tenets of [his] own party" in favor of "State socialism."[4] Hoover, the much-heralded commerce secretary and Republican standard-bearer, was seeking the White House as the engineer of the political economy of the 1920s, promising to "go forward with the policies of the last eight years"; he and his supporters saw Smith's progressive agenda as a threat to their "New Era."[5]

Forty-eight hours later, Smith responded to Hoover's indictment. It was an attack with which he had been grappling for his entire career, and thus the charges invited the governor to review his progressive bona fides. "Take the workmen's compensation act," he implored his Boston hearers.

> What was the argument against that? Because it set up an insurance company under State ownership and State operation, it was referred to as socialism. Take all the factory code. Take the night work law for women, the law prohibiting manufacturing in tenements, the [law] prohibiting the working of children in the tanneries of the State, the bill prohibiting the working of women in the core rooms of foundries. That great factory code in New York, designed to protect the health, the welfare and the well-being of men, women and children at some time or the other in the last twenty-five years has been referred to as paternalistic and socialistic.[6]

Smith vigorously agreed with at least one of Hoover's assertions: that the Democrat's proposals were "serious" and that articulation of these controversies "submitted to the American people a question of fundamental principle."[7] Therefore Smith not only catalogued the past; he applied that record to the present. Dissenting from popular accolades for the Coolidge economy, he outlined the ongoing depression of New England's textile industry and contrasted that widespread suffering with Hoover's sanguine remarks on workers' living standards to postulate a general Republican neglect of the laboring classes. Smith's alternative policy approach was revealed in his record of progressive social welfare and labor reforms in New York—and so Republican cries of socialism were portrayed as a renewed attempt by "selfish" groups to derail "forward-looking, constructive suggestions" for the "betterment of the human element."[8]

Smith was running against the Harding-Coolidge-Hoover status quo, and while subsequent historians—like contemporary élites—have failed to appreciate this fact, Smith's followers were quite receptive to the message. Understanding Smith's presidential aspirations within the context of his progressive governorship, an Irishman from New York's Lower East Side prodded the maverick Nebraska Republican George W. Norris to back the Democrat, boasting that "the New York 'Wonder Man'" had "lambasted the reactionaries here . . . so that their lives are hardly worth living."[9] The Smith-boosting *Brooklyn Eagle* invoked a similar understanding of the Democrat's agenda—portraying him in one political cartoon "stepping out" into "national affairs" from the foundation of his "record as governor of N.Y." and armed with his set of progressive "issues."[10] Working-class voters beyond the Empire State also understood Smith's progressive challenge to the Republican political economy and made it their own: an Italian American voter in Newark composed a scathing denunciation of employment conditions by citing numbers and arguments propagated by the Smith campaign; a pseudonymous Hartford worker assailed the "insulting" notion of Republican prosperity; a Polish American in western Massachusetts excoriated the incumbent party for having "furthered, protected, and fostered the special interests of a certain few against the common interests of the many"; an Italian American Rhode Islander decried the Coolidge administration's "favoritism" toward powerful industrialists in justifying his community's support for the Democratic nominee.[11]

Smith, dubbed "the Happy Warrior" by his ally and gubernatorial successor, Franklin Delano Roosevelt, is rightly remembered as a progressive executive.[12] One study of his governorship, by the historian Paula Eldot, goes as far as to suggest that "Smith represents a transitional stage between progressivism and the New Deal."[13] However, historians have not similarly understood Al Smith's campaign for the presidency. Eldot's study, while recognizing the "transitional" nature of Smith's administration in New York, did not scrutinize his presidential run. Meanwhile, scholars concerned with 1928 have portrayed Smith's national campaign in a different light than his years as governor. The historian David Burner, in his crucial work on 1920s Democratic politics, suggested that Smith's campaign was essentially conservative, and this position has proved to be the prevailing academic interpretation.[14]

Historians have thus determined that, as Smith biographer Robert Slayton suggests, 1928 saw "no substantial issue to differentiate the parties," rendering the campaign "a contest between personalities."[15] Indeed, Smith's personality has come to dominate the scholarly understanding of his presidential run. A typical description in a 1992 academic work introduces the 1928 Democratic presidential nominee thus: "Al Smith was as urban as the Brooklyn Bridge near which he had grown up, as Irish as the Blarney Stone, and as Catholic as St. Patrick's Cathedral."[16] Such caricatures, however poetic, divert scholarly attention toward a total fixation on the candidate's personality, obscuring the serious policy ideas of Smith and his closest associates. This historical interpretation draws from a long tradition of élite dismissiveness—a reality lamented by contemporary Smith supporters: "Some of our best people make the mistake of forming their impressions of this man Smith from the comic cartoons which overemphasize his back-slapping, hand-shaking, hat-waving, his very evident joy in political contest and taking his message to the people. They have not looked into the record of his victories for progressive legislation, for conservation of natural resources of the state, for public health, for better administration of the state's business, for the welfare of men and women in industry, for protection of children, for honesty in government."[17] Smith continued throughout his presidential campaign to argue doggedly for his progressive vision of the government's responsibility to implement a broadly defined social welfare regime, improve the lot of the working class, and respect the dignity of the diverse members of modern American society.

With a focus on the political implications of policy ideas, my work seeks to revise the prevailing view of the Happy Warrior and his fervent followers. Understanding Smith as his time's leading exponent of an important branch of the progressive tradition helps place him in proper perspective: squarely at the center of an evolutionary process that connected aspects of progressivism with central portions of the New Deal. Recognizing that his supporters—like his opponent—understood the seriousness of the Smith program reveals the early manifestations of a popular political movement that transformed the Democracy into the party of working-class pluralistic liberalism.

In fact, the urban, ethnic, working-class voters who would soon constitute the backbone of the Roosevelt coalition embraced *both* the cultural symbolism of the Smith candidacy *and* the progressive initiatives the candidate expounded. Smith's Catholicism, his working-class roots, his disdain for Prohibition and for the Ku Klux Klan—these attributes all had a clear influence on voters in 1928, and they benefited Smith greatly among urban workers, just as they would prove unpalatable among voters in other parts of the nation. But leaving the story at that is superficial—perhaps even condescending.

I have proceeded from the hypothesis that, like any other human actors, the real people who became Smith Democrats in 1928—the ones who did the working and praying and suffering and voting that historians have attempted to decipher—were complex beings with complicated motivations. There is no question that there were many voters like Nazzareno Marconi of Wilkes-Barre, Pennsylvania, who wrote to Smith, in Italian, to assure him that "we Catholic people do not get tired of working for your victory."[18] But there were others, like Joseph F. Nolan of Westfield, New Jersey, an Irish American first-time voter, who explained to the *Newark Evening News* that Smith's gubernatorial résumé was "ample proof of his ability. If that record is indicative of what is to be expected of him in the event of his election the United States is destined for one of the most distinguished administrations in its history."[19] In fact, this is not an either-or proposition. Most Smith voters were sophisticated enough to understand the Democratic candidate as representing *both* cultural pluralism *and* social and economic reform—and most of those voters were clamoring for each by 1928. This combination of cultural empowerment with social welfare appeals had been the formula of Smith's progressive governorship, and it was the platform from which he sought the presidency. In 1928, Al Smith nationalized his particular brand of progressivism; and while he went down to a bitter defeat that year, the ideas he promoted were taken up by his enthusiastic supporters and, through their efforts, infused the reforms of the New Deal with those earlier progressive priorities.

In 1927, the journalist Walter Lippmann delineated what would become the consensus view on the national significance of Al Smith, then in his fourth term as governor of New York: "Smith is the first child of the new immigration who might be President of the United States. He carries with him the hopes, the sense of self-respect, and the grievances of that great mass of newer Americans who feel that they have never been wholly accepted as part of the American community. . . . Many of them are Catholics, most of them are wet, most of them live in cities. Those are all superficial facts as against the fundamental fact that they are all immigrants. . . . He comes from a class of citizens who are felt to be alien to the historic American ideal."[20] In this passage, Lippmann set down many of the important tropes that continue to dominate the historical understanding of Alfred E. Smith.

Indeed, these themes have retained their prominence with justification. In 1928, Al Smith became the first Roman Catholic to secure a major party presidential nomination. He openly opposed Prohibition, rhetorically bludgeoned the Ku Klux Klan, and thoughtfully challenged immigration quotas that had been rooted in an Anglo-Saxon conception of Americanism. His campaign theme song was "The Sidewalks of New York," and his trademark brown derby—along with his perpetual cigar—became a staple within contemporary political iconography. His speeches were delivered, unapologetically, in the raspy tones, dubious pronunciation, and proletarian diction of the Bowery.

All of this reflected Smith's background. Indeed, in order to understand Al Smith's personality and his politics, one must understand Manhattan's Fourth Ward. A geographically small community on New York's Lower East Side, it had absorbed thousands of Irish refugees during the mid-nineteenth century. The historian Oscar Handlin described the neighborhood as "a motley array of tenements, of converted warehouses, of dwellings in every stage of repair and decay, and of shacks and shanties" that, as a waterfront district, had acquired an "unsavory" reputation as a den of ruffians. Nevertheless, it was cheap to live near the wharves along the East River, and so the Fourth Ward's population of impoverished, unskilled laborers continued to swell, while these families struggled mightily to raise their children in an environment secluded from the surrounding vice.[21]

The son and namesake of a Civil War veteran, Alfred Emanuel Smith was born December 30, 1873, and grew up on South Street, one of the Fourth Ward's many narrow, bustling cobblestone roads.[22] Like the lion's share of their neighbors, the Smiths were Irish, Catholic, and poor.[23] Young Al Smith started to work part time at age eleven; the next year, when he was in the eighth grade, his father died, and the boy was forced to leave school and go to work full time.[24] For several years he labored twelve-hour days (that began at 4:00 a.m.) as a checker at the Fulton Fish Market and later moved on to a position at a pumping station in Brooklyn.[25] In the decades that followed, Smith would often joke that "his only academic degree was an F. F. M., standing for Fulton Fish Market."[26]

As with so many ethnic, working-class ghettos throughout Manhattan, another fundamental characteristic of the Fourth Ward was the omnipotence of Tammany Hall. The most notorious political machine in U.S. history, Tammany emerged from the tumultuous political reshuffling of the Civil War era with a working-class immigrant following that powered its dominance of New York City until the election of Fiorello La Guardia as mayor in 1933.[27] Its formula for success, according to Gilded Age district heeler George Washington Plunkitt, lay in the organization's ability to satisfy basic human needs: through patronage, mostly in the form of municipal jobs; and with benevolent acts to ease the daily burdens of constituents—a bucket of coal when money was tight, bailing a son out of jail after a night of hooliganism, and other such favors.[28] All of this forged a sense of community and a spirit of fealty between machine and constituent, securing generations of political loyalty in the process.

These operations also required exorbitant sums of money—funds easily obtained over decades of extortion, looting the city treasury, and accepting kickbacks for lucrative municipal contracts.[29]

Such was the political school in which Al Smith was educated. The Plunkitt of the Fourth Ward was "Big Tim" Sullivan, but for Smith the most important political lessons were learned from saloonkeeper Tom Foley, considered the "real boss" by many in the neighborhood.[30] As *Time* magazine would later note, "His college was the Society of St. Tammany and his freshman courses were in addressing postcards to voters" and "watching the polls," until "Tammany promoted him to speechmaking in his district and his name began to get into the newspapers" as he "worked for other men's elections."[31] During this period the young Tammany man, who was also an aspiring actor, married Catherine Ann Dunn, and within a few years the couple moved to the Oliver Street home that would be forever associated with Al Smith.[32] By 1903, Tom Foley, frustrated with an assemblyman who "seemed to have forgotten his friends," sent the faithful Smith to Albany.[33]

During his first legislative session, Smith did not make a single speech.[34] He "found himself entirely disregarded and completely confused."[35] Amplifying Smith's frustration was his total inability to comprehend the stacks of arcane legislation that daily cluttered his desk and his mind with legalistic esoterica. Yet the young assemblyman was tenacious. Each night, while other legislators caroused in local pubs, Smith would retire early and thoroughly dissect each bill—developing not only an understanding of specific pieces of legislation but also a critical eye for the mechanics of state government. With time, he earned a positive reputation among his colleagues; and in 1911, after revelations of corruption among legislative Republicans ushered in a Democratic majority, Smith was the logical choice for Tammany sachem Charles Francis "Silent Charlie" Murphy to promote for majority leader.[36] After a brief foray into New York City politics as sheriff and then as president of the board of aldermen, Alfred E. Smith was elected governor of the Empire State in 1918. A decade later, his party nominated him for the White House.

My understanding of this period necessarily builds on the works of many past historians. Some of the most significant contributions to my thinking have come from the scholarship of J. Joseph Huthmacher and John D. Buenker on "urban liberalism"; Robyn Muncy and Elisabeth Perry, among others, on women's social work progressivism; and William E. Leuchtenburg on the New Deal era. I have also considered the works of numerous scholars of Alfred E. Smith, from Oscar Handlin (1958) to Robert Slayton (2001).

However, it will be equally apparent that what I am proposing is a revisionist argument, and I intend to present points of strong disagreement both with the aforementioned scholars and with a large number of other excellent historians of the period. My interventions are fundamental but not sweeping. I do not contend that Al Smith was the father of the New Deal; nor do I suggest that the connections between progressivism and New Deal liberalism can be understood solely through consideration of Smith's political career. The origins of the liberal reforms of the 1930s were too fantastically complex, diverse, and situational for any hypothesis of singular causation to be useful or tenable.

What I am arguing is that (1) during the 1920s, Al Smith consistently pursued a specialized progressivism—centered on social welfare, labor protections, and cultural pluralism—the roots of which are discernible within the broader sweep of Progressive Era reform; (2) Smith and his allies grounded his presidential aspirations in his record of battling for those priorities as governor of New York and continued throughout the 1928 campaign to offer voters a vigorous economic reformism along with a pluralistic interpretation of Americanism; (3) new-stock, working-class voters in the nation's great industrial cities, and especially throughout Depression-ravaged New England, understood and were attracted to Smith's candidacy on both economic and cultural levels and responded electorally, forging new, durable state-level coalitions and precipitating a metamorphosis of the national Democratic Party; and (4) the cohort of northeastern urban liberals who ascended to congressional prominence during the 1930s continued to pursue the agenda Smith had nationalized in 1928, expressing the specific economic and cultural priorities of their constituents and exerting a fundamental influence on the direction of New Deal liberalism from within an evolving Democratic Party.

Clearly, then, this is not a political biography. Rather, this study's purpose is to trace the development of a particular reform vision that was profoundly influential among the urban, ethnic, working-class voters who emerged as the core of the Democratic coalition during the New Deal era. Al Smith was the premier proponent of that vision and the foremost practitioner of its concomitant policy program, and so his career provides the ideal means for understanding this idiomatic progressivism. Comprehending this humane vision of labor protections, social welfare initiatives, and pluralist tolerance while tracing the sources of that vision within recent-immigrant and working-class communities in the early decades of the twentieth century contextualizes the politics of the 1920s and 1930s at the vibrant intersection of grassroots experience and partisan competition. Exploring that partisan electoral competition in depth, moreover, yields a more holistic and historical understanding of that idiomatic progressivism and its interaction with the broader polity; for, as the historian Julian E. Zelizer asserts, "a focus on elections forces historians to see the political landscape as historical actors did."[37]

The first two chapters chart the development of Smith's progressivism and its implementation during his gubernatorial administration. In chapter 1, I explore how the progressivism of Smith's New York Democratic Party emerged from the interaction of female social welfare activists and urban ethnic machine politicians during the 1910s and 1920s. Chapter 2 considers specific policy initiatives undertaken by Governor Smith and demonstrates ways in which these programs were tangible manifestations of Smith's progressivism—through both the establishment of a broadly defined social welfare regime and key administrative reforms. Smith was an economic reformer with a robust agenda *as well as* a symbol of urban-immigrant America, and since I maintain that voters in 1928 were amply abreast of Smith's gubernatorial progressivism, these chapters contextualize the presidential politics that followed.

Chapters 3 through 5 present my interpretation of the 1928 presidential contest, answering those fundamental questions about why voters were interested in Smith's candidacy; what they heard from the candidate; and how they responded to the politics of the day. Chapter 3 focuses on the "what" question, exploring the major policy debates of 1928 and presenting them as part of a revisionist narrative of the campaign. Chapter 4 addresses the "how," by dissecting the popular response to that campaign and providing quantitative analysis of the electoral results and their significance, while situating my findings within the long-running "critical election" debate. Chapter 5 delves into by far the trickiest issue—the "why" question—through a regional case study of southern New England, where Smith experienced his greatest triumphs. Charting in detail developments in Massachusetts, Rhode Island, and Connecticut reveals the complex origins of the political upheavals of 1928, demonstrating how Smith's progressive rhetoric interacted with working-class ethnic New Englanders' sense of isolation from the 1920s American polity on both economic and cultural levels to fuel a revolutionary political transformation. I conclude by following the developments of 1928 into the 1930s, suggesting ways in which the many enduring proponents of Smith's particular progressivism exerted a primal influence on the development of New Deal liberalism.

CHAPTER 1

The Making of a Progressive

The period between the unofficial close of the Progressive Era (sometime shortly after the Armistice and the precipitous decline of Wilsonianism) and the inauguration of Franklin Delano Roosevelt to the presidency was not simply an unchallenged conservative interregnum.[1] To be sure, this "long 1920s" was marked by the cult of the businessman, cultural clashes, and laissez-faire governance. But even as Bruce Barton preached the virtues of corporate prowess, even while William Jennings Bryan delivered jeremiads on the decline of traditional values and Calvin Coolidge made laconic indifference a heroic trait, a progressive ideology and style persisted that would serve to link the two periods of reform within a longer liberal tradition.

During the long 1920s, New York Democratic governor Alfred E. Smith, along with a motley group of reform-minded allies, practiced a specialized, idiomatic progressivism that affected both public policy and electoral politics in the Empire State. This particular progressivism drew from various "progressivisms" of the past, arranging previously unrelated or even antagonistic elements within one consistent agenda for the state and eventually the nation. Of equal significance, Smith and his progressive colleagues politicized this agenda in a radically new way, transposing their reform platform into Democratic partisan dogma. Although the political ramifications were novel, this reformism emerged from long-established elements; identifying those elements and tracing the process by which they were blended reveals the complex heritage of Al Smith's progressivism, as well as the peculiar conditions under which that progressivism was forged.

The diversity and inconsistency of American progressivism have vexed historians for generations. In response, scholars have defined progressivism as everything from a reactionary defense against a "status revolution" to a rationalization of government in response to modernizing technological and economic forces; from a movement to homogenize the citizenry and control social conflict on the part of the middle class to a set of tools for dealing with industrial society imported from late nineteenth-century Europe by cosmopolitan intellectuals, to a drive to establish the political ascendancy of the "public interest" over interest group, class, or partisan goals.[2] Studies have thus located the core progressive constituency variously: old-money "Mugwump" reformers, the professional middle class of the new industrial order, worldly scholars and social activists, settlement house pioneers—even urban machine politicians.[3] Moreover, some scholars have questioned whether a "progressive movement" existed at all, and others have suggested that there was no ideological uniformity across the various political drives of the reputedly progressive decades, merely shared "clusters of ideas" and "social languages" that were drawn on by sundry interest groups.[4] Indeed, some studies have demonstrated that the rhetoric of progressivism was easily appropriated by partisans and injected into the public sphere toward nonreformist, highly divisive ends.[5]

Amid this whirl of academic ambivalence over the "age of reform," there is room for a diversity of "progressives" or even "progressivisms" within the working definition of that concept.[6] The objective of the present study is more tangible and precise: to chart the historical forces that produced the specific progressivism practiced by Alfred E. Smith as governor of New York. At its core, Smith's reformism represented the confluence of two important streams of progressive ideology: urban liberalism and social welfare progressivism.

Urban liberalism was a form of progressivism prevalent among machine politicians, who realized that ameliorative social and labor legislation was an increasingly effective way to retain the political loyalties of their urban ethnic working-class constituents.[7] It grew out of the pragmatic machine tradition of urban politics and adopted reform and welfare legislation as means of securing power in lieu of the more traditional, feudalistic system of building fealty to the machine through personal favors.[8] The introduction of this concept to the study of progressive politics by scholars such as J. Joseph Huthmacher and John D. Buenker in the 1960s represented a significant shift in the analysis of early twentieth-century reform. It directly challenged previous treatments, most of which had portrayed progressive reformers as "likely to be from urban, upper middle class backgrounds" and as "native-born Protestants of old Anglo-American stock" and college graduates, who were usually "either professional men, particularly lawyers, or businessmen who represented neither the very largest nor the very smallest businesses."[9]

Urban liberalism scholars agreed with earlier analyses that during the Progressive Era the "sovereign individualist" culture of old-stock Anglo-America, represented by the progressive profile quoted above, was in conflict with the "organic network" culture largely retained by recent immigrants and central to the success of urban political machines.[10] However, these revisionists differed from their predecessors' exclusive assignment of the label "progressive" within this cultural contest. Indeed, the political disciples of the organic network culture often supported progressive reforms as strongly as the sovereign individualist politicians.[11]

To be sure, the reformist tendencies of urban machines were often masked by their scandalous administration of city affairs and relentless plundering of the municipal treasury. Indeed, many of the politicians who would later be identified as urban liberals had benefited directly from the machines' sprawling patronage operations—and since patronage was one of the most distressing targets of old-stock middle-class progressivism's ire, these figures could at best be viewed by contemporaries as an ironic source of progress. Nevertheless, urban liberalism analyses of progressive politics were able to sift through these incongruities, rightly presenting urban ethnic politicians as at least opportunistic reformers and demonstrating how rank-and-file urban ethnic voters developed an increasingly astute understanding of government's potential to improve living and working conditions.

Social welfare progressivism was a manifestation of the reform impulse that grew largely out of the settlement house tradition and was generally the progressivism of female social workers.[12] It focused on improving the living and working conditions of the urban poor through settlement house work, education campaigns, and pressuring industry with protests and boycotts by organizations such as the National Consumers' League—as well as through lobbying state legislatures for specific welfare and labor laws. As the large majority of the movement's leaders were college graduates, a central aspect of these reformers' modus operandi was scientific surveys of conditions to determine appropriate social remedies. Social welfare progressives often fit the classic progressive profile rather well—they tended to be well-educated, middle-class, old-stock Protestants—except they were women. Indeed, essential to understanding social welfare progressivism is consideration of its development as a largely female enterprise.

The Progressive Era witnessed the entry of more women into public life than any previous age; but this influx of female activists did not occur unhindered, for Victorian ideas about "separate spheres" for the sexes persisted into that period, often excluding female reformers from "professions traditionally dominated by men" and forcing these women "to create within the public realm a new territory they could rule themselves . . . that territory of policy and professional expertise which affected women and children exclusively."[13] Thus barred from established policy-making institutions, female reformers entered public life at the end of the nineteenth century by opening settlement houses, most notably Jane Addams's Hull-House in Chicago. Experiences like those at Hull-House "supplied the values and strategies" that made it possible for these women to create what the historian Robyn Muncy has called "a female dominion within the larger empire of policymaking."[14] Critically, these progressive women were not only constructing their own institutions; they were also formulating a unique reform ideology within those institutions— an ideology that heartily endorsed labor regulations and government welfare programs, particularly on behalf of children, mothers, and the poor.[15]

The alliance between the cigar-chomping, glad-handing, opportunistic ward heeler and the college-educated, old-stock, often moralistic female reformer is a strikingly unnatural one at first glance. Machine politicians often benefited from (or participated in) unsavory or illegal activities, were primarily interested in retaining power, and generally held chauvinistic attitudes toward female civic participation—fittingly summarized by the Boston boss Martin "Mahatma" Lomasney, who declared that in politics, "you can't trust these women, they are apt to blab everything they know."[16] Meanwhile, female reformers could at times be culturally insensitive toward immigrants, generally favored Prohibition, and often advocated dismantling political machines.[17] Nor was this alliance, once forged, unproblematic—for example, during a heated exchange, Al Smith once called National Consumers' League founder Florence Kelley a "Protestant bigot."[18] Nonetheless, during Smith's governorship, these two political traditions merged, producing a unique and fruitful reformism that transformed New York State and held revolutionary implications for the entire nation.[19]

It was unforeseeable in 1904 that Al Smith, freshman assemblyman and Tammany stalwart, would one day become the gubernatorial embodiment of progressive reform. Young Smith learned politics under the tutelage of saloonkeepers and worked his way up the hierarchy of the infamous New York machine until he was rewarded for his loyalty by ward boss Tom Foley with a seat representing Manhattan's Lower East Side in the state assembly.[20] While set apart from many of his machine brethren by what Franklin Roosevelt's secretary of labor, Frances Perkins, later described as "a receptive mind" that drew him to reform and allowed him to function with a certain degree of ideological independence, Smith always remained true to the Democrats and to Tammany sachem "Silent Charlie" Murphy.[21] As partisanship and bossism were precisely the sort of civic vice the extermination of which was New York progressivism's raison d'être, Al Smith was an offensive character to most reformers. His early career in Albany was dismissed as hackery by progressives, and in fact he did not make a single speech in his first term.[22] Yet over time Smith matured as a legislator, and he slowly earned respect within the reform community. Joseph Proskauer, a member of New York's progressive Citizens' Union and an eventual Smith confidant, noted that his organization began to change its opinion of the Tammany assemblyman as they witnessed time and again "the whole high caliber of Smith's service in the legislature."[23]

Al Smith gained a forum to demonstrate his capabilities further in 1911, when his party won control of the state legislature. Charlie Murphy had Smith elected majority leader of the assembly; Robert F. Wagner, a German immigrant representing the Upper East Side, was made majority leader of the state senate.[24] Wagner and Smith's relationship dated to 1905, when then-freshman assemblyman Wagner was a roommate of second-term assemblyman Smith at Albany.[25] Not only would the two Manhattan Democrats' careers be inextricably linked over the ensuing decades, but they would also develop a close friendship—Wagner even naming his son Alfred in honor of Smith.[26]

During this period a tragedy occurred that would change the course of both men's careers. On March 25, 1911, a fire erupted in the tenth floor workroom of the Triangle Shirtwaist Company in Manhattan. One hundred forty-six of the workers who toiled at the sewing machines—most of them Jewish immigrant girls and young women from the Lower East Side—died in the inferno.[27] In response, a Committee on Safety was established, culminating with Wagner and Smith's sponsorship of legislation to form an investigative commission; Wagner served as chair and Smith as vice chair of the body.[28]

The commission "was one of the first experiments in the utilization of the volunteer citizen in a governmental project to discover what was wrong and what to do."[29] Consequently, this was an important opportunity for nonpartisan reformers to participate directly in the regulatory process. Female reformers served crucial roles: Mary Dreier of the Women's Trade Union League was named a commissioner, while Frances Perkins, who had served as secretary of the Committee on Safety, was consistently called as an expert witness on factory conditions, having established her credentials as an investigator with the National Consumers' League.[30]

After repeatedly testifying before the commission, Perkins became one of its lead investigators. In this capacity, she resolved to "educate" Smith and Wagner on the abhorrent working conditions prevalent across the Empire State. Perkins later recalled that "Smith said it was the greatest education he'd ever had. He had no idea life was like that. He'd grown up in the slums of New York, but he didn't know what factory life was like. Neither did any of them. It was an astonishment for them to see the frightfully filthy conditions, the obvious fire hazards and the very great accident hazards. We took them to everything before we got through."[31]

Perkins and her fellow investigators "[made] it our business to take Al Smith . . . to see the women, thousands of them, coming off the ten-hour night-shift on the rope walks in Auburn." They "made sure that Robert Wagner personally crawled through the tiny hole in the wall that gave egress to a steep iron ladder covered with ice and ending twelve feet from the ground, which was euphemistically labeled 'Fire Escape.'" Wagner and Smith and other legislators witnessed "five-, six-, and seven-year-olds, snipping beans and shelling peas," and saw "the machinery that would scalp a girl or cut off a man's arm."[32] Huthmacher has argued that for Wagner (and the same can certainly be said of Smith), "service on the commission was the most important event in his public life up to that time, for it focused and made impregnable the reformist leanings he had exhibited earlier. It also made him, and the political organization he represented, essential links in the chain of reform that spanned the Progressive Era and marked the emergence of modern, urban liberalism on the American scene."[33]

Through investigations and interrogation of experts—experts hand-picked by Perkins—Smith and Wagner became "considerable fellows" on industrial policy.[34] They heard testimony from such social work luminaries as Jane Addams and Lillian Wald and developed a reform program that gained the endorsement of "every important civic and social work organization in the city of New York."[35] The commission sponsored thirty-six bills on fire regulations, workplace safety, and working hours and conditions for women and children between 1912 and 1914, venturing well beyond the original scope of the investigation, into some of the labor and welfare crises that had been so vividly exposed through the Perkins-led field trips.[36] Many of these bills were crafted by Smith and Wagner, along with reformers including Perkins and Boston's "people's attorney," Louis Brandeis, in the law office of Abram Elkus, counsel to the commission.[37] On the floors of the assembly and senate, respectively, Smith and Wagner championed the reform bills. Such issues came to dominate the agenda of the two Tammany leaders. By a conservative estimate, 47 percent of the bills introduced by the pair in the three sessions following the initiation of the factory investigations concerned labor reform and other questions of social welfare; in the two previous sessions, that figure had stood at just over 4.5 percent.[38]

The Factory Investigating Commission experience certainly affected each legislator's worldview. Nevertheless, the two remained loyal party men, retaining their "profound affection for Tammany Hall and all that it stood for."[39] In the 1910s, being a Tammany stalwart was still often irreconcilable with favoring aggressive social welfare programs by an active state. For example, in a 1912 campaign speech, Robert Wagner raged against Theodore Roosevelt's New Nationalism, exclaiming: "Whatever advance its adoption would bring is advance toward socialism. . . . Such a 'new nationalism' would lay the meddling hand of bureaucracy upon every industry, increasing the burdens of taxation."[40] Moreover, when Murphy ordered his legislators in 1912 to block passage of Perkins's fifty-four-hour women's work week, Wagner—while sympathetic to the bill—dutifully employed his powers as temporary president of the senate in an attempt to prevent a vote on final passage (he was ultimately outmaneuvered by a fellow Tammany man, Big Tim Sullivan, who had less to lose by flouting Murphy's edict).[41] Over time, a combination of political expediency and genuine interest in social welfare policies would soften and eventually eliminate the opposition of Wagner, Smith, and other urban ethnic Democrats to the dynamic state. The 1911 fire and the investigations in its wake initiated this process.

Providing further impetus for reform was the Democrats' realization that their ethnic working-class constituents would reward them for strongly supporting ameliorative social welfare and labor legislation. Throughout the 1910s, Tammany began to lose its stranglehold over new-immigrant neighborhoods, ceding these wards—especially the Jewish ones—not to the conservative GOP but to Progressives and Socialists.[42] The East Side of Manhattan thrice elected Socialist Meyer London to Congress (in 1914, 1916, and 1920), and in the 1917 municipal elections, seven Socialist aldermen were swept into office from "chiefly Jewish districts" on a wave of support for mayoral candidate Morris Hillquit.[43] Over the decade, a series of nativist attacks by Republicans, as well as some Democratic social welfare initiatives (especially those championed by Smith and Wagner as a result of the factory investigations), along with Smith's large and visible group of progressive Jewish supporters in 1918, would help bring many of these voters back into the Democratic fold.[44] The Democrats, pragmatists still, keenly interpreted and acted on these trends. In a 1918 article in *Outlook*, former Progressive Party congressional nominee Henry Moskowitz analyzed the politics of the East Side thus: "The Tammany group is constantly jockeying with the Socialists to prove that they are the real 'people's friend' . . . skillfully maneuvering 'to beat them to it.' . . . In the recent city election [Tammany] advocated radical municipal reforms. . . . It gained the appearance of a progressive party and left the re-formers appearing as reactionaries."⁴⁵ Significantly, while Moskowitz remained generally skeptical of the machine, he credited much of this strategy to the sincere reformism of several young Tammanyites, especially "Alfred E. Smith, a brilliant East Side product."⁴⁶

The new generation of urban ethnic working-class Democrats—the "urban liberals" of the Progressive Era, with Smith and Wagner in the vanguard—was evolving to champion aggressive social welfare and labor reforms.⁴⁷ Indeed, the very nature of the urban Democracy was beginning, ever so slowly, to trans-form. Perhaps the most vivid example is that of the state senator who had supplanted the famous Tammany apologist George Washington Plunkitt in New York's Fifteenth District. Thomas J. McManus, better known simply as "the McManus," whom Plunkitt had described as "my Brutus," certainly in-herited his predecessor's propensity for graft, and reformers like Perkins saw him as "obviously very much of a roughneck and not too bright"; but he was also, with Tim Sullivan and others, one of the "heroes" of the 1912 battle for the fifty-four-hour law in the state senate and was the chairman who was first able to recover that bill and others affecting workplace standards from the leg-islative purgatory of the Committee on Labor and Industry.⁴⁸

Thus, in the 1910s, machine politicians were beginning to evolve, employ-ing their time-tested shenanigans not exclusively to line their own pockets, but also to promote social welfare and labor reforms. Critically, as Moskowitz noted, the urban Democrats had tutors during this transformation: "Settle-ment workers . . . have helped to modify the point of view of Tammany's elementary neighborliness."⁴⁹ Simultaneously, New York's social welfare pro-gressives had an evolutionary process of their own to undergo before their reformist vision could be fused with the political aspirations of urban ethnic Democrats.

In 1919, when Al Smith was inaugurated for his first term as governor, he named Frances Perkins to the State Industrial Commission. After years of leg-islative collaboration, Smith considered Perkins the ideal candidate to pro-mote his vision for the commission, and in fact saw Perkins as "*his* member on the Industrial Commission." Nevertheless, at this time Perkins was not a Democrat. Although an ardent Smith supporter, she chose to remain a regis-tered independent, free from partisan responsibilities. "I voted for whom I thought was the right man and the right program. I certainly didn't call my-self a thorough-going *bona fide* Democrat. . . . I thought Al Smith was the right person and I was very enthusiastic about him. I wasn't voting for him as a Democrat."[50]

As with many female reformers, much of Perkins's nonpartisanship resulted from the experiences of the pre-suffrage era.[51] She had attended the 1912 Democratic convention at Baltimore because "I'd never seen one. . . . I went for the show." And while she "also went because I was deeply interested in political principles," the "convention didn't make too much difference to me. . . . I was not . . . a Democrat. Woman didn't have the vote, so women didn't have to be anything." Furthermore, while admiring "the Wilsonites," Perkins did not favor the progressive Democrat in 1912, considering herself "nearer a Bull Mooser," and only missing the Progressive Party's convention in Chicago due to a death in the family.[52]

When, in the fall of 1919, Governor Smith became aware of Perkins's nonpartisanship, he called on the commissioner to meet him at his suite in Manhattan's Biltmore Hotel. Smith inquired if Perkins considered herself a Democrat; she responded that she did, insofar as at Albany Democrats had been much more amenable to the reform legislation she was promoting. Well, that makes you "a Democrat in theory at least," responded the governor, but "they tell me you're not an enrolled Democrat." "I never enrolled, I wouldn't think of enrolling in any party," confirmed Perkins; "that sort of ties your hands." Smith, who by this time greatly admired Perkins and many of her progressive associates, took the opportunity to articulate his vision of their place in his party, in a manner that mingled their reformism with old-fashioned machine politics. "That's the kind of mistake a lot of good people are likely to make," he warned his commissioner. To Smith, the party was necessary as a rallying point: "Suppose you got some good ideas. . . . You can't go out and say that to the public because you just sound like a fool." But "if your party is all ready set," he continued, "they're all for it and they put it over. They make it popular. It doesn't seem like a one-man crank idea."[53]

In Smith's conceptualization, the Democratic Party could serve as an apparatus for channeling reformist energy to produce profound political changes. But in order for this to occur, "good people need to be in the party, not outside looking in. They don't have any influence at all if they're outside looking in. If they're inside, doing their full duty by the party, voting, getting out the vote, helping with the campaigns, and making what they know available to everybody, then they have some influence. . . . Then the party takes up a good and wise program."[54] Perkins protested quite reasonably that she wanted to know whom specifically she was supporting before joining a party. But Smith retorted that she and other progressives needed to enroll first, "so you have something to say inside the party." Referring to "these people who jump around from one party to another," he asked, "Have any of them ever accomplished anything? No. You've accomplished more in a couple of years than they have in twenty years by always being so independent. But you won't get far if you won't line up with a party so that the Democrats know that you're a Democrat and that they can rely on you." Perkins, taken by this logic, registered as a Democrat "as soon as they opened enrollment" and "never had any doubts about it afterwards."[55]

This is an extreme case. It is doubtful that a significant number of social workers were proselytized for the Democracy through a colloquy with their state's governor. But this anecdote aptly demonstrates the initial philosophical discordance between reformers and partisans, as well as the thinking behind so many New York progressives' abandoning their independent posture in favor of Al Smith and the Democrats.

Furthermore, speeches delivered by Perkins throughout the 1910s in her capacity as executive secretary of the New York Consumers' League suggest an evolving concept of the role of politics in reform. Earlier addresses focused on women's place in economic life as consumers: "Their duty in the life of family is purchases. So after all it lies in their hands to . . . change conditions" through boycotts.[56] As the factory investigations progressed and the commission's work continued, Perkins would pronounce "legislative work" the "most important phase" in reform.[57] In 1912, Perkins declared that the "purpose of Gov[ernment] is to make things better for the children," and later that year called for government studies of industries and imitation of German and English "social measures" to combat unemployment.[58] Perkins had begun legislative lobbying activities prior to developing relationships with Albany politicians, but through her work on the factory commission she was increasingly crafting bills not for the Consumers' League but for partisan legislators such as Smith and Wagner. By 1919, she was a total insider, appointed by Governor Smith to the State Industrial Commission.[59]

Certainly social welfare progressives had petitioned the government prior to 1911.[60] Perhaps the most famous example of such engagement was the National Consumers' League's central role in the landmark 1908 Supreme Court case *Muller v. Oregon*. Moreover, it was through the league's legislative lobbying that *Muller* and similar cases were precipitated.[61] Nor was Perkins the first social worker to gain a prominent position within government; she was preceded in this by notables including Florence Kelley as chief factory inspector in Illinois and Julia Lathrop as head of the federal Children's Bureau.[62] In fact, settlement activists had been lobbying for local and state ordinances, pressuring local politicians, sponsoring reform candidacies, and advising municipal governments for decades before Al Smith met Frances Perkins.[63]

Yet these highly political drives operated outside of traditional partisan divides and did not serve to inculcate the old parties with reformist zeal. Social progressives tended to gravitate toward government service under reform and "fusion" administrations, and certainly not under machine politicians, with whom they instead battled tenaciously and only occasionally struck a reluctant détente (Jane Addams finally abandoned attempts to upend the political organization in her Chicago neighborhood only after her candidates were twice defeated by local kingpin Johnny Powers).[64] The closest these reformers came to concerted partisanship was in 1912, when many from the settlement community flocked to Theodore Roosevelt and the Progressive Party; but that campaign would ultimately produce nothing in the way of long-term partisan alignment, and in retrospect seemed "in some ways more like a crusade than politics."[65] Thus, despite their record of political activity and the inherently political nature of their program, most social work progressives adopted the posture of Mary Kingsbury Simkhovitch from the Greenwich House settlement in New York, another future Smith partisan, who concluded that "in political action the settlement has held aloof . . . because of the conviction that political parties do not express in any vital way the desires of the people of the neighborhoods where settlements are situated," leaving reformers with "an inability to regard existing forms as adequate to meet the real situation."[66]

So while the story of Perkins's evolution is telling, what begins to make it outstanding is that the desire to work within government to implement a progressive social vision led to partisan political commitments. By 1920, Perkins was an active Democrat and promoted her social welfare vision within the context of Democratic politics, articulating her progressive beliefs in speeches on behalf of Smith throughout his governorship.[67] As Smith had suggested, this facilitated Perkins's ambitions: in 1923, the governor appointed Perkins to the State Industrial Board, and in 1926 he made her the board's chairperson.[68] Meanwhile, Perkins continued her political activities, helping craft Democratic strategy and composing materials for "a good many of Governor Smith's speeches."[69] Her star would of course ascend further still under Smith's successor and fellow Democrat, Franklin Roosevelt.

Perkins's increasing partisanship helps illustrate social workers' centrality to the progressive Democratic alliance marshaled by Governor Smith in 1920s New York; but hers is hardly the only case in point. Lillian Wald, who ran the Henry Street Settlement on Manhattan's Lower East Side and was a prominent advocate for public health nursing services and other pieces of the social welfare agenda, underwent a similar transformation in the 1910s and 1920s.

As with Perkins, the more established Wald came out of the settlement house tradition and was lobbying Albany for social welfare measures long before the factory commission produced its blizzard of reform bills.[70] Like many progressives, she was drawn to "Governor Wilson's splendid record in social reform" during the 1912 presidential campaign.[71] But when members of the Democratic National Committee solicited Wald's official support, they were rebuffed. "As a suffragist," she explained, "I find it illogical to assume even a minor responsibility for a platform that has no suffrage plank."[72] Here again the influence of women's exclusion from the franchise by the traditional parties foreclosed the potential for partisanship by politically active social welfare progressives—not only technically, through the legal denial of votes, but also philosophically, creating intellectual barriers to partisan involvement by otherwise engaged individuals.[73]

Even after New York women gained suffrage in 1917, Wald was not involved in Smith's first campaign for the governorship, instead continuing to offer her services to the new governor just as she had to legislators, aldermen, and mayors for decades.[74] By 1920, she was increasingly enthusiastic over the governor's agenda, assuring Smith of her "whole-hearted support for your admirable, progressive administration."[75] In that year, Smith was turning to Wald for advice in specific policy areas that had defined her career—especially public health.[76] By the fall, she was no longer only an interested progressive or an enthusiastic observer; she was now a Smith partisan. In October, Wald promised the Citizens' Committee for Alfred E. Smith that she would "be very glad indeed to do what I can" to aid the campaign, adding that "the residents of the Settlement agree with me in that the Governor has given us an admirable administration. Appreciation of voters should enable him to continue his good work." Three days later she fulfilled this pledge by writing a more formal letter for the campaign, which noted that Smith "should be re-elected and that voters irrespective of party affiliations should keep in office one who has served the state so well." The next week Wald donated ten dollars to the governor's reelection fund.[77]

In spite of Smith's defeat that year, Lillian Wald's commitment to him in both politics and policy abided. Upon Smith's return to Albany in 1923, Wald served on the governor's committee to study rural health.[78] She also continued her political activities for Smith, delivering a speech on the governor's behalf at Nyack in August.[79] Furthermore, Wald's activism spread beyond a personal attachment to the governor: Smith allies (and partisan Democrats) like Joseph Proskauer and Herbert Lehman would soon gain the endorsement of the noted social work leader.[80]

A most striking example of a New York social work progressive turning to partisanship is that of Belle Moskowitz. Moskowitz spent the first two decades of the century struggling for social reforms in New York City, with a particular interest in dance halls and other working-class recreational outlets. In this mission she looked to the government, for, as the historian Elisabeth Israels Perry notes, "she wanted the state to act as a beneficent parent, sheltering the weak and leading the strong to serve society as a whole." Like many reformers, Moskowitz was wary of the major political parties and of Tammany Hall, and like Frances Perkins she was a supporter of Theodore Roosevelt and the Progressives in 1912. Over the course of the 1910s, Moskowitz remained a nonpartisan reformer, but she was drawn increasingly toward political activities both by the nature of her work and by her new husband, Henry Moskowitz (whose résumé included a 1912 congressional campaign). Also during that period, her apprehensions about Tammany politicians began to wane with exposure to Al Smith and the New York Democrats' increasing commitment to social welfare measures.[81]

Moskowitz joined with other prominent progressives to support Smith's gubernatorial candidacy in 1918; the following year, she was appointed executive secretary of the new governor's State Reconstruction Commission. As "linchpin" of the commission, Moskowitz directed its work toward such social reforms as unemployment insurance, a state milk commission, a coordinated housing policy, state maternal and infant welfare campaigns, and compulsory health insurance for industrial workers. As Smith's closest adviser throughout his governorship, Moskowitz crafted not only public policy but also Democratic partisan strategy.[82] By 1928 she was a leading force within the party and began gaining national recognition—the *Charlotte Observer* described her as "Smith's Colonel House," while a profile in the *Jewish Criterion* noted that "at no time is the French expression *cherchez la femme* more in place than in a consideration of Smith's career."[83]

To describe a "politicization" of female social workers informing Smith's gubernatorial progressivism would be misleading, for these women's project was inherently political. Through lobbying, lawsuits, public service, and support for progressive candidates, these activists had led a thoroughly political existence from the inception of the settlement house movement. But what developed in New York in the late 1910s and the 1920s was something more. The adoption of political *partisanship* by some of these progressive women represented a new threshold of politicization, one that could only be reached after much ideological negotiation between the old parties and these new voters. Only after the Democrats embraced not only women's suffrage but also the progressive social welfare agenda, and only after they had demonstrated the utility of partisan politics and politicians to the achievement of social work's broader goals, could these women be not only politicized but also evangelized for the party.

The activities of politicians like Smith and Wagner—and even the Mc-Manus—in the 1910s reveal how the Democratic Party in New York was transforming; and Smith's ascension to the undisputed leadership of the state party by 1920 signaled that this transformation would continue. Through appointments, policy innovations, and some old-fashioned political haggling, the increasingly progressive New York Democracy made a strong appeal to the newly enfranchised social work women and their allies. The outlook of many Democratic partisans had been adjusted to include a broad vision of state action for social welfare; adopting much of the progressive women's agenda, Smith and his confrères could challenge those women likewise to modify their outlook.

In a speech before the Women's State Democratic Forum at the Hotel Astor on November 22, 1917, Anthony Griffin, an Irish-Catholic Tammany politician who the following year would begin a nine-term career representing parts of Harlem and the Bronx in Congress, asked women: "Now having obtained the suffrage, the question is 'What are you going to do with it?'" A progressive as well as a Tammanyite, Griffin had his own suggestions. "You come into possession of the franchise after the battle for political independence is won. The issues of the present hour are purely economic, and to meet them, women are equally qualified with men." With ongoing clashes over tariff rates, struggles against trusts, and a ballooning cost of living, "the battles of the future for economic independence will be by the ballot. We ought, therefore, to welcome the aid of women in this conflict."[84]

Moreover, the "we" that would fight economic inequality would be the Democratic Party, with the strong support of progressive women interested in such issues. Like Smith, Griffin declared that it was not enough to profess these things and then shift mercurially among Democrats, Socialists, and independents. Instead, women should sign on with the Democrats, because they had demonstrated the value of partisanship for progressive advances. After all, claimed Griffin, "the eight hour law; better working conditions for men, women and children in factories; the Workmen's Compensation Law and the Widows Pension Law were all enacted by Democratic Legislatures without the aid of Socialist agitation."[85] Two weeks later, Griffin made the case for a progressive alliance crossing lines of gender within the Democratic Party even more explicitly: "Man and woman stand together in loyalty to our country at large and in their interest in community welfare. In order to make her ballot most effectual, she must align herself politically in accordance with the cleavage of political parties. She must find her political home among the parties which have hitherto claimed only men among their membership."[86]

The following fall this alliance began to crystallize when the now unabashedly progressive Al Smith gained the Democratic nomination for governor. By then, Smith's progressive credentials were such that he enjoyed the solid support of New York's reform community in his gubernatorial bid. To help corral Smith's non-Democratic admirers, Abram Elkus formed the Independent Citizens' Committee for Alfred E. Smith, reviving the progressive coalition that had fought for reform after the Triangle fire. Many of the members of that committee, including the Moskowitzes, would become ardent Smith Democrats in short order. Significantly, about one-third of the committee members were women.[87]

In New York, then, the 1910s into the early 1920s was a period of negotiation between largely old-stock female social welfare progressives and largely ethnic male machine Democrats turned urban liberals. As each side shed its inhibitions about coalition, as well as some of its own attributes that were anathema to the other party, they were able to coalesce to fuel the extraordinarily ambitious gubernatorial progressivism of Alfred E. Smith in the 1920s. As is often the case, personalities also aided in this fusion. Al Smith and Robert Wagner, unlike many of their Tammany brethren, were never associated with vice or scandal, and Tammany sachem Charlie Murphy is known to have sensed their promise and granted them a certain degree of ideological autonomy.[88] Furthermore, reformers like Frances Perkins and Belle Moskowitz did not project the same cultural condescension as some social workers, and unlike some within the reform sorority, did not prioritize Prohibition over social welfare.[89]

The progressivism that developed through this confluence of traditions focused on certain strains within the wider reformism of the Progressive Era—specifically those that concerned urban laborers. The one common denominator between settlement house activists and socially engaged ward bosses was a desire to ameliorate the ills of the urban industrial order. This interaction, then, featured the formulation of a social welfare agenda by enlightened urban ethnic politicians and savvy female reformers and ultimately spurred the institutionalization of that agenda as Democratic partisan dogma. The first fruits of this coalition were to be harvested during Al Smith's remarkably progressive governorship.

Predictably, Smith expanded on the labor laws championed by the alliance that had emerged in the wake of the Triangle disaster. The number of workers covered by the fifty-four-hour week was expanded in 1919 and again in 1924, and a series of bills were passed to regulate conditions in specific industries.[90] The apogee of these efforts came in 1927 with the passage of the forty-eight-hour week for women. Mary Dreier, another crucial member of the

New York coalition, recognized the important role Smith and the partisans had played in this achievement, cabling the governor that "had it not been for your courageous and generous support throughout all these years and your persistent effort in behalf of the forty eight hour week for the working women of this state this bill would never have gone through."[91] (Indeed, Dreier and others had been working with Smith since the early years of his governorship on a series of unsuccessful bids to pass similar legislation.)[92] Smith responded that Dreier gave "me too much of the credit for the final success of our forty-eight hour bill," for "you . . . and the women associated with you have worked unselfishly for its success, and I feel that you are entitled to more credit than I. However, we will not quarrel about it." Smith was indeed sincere when he remarked that he considered the forty-eight-hour bill "*our* bill"—he saved the pen used to sign the legislation and sent it to Dreier as a token of thanks.[93] In the final year of his incumbency Smith reflected: "It is a matter of record that I have had my strongest and most vigorous support from the women of my State. They have a deep interest in the human side of government." He stressed that these progressive women had not necessarily come from the ranks of the Democratic Party, and yet "they fought side by side with me . . . in the struggle to obtain factory laws for safeguarding the lives, health and welfare of men, women and children in industry; to secure social legislation like widowed mothers' pensions, designed to keep the orphaned child in its mother's home; to protect society against the evils of child labor and the overwork and exploitation of women and children in industry; to improve the care of afflicted veterans, tubercular patients, of the mentally deficient, and to restore to usefulness the lives of crippled children."[94]

In fact, this social welfare progressivism influenced nearly every facet of Smith's executive tenure, manifesting itself in a number of initiatives that placed New York in the forefront of reform legislation in the United States. During his four terms as governor, Smith championed unemployment insurance, better compensation for victims of industrial accidents, improved benefits for injured workers, and increased death benefits for industrial widows.[95] He also pressed for labor measures including the eight-hour day and a minimum wage.[96] In the realm of housing, which was the Smith initiative "most energetically attacked as socialistic," the governor fought for state credit for builders of moderately priced homes, municipal development of low-cost housing, and the establishment of state and local housing boards to plan and organize further endeavors.[97] On recreation, the administration battled for the development of state parks and beaches and for parkways to provide easy access from New York City to these facilities on Long Island.[98] On power, Smith tirelessly advocated development of hydroelectric plants under state rather than private control, for the conservation against private exploitation of those water resources left undeveloped, and for the formation of a state power authority.[99] On education, Smith promoted improved salaries for teachers, equal pay for women, capital improvements, rural school consolidation, and an aggrandized state role in funding public schools—to be financed through increased taxation: in Smith's first year as governor, New York spent $9 million on education; by 1927 that figure was $82.5 million.[100] On public health, Smith and his administration pushed for development of a state milk commission to ensure the quality and availability of milk by making it a regulated public utility; pressed for maternity education and state grants for maternal and infant welfare, including participation in the federal program developed under the Sheppard-Towner Act; proposed increased child welfare services, hot lunch programs, and mandatory physical education; and promoted compulsory health insurance for industrial workers.[101] Smith was not able to institute all of these programs during his governorship, largely because Republicans controlled at least one chamber of the state legislature for his entire tenure. Nevertheless, much of this platform was achieved, and all of it was pursued doggedly by the newly minted Democratic social welfare progressive alliance.

Throughout the 1920s, Governor Smith distinguished himself by pursuing an agenda driven by this particular style of progressivism. Owing partly to its roots in the social work tradition and partly to its constituency within the urban ethnic working class, Smith's progressivism shifted emphasis away from the retention of small-town Yankee values and the veneration of American individualism or the fear of an overthrow of the social hierarchy, and applied all of its reformist energies to causes of social welfare, industrial justice, and a general improvement of the quality of working-class life. Radically absent was the erstwhile preoccupation with personal behavior and cultural assimilation; lives would be uplifted not through forced temperance or compulsory Americanization, but through better working conditions, adequate health care, and ample recreation. Here at last was a progressivism of which working-class immigrants and their progeny could imbibe; here as well was a progressivism that retained the social work agenda and that offered pragmatic means of widespread implementation. This idiomatic progressivism informed the administration of Alfred E. Smith in New York, and it was on this progressive platform that Smith sought the presidency in 1928.

While the nascent progressivism of rising Democratic stars like Wagner and Smith revolved around ameliorative labor and social welfare measures for the benefit of the urban working class, another facet of this progressivism was public policies reflective of an increasingly heterogeneous society, in the interest of Tammany's diverse constituency. Historians have often assigned such issues as religious and racial tolerance, immigration restriction, and Prohibition to a unique ethnocultural category of analysis, segregating them from questions of economic justice. Yet, when considering the developing ideology of the ethnic working class and their political representatives, such a bifurcation proves artificial. Justice for these workers meant *both* industrial democracy *and* social respect. Indeed, while the progressivism of Smith and his allies was centered on social welfare, the very nature of their intended beneficiaries also compelled them to denounce bigotry and cultural condescension.

Tammany's constituents had always been the ethnic working classes of New York City. For decades, this had meant the Irish, and so Democratic candidates could succeed while maintaining a clannish insularity. But as the late nineteenth and early twentieth centuries brought waves of new immigrants from southern and eastern Europe, as well as a deluge of African American refugees from the Old South, wily Tammanyites modified their tactics not only to outflank Socialist challengers but also to avoid ethnic dissension.[102] In 1898, the "United Colored Democracy" was established by Tammany to distribute patronage among New York's growing African American community in return for electoral support in much the same way the machine operated in predominantly white wards. This was a minor advance made all the less meaningful by intransigent racism within the party and city bureaucracy, and it did not yet translate into black Democratic nominees for high office.[103] Within other communities, however, representation became an increasingly important tactic for securing partisan loyalties.

To give only a brief sampling: Yorkville, on the Upper East Side, was represented not by an Irishman but by a German immigrant (Robert Wagner), reflecting its status as New York's "Little Germany."[104] This was not particularly pathbreaking given Germans' long history in the city, but many newer groups would slowly receive similar treatment. In the opening decade of the twentieth century, Tim Sullivan responded swiftly to population shifts on the Lower East Side with ethnic outreach—"the Big Feller" was far ahead of his Tammany cohorts in extending "a welcome to Jewish advisors and captains" and "started many successful Jews in their careers."[105] So too did John F. Ahearn's Fourth District organization—also on the Lower East Side.[106] While Sullivan and Ahearn, largely prompted by demography, outpaced the citywide machine, this pragmatic inclusiveness would cease to be exceptional in the decades to follow. In 1923, when seeking a congressional candidate for a previously Republican-dominated seat in a heavily Jewish district, the Democrats drafted Sol Bloom, who recalled, "I had been chosen because I was an amiable and solvent Jew." Bloom, a colorful impresario and son of Polish immigrants, would go on to serve for nearly three decades in the U.S. House of Representatives.[107] In East Harlem, Tammany survived both a party insurgency and a Republican challenge from the neighborhood's burgeoning Italian community in 1911; in 1912, Twenty-Eighth District boss Nick Hayes reluctantly but presciently acceded to popular demand and nominated Salvatore Cotillo to stand for assemblyman as a Democrat. During a distinguished career in Albany, Cotillo would join Wagner and Smith as a leading advocate for labor and welfare reforms, and in 1923 he would become the first Italian American elected to the New York State Supreme Court.[108] The Democrats in New York were not the only political machine in the United States that appealed to a polyglot constituency to ensure their own survival.[109] Yet while Tammany's adoption of such pragmatism toward ethnicity seems almost too obvious to mention, Irish political organizations in places like Boston, Providence, and Chicago had antagonized newer immigrants by excluding them from representation—to the extent that Italians, Poles, French Canadians, and others tended to coalesce around the Yankee-dominated Republicans in such cities.[110]

Nevertheless, Tammany's small strides toward more diverse representation were only a minor piece of its ethnocultural agenda. Heeding their constituents, these Democrats fought strenuously against repressive social measures such as Prohibition and Sabbatarian restrictions, while battling discriminatory immigration policies such as literacy tests and national origins quotas.[111] The question of alcohol is complex. It is true that aspiring politicians like Al Smith received much of the Tammany catechism at the saloon. Yet many of the notorious bosses were teetotalers—perhaps most notably George Washington Plunkitt, who although "no fanatic" and a friend of saloonkeepers, made certain "as a matter of business I leave whisky and beer and the rest of that stuff alone." Of equal significance, he remarked, "As a matter of business, too, I take for my lieutenants in my district men who don't drink." According to Plunkitt, sachems like Richard Croker and Charlie Murphy were of the same disposition, the latter taking "a glass of wine at dinner sometimes, but he don't go beyond that." The same even applied to Bowery leaders "Big Tim" and "Little Tim" Sullivan, neither of whom had "ever touched a drop of liquor in his life."[112] This is not to say that Tammany men had no stake in the issue: Murphy and the Sullivans were saloonkeepers with an obvious financial interest in alcohol; drinking establishments provided infusions of funding for the machine; and Plunkitt is noted for hyperbole and generalizations. Still, the battle on behalf of the saloon ought not to be seen as a purely personal and emotional crusade by the Democrats. If Plunkitt exaggerated, so did those who caricatured the ward boss as a souse (as much of the more scurrilous anti-Smith propaganda would do in 1928). A more representative figure would probably be the real Al Smith. Franklin Roosevelt testified that Smith had never been a "drunkard," and biographer Robert Slayton reports that the Happy Warrior "was a light to moderate social drinker who enjoyed an occasional beer." More significantly, Smith did not view Prohibition as "a critical political issue."[113] With Smith, as with the earlier party leaders, standing up for the saloon was a way of standing up for the legitimacy of his constituents' folkways.[114] Fighting against Prohibition was a way to resist cultural domination of urban ethnic workers by élites, just as fighting for social welfare measures was a way of battling for economic justice for those workers. Indeed, Plunkitt summarized Tammany's position on alcohol succinctly: good political leaders "don't make no pretenses of being better than anybody else."[115] Thus, the Smith Democrats repealed New York State's Prohibition enforcement mechanism, the Mullan-Gage Law, in 1923.[116]

If Al Smith and his allies imbibed this democratic approach to drink, they adopted even more passionately urban ethnic workers' disdain for immigration restriction. It is well known that political machines like Tammany Hall thrived on the votes of recent immigrants, providing newcomers with connections and social services in return for political loyalty. In a new and often overwhelming setting, immigrants' unfulfilled needs were satisfied and abstract democratic concepts were humanized.[117] This in turn earned the machine votes and enabled its operations to persist indefinitely. Clearly there was strong incentive for machine men to oppose immigration restrictions. But in seeking to serve the interests of their constituents, these politicians were also compelled to defend the newcomers' legitimacy as citizens by opposing legislation that implicitly denied their social worth. Thus Tammanyites objected to literacy tests, national origins quotas, and other immigration restrictions grounded in an Anglo-Saxon vision of Americanism.

In fact, machine progressives framed these issues as questions of democratic justice. In proposing a resolution that the state senate petition Congress in opposition to a literacy test in 1917, Robert Wagner proclaimed that "the question of a literacy test for immigrants does not belong to this day of toleration and liberal thought. It is an echo sounding from the past, from a very brief period in the history of our country." Significantly, Wagner insisted that his vision—and that of his urban ethnic constituents—was *the* legitimate understanding of American democracy, concluding that "the imposition of a literacy test for admission to our shores is un-American."[118] After passage of the Johnson-Reed Immigration Act in 1924 established national origins quotas based on the 1890 census, New York Democrats decried the "sinister" attempt to institutionalize ethnic hierarchies.[119] Brooklyn congressman Emanuel Celler denounced it as an affront to southern and eastern Europeans, while Meyer

Jacobstein, a New York–born representative from Rochester, agreed that the act "arbitrarily and unfairly discriminates against certain nationalities."[120]

Such progressives were devoted both to their party and to their inclusive vision of the U.S. polity. This at least partly explains the debacle at the Democratic National Convention at Madison Square Garden in 1924, when Al Smith and his allies battled unsuccessfully for both the presidential nomination and a platform provision denouncing the Ku Klux Klan, while the Tammany-packed rafters repeatedly erupted into raucous choruses of heckling at opponents like William Gibbs McAdoo and William Jennings Bryan. Smith and his allies wished to jettison some of the most intolerant traditions of the Democratic Party while retaining an unswerving loyalty to that party; they believed that their understanding of the Democracy was rooted not only in their own aspirations but also in historical fact.[121] Thus the cheerfully naïve and blatantly ahistorical sentiments of Congressman Celler, who declared in 1928 that "the clause of the Immigration Act of 1924 providing for immigration by 'National Origins' should be repealed. The Democratic Party, *which has always been opposed to discrimination against races*, should be the first to urge this repeal."[122]

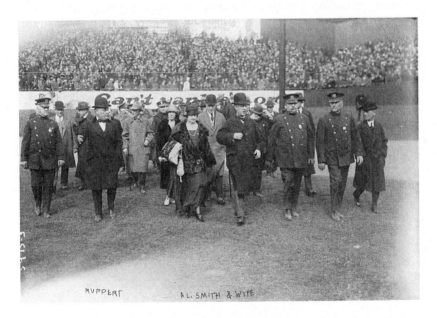

FIGURE 1.   Al Smith, who had fought the state's proscription against Sunday baseball as a legislator in 1907, preparing to deliver the first pitch ever thrown at Yankee Stadium, Bronx, NY, April 18, 1923. Jacob Ruppert, "Gov. Al Smith & wife at opening of Yankee Stadium, 4/18/23," George Grantham Bain Collection, Library of Congress, Washington, DC.

Tellingly, the social workers who aligned with machine Democrats to concoct and cultivate Smith's progressivism tended to be either those least inclined to press for measures such as Prohibition (like Belle Moskowitz) or those who were willing to set such questions aside in favor of the social welfare and labor reforms that they valued far more (like Lillian Wald). Indeed, these social welfare progressive women often shared the cultural positions of the Tammany Democrats outright: in 1921, Mary Dreier berated President Warren G. Harding for remarks made by his secretary of state suggesting that "Armenians, Jews, Persians, and Russians cannot be regarded as desirable population."[123]

In both social welfare and cultural pluralism, Smith and his progressive coalition sought to represent their urban ethnic working-class constituents—to battle for both their economic welfare and their social dignity. As Wagner saw it: "There are in America two schools of political thought . . . one conception of government which believes that there should be a governing class and a class to be governed . . . [and] the other . . . which holds that governments are created by the people themselves as instruments for the working out of the happiness and welfare of all."[124]

By the time Alfred E. Smith became governor of New York in 1919, he had emerged as the foremost practitioner of this specialized progressivism, with its threefold focus on social welfare, labor protections, and cultural pluralism. This particular progressive ideology never completely conquered the social work community (many reformers remained ardent Prohibitionists or staunchly nonpartisan) or Tammany Hall (many Democratic politicians remained more interested in personal enrichment than social welfare). But it was, absolutely, the guiding credo of the Smith administration, which was stocked by the creators of this progressivism and which doggedly pursued their agenda. By 1928, when Smith ran for president, these ideas would be adopted by the national Democratic Party. In the meantime, Smith's progressivism made New York State an island of reformism in an ocean of normalcy.

CHAPTER 2

Progressive Governor

[handwritten annotation: a braRless sense of ... new ideas ! That Sm. was rvl/? a progressive]

From the moment of Al Smith's gubernatorial inauguration on New Year's Day 1919, it was clear that his administration would be marked by a progressive ethos. Fueled by a genuine interest in developing state solutions to social ills, informed by the social welfare tradition, and championed through pragmatic politics, Smith's progressivism would continue to develop over the next decade, expressing itself consistently throughout his executive tenure. Smith's gubernatorial record demonstrates unwavering support for a uniquely broad social welfare regime; attention both to these policies and to the governor's accompanying political rhetoric elucidates the centrality of Smith's progressivism to his executive priorities and, later, to his presidential run. Health care, conservation, and administrative reform are but three of the many policy areas in which Smith transformed life in New York State. Exploring the governor's treatment of these areas of public policy reveals both the profundity and the breadth of Smith's commitment to his particular progressivism during the 1920s. Indeed, the administration's posture toward these issues demonstrates how expansively Smith and his allies defined social welfare and how liberally they were willing to exercise state power in order to promote the public good.

Public Health

When Al Smith was inaugurated governor of New York in 1919, he was already widely known as a progressive reformer, and supporters anticipated that his administration would reflect such an agenda. These hopes were amplified by the fortuitous timing of Smith's ascension to the governorship. Coming less than two months after the conclusion of the Great War, the first year of the Smith administration would be marked by the work of the State Reconstruction Commission, a body appointed by the governor to craft a response to the many public welfare crises made plain by mobilization.[1] Smith elucidated the administration's philosophy in his first inaugural address: "The lessons of the war must not go unheeded. We must benefit by the war as a nation and as a State. It has taught us that more stringent and more universal laws are required for the protection of the health, comfort, welfare, and efficiency of all our people."[2]

The most embarrassing wartime lesson was learned when the state draft board had deemed "one-third of all the male population in the State of New York between the ages of twenty-one and thirty-one years . . . unfit to fight because of diseases or other physical unfitness."[3] The governor proposed two categories of solutions to this disgraceful situation, both of which would be addressed by the Reconstruction Commission and both of which would inspire legislative battles.[4] The first was legally reforming health policy in the state, most notably by supporting compulsory health insurance for all laborers. The second was expanding and modernizing the state's health care infrastructure.

In his first inaugural address, Smith "strongly urge[d] . . . the enactment of a health insurance law," to remedy the "unfair condition" in which "the worker and his family bear . . . alone" the burden of illness, injury, and incapacitation. The governor believed that this plan would "lead to the adoption of wider measures of public health and hygiene, and . . . operate to conserve human life." Smith also proposed a maternity insurance program "in the interest of posterity and of the race." For a model, he looked overseas, lecturing the legislature that "other countries are far ahead of us in this respect, and their experience has demonstrated the practical value and economic soundness of these principles."[5]

As with much of his agenda, Smith was not creating this program himself. As he noted, compulsory insurance laws or national sickness insurance had been implemented in a number of European countries.[6] Domestically, the American Association for Labor Legislation (AALL) had drafted a "standard bill" that was promoted in numerous state legislatures beginning in 1915.[7] This bill called for a system of local mutual funds administered by a state health insurance commission. A program based on the bill had been proposed in California but was defeated soundly in a 1918 referendum.[8] Meanwhile, in New York, Republican state senator Ogden Mills had proposed an insurance bill modeled on the AALL program during the 1916 and 1917 legislative sessions, with the senate agreeing to create a commission to study the question.[9] As Smith took office promoting state health insurance, another iteration of the standard bill began meandering through the legislature that would become tied to the rest of the governor's welfare agenda.[10]

The 1919 bill was introduced by Frederick Morgan Davenport, a Republican state senator from Clinton who had run unsuccessfully for governor on the Progressive ticket in 1914.[11] In the assembly the bill was sponsored by Charles D. Donohue, a Manhattan representative and the leader of the Democratic caucus, further indicating Smith's support. Based on the AALL model, the proposal would promote preventative care and create a system in which employers and employees would contribute equally to a state-managed fund to cover medical costs in times of illness.[12] "Local mutual funds" would be administered by boards of directors with equal numbers of employers and employees, and each board would set premium rates and manage health care in its region. "Special provision" was made for medical, surgical, and nursing care for mothers and their babies, and working women were provided with a cash benefit for two weeks before the birth of a child and six weeks thereafter.[13] In addition, Davenport's plan would provide "minimum benefits" to cover costs associated with medical, surgical, sanitarium, and dental treatment, and cash benefits would be provided for maternity, sickness, and funerals.[14] The program was projected to cost employers twenty-four cents per week per employee and cost each worker the same.[15] The bill was amended by its sponsors in March, "in an endeavor to meet objections advanced by physicians" by affirming beneficiaries' ability to choose their own doctor, rather than having one assigned by the local board, and by placing all of the boards under the strict supervision of the State Industrial Commission. The amendments were also designed to mollify businessmen by explicitly defining what sort of employee would be covered by the program.[16]

This failed to impress the opposition, however, and while compulsory health insurance became a key piece of Smith's welfare agenda, it quickly earned denunciations from numerous professional organizations and interest groups.[17] The New York City Bar Association denounced the Davenport-Donohue Bill as "socialistic"; the Associated Manufacturers and Merchants of New York State expressed alarm at the burdensome costs associated with the program;

and other business and medical organizations vociferously objected.[18] Encouraged by these developments, legislative Republicans derailed the bill, as well as the entire Smith program. Indeed, even after a brief insurgency led by Davenport, wherein a small group of "radical" Republicans aligned with the entire Democratic caucus to pass the insurance proposal through the state senate, the iron-fisted assembly speaker, Thaddeus Sweet, was able to halt any progressive momentum by having his chamber vote to adjourn—trapping Smith's welfare bills in committee.[19] With the crumbling of the insurgency and the suffocation of the Smith reconstruction program, that year's session would be aptly summarized by the *New York Times* with the headline "Legislature Noted for Little It Did."[20]

But this was not the end of the battle. Late that summer, Smith addressed the convention of the New York State Federation of Labor at Syracuse and promised to demand health insurance, a minimum wage, and an eight-hour day for women from the 1920 legislature; the governor charged that "reactionaries" and "men of little foresight" had blocked his industrial reforms, including health insurance, and threatened that these politicians "must see the light or they will be replaced by men of our modern day." Senator Davenport also appeared before the convention, heralding an emerging consensus for insurance, "even among employers who opposed it at the outset."[21] Indeed, the very support of the state federation, expressed at the summer convention, was quite significant, for the American Federation of Labor opposed compulsory health insurance, and its president, Samuel Gompers, had resigned from the AALL over the "socialistic stuff" he felt the organization was producing.[22]

As the next legislative session opened, Smith fulfilled his pledge to labor, using his January 7, 1920, message to demand swift action on his welfare agenda, noting in particular maternity insurance, workmen's compensation, and health insurance for workers, as well as an expansion of the state's public health activities.[23] These remarks were received enthusiastically by New York's social welfare progressives. From Henry Street, Lillian Wald wrote the governor: "I am . . . very much interested in your recommendations for reform in the health protection of the state, and naturally personally interested in your recognition of the need of the public health Nursing Service," while pledging her personal support for his agenda.[24]

In March, Davenport again proposed insurance legislation. Yet the senator was less optimistic, suggesting that he would "not press for final passage of the bill until there was an intelligent public opinion back of it." Davenport linked a perceived loss of momentum to postwar paranoia, citing "a subtle and organized propagandism" against social welfare measures in the context of the state legislature's anti-Bolshevik Lusk Committee investigations of socialist politicians and educators and the U.S. Justice Department's ongoing hunt for subversives under Attorney General A. Mitchell Palmer.[25] In fact, only three weeks after this announcement, the bill was "bitterly denounced as 'pernicious and un-American'" at a hearing of the Senate Labor and Industrial Committee.[26] The National Association of Manufacturers assured the committee that the bill was "unsound," while the Women's Betterment League of the Lady Maccabees of America execrated not only the bill but also its supporters within the League of Women Voters, whom they skewered as a socialist cabal. Not everyone agreed with these sentiments: the same day, a group of progressive Republican women "bearded Speaker Sweet in his den" and upbraided him over his stifling of Smith's welfare agenda, arguing that such actions were "more fertile of Bolshevist propaganda and of disloyalty toward Government than a thousand radical schools and soap-box orators."[27] In any case, it was clear by April that the insurance bill was doomed for 1920—a casualty of the Red Scare.[28]

While compulsory insurance appeared moribund by the spring of 1920, the governor remained responsible for dealing with the state's lingering health crises, and Republican leaders in the legislature offered a compromise. Henry M. Sage, chairman of the state senate Finance Committee, and his assembly counterpart H. Edmund Machold, proposed a bill to establish "a system of statewide health centres, supported in part by State funds"—a program already being urged by the governor, who had called for "a law extending a State subsidy to localities which would establish health centers in order that doctors and nurses might be available for the entire population." The bill's supporters claimed that it would allow "persons of small means and dwellers in rural and industrial communities . . . access to the best that modern medicine provides."[29]

This was especially critical given the failure of compulsory health insurance, for the advocates of that bill had long recognized that uninsured laborers in New York's cities were inundating charitable dispensary clinics and public health centers originally intended for the very poor. Accordingly, one motive behind insuring laborers was easing the increasing burden on these clinics wrought by growing numbers of working-class sick seeking free treatment.[30] If these workers could not be insured, at least their access to care at public clinics could be expanded. Furthermore, the program would be especially advantageous to rural areas of the state, where thirty-seven communities were "entirely without the services of a physician," according to a study by State Health Commissioner Hermann M. Biggs.[31]

Despite this apparent incentive for Republican cooperation, Smith's health program, like his entire welfare agenda, went down in flames in the 1920 legislature.[32] That fall, the governor was narrowly defeated for reelection by Republican judge Nathan Miller of Syracuse. Restored to office after a 1922 rematch, Smith would resume the health policy course semaphored by the clinics proposal: heavy spending to improve the state's public health infrastructure and thus open access to care for the entire population.

It will be recalled that one of the most important periods of reform in New York history was spurred by the infamous Triangle Shirtwaist Fire of March, 1911: in the wake of this horror, protective labor legislation was passed at a frenzied pace, informed by the State Factory Investigating Commission and shepherded through the legislature by Al Smith and Robert Wagner. It is a tragic—even shameful—irony that the Empire State's major initiative for improving one aspect of its health care infrastructure was to be inspired by another, less-well-known conflagration. On February 18, 1923, only seven weeks after Smith was inaugurated for his second tenure as governor, a fire at a hospital for the mentally ill on Ward's Island in New York killed twenty-four patients and three state employees.[33]

The blaze caused a sensation in the media and scandalized the New York public. It was revealed that there had been warnings of a possible cataclysm by a series of previous fires at the facility; the antiquated fire apparatus on the island was lambasted; a slew of investigations into various aspects of the tragedy commenced almost instantaneously; and the *Times* editorialized that "responsibility for the failure to provide a fireproof building for the insane must be assumed by the State authorities."[34] The fire had a significant effect on the psyche of New Yorkers well after the flames were extinguished: in June, a grand jury in Brooklyn admonished Mayor John F. Hylan's administration over conditions at Greenpoint Hospital and Kings County Hospital, fearing "a repetition of the Ward's Island disaster."[35]

At Albany, Tammany assemblyman Louis Cuvillier demanded immediate consideration of his proposal for a "tri-borough" bridge, which had been blocked the previous year by Hylan, and which acting mayor Murray Hulbert claimed would have allowed fire vehicles access to Ward's Island. Meanwhile, the governor immediately launched an offensive, declaring from Albany the day after the fire that "the overcrowded condition of the Manhattan Hospital, to my mind, was the main cause for the great loss of life. The only remedy seems to me to be new buildings, or additions to those already in use. No amount of fire apparatus could have prevented what has occurred, I am told."[36]

Since 1916, the state had been moving to remedy its "acute hospital problem" through new construction and repairs, but "the exigencies of war halted the program until 1920," and after Smith's defeat that November, the Miller administration "slowed up that program."[37] The renewed scrutiny of conditions in hospitals for the state's dependents offered Smith an unparalleled opportunity for action, for the fire presented a graphic case in his larger point that the state needed to expand and modernize its health care infrastructure. Swiftly, the point was made. Within twenty-four hours of the fire, officials in New York were warning of "death trap" conditions at Bellevue Hospital and at the City Home on Welfare Island.[38] Within seventy-two hours, the governor had sent a special message to the legislature urging approval for submission to the voters of at least $50 million in bonds "for the erection of new State hospital buildings to check overcrowding, as well as an immediate appropriation of $1,438,950 for urgent repairs and removal of fire hazards at these institutions."[39]

When the State Hospital Commission submitted its final report to the legislature in mid-March, they confirmed Smith's theory, declaring overcrowding the primary culprit in the deaths.[40] These revelations bolstered Smith, and by April it appeared that his bond proposal, sponsored in the assembly by his insurance-war ally Charles Donohue, would pass the legislature and face a November referendum.[41] That fall, the governor campaigned vigorously for the bond, reminding voters of the Ward's Island tragedy and the looming threat of further devastation.

At Yonkers on October 11, Smith stated that he could "think of no more sacred duty resting on the State today than the proper care of the unfortunate sick and afflicted whom we promised to care for, and we are not doing it." Smith noted that "the structures themselves are too old."[42] Thus it was of fundamental importance to develop these facilities not only because of overcrowding but also because of dilapidation. Indeed, a report issued to the governor days after the Ward's Island fire illustrated this point. The youngest of the state hospitals had been constructed in the late nineteenth century. Binghamton State Hospital had been opened as an inebriate asylum in 1860; Manhattan State Hospital had been in use since 1855 and had gone through phases as a homeopathic hospital, a holding facility for immigrants, and an insane asylum before its ultimate conversion to a hospital in 1896; construction on Utica State Hospital had been completed in 1843—three years before the first shots were fired in the Mexican War.[43]

If humanitarianism obliged the state to rebuild these facilities, "good sound business principles" demanded that the state finance these operations with long-term debt, for "hospitals built to-day on modern plans, built of steel and concrete, are destined to last for a hundred years at least to come, and why should the taxpayers of to-day pay for them?" The maneuver offered a means of bypassing legislative politics, which in past sessions had so often quashed

Smith's program. Smith had witnessed how the election of a new governor in 1920 begat substantial cuts in construction spending the following year, and feared that when annual appropriations were used to finance these projects they would be subject to political whims: "When you don't pay for them as the result of bonds they fall into the politics of the State once in a while when there is a wave of alleged economy and there is a cut down in the building." To Smith, such frugality bequeathed a deleterious legacy: "We have an over-crowding to-day in State hospitals throughout the whole State of very nearly 35%. 37,000 people are in these institutions alone and 35% of them are not being properly cared for."[44] Smith sought further to ease voters' anxieties by suggesting that costs would be minimal: repaid over twenty-five years, the ostensibly large deficit "would mean, for each individual, a debt of [$]4.65, and each individual would have 25 years in which to pay that debt, or about 19¢ a year. . . . Now, tell me, what citizen of this State would not pay 19¢ a year, or a good many times that amount, for the sake of knowing that the unfortunate dependents upon the State were cared for safely and properly."[45] That November, the bond was widely approved, and so the governor could now set about modernizing the state's hospitals.

Twenty-five months after this victory, an infusion of funds had spurred a spending and building spree, with robust projects breaking ground in all corners of the state. In Binghamton, work began on a 150-bed tuberculosis pavilion; in Buffalo, on a 100-bed reception hospital and housing for one hundred nurses; on Long Island, on buildings for 500 beds at an inpatient colony in Central Islip; in Gowanda, on a 200-bed reception hospital; on 300 beds' worth of rooms at Hudson River Hospital in Poughkeepsie, 764 at Kings Park on Long Island, 200 at Manhattan, 873 at Rochester, 550 at St. Lawrence, and so forth.[46] By 1927, bond funds had provided accommodations for 12,691 additional patients in the state's hospitals and charitable facilities, as well as housing for 2,846 doctors, nurses, and staff.[47] In the decade preceding this growth spurt, the state had provided for a total of 7,060 new patients—an average addition of 706 beds per year; from 1924 through 1927, the state added 3,173 beds per year.

While delighting in these advances, the governor was far from satisfied. In 1925, adviser Belle Moskowitz calculated that existing overcrowding and continued population growth meant that the new accommodations yielded a statewide surplus of only one hundred beds—hardly enough to assure the long-term adequacy of state hospitals. Moskowitz concluded that "if provision . . . is not made by appropriations from current revenues year by year to take care of the reconstruction items and to provide new accommodations for the annual increases it is only a question of time when the State will be again confronted with the problem of overcrowding and face the need of another bond issue to 'catch up.' "[48]

Smith's solution was to double down: to seek further bond revenue to allow the state to keep pace with demand for hospitals and all other public works. In 1925, only two years after the $50 million was approved specifically for hospitals, the governor pushed an even more ambitious debt scheme: an amendment to permit the legislature to bond $10 million a year for the next ten years "without further reference to the people." Smith saw the proposal as a way to avoid "the temptation that looms in front of every man . . . that the way to gain popular favor is to have low appropriations bills," as well as a means of circumventing New York's constitutional prohibition against holding referenda on multiple bonds at a single election. Smith reflected again on the hospital experience, detailing how the State Hospital Commission had requested $49 million for construction between 1919 and 1923 but had received only $15 million, "because every succeeding Legislature and most of the Executives had in mind low appropriation bills as an indication of their ability to economize in the government of the State." The governor understood that this ten-year bond scheme was a radical departure from the legislative and constitutional traditions of the Empire State—but he did not care. He proclaimed that he and his allies were "not thinking of some holy economic law," nor were they particularly interested in "what Silas Wright said in 1846." His interest was not orthodoxy, but that "what the State of New York is doing tonight and today with regard to tubercular patients is a crime and a disgrace." His interest was in the fact that "we have in this State the greatest group of dilapidated, worn out, sickly looking, old buildings devoted to public use that anybody will find in the United States."[49] The $100 million bond carried with bipartisan support, and Smith was able to cooperate with the legislature to direct funds toward projects ranging from government offices in Albany, to major construction at Sing Sing Prison, to land acquisitions for the Taconic State Park, to improvements at state hospitals like Brooklyn, Creedmoor, Harlem Valley, and Rockland.[50]

Smith's immense building program for state hospitals is a particularly striking example of his campaign to expand and modernize New York's health care infrastructure. But this was in fact only one portion of his broader agenda. Of equal significance is the way in which his administration expanded health clinics, research facilities, and access to medical personnel statewide.

In 1920, Governor Smith had urged the legislature to establish an "adequate system of public health centers in conjunction with local health activities" and to provide state subsidies for local health efforts.[51] Additionally, the governor suggested that improvements in health care would require "good salaries to get good people."[52] Smith accomplished none of this in his first term. Returning to Albany in 1923, he began again to pursue this public health program. In February he summoned a group of physicians and experts to the executive chamber to craft a plan for improving rural health care.[53] The Conference on Rural Health and Medical Practice concluded that many rural areas lacked adequate services not because of poverty but due to inaccessibility.[54] They recommended against state subsidies for country doctors, calling instead for development by the counties of small, centralized rural hospitals.[55]

In response, the governor summarized the need for rural health reform in an April message to the legislature, declaring, "Sickness is no respecter of geographical location, and tragic conditions prevail in the more sparsely settled areas of the State where, especially in the winter months, it is difficult for physicians to go." This was in contrast to the city, where citizens, "however poor or unfortunate, [have] hospitals and nursing services at hand and never need experience the suffering that now falls on the lot of some parts of our farm population." Echoing the physicians' conference, Smith prescribed the establishment of "small community hospitals to serve rural districts where . . . physicians would have the advantages of being able to take care of several patients at a time, and thus avoid the long rides in the winter time over difficult roads to scattered homes."[56] The governor asked counties to establish such hospitals, but diverged from the conference recommendations and promised state matching funds for all projects—reasoning that "it is sometimes necessary to apply a stimulus to secure local activity."[57] The legislature approved the program that spring.[58]

The administration's rural health initiative went beyond encouraging hospital construction. By 1925, Smith could also point to increased provision of nurses for rural communities. Through January of that year, $26,000 had been granted in aid to sixteen counties, and fourteen of those grants went directly to nursing services.[59] By 1927, he could claim credit for "twenty-four counties of New York State receiv[ing] a total of $91,732.00 for aid in providing public health nursing services and other urgently needed public health activities that would not otherwise have been available to these communities."[60]

Perhaps most significantly in 1923, Smith pressed successfully for New York's participation in the federal Sheppard-Towner maternity education and health program—a reform that had been blocked by Governor Miller.[61] Smith credited generous state appropriations for public health, along with participation in Sheppard-Towner, with providing a quick return. "The decrease in the death rate of infants is especially remarkable. For the first ten months of 1924, sixty deaths per 1,000 infants under 1 year of age is much the lowest ever recorded in the State. If we compare it with the average annual death rate of infants for the five-year period of 1917–1921, it would mean that 3,455 infants now living would have died." These programs were also effective in promoting maternal welfare, producing a "most gratifying decrease in deaths among women from causes directly connected to childbirth" of about forty-five per year since the organization of the Division of Maternity, Infancy, and Child Hygiene in 1921.[62]

The 1923 reforms initiated a period of expansion of health services and spending under Smith, so that by 1927, the state was granting counties $91,000 for public health work, $80,000 for laboratories, and $62,000 for maternity programs.[63] In 1917, the State Health Department spent $732,095; by 1927, that figure stood at $1,748,477.18.[64] The state created a traveling preschool children's health unit, which was performing 220 clinics in twenty-three counties by 1927. Two obstetrical units toured the state, performing 284 clinics in twenty-two counties by the same year. Also that year, ninety-two orthopedic clinics examined 1,935 patients, with 500 additional exams by the unit's orthopedic surgeons and over 7,000 home visits by orthopedic nurses. Meanwhile, a tuberculosis consultation unit traveled to twenty-seven counties, performing 132 clinics for 3,249 patients.[65] Funds for hospital improvements continued to flow, and salaries for state nurses and attendants were raised.[66] Simultaneously, a newly created Department of Mental Hygiene established outpatient mental health clinics, modern children's programs, and "an active social service" arm charged with distributing information about mental health issues to social and civic organizations.[67]

Smith argued that the results of this largesse were reflected in the state's health statistics. Vaccinations and children's clinics had led to a reduction in childhood illness; prenatal care translated to lower infant and maternal mortality rates; better buildings and better-paid staff facilitated better patient care; preventative mental hygiene promised "far-reaching influence on the character and mental health of these cases."[68] The governor could cite specific instances of success: the state had initiated a major campaign against diphtheria, and by 1926 the number of deaths from that disease had fallen below 700—an all-time low from the high of 6,500 in 1888. Scarlet fever had "almost ceased to be a factor in childhood mortality," while tuberculosis had fallen to a record low, halved from the number of cases two decades earlier. Within three years of commencing participation in the Sheppard-Towner program, maternal mortality rates reached an all-time low in 1926, beginning to parallel the fantastic successes in infant health noted in previous years.[69]

"Public health is purchasable" was the favorite saying of Dr. Hermann Biggs, who served as state health commissioner in the early years of the Smith administration, until his death in 1923. Al Smith was fond of Biggs's aphorism, to the extent that he quoted it in his annual message to the legislature in 1925, 1926, and 1927, and included it in policy speeches long after his tenure as governor had concluded.[70] This belief was reflected not only in Smith's rhetoric but also in his policies. Health care spending more than doubled under Smith, and investment in new facilities reached unprecedented levels through unprecedented means.

All of this was a clear reflection of the governor's progressive sensibilities. His program for public health was in many ways a manifestation of his ideological roots in the social work tradition. His eagerness to mobilize the power and the purse of the state in behalf of constituent welfare irrespective of fiscal concerns also grew out of the Tammany tradition—especially the post-Triangle machine's increasing openness to the dynamic state.

Meanwhile, Governor Smith himself proved an able executor of this progressive amalgam of machine and reform. He articulated the reformist message in clear, relatable, human terms, while employing his own governmental prowess to achieve long-thwarted public health aims. In 1925, as his program began to gain momentum, Smith alluded to the former commissioner and the enduring credibility of his ideas: "The late Dr. Biggs was noted for his statement that public health is purchasable. I believe we have demonstrated it."[71]

Public Property

Like that of health care, the story of Al Smith's conservation program provides great insight into his broader political ideology.[72] In this case, Smith's policies link him with a long progressive conservationist tradition, while demonstrating the breadth of his social welfare vision—one that encompassed recreation, environmental protection, and affordable electricity.[73] The conservation story is also telling in terms of execution, for it reveals ways in which Smith employed the might of the state vigorously to pursue his progressive ambitions.

On April 18, 1923, in a special message to the state legislature, Governor Smith advocated a statewide system of parks with a centralized administrative apparatus. Smith argued that "there is undoubtedly great need of large open spaces outside of our cities for camping and recreation," pointing out that "the cheap automobile has brought the country and the forests and lakes to the doors of hundreds of thousands of people" who had never ventured "more than a mile or two away from their homes before." With these developments, "people in great numbers, not the rich, but the great rank and file of citizens and particularly the children visit our forest playgrounds, even going as far as the Adirondacks to do so." This "enthusiasm for outdoor life" represented "one of the healthiest developments of recent years," and as such, "the State ought to do everything in its power to provide forests and streams and parks to satisfy not only this generation but future generations who must live in even more crowded places." Beyond recreation, there was an underlying conservationism that influenced Smith's thinking. "Our water supply, the protection of watersheds, and the flow of streams, the protection of trees which are being cut four times as fast as they are grown, the wild life of the forests, the rainfall and the very temperature of the State depend upon our forest preserves. . . . I am convinced that timely expenditures for the extension of our forests and parks is a real economy."[74]

Smith understood that his proposal would be quite expensive; yet he was constitutionally prohibited from pursuing a bond for his parks program that year because he was already seeking the $50 million hospital bond. Nevertheless, the pace of ecological destruction and the rising costs of lands that the state might someday wish to acquire necessitated quick action, so the governor requested, and received, $850,000 in immediate appropriations. Additionally, Smith proposed the issuance of a $15 million bond in 1924, so that the program might be funded more robustly.[75] The bond, argued Smith and other proponents, would help meet the demands of a growing population by funding a unified park system, campsite development, and extensions of the state forest preserves in the Adirondacks and the Catskills. It would foster development of existing holdings like the Palisades Interstate Park on the New Jersey border, the Niagara reservation on the falls at the Canadian border, and Letchworth Park along the Genesee River; as well as the creation of new parks—an Allegany state park in the west, a Taconic tristate park on the border with Massachusetts and Connecticut, and numerous projects on Long Island.[76]

Prior to this, New York had no systematic program for the acquisition or supervision of parks.[77] The Empire State had been actively preserving the Adirondacks since the nineteenth century, several scattered state park systems had been established, and a $10 million bond approved in 1916 for development of the Palisades Park had been the largest such measure in American history; yet there existed neither a coordinated administration of these lands nor a vision for the extension or even the maintenance of such holdings.[78] Although Smith received the funds he requested in 1923, he did not yet win the overarching parks commission necessary to implement his broader vision.

The following year, the governor called again for a unified parks system. Responding with surprising alacrity, the legislature created the State Council of Parks to act as the central advisory agency for all parks except the forest preserve. The legislature further gladdened the governor by approving his $15 million bond proposal for referendum, appropriating an additional $850,000 for immediate use, and creating commissions to oversee state parks at the Finger Lakes and on Long Island. Smith's winning streak rolled into the fall, when voters approved the bond issue by a margin of almost three to one. Smith noted that nearly nine-tenths of this majority came from the larger cities of the state, claiming that this demonstrated "the desire of the congested populations for summer breathing spaces outdoors."[79] Notably, these jurisdictions were also the source of much of Smith's strength in his reelection bid, and his influence likely affected the outcome in the urban districts.

Armed with $15 million and bolstered by a countercurrent reelection victory, Smith returned to Albany in 1925 intent on developing his coveted parks system. Here, however, the governor's yearlong rally reached its conclusion—the Republican legislature suddenly turned against the Smith agenda. It swiftly became apparent that this shift was due to the administration's plans for Long Island.[80]

The battle of Long Island dramatizes a primary motive behind the governor's crusade for state parks: a belief in the fundamental value of the outdoors to the welfare of the working masses. Furthermore, Smith asserted that the power of the state ought to be wielded to wrest control of potential recreation destinations from the rich and open them up to those masses—a sort of redistribution of environmental wealth.[81] Many Long Islanders vociferously opposed such notions. North Shore residents battled plans for parkways to provide access from the metropolis to new parks, while on the South Shore members of the Timber Point Golf Club filibustered plans for a state park on a tract known as the Taylor Estate.[82]

Under intense lobbying from North and South Shore residents, the Republican assembly moved to thwart the activities of Robert Moses, appointed by Smith as president of the new Long Island State Park Commission. This legislation, dubbed the Thayer Bill after its sponsor, a Republican senator from Franklin County, smothered the condemnation process in bureaucracy and introduced a cumbersome mechanism for approving park expenditures that would feature the Republican-dominated State Board of Estimate and Control. While the bill drew a forceful rebuke from Smith, the now-defiant legislature passed it over the governor's protests, and although Smith vetoed the Thayer Bill, another burdensome method of appropriations was soon established.[83]

With Long Island at the root of this legislative pertinacity, Smith took to the airwaves on June 11 to discuss the controversy over funding that region's park projects. The speech is an astounding document that reveals the strong class motivations behind the governor's dogged support for Moses's Long Island ambitions, as well as a willingness to politicize class on behalf of his policy program. Smith described "wealthy residents and golf club members" who "started an agitation . . . about the hordes of people from New York that would come down tramping over the country and leaving empty sardine and cracker boxes behind them," and denounced this "small group of wealthy men" who felt that "a public park to serve all the people was not desirable in that section of Long Island."[84]

The governor reported further that these objections were reinforced at a hearing he had hosted: the State Parks Commission "declared that they desired this large acreage to find a breathing spot on the south shore of Long Island for the millions of people living . . . throughout the Greater City and metropolitan section," while "their opponents, a very few wealthy men . . . reduced their entire argument against the State to the bare statement that they desired to get control of the property for themselves in order that they might . . . have a kind of exclusive community there with the golf club as the center of attraction." For Smith, the choice was clear: "As between the few and the many to be benefited, I cast my lot with the many and I signed the papers necessary to acquire the property by entry and appropriation."[85]

But these ravenous patricians proved implacable. "High-priced legal talent was brought in," because, as Smith saw it, "this small group of Long Island people desired that great playground to themselves and wanted to keep the people from it." So the question, according to the governor, was, "Will the law of this State be so shaped to give power and influence to a small group of selfish men as against the best interests of the great mass of our people?" Then, pledging to "battle it out right in the shadow of the Capitol itself," Smith demanded in archetypically progressive tones that New Yorkers must "not permit the impression to go abroad in this State that wealth and power can palsy the arm of the State and stall the machinery of Government in the performance of a duty that has so much to do, now and in the future, with the health, happiness and the comfort of our ten million people, and of the millions more who will follow them."[86]

This speech is not important because it convinced legislators to abandon their protests—it did not. A special session was called the following week, and the same bill was passed, again to be vetoed by the governor. But the speech, as well as the entire episode, provides important insight into Smith's beliefs about parks and about state action more broadly. It demonstrates that an important part of his motivation was the provision of what he considered a key welfare service—recreation—by the government to the masses of crowded workers in New York City and throughout the state. It also reveals Smith's willingness to arouse class antagonism on behalf of what he considered a progressive cause.[87]

Meanwhile, progress continued, and by 1928, the State Council of Parks administered 2,218,993 acres divided into about seventy parks and reservations.[88] Such a widely dispersed and expensive system was facilitated largely through the centralized administrative apparatus that Smith had envisioned, as well as by the use of bonds, rather than annual appropriations, to fund condemnations and improvements. Bonds were vital to the project for two related reasons: first, because legislative appropriations for all sorts of public works tended to suffer delays, so that in the pay-as-you-go system, "we do not 'pay' and therefore we do not 'go'"; and second, because swiftness was key in the interest of economy, since "prices for land are continually rising."[89] As with his hospitals program, Smith justified incurring long-term debt for these projects by reasoning that they were undertaken not simply for immediate needs but with an eye toward the future.[90] Moreover, this did not burden the state with an especially onerous bond obligation: in 1927, the per capita debt of New York State was $21.80, while for the federal government it was $165.92.[91]

This expansive statewide project reflected the governor's understanding of recreation as an important facet of the welfare services of the progressive state. But it also reflected a genuine interest in preserving the state's natural heritage from destruction.[92] This is particularly striking, for while Smith's interest in the welfare of the urban worker has been well chronicled, his interest in conservation has not.

Smith loudly lamented New Yorkers' "reckless" destruction of their woodlands and other natural blessings, and in response recorded a catalogue of conservation achievements that transcends parks and recreation.[93] During his tenure, eleven million acres were brought under fire protection; more than 300,000 acres were added to the state forest preserve; a similar acreage was cleared of ribes to protect white pines from blister rust; a 5,000-square-mile "barrier zone" was established along the state's eastern border and on Long Island's North Shore to check the advance of the gypsy moth, which had done millions of dollars' worth of damage in New England and by 1922 had begun "invading [the] state from Massachusetts."[94] By the late 1920s, New York was the national pacesetter in reforestation—"a conservation achievement of the very first importance," in the administration's view. Within one year of Smith's 1925 demand for increased funding to expedite reforestation, output at state nurseries had swelled from 10.5 million trees to 20.5 million, and by 1928 it stood at 25 million. In that year, idle land was "being planted to forests at the rate of about 25,000 acres . . . a year, an increase of 500 per cent over the average annual planting for the ten years prior to [Smith's] incumbency."[95]

Forests were planted and preserved with enthusiasm, and then made available to the citizenry. State parks were expanded greatly—and not only on Long Island for quick weekend escapes by residents of Manhattan and Brooklyn, but throughout the state for excursions by all the people. Six hundred miles of trails were blazed in the Catskills and in the Adirondacks. Campsites were established in these places with a capacity for two million—a figure that they attracted annually. Hundreds of islands on Lake George were purchased and preserved by the state, and of these 155 were opened to the public.[96]

All of this demonstrates the Smith administration's commitment to the protection of New York's natural resources and the governor's willingness to employ the power of the state expansively for such purposes. Such initiatives gained the governor effusive approbation from scores of outdoorsmen—in a representative statement, the Southern New York Fish and Game Association named the governor an honorary member, remarking that his administration had been conducted in accord with their motto: "For the Good of All."[97] Across the state, citizens were aroused by the governor's initiatives and encouraged him to acquire idyllic tracts that were yet unprotected—from glens near the Finger Lakes, to Dome Island in Lake George, to Montauk Point on Long Island.[98]

Twin impulses to assuage the condition of ordinary New Yorkers and to preserve the state's natural heritage are discernible among the sundry parks and conservation initiatives of the Smith administration. These impulses converged in what was to become not only one of Smith's signature issues as governor, but also one of the fundamental concerns of his national campaign: water power. The experience of water power development in New York State prior to Smith's tenure was a haphazard comedy of errors marked by a deficit of foresight and an absence of coordination. At the turn of the century, the legislature had granted charters for development on the Niagara River so recklessly that in 1905 the federal government, "fearing the ultimate destruction of the Falls themselves, reached its hand into the State"—stopping for a time these "promiscuous legislative grants." Within two years, the St. Lawrence was in similar jeopardy, as the Long Sault Development Corporation was chartered to pursue power projects on that river. This continued until 1913, when the Democratic-controlled legislature, under Al Smith and Robert Wagner, repealed Long Sault's incorporation.[99]

Partially in response to the Long Sault giveaway, progressive Republican governor Charles Evans Hughes had called for public development of state water resources in 1907, but his program encountered a legislative blockade. In 1912, legislative Democrats including Assemblyman Smith went further, demanding state ownership of water power projects—to no avail.[100] The consolation prize was creation of a conservation commission to oversee state resources, but this body's work was encumbered in bureaucracy in 1915 when Republicans, led by Governor Charles Whitman, enacted a provision requiring all of the commission's plans to secure approval from the attorney general and the state engineer.[101]

After Smith assumed the governorship at the close of the decade, he began urging public water power development. The 1919 legislature responded with a program of private control, which Smith vetoed.[102] Meanwhile, the governor's proposal for public development died unceremoniously in the assembly's rules committee and was "flatly rejected" again the following year.[103] As with so many of his early proposals, public hydroelectricity was held in check by obdurate legislative Republicans; and as with so many of those proposals, Smith opted to present his case directly to the voters.

Running for reelection, Smith proclaimed at Elmira his stand for water power's "public ownership, public development, and public control in the interest of all our people."[104] A week later, the governor explained before 4,000 at the Wieting Opera House in Syracuse that experience had demonstrated the dangers of private control. "I am for State development, State ownership and State control because I am sure that is the only way in which the people themselves will get any benefit from this God-given resource, because under private development the price of electricity is exactly the same in Buffalo, where it is developed from the falls, as it is in the City of New York, where every bit of it is developed from coal which is dragged all the way from Pennsylvania."[105] Smith believed that hydroelectricity should be cheaper than coal power once developed, speculating that if the profit margins of private capital were removed from the price of this energy, electricity rates for New Yorkers would decline appreciably. He reiterated his stance October 30, before 10,000 supporters at Madison Square Garden: "The great natural water power resources of this State must be developed by the State itself under State ownership and State control. . . . That is the only way that the rank and file of the people can ever get any distinct benefit from the property that belongs to themselves." Smith distinguished his stand from that of the Republicans, whom he claimed were directed by "a small and an influential and a rich and a very powerful group" who intended that "the great water power resources of this State should be developed for private interests and by private capital."[106]

Accepting the Democratic nomination to challenge Governor Miller in 1922 in the wake of his narrow reelection defeat, Al Smith assailed his successor as "a reactionary Governor of the old-fashioned Republican school" whose reign had benefited the "water power interests," among other nefarious plutocrats (this attack was in fact tame by the standards of the evening, during which Albany mayor William Hackett denounced Miller as a "dictator").[107] While this was a night for political histrionics, the underlying assumptions of Smith's broadside were factual, for Miller had created a new water power commission authorized to license private development—reversing what had been state policy since the Hughes administration.[108] At Troy on October 16, Smith concluded that on the power question, Miller had turned "back the hands of the clock more than fifteen years."[109] On this and many other points, the voters ostensibly agreed with the challenger, and Smith won in the greatest landslide of his career.[110]

Yet this was no deathblow for private power interests. Prior to Smith's restoration, in early 1922, Mortimer Ferris, a Republican state senator from Ticonderoga, proposed to relax state constitutional protections of the forest preserve to allow private exploitation for water power development.[111] The scheme would have empowered the legislature to grant fifty-year leases to private firms, at as low a price as legislators found agreeable.[112] The amendment passed both houses that spring.

Because the 1894 state constitution required any amendment to gain approval from two consecutive legislatures before being submitted for referendum, the Ferris Amendment, which quickly earned the epithet "the Adirondack Raid," underwent a second test in 1923, now facing a Democratic senate. The amendment again passed the assembly and was "railroaded" through the upper house with enough bipartisan support that the majority leader, Smith protégé Jimmy Walker, was left utterly impotent. Resigned to legislative futility, the future Gotham mayor declared, "We will refer this resolution to the people and let them defeat it."[113] Walker's confidence was grounded in his awareness of the governor's campaigning prowess; the senator understood that with the battle now taken to the public, Smith would be the most formidable contestant in the arena.

Across the Empire State, a torrent of objections was unleashed in response to the legislative ascent given the Ferris Amendment.[114] Diverse opponents warned of the mutilation of Saranac Lake, shuddered at "the erection of private power plants on State lands," feared for the very "ruggedness of the country, its wild grandeur," and alerted voters to "a gigantic conspiracy . . . to impose forever upon all the people of New York an onerous tax from which they can never escape" in the form of a monopolistic "super-power combine."[115] To such voices was added that of the governor, who abhorred both the denuding of the forest preserve and the invasion of the region by rapacious private developers, "well-known exploiters of public resources . . . eager to get their grips on the people's lands."[116]

Determined to scuttle the Ferris measure, Smith took to the campaign trail in opposition to ratification. In doing so, the state's chief executive became its chief crusader for the protection of state lands and the retention of public water properties. At Yonkers, Smith railed against the "raid," invoking the progressive trope "the people" versus "the interests": "Now that great big natural park is the property of the people of the State and if water power is going to be developed from it, it should be developed for the people themselves, and not for the private owners that are spoken of in the water power plank of the Republican declaration of principle." Ultimately, the episode yielded one of Smith's few total victories on the issue: voters overwhelmingly sided with the governor, 965,777 to 470,251.[117]

The belligerency of the Ferris Amendment positioned the state GOP as the unabashed champions of private water power development. With sustained Republican power in the legislature, the governor and his allies realized that the defeat of the Adirondack Raid did not assure public control. Acknowledging these realities, Smith recalibrated his political tactics in order to promote his public power program.

Shortly after thwarting Ferris, Smith sent a special message to the legislature outlining in the most specific terms yet his alternative to private development. For inspiration, the governor looked northward, where the province of Ontario had "boldly developed a successful policy of control by a public agency representing the municipalities of the Province."[118] For Smith, the Ontario system suggested the possibility of a middle way for his own jurisdiction—and one offering palpable benefits: in Toronto, Hamilton, and London, Ontario, the average cost of household energy was two to four cents per kilowatt hour, while in New York's cities, power cost from eight to fifteen cents per kilowatt hour.[119] Further, Smith sought to assuage popular apprehensions, suggesting that a total state takeover of the entire power system would be unnecessary, "provided that the State controls the situation at the source, from which it can direct where the power derived from public sources can go and at what rates it can be sold." Accordingly, Smith advocated a public corporation—a state power authority.[120]

The controversy really boiled down to a fundamental philosophical discordance between the governor and the private interests—one that reveals the extent to which Smith's progressive views of an expansive state role in social welfare informed his administration. The week before Smith unveiled his new policy, Robert Moses had fumed that "it is to the everlasting discredit of the corporations which have engaged in the electric light and gas business that, generally speaking, they have been interested primarily—almost exclusively—in development for profit."[121] Of course prioritization of profits was a perfectly reasonable posture for these capitalist outfits; yet it threatened the governor's alternative view of the use of state resources. For Smith, the proper disposition of these natural blessings was preservation from private exploitation, in favor of cautious state development for public benefit.

Meanwhile, recent events had served to calcify Smith's opposition to private exploitation of New York's untapped rivers. Indeed, the administration believed that, once established, corporate developments would prove unmanageable. If the legislature were permitted to "throw" the Niagara or the St. Lawrence "into private hands," warned Moses, "the possibility of regulation as a solution of this whole question becomes somewhat dubious." Given all of this, the answer was a state power authority.[122]

Smith pursued this new tactic with the 1924 legislature, proposing a commission to control and develop state power resources with a structure similar to that of the Port of New York Authority—featuring "no private stockholders" and deriving "its powers from the State," including bond-issuing prerogatives. The proposal encountered dilatory amendments and ultimate rejection; and although Smith was reelected in 1924 despite the second of three quadrennial triumphs by the national Republicans, proposals in 1925 and 1926 met with similar results. After sustaining repeated frustrations, Smith declared this struggle "the greatest single issue" of his 1926 reelection campaign.[123]

By now, both sides had grown truculent. Republicans were aggressively denouncing Smith's proposals as socialistic, a charge the governor dismissed as "foolish talk" and "an insult to the intelligence of the people of the State." Delivering haymakers of his own, Smith attacked by name Congressman Ogden Livingston Mills, a virulent critic of the power program and a potential challenger for the fall campaign: "No wonder Mr. Ogden Mills has the point of view of a well-entrenched advocate of private interests. Mr. Mills, who is shrieking so loudly about Socialism, was a director in this power company in 1923 and in all probability is still interested."[124]

If Smith's statement was that of a frustrated politician, it nevertheless portrayed accurately the nature of Mills's opposition by mentioning the charges of socialism. Mills was indeed the Republican gubernatorial nominee in 1926, and his major critique of Smith was to attach the epithet "socialist" to the proposed power authority. While Smith had repeatedly called for "perpetual ownership and control by the people of the State of the State-owned water-power resources," in contrast to development "by private capital," the governor was no doctrinaire socialist.[125] Like other progressives, he sought within reasonable limits the decommodification of life's basic necessities—health care, milk, housing, education, and in this case, electricity.[126] As a pragmatist who prioritized human welfare over rigid adherence to any specific theory of government, when he recognized that the private sector could not adequately or responsibly perform one of these social functions, the governor had no qualms about state intervention.

Thus Smith had no particular objection to socialistic solutions to the failures of the market. In defense of his plan, the governor pointed to precedents for state involvement in public works projects to encourage economic development, adducing the case of the Erie Canal and querying, "Does Congressman Mills suggest that DeWitt Clinton was a socialist?"[127] He later grew blunt: "The Congressman's talk about Socialism is, using a mild term, stupid."[128]

Indeed, with charges of plutocracy and Bolshevism flying about, the 1926 contest became a particularly bellicose affair. One Smith stalwart declared Mills "unqualified to be governor of New York" because of his recent directorship of an energy combine in New England and because of his noble family's vast holdings in power concerns.[129] Smith himself produced one of the most hotly populistic speeches of his career at Flushing that October: "Here we have a service promised by the Republican party but promised to whom? To the people of the State of New York? No. Promised to the water barons of the State, to the group of millionaires who now control practically all the water power resources in the northern and northwestern part of the State."[130] Such attacks were common throughout the campaign.[131]

Meanwhile, the Republicans could rely on anti-Smith propaganda bankrolled by the very businessmen Mills and the GOP were being accused of abetting. A 1928 Federal Trade Commission investigation revealed that power interests had, since 1922, invested more than $227,000 against the Smith power scheme. Materials distributed included 196,000 copies of a pamphlet entitled *Water Power in New York State*, given to educators, businessmen, the press, and civic organizations; another entitled *River Regulation in New York State*, of which 40,000 copies were dispersed among similar groups; and, most egregiously, 106,000 copies of two propagandistic textbooks, disbursed to students at 491 high schools. Furthermore, utilities were estimated to have spent between $28 million and $38 million on publicity annually—sponsoring in one six-month period 3,479 speeches. One architect of this public relations bombardment "admitted, upon close questioning . . . that the object of the literature was to oppose" Smith's power program.[132]

As another legislative session commenced, the reelected Smith penned an article for the periodical *Survey Graphic* in which he explored the obstacles his program had theretofore endured. "You know as well as I do that in democratic government you can get too many blocks ahead of the parade. You have got to be able to look around and see whether all of the members of your regiment are with you or not." The governor now recognized that public ownership schemes left proponents exposed to the toxic charge of socialism. Yet he saw an antidote. "It is possible to create . . . an agency of the state for the purpose of progressive public development without any public responsibility," he contended. "How any man who voted for the New York Port Authority or to set up the Port of Albany can talk about a power authority as a socialistic proceeding is more than I can understand."[133]

In making the Port Authority analogy, Smith invoked the Holland Tunnel, which would open later that year as the first of several Hudson River crossings constructed under the auspices of the authority (in fact, construction on the Outerbridge Crossing, the Goethals Bridge, and the George Washington Bridge was well under way by the end of Smith's administration): "How many of us know how much we really cut from our annual tax roll for this tunnel? Between 1919 and 1926 we put twenty-one million dollars in cash into it—and nobody knows anything about it because we just put it up. . . . Now that we are satisfied with it, everybody is going to go down when it opens and ride out into Jersey and sing 'Three cheers for the red, white and blue.' Yet it was just as much of a risk as would be the pledging of the credit of the state in the development of dams and powerhouses on the St. Lawrence River."[134]

Despite his reelection triumph and his increasingly tangible rhetoric on the issue, Smith would never succeed in creating a state power authority. Indeed, such a body would not be inaugurated until the second gubernatorial term of Franklin Roosevelt, and real work on state power projects would not commence for another two decades. Thus the lesson from the water power fight is not about Smith's tactics as much as it is about his fundamental convictions. State hydroelectric development represents the confluence of two: the belief in the inviolability of public resources, and the belief that, when necessary, the government must be employed in full to assuage the hardships of modern life—even to the point of "socialistic" policies. Smith's militant rhetoric, teetering as it did on the brink of class warfare, was but a manifestation of his interest in preserving the tranquility of the Adirondacks, asserting the state's riparian rights, and providing cheap energy to the working class. By the mid-1920s, Smith's political activities were driven by his policy ambitions.

This demonstrates a great deal about Smith as an executive, while presaging his emerging national agenda. Indeed, Smith would plunge into the national fracas over water power during his governorship, engaging in a series of skirmishes with the federal administration over questions of authority and of economics.[135] In June 1920, during Smith's first term, Congress enacted the Federal Water Power Act, or "Esch Law," to bring hydroelectric development under federal control. Although the implications of the act might not have seemed so pernicious to the governor when executed by the relatively friendly Wilson administration, upon his return to office in 1923 Smith would find water power policy being piloted by the Harding and then the Coolidge administration.[136] Smith challenged Washington's assertions of authority on the grounds that "for years it has been our understanding that Federal control over navigable streams was only and solely for the purpose of regulating navigation. In other words, we believe that the bed of the stream is the property of the State and over it flows the water that generates the electrical energy." New York pressed a suit against the federal government challenging the Esch Law that was to be heard by the Supreme Court of the United States, with Smith rejecting entreaties from another progressive conservationist governor, Pennsylvania Republican Gifford Pinchot, to abandon the case, by insisting that the streams were "the property of the State and should be preserved for the benefit of the people of the State."[137] To avert such a judicial spectacle, a conference was held on May 10, 1923, between federal and state authorities, at which the federal government ceded to the New Yorkers exclusive jurisdiction over water power development in the Empire State.[138] The litigation was dropped in response.

This arbitration did not end the quarrel between Washington and Albany, and in fact the episode only masked the most crucial issue behind the rhetoric of states' rights. Friction between Smith and the conservative administrations in Washington over questions of national authority has led scholars to ascribe to the governor's activities an overriding constitutional purpose of state empowerment. But in these battles, state control was not an end unto itself; rather, Smith wanted to retain the rivers to prevent their exploitation and monopolization by private developers.

Indeed, the governor remained openly critical of the national administration on this point, warning New Yorkers in 1924: "If Republicans are the same in the State as they are nationally, bid good-bye to your water power resources. Say a farewell to the Adirondack Preserve, be prepared to deliver the inland streams and rivers to the power combine."[139] The White House was no more impressed with the direction being taken in New York. Watching the critical events of 1926 unfold, the Coolidge administration decided to push back against Smith's drive for state-run hydroelectric plants. Private communications between the parties demonstrate that economic rather than constitutional questions were the real points of contention. In a December memorandum for the New York governor summarizing the position of the White House, the president's very different philosophy on the purpose of hydroelectricity was set forth—a philosophy much more in tune with the polity of 1920s America. State regulations that encumbered the freewheeling development of power by private capital were "illegitimate items of cost" which "must be eliminated."[140] Indeed, the national administration had different priorities: "The consumers are being taxed in order to make for these large profits for investors. IT IS THESE PROMOTERS' PROFITS WHICH ARE SENDING UTILITY STOCKS BOOMING AND WHICH GIVE TO STOCKHOLDERS A RETURN ON THE GRANT OF SOVEREIGN POWER OR GRANT OF SOVEREIGN RESOURCES WHICH THE CONSUMERS OR USERS ARE PAYING FOR."[141] The White House argued that such economic dynamism would be impossible under a scheme similar to that governing the Port Authority, where tolls were charged only to cover costs, and thus profits were not accumulated.[142] Port Authority general counsel Julius Cohen, who compiled these administration arguments for Smith, provided a less favorable summation: "All these profits are made under legal sanction. In the last analysis, it means consumers are paying in their light and power rates huge dividends to the owners of common stock in power and light securities. Of course the Insulls and the Carlisles know it. . . . That is why the fight against the governor's plan is so intense and so bitter. He has touched a delicate pocket nerve."[143]

Smith was enthusiastic to mobilize the power of the state on behalf of his conservationist agenda. He was also willing to spend liberally on these initiatives, denouncing the "kind of false economy that means a weakening of our efforts to preserve forests and streams, the great gifts of nature herself."[144] His genuine interest in a variety of preservation projects throughout New York State helps discredit the suggestion that Smith was a myopic urbanite who knew—and cared—nothing for the world beyond the five boroughs. Furthermore, his understanding of parks and recreation as an important facet of social welfare, especially for urban workers who lacked regular access to such facilities, expands the academic understanding of 1920s urban liberalism: the welfare state was defined not only as laws to protect workers, shelter the poor, or extend health services, but also as initiatives to provide ample recreation and engagement with nature. In the water power debate, Smith simultaneously took stands for the preservation of the people's natural inheritance and for responsible state development of hydroelectricity to alleviate the burdensome cost of energy—revealing an expansive view of the appropriate role of government. In both parks and power, there was a socioeconomic element to Smith's thinking—the state needed to prevent resources from being monopolized by the influential and the wealthy, whether they be buccaneering power trusts or Long Island barons.

Smith's maneuvers on parks and hospitals are linked by the state's assumption of a sizable bonded debt for social welfare purposes, which enabled him to accomplish much of this agenda in his own time. Moreover, the governor established a two-pronged precedent for those who would follow. First, he claimed for the state an expansive role in public welfare. Second, he blazed a path for the heavy use of bonds for public works. The ramifications of this double legacy would become immediately apparent under Smith's successor, Franklin Roosevelt, who like Smith expanded the state's role in public welfare and like Smith sought to finance many of his public works with bonds.[145] Over the succeeding administrations of Smith, Roosevelt, and Herbert Lehman, this broadened state engagement in matters of social welfare was legitimized both through repeated use and—eventually—through the desperation of the Depression years. But it must be noted that long before the Great Depression compelled the state and eventually the nation to expand services and endure debt, Al Smith was already pressing such an agenda, urging that New York fulfill its obligation for the well-being of its citizens, at whatever cost necessary.

Public Administration

As governor, Al Smith demanded swift implementation of a broadly defined and generously funded social welfare regime. As the story of Smith's ardent labor on behalf of this agenda demonstrates, these initiatives were often frustrated—not only by conservative politics, but also by technical and constitutional hurdles. In order to promote hospital construction, for example, the governor needed to improvise new administrative tactics—in that case, a redefinition of the appropriate use of the state's bonded debt. The bond innovation was a remarkable one that would be of fundamental significance to the future of New York state governance, and it elucidates Smith's priorities as well as his mastery as an executive tactician. These themes are demonstrated even more profoundly by the governor's battle for administrative reorganization and the executive budget. Like partisan blockades and fiscal scruples, the Empire State's antiquated administrative apparatus would hobble and halt many of the governor's social welfare initiatives. Therefore, the governor's progressive agenda, as well as traditional concerns over "good government," compelled Smith to take up the mantle of administrative reform in the name of efficiency and economy.

Numerous studies have agreed that Smith's pursuit of executive reform was intertwined with his social welfare agenda; as the historian Elisabeth Israels Perry put it, Smith quickly "discovered" that "a powerless governor presiding over an array of uncoordinated agencies staffed by political hacks could never implement the reforms the Reconstruction Commission was proposing."[146]

Of equal significance, this episode is instructive regarding strategy. Smith pioneered a political style to accompany his progressive ideology, and he employed those tactics vigorously throughout the reorganization fight: the byzantine machinations of state government were made plain to uninitiated voters; abstract reforms were promoted in palpable terms; and a long-standing objective of élite progressives was transformed into a popular cause.

Throughout 1919 and 1920, Governor Smith's State Reconstruction Commission, with Belle Moskowitz as executive secretary, produced a series of twelve reports exploring all facets of state governance—including administration and efficiency. While the governor's interest and energy focused on the commission's social welfare and regulatory proposals, he soon realized that his ability to put into effect reforms of any kind would be impeded without administrative reorganization. Smith could not effectively implement his coveted social programs without crafting his own budget; yet the governor of New York lacked such authority.[147] Meanwhile, the Republican legislature refused to act on any of the governor's proposals, capping what was widely decried as a do-nothing session.[148] At the end of his first term, a frustrated Smith accurately grumbled that it had become "notorious throughout the State that much of my administration so far as constructive suggestions requiring legislation were concerned was fought by a Republican majority in the state legislature with no regard whatever to the merit of my proposals."[149]

With those proposals—influenced by both the urgency of social workers and the pragmatism of Tammany men—Smith had departed the realm of the abstract to pursue a catalogue of initiatives in areas such as housing, recreation, and public health. Yet while the governor and his forces fought doggedly for such reforms, they lost the first round of each bout. It took three years to create a housing board. This triumph came comparatively briskly, as most reconstruction programs would not be approved until Smith's third term. The development of state parks on Long Island did not begin in earnest until Smith's fourth term, and only after a protracted court battle. Proposals for workers' health insurance, a milk commission, and a power authority never fructified in the Smith era.[150]

Through such frustrations, the governor came to prioritize administrative reforms. In fact, he had endorsed such reforms conceptually as early as the New York State Constitutional Convention of 1915, where as a delegate Smith had supported Republican Elihu Root, former U.S. senator and secretary of war and of state under Theodore Roosevelt, in his efforts to modernize state government through administrative reorganization, executive budget making, and the "short ballot."[151] The convention's proposed constitution included all three of these progressive desiderata: New York's tangled web of 169 state agencies, boards, and commissions would be consolidated into seventeen departments; rather than preserving popular election of executive officers like the state engineer or secretary of state, ten departments would now have their leaders appointed by the governor, while only two positions would remain elective—the comptroller and attorney general; and the new document required that the consolidated state departments "furnish the governor in ample time a statement of . . . needs," which the governor was then charged to "revise . . . and cut . . . or hold himself responsible for the amounts," presenting the final tally "before the legislature side by side with a statement of the resources from which the appropriations are to be paid"—thus establishing the executive budget.[152]

Al Smith had advocated these reforms during the convention, adopting the traditional progressive interest in efficiency. However, the new constitution was submitted to delegates for approval in toto rather than in individual sections, and New York City Democrats like Smith voted against the document, largely because the proposed charter did not remedy the gross underrepresentation of the city in the state legislature.[153] While the new constitution limped out of the convention, it was rejected at the polls in November, with Smith campaigning against the document that contained administrative innovations for which he had fought.[154]

Four years later, Smith recognized that his social welfare agenda would be bolstered by a progressive reorganization scheme. Thus the governor became the foremost champion of administrative reform in New York. To Smith, reorganization could yield tangible social improvements beyond a more businesslike state government. Consolidating budget-making authority and other powers in the governor would enhance the executive's ability to set the state agenda; while streamlining state administration would provide resources for aggressive social programs and improve the efficacy of existing initiatives.

After the failure of the 1915 constitution, reorganization could be achieved only through constitutional amendments, which required approval in two consecutive legislatures and then ratification by the voters. During the second legislative session of Smith's first term, the governor was able to "bludgeon" the legislature into passing a reorganization amendment.[155] The *New York Times*, criticizing the bloated state budget, editorialized in favor of reorganization as it lay before the legislature, declaring, "There must be a halt to this extravagance. There can be none until the machinery of government is simplified, until there is a responsible and effective administrative control."[156] Here was a pithy articulation of the traditional motivation for such reforms: bringing a measure of sobriety to an unruly appropriations process to save taxpayers' funds.

Yet during that autumn's gubernatorial race, Smith presented his alternative argument for an executive budget. In a speech at Brooklyn, Smith countered charges by his opponent, Judge Nathan Miller, that the governor's "paternalistic" programs were draining the state treasury: "The Judge well knows that the real solution of the cost of government in this state is a change in the present method of making appropriations, and well knows that the cost of this government is made necessary because of its cumbersome organization. . . . I have declared for an executive budget at Albany, in the interest of economy. . . . I have declared in favor of reorganization and consolidation of the state departments, not only in the interest of economy, but to promote efficiency in the government of the state."[157]

There was no question that state government was wasteful—actors on all sides sought to remedy this in varying ways. Smith sought to do so not by scaling back social welfare programs but by making government run more efficiently. The governor rhetorically asked his opponent just which of his "paternalistic" initiatives he would cut—would it be care for orphans? Or would he reduce hospital funding? Or would he eliminate care for the mentally ill? To Smith, a miserly campaign of whittling necessary programs down to austerity—or eliminating them outright—was not a serious solution. The only "real solution of the cost of government" was reorganization.[158]

Although Smith lost in November, it was clear that his message had resonated in reform circles. The incumbent had retained the backing of many independents and progressive Republicans and managed to run well ahead of the national Democratic ticket.[159] In New York City, Republican presidential nominee Warren G. Harding won by 443,000 votes; simultaneously, the Democrat Smith won the city by 325,000 ballots.[160] Moreover, there was a "record vote for Smith in districts normally Republican," and many considered his showing "a great personal triumph." Meanwhile, Miller's allies expressed disappointment with the judge's relatively weak showing in the midst of a national Republican landslide.[161]

Nevertheless, the election of Nathan Miller imperiled reorganization. To appear on the ballot, the amendment was required to pass two consecutive legislatures—it had thus far progressed only half way. The new governor signaled his opposition to the reorganization and executive budget amendments, and in response the Republican legislature did not allow them out of committee.[162]

Meanwhile, Smith had not recoiled from political life after his 1920 defeat, and public appearances in 1921 and 1922 signaled the vanquished Democrat's enduring interest both in reform and in reclaiming the governorship. In a speech at the Lexington Opera House on November 4, 1922, just days before the next election, challenger Al Smith accused incumbent Nathan Miller of exacerbating statewide dysfunction by killing reorganization. "By his action he continued the disorganized and disjointed government that he claims he was able to make run, although nobody, not even the progressive members of his own party, believes that to be possible." In their rematch, Smith cruised to victory, winning by 387,000 votes statewide—to that time the largest plurality for any gubernatorial candidate in New York.[163]

Restored to office, Smith pushed with renewed vehemence for his reorganization program. In his inaugural address on New Year's Day 1923, Smith briefly discussed the topic, imploring the legislature to cooperate during the new term.[164] He began making allusions to his noted Republican forerunner, Charles Evans Hughes, and analogizing his difficulties with the Republican legislature to those faced by Hughes when he had grappled with party bosses fifteen years earlier.[165] Smith had political capital to spend, having won the most decisive gubernatorial victory in New York history, and he compounded this advantage through both his political cunning and his ability to garner the support (and invoke the legacy) of progressive Republicans. That spring, as the administration continued to concentrate on the question behind the scenes, the assembly passed the reorganization amendment, setting the program back on track for a referendum.[166] A triumphant Smith crowed that legislative assent had "lifted this important issue out of the realm of controversy."[167]

Smith called also for an executive budget, a reform which in his view went "hand in hand with reorganization of the Government itself," but which had theretofore floundered in the legislature.[168] By October 1924, the governor could announce that "the Constitutional amendments providing for the reorganization of the Government were passed by both houses and are now awaiting passage by the new Senate to be elected this Fall"; yet the legislature, loath to surrender fiscal prerogatives, still "refused absolutely to provide by constitutional amendment for an executive budget."[169] Momentum, however, was now with Smith, and in light of his 1924 reelection it was increasingly clear that legislators would be compelled to acquiesce and that 1925 would be the year in which the battle over these reforms would leave the halls of Albany and be taken to the voting public. Therefore, Governor Smith's talents as a speaker, debater, and campaigner would become vital to the cause.

Smith received a major opportunity to employ those talents on March 7, 1925, at a debate sponsored by the Women's City Club in New York. Thanks largely to the work of Belle Moskowitz—a board member since 1922—the club had energetically backed Smith's executive reform proposals for several years.[170] Now they decided to host a debate on the issue. Molly Dewson, the organization's civic secretary, sent invitations to Lieutenant Governor Seymour Lowman and State Senator Jimmy Walker to represent the Republican and Democratic viewpoints, respectively. Detecting an opportunity to rally support before a friendly audience, Smith announced his intention to substitute for Walker. Smith's forensic dexterity was so renowned in New York that when it was learned that the governor intended to engage Lowman personally, Dewson and club president Ethel Dreier traveled to Albany to inform the lieutenant governor of the change—and to give him the opportunity to withdraw.[171] Dewson recalled that "it was in the winter yet great drops of perspiration came out on his forehead"; but although visibly nervous at the prospect of jousting Smith in public debate, Lowman "was a sport and did not back out."[172]

The event was a tour de force for a politician already notorious for his prowess in debate. Lowman fired the opening salvo the afternoon of the event, deriding Smith for taking "his usual holier-than-thou" stance and professing that "no twisted vision of intoxication can be more arbitrary and more dangerous than the mind of an ambitious man who is drunk with power." While adopting a slightly more amicable posture in face-to-face debate, the lieutenant governor nevertheless accused the governor of engaging in an unabashed power grab, while insinuating that Smith was merely spouting other progressives' ideas, claiming that "very rarely does he advance a plan or policy that is original with him." At this, Lowman was "roundly hissed" by the audience of progressive women, but, undeterred, continued his aggressive indictment of Smith's agenda: "Governor Smith . . . is the first ruler of an Anglo-Saxon State to demand executive power over the purse since the days when the English yeomen on the field of battle overthrew the right of the King to levy taxes and appropriate money. Revolutions . . . rocked kingdoms to take away from Kings and Emperors the power of raising and spending money."[173] Addressing the irony of Lowman's analogy between the well-born King John and Al Smith, a poor grandson of immigrants who grew up in the slums of the Lower East Side, the governor opened his remarks by proclaiming himself the "king from Oliver Street."[174] Lowman, reassessing the situation, fled the hall.

In his rebuttal, Smith rejoined the argument that the executive budget and administrative reorganization proposals were aimed at reducing the influence of the legislature: "After the appropriation bill becomes a law, the legislator is as free as he can be to get up and build all the bridges and all the roads, to dig all the canals and to do any God's thing he wants, but the terrible thing is that he must show where the money is coming from." He also noted Republican support for his plan, including that of Elihu Root, and repeatedly quoted Root's 1915 speeches on the subject.[175] Such invocations of prominent New York Republicans would yield continuous benefits to Smith throughout the reorganization battle. For the moment, the governor enjoyed a lopsided triumph. The front page of the next morning's *New York Times* announced: "Governor Cheered, Lowman Is Hissed in Budget Debate."

This episode is demonstrative of Smith's ability to apply his political talents—working an audience, sharing compelling illustrative anecdotes, reaching across the aisle for support—to the battle over his reorganization plan. In the following months, the governor continued to campaign vigorously for the proposal, tying it to his broader agenda.[176] In a July debate with former governor Miller, Smith blamed Republican procrastination over reorganization and the administrative chaos that ensued for causing overcrowding in state hospitals that, by Smith's first term, "constituted a disgrace to the State of New York."[177]

Indeed, Smith's March debate with Lowman was but the opening skirmish in a very public battle over reorganization. The governor's decision to engage the populace on this question is striking on its own merits, for as the historian C. K. Yearley notes, proponents of administrative reform had always eschewed appeals "to the masses," partly as "a matter of style" and partly because "they could rarely count on much from the general public except indifference."[178] Contrastingly, Smith's argument for reorganization, crafted in layman's terms by a well-liked politician, effectively popularized the subject.

Furthermore, the Lowman debate reveals the centrality of the progressive Republican tradition to the governor's rhetorical strategy. A Democratic executive who was consistently confronted with Republican legislative majorities, Al Smith understood the necessity of partisan cooperation. His experiences as a caucus leader in Albany had trained him in the art of bipartisan negotiation; his upbringing in the culture of Tammany had taught him the value of public munificence for securing political loyalties. In his protracted battle with the legislature, Smith would offer progressive Republicans both coveted reforms and effusive acclaim.

By 1925, the governor enjoyed public support from prominent Republicans, including Elihu Root and Henry L. Stimson, secretary of war under William Howard Taft; but he still struggled to convince his partisan rivals in the legislature to back his reorganization program. Smith was increasingly able to count on progressive Republican allies to break party ranks and denounce the obdurate posture of the legislature.[179] Through such Republicans, the Smith camp began making overtures to Charles Evans Hughes—by now a former governor, U.S. Supreme Court justice, secretary of state, and presidential nominee, who happened to be an erstwhile spokesman-in-chief for administrative reorganization in New York. As governor in 1910, Hughes was the first to raise the cry for "administrative reorganization and consolidation" in the Empire State, responding in large measure to his own frustrations with the feebleness of the office.[180] His futile attempt to evict an inept official from the executive bureaucracy in 1907 revealed that in New York, a governor was simply incapable of managing personnel within the executive branch—indeed, many retained office despite the governor's wishes. The state senate was the only body empowered to remove individuals from office, and there the spoils of patronage and the power of political machines and corporations trumped any reformist impulse. While Hughes achieved nothing in the way of reorganization, he would lay the intellectual groundwork for future endeavors, concluding with many progressives that "a concentration of executive powers in the hands of the governor" was the antidote to bureaucratic dysfunction.[181]

More than a decade later, Smith and his allies saw the former governor as an ideal field marshal in their rekindled battle for reform. Hughes's gubernatorial activities demonstrated that he was ideologically committed to the cause, while his Republican bona fides were indisputable. Here was a credible Republican who had been a trailblazer for reorganization and, significantly, was completely trusted by Smith's progressive Republican allies.[182] But Hughes was reluctant to involve himself in the issue due to the partisan nature of the contemporary debate.[183] Ultimately, a colorful series of Republican misfires and Democratic entreaties during the summer of 1925 prompted the former governor to terminate his recent quiescence on the issue: legislative Republicans preempted a rumored gubernatorial announcement of a reorganization commission by announcing their own group to work on the details of administrative reform—furnishing an impressive list of notable New Yorkers to fill it. They had not, however, contacted any of these figures beforehand, leaving potential commissioners, including Hughes, baffled. Smith pounced, accepting the proposal in principle but nominating fifteen additional members and suggesting Hughes for chairman. Smith's Republican allies then entreated Hughes to accept, warning that other rumored commissioners, including former governor Miller, would imperil reform should they gain control of the body.[184] The once-reluctant Hughes agreed to serve on the commission, and while "there had been some speculation as to the chairmanship," Smith's suggestion of Hughes "practically ended the discussion."[185] That November, reformist optimism was vindicated, as nearly 60 percent of voters ratified the constitutional amendment allowing for reorganization of state government.[186]

Ratification was but a single step—now the commission needed to draft concrete proposals. Guided by Hughes, commissioners prepared their report for the upcoming 1926 legislative session. Subcommittees began developing reorganization plans for specific arms of the state bureaucracy, reporting their findings to Hughes's executive committee, which in turn authored the final product, known as the *Hughes Report on the Consolidation of State Departments*.[187] The report, submitted to the legislature on March 1, 1926, began by collapsing 187 agencies into sixteen executive departments, defining with precision the jurisdiction and operating procedures of this realigned bureaucracy.[188] The herculean feat of streamlining state government through consolidation promised to curb redundancy, cut costs, and facilitate the governor's reaffirmed duty to coordinate state functions.[189] Furthermore, by calling specifically for gubernatorial appointment of most department heads, the Hughes Commission finally established the short ballot in New York.[190] Proclaimed Smith: "I shall have . . . the prayers of my successor—because he will talk to seventeen men. I have been trying to talk to nearer 17,000 for four years."[191]

Perhaps the most dramatic proposals were those involving the executive department—an entity without precedent in other reorganized states. It was in this department that many of the most important reforms that Smith and others had desired were realized. Hughes's executive department would be headed by the governor, to "increase [the governor's] power of supervision and to make him exercise the necessary duty of coordinating the activities of . . . the executive branch of the State Government." Moreover, the new department would include a division for "formulating the budget and exercising supervision and control over the estimates, requests and expenditures of the various departments of the State." In that body, the commission took steps toward establishing the long-coveted executive budget.[192]

No longer would the Empire State be noted for its archaic fiscal process. Under the new method, the heads of the concurrently overhauled departments would be emancipated from their annual pilgrimage to the legislature. This was to be the end of department chiefs groveling before legislative committees, their budget requests honored only after they had paid tribute in the form of patronage to powerful chairmen. Instead, these officers, who were now to be appointed by the governor, would present their requests directly to the executive. The plan also allowed the governor to submit supplemental budget requests and amendments to the original budget.[193]

The conclusion of the decade-and-a-half-long struggle was anticlimactic. The Hughes Commission's prestige was so great that the legislature "hastened to accept not only the organizational pattern but also the recommended changes in the law."[194] The legislature voted to enact the proposals and referred those necessitating further constitutional alterations to the people for approval; in the fall of 1927 amendments were ratified establishing the governor as head of the executive department and instituting the executive budget.[195] Smith, in his final term as governor, was able to oversee implementation of the consolidation program and was the first governor of New York to produce his own budget.[196]

After more than fifteen years of political maneuvering, administrative consolidation and the executive budget were now constitutionally mandated in New York. But this was not a progressive triumph on its own. Indeed, these reforms failed to reduce the size of government, either in cost or in staff—and so the traditional progressive goal of promoting economy had not been achieved.[197]

But Smith had not pursued reorganization exclusively "in the interest of economy, but [also] to promote efficiency."[198] Indeed, it was efficiency that was a sine qua non for Smith's progressivism, for through efficient administration, social needs could be effectively met by good government. The governor had contended that the state had a responsibility to improve the lives of its citizens through a robust social welfare regime. Frustration over his administrative inability to fulfill this promise had led him to crusade for executive reorganization. Now reorganization would empower the government to respond more swiftly and effectively to desperate social conditions.[199] For Smith it was this goal, rather than reducing the cost or size of government, that was paramount.

Smith had sought classic, technocratic progressive reforms (efficiency, economy, accountability), but did so largely out of a desire effectively to provide necessary welfare services through a dynamic state. Progressives had long championed a professional, rational, scientific administrative structure. But this in itself is not a social welfare initiative: one could favor reorganization in order to justify retrenchment, or promote efficient administration to ensure domination of government by educated élites. Indeed, many adherents of the "cult of efficiency" were hostile toward "a democracy more plural than they preferred."[200] Moreover, the push for economy could just as easily cause one to decry social programs as baneful extravagancies. Smith's reorganization ally Elihu Root, for one, had long lamented such programs: "We are setting our steps now in the pathway which through the protection of a paternal government brought the mighty power of Rome to its fall."[201] Smith pursued reorganization to enable government to engage in the sort of programs that

Root would have censured as "paternal." The reorganization narrative thus elucidates the distinctive nature of Al Smith's political sensibilities by revealing his zeal for, and intended use of, a quintessentially progressive reform; it sets Smith's progressivism apart from that of many of his contemporaries, placing him at the crossroads of traditional progressivism and the modern social welfare liberalism that would follow.

"THERE'S NO USE IN TRYING TO FIGHT THAT MAN SMITH."

FIGURE 2. Cartoonist Rollin Kirby's assessment of Smith's mastery of state politics, "There's No Use in Trying to Beat That Man Smith," 1925. By permission of the Estate of Rollin Kirby Post. Credit: Rollin Kirby (1875–1952) / Museum of the City of New York. 43.366.748.

This history is equally instructive for comprehending Smith's unique progressive style. Advocates of executive reorganization, as well as other progressive reforms, had instinctively avoided popular political appeals in favor of more academic or legalistic exercises. And why not? After all, when presented to voters, the reformist 1915 constitution was roundly rejected, largely over regional rivalries. Surveying the political disposition of urban workers in 1917,

FIGURE 3. The *Brooklyn Eagle*'s interpretation of the foundation of Smith's presidential ambitions. Michael E. Brady, "Stepping Out," *The Brooklyn Eagle*, August 28, 1928.

social worker Mary Simkhovitch would conclude that "'good government' is a cold idea and does not lend itself to popularisation."[202] Yet rather than being theoretical and even élitist, the reform program proffered by Smith, while often esoteric, was transformed by its sponsor into a people's initiative. This was in fact the political essence of Smith's progressivism. According to Robert Moses, the governor "had a way of getting at the heart of things and popularizing very abstruse questions so that the average fellow could understand them."[203] Others shared this evaluation: future New York City mayor Robert F. Wagner Jr. opined that his father's longtime ally "could get people, the rank and file of America, to understand what the problems were—make complicated issues plain to them, so they could understand"; while future New York governor Charles Poletti "liked [Smith's] mind because he was able to . . . strip any problem into simple terms and get those simple terms over to the people."[204] Even Franklin Roosevelt concurred, writing that "Governor Smith reminds me of Theodore Roosevelt in his instinctive method of stripping the shell of verbiage and extraneous matter from any problem and of then presenting it as a definite programme which any one can understand."[205] Thus, the Happy Warrior's battle for administrative reorganization, perhaps the most arcane of progressive initiatives, demonstrates one of the most important qualities of Smith's progressivism, both in New York and during his presidential campaign: the ability to "popularize the abstruse."

CHAPTER 3

The Campaign of the Decade

As governor of New York State, Al Smith earned a reputation as an efficient administrator and a champion of social welfare. Over the course of his four terms as chief executive, Smith's progressivism was distilled into a discernible cluster of policy initiatives and political beliefs and matured into a coherent reform program. Moreover, the governor's political skills had been refined over a decade of communicating that program to his constituents. It is therefore unsurprising that Smith's 1928 campaign for the presidency featured the nationalization of his progressive platform.

Al Smith and the alliance that had crafted his unique progressivism in New York unremittingly invoked his gubernatorial record to substantiate his reformist credentials and promulgate his national agenda. Yet most studies of 1928 focus on cultural questions, including Prohibition, Smith's Roman Catholicism, and the urban-rural divide. Indeed, the dominant scholarly interpretation has been that "on most important questions facing the American people, Democratic and Republican positions could not be distinguished."[1]

The myopic gaze the literature has fixed upon the cultural controversies of 1928 has obscured the fundamental policy debates that occurred in that year. In fact, the campaign represented the apogee of Smith's progressivism and imbued the emerging urban Democratic coalition with a set of political values and policy prescriptions that reflected those voters' economic *and* cultural struggles and aspirations. Considering the events of 1928 with an understanding of the Democrat's peculiar style of progressivism and thus recognizing Smith as both an economic reformer with a robust agenda and as a symbol of urban-immigrant America places the election squarely at the center of an evolutionary process that connected portions of the progressive tradition to key elements of New Deal liberalism.

It is clear that cultural battles over alcohol and urbanism and particularly over Smith's Catholicism were of great significance to the candidates and voters of 1928. But far from monopolizing the debate, these questions were often relegated to the periphery by Smith and his allies in favor of issues that, in the context of their time, represented important ideological divisions between the parties and the nominees. Smith went into great detail enunciating and defending his positions on fundamental problems, including farm relief, water power, labor relations, social welfare, and administrative efficiency. On all of these questions he challenged, in some cases very profoundly, the Harding-Coolidge status quo. Smith's opponent, Herbert Hoover, had engineered much of that status quo from his powerful post as secretary of commerce for the previous two administrations, and in his campaign for the White House the Republican nominee proudly became the chief exponent of the virtues of the political economy of the 1920s. Smith never sought the total destruction or even the dramatic reconstruction of that political economy—to expect such things from a mainstream candidate in a period of general economic strength would be absurd. Nevertheless, the Democrat shone a critical light on the neglected corners of Calvin Coolidge's America, challenged many accepted policy doctrines, and presented in the form of his progressive governorship the blueprints of an alternative approach to national administration.

Toward the Nomination

During what could be called the "long Gilded Age," being governor of the Empire State made one an ex officio contender for a presidential nomination. From the end of the Civil War through the election of Franklin Roosevelt in 1932, New Yorkers secured major party nominations for the presidency no less than eleven times, including those for seven sitting or former governors and three men who would eventually reside in the White House. By 1928, Alfred E. Smith was the four-term governor of the wealthiest, most populous, and arguably the most politically significant state in the union, with an impressive catalogue of achievements and a considerable national following. Moreover, there was not in the waiting an eager battery of prominent Democrats clamoring to contend for the presidency that year. At least as early as 1927, it was clear that the last election of the Roaring Twenties would be Al Smith's best chance at the nation's highest office.

Smith's name had already been placed before Democratic delegates twice that decade: in 1920, in a largely ceremonial "favorite son" nomination by noted orator and sometimes-congressman Bourke Cockran; and in 1924, when he was introduced by former vice presidential nominee Franklin Delano Roosevelt as "the Happy Warrior." At the latter convention, the New York governor and other northeasterners waged a fierce if unsuccessful battle to wrest the party away from southern and western domination by thwarting the presidential ambitions of William Gibbs McAdoo and demanding a direct rebuke of the Ku Klux Klan.

While McAdoo, the son-in-law and treasury secretary of Woodrow Wilson, was considered the front-runner, Smith enjoyed the benefit of home court for the 1924 contest, which was held at Madison Square Garden. Seeking to exaggerate this advantage, Tammany operatives packed the rafters with their constituents, whose bawdy taunts of the speakers and constant bickering with the delegates transformed the proceedings into a burlesque of the decade's culture wars. Sectional antagonisms raged, especially over the Klan issue. Oklahoma senator Robert Owen was hissed from the bleachers when he suggested that "a large number" of Klansmen "joined the order to protect the Constitution and the law." When delegate Andrew C. Erwin, "a tall young Georgian" and veteran of the world war, implored the nation to help the South put down the Invisible Empire and denounced his fellow southerners as "unworthy of their ancestry" if they refused to join the fight, he was jeered by McAdoo's forces and ignored by his cohorts. He was not ignored, however, by representatives from twenty-three other states, who paraded and then mobbed in celebration of Erwin's righteousness, "pushing in so hard that police had to protect the Georgians," as Isabella Ahearn O'Neill, an actress from Providence and the only woman in the Rhode Island delegation, "rushed up to the youthful orator and kissed him on the lips." Dixie delegates reacted with indignation as the house band struck up the popular Sherman tribute "Marching through Georgia" in the midst of the brouhaha. Fistfights were rampant. When a North Dakotan gave a speech endorsing McAdoo that included the line "I condemn the order known as the Ku Klux Klan," only the New Jersey, Pennsylvania, and Rhode Island contingents marched in approval; McAdoo's own California delegation refused even to applaud. An Ohio jurist was shouted down ("Oh, shut up!"), and the audience laughed mockingly at the governor of North Carolina.[2]

After more than a week of balloting, McAdoo, whose name was consistently met with acrid chants of "oil, oil" (a reference to his past legal work for Teapot Dome offender Edward Doheny), was indeed denied the nomination; so too was Al Smith.[3] Meanwhile, the proposal to denounce the Klan by name had been rejected by a single vote out of over a thousand cast. In the sweltering July heat, in the exhaustingly heavy air, with the delegates' lethargy checked only by the cacophonous anarchy within the hall, decades of Democratic contradictions were betrayed, and the party was torn asunder. Even a three-time presidential nominee was not immune from the infectious disrespect. In the midst of the chaos William Jennings Bryan, a year away from his grave, had taken to the podium. Portions of the Commoner's speech were "met with such a storm of hisses and booing that it was impossible for him to make himself heard." Reprimanding the rowdy Tammanyites and their northeastern allies on the convention floor for their indecorous conduct, Bryan forecast that if the present Democracy failed in its historical mission against privilege, "some other party will grow up to carry those issues and take our place." "But," he added contemptuously, "that new party will never find the leaders of a noble cause in the gallery." The progressivism of Wilson, Bryan's own populism— these would surely be carried on, but not by these New York hooligans.[4]

Al Smith had other ideas. Crude shenanigans aside, historians have allowed that within the mêlée the Smith forces "had represented the good fight . . . had stood before the most powerful politicians the Klan could muster and never backed down."[5] Indeed, many ordinary New Yorkers, like John Vincent Donahue, a postal employee and low-level Tammany operative, believed by 1924 that "the poor little boy from Chatham Square and Fulton Fish Market is without doubt the Moses who is going to lead the masses of this country out of the wilderness of the rottenness created by the present situation in Washington."[6] Nor had all of the visiting delegates shared Bryan's revulsion with their Gotham hosts. A Texan wrote Brooklyn congressman Loring Black that he had been impressed by "the great demonstration given [Smith] at that memorable Convention . . . because of the great love the common people manifested for him" and "the spontaneous explosion of sincere devotion by a people in admiration of their great leader."[7]

Moreover, Smith's campaign was only partly aimed at making an ethnocultural point. Prior to the convention, Smith suggested that his candidacy was rooted in his record as a progressive governor; he referred those interested in his ideology to his purposeful annual messages to the legislature; he reproached those "progressives who only talk about progress in government" but "never do anything about it"; and he demanded that his "stand on the 'wet' issue . . . not be stressed," but rather that it be "left alone."[8] This might be dismissed as

FIGURE 4. Alfred E. Smith at the Guild Theater, 1924. Bain News Service, "Al Smith," undated (other photos in the series establish the year). George Grantham Bain Collection, Library of Congress, Washington, DC.

political posturing were it not for Smith's address on the final night of the convention, in which he boasted of the greatness of his home town but then guided delegates through an extended tour of his progressive achievements and his ambitious agenda—highlighting administrative reforms, liberal appropriations for education, the water power fight, "the most enlightened factory code in the world, bar none," widows' pensions, parks development, and public health programs, among other important state initiatives.[9] He made only a veiled reference to Prohibition and did not discuss the KKK or any other contemporary cultural controversies.[10] Responding to the New Yorker's disposition throughout the convention, the journalist Walter Lippmann, a friend and adviser of the governor, wrote to Smith that "working for the best things in sight meant working for you. . . . Let me thank you."[11]

Indeed, despite his loss at the convention, 1924 was a good year for Al Smith: while the national Democratic ticket of John W. Davis and Charles W. Bryan went down to ignominious defeat, Smith was reelected governor, vanquishing Theodore Roosevelt Jr. by 100,000 votes in spite of New York's going to Calvin Coolidge by a margin of almost one million ballots.[12] The following summer, during a debate at Carnegie Hall over the ten-year, $100 million bond proposal, Smith's opponent, Nathan Miller, received what was probably his most enthusiastic applause of the evening when he quipped: "I do not suppose the Governor intends to stay in Albany all of the next ten years. . . . I have heard that he had ambitions to go somewhere else."[13] As the *Newark News* concluded, Smith had "emerge[d] from the Democratic wreck a bigger figure than ever before"; from 1924 forward, the governor was a serious contender for the 1928 Democratic presidential nomination.[14]

Revealingly, as Smith's reputation grew, so too did his emphasis on his progressive agenda. The governor marked his return to national prominence on September 27, 1925, in Chicago, at a picnic event dubbed "Al Smith Day" by the Cook County Democratic Party. With an estimated 100,000 people present, he refrained from discussing issues popular with this largely ethnic audience—namely, "his well-known views on prohibition," which "could have set the crowd . . . aflame"—and instead used the venue to promote his reformist ideals. Before what was described as an attentive audience, Smith highlighted his battles for workmen's compensation and widows' pensions and outlined the need for reorganization of both state and federal government to meet the demands of modern society.[15] By that December, Lippmann was writing in *Vanity Fair* that for those following Smith, it had become "impossible any longer to ignore the signs of an impending fate. For with each new proof of his power in New York the tension throughout the country becomes more ominous. His victories have ceased to be victories merely; they are premonitions."[16]

Smith carried his national progressive advocacy into Pennsylvania the following May, speaking on behalf of a hospital bond proposal in that state similar to the one he had championed at home in 1923. The governor appeared at the invitation of Philadelphia public health activists who had been impressed by his New York success. Smith provided insight into his own progressive style, suggesting from experience that when skeptical voters learned the specifics of welfare proposals, they became much more favorably disposed to state assumptions of debt. Then he challenged his enthusiastic Philadelphia audience: "Does it not occur to the individual that every now and then there is expected some offering in the nature of gratitude or in the nature of thanksgiving?" If so, the hospital bond offered an ideal opportunity "for every man and every woman in Pennsylvania to be able to say to the ruler of the Universe Himself, 'Inasmuch as the poor, the weak, the sick and the afflicted were special charges of Thy Divine Son during His life on earth, their care, their proper and adequate care, will be given by the Commonwealth of Pennsylvania.'"[17] As the next presidential contest drew closer and the press increasingly scrutinized the front-runner's every public pronouncement, Smith amplified these calls for active government on behalf of social justice. Appearing before the Child Welfare Committee of America in early 1928, he summarized these beliefs to "great applause": since "we have been particularly blessed . . . we owe something . . . to take care of the poor, of the sick, the afflicted and particularly of the children."[18]

Meanwhile, Smith's national following continued to grow. Loring Black reported that Dubuque, Iowa, was "quite enthusiastic" for the New Yorker by 1926; the next year Congressman William Cohen, another New York Democrat, dispatched similar news from Dallas and Miami. In Tampa, Florida, the city fire department followed Smith's 1926 reelection campaign, tauntingly cabling his Republican challenger: "Straw vote here Smith ninety eight and you nothing." On March 10, 1927, the wife of an infantryman stationed at Fort Benning, Georgia, gave birth to Alfred Smith Washington.[19]

By 1927, speculation about Smith's ambitions routinely appeared in the press.[20] The candidate's religion remained an albatross during these discussions. Anticipating a Smith presidential bid, Alabama senator Thomas Heflin, a fellow Democrat and a noted anti-Catholic, "assailed" the governor of New York in March of 1927 (such tirades would become banal by the end of the campaign).[21] On a more sophisticated plane, an essay was published in the April 1927 issue of *Atlantic Monthly* by New York attorney Charles C. Marshall questioning whether a Roman Catholic president could uphold the

Constitution, respect religious freedom, maintain military neutrality, and support public education.[22] Walter Lippmann exhorted Smith that the article offered "a tremendous opportunity" for him "to answer not only for yourself but for this whole generation in a way that would be final and conclusive."[23] Smith concurred. The following month he composed a rejoinder with guidance from Father Francis P. Duffy, a parish priest in Manhattan's Hell's Kitchen neighborhood who had been copiously decorated for his service as chaplain to New York's conspicuously Celtic "Fighting Sixty-Ninth" infantry regiment when it was federalized during the Great War, as well as from long-time adviser Joseph Proskauer, a Jewish progressive and a justice of the New York State Supreme Court.[24] The essay cited episodes from the governor's career as well as writings by Catholic theologians to confirm both Smith's and his co-communicants' patriotism and fidelity to democratic government. Unlike any previous candidate, the Catholic Smith was forced to defend openly his faith and to declare, "I recognize no power in the institutions of my Church to interfere with the operations of the Constitution of the United States."[25] Smith would later discover that his response on the religious question was neither final nor conclusive; but, believing it was, he continued to ground his presidential ambitions in his progressive agenda and his gubernatorial résumé.

Unquestionably, by the fall of 1927 Al Smith's career plans were the talk of the nation, and in that context the governor released a public report that served as a sort of capstone to his tenure, entitled *Progress of Public Improvements: A Report to the People of the State of New York.* Officially a review of the application of bond funds, the document was really an apologia on Smith's progressive predilection for generous expenditures in the name of social welfare and civic progress. In the introduction, the governor rejected the narrow reading of the appropriate use of bonded debt employed by his conservative critics and touted his record of fighting recalcitrant legislators in order to fund public works. Then, displaying again his characteristic talent for popularizing the abstruse, Smith presented ninety-eight pages of captioned photographs demonstrating just where these public funds were being spent—many of them before-and-after shots of bridges, parks, beaches, hospitals, and schools.[26] Here was the increasingly scrutinized governor of New York, boasting of his liberal funding of active government on behalf of social welfare and demonstrating the tangible benefits attained through such investment. More than 10,000 copies of this extended advertisement for the virtues of Smith's executive temperament were issued to the public on the eve of his campaign for the White House.[27] Smith clearly intended to present himself as a vigorous, kinetic progressive.

As the governor girded for his national campaign, another revealing development occurred that was popularly linked to the presidential ambitions of the New Yorker. In 1926, Smith had strongly supported his friend Robert F. Wagner's bid to unseat Republican U.S. senator James Wadsworth. Wagner, with Smith, had been among the most influential architects of New York's robust social welfare regime, and in 1926 he campaigned for the Senate as a sort of "Al Smith candidate."[28] Victorious, Wagner went to Washington intent on pursuing progressive labor and social welfare legislation and committed to serving the interests of the working-class voters who were largely responsible for his narrow election. With these goals in mind, Wagner took to the Senate floor on March 5, 1928, and introduced legislation to compel a thorough Department of Labor investigation of unemployment. Rejecting persistent claims of general prosperity and a "full dinner pail," Wagner cited the "growing bread lines . . . the larger number of men and women seeking work . . . a constantly decreasing return for the worker . . . [and] a lowered standard of living for a large portion of our people" that he witnessed among his working-class neighbors; and he demanded federal action. Wagner charged that "four million people . . . is a conservative estimate of the number of those out of work. . . . One in every ten of our wage earners is in idleness"; he derided President Calvin Coolidge's persistently sanguine reports of high wages and "plentiful" employment as unsubstantiated and unrealistic; and he censured Secretary of Commerce Herbert Hoover for looking "all across the Nation, to discover not a single idle man."[29]

Wagner's speech was given from the perspective of his core constituents—ethnic urban workers—many of whom were "not sharing much in [the] prosperity" of the Coolidge years.[30] It was a broadside against the Republican administration on behalf of such Americans, and it was framed in progressive terms, proposing systematic surveys as the first step toward ameliorative legislation. Significantly, the speech was widely interpreted in the press as an opening salvo by the forces of Alfred E. Smith against the Republican administration in anticipation of an imminent conflict between the governor and either Coolidge or one of his lieutenants.[31] Just four months in advance of Smith's nomination for the presidency, his particular friend and steadfast political ally Robert Wagner was attacking the Republican administration in progressive terms from a working-class perspective—in a move linked to the governor himself.

The columnist Mark Sullivan wrote that for the Democrats to nominate anyone but Al Smith for the presidency in 1928 "would be an act so calling for explanation as to weaken them in the country."[32] The party obliged. The convention, held at Houston in late June, was "all sweetness and light," recalled Bronx County Democratic boss Edward J. Flynn—particularly as a sequel to the 1924 pandemonium at Madison Square Garden; another delegate noted that "there was no doubt from the beginning that Smith was to be the candidate," and indeed the Happy Warrior was nominated handily, as was Joseph T. Robinson, a senator from Arkansas and the party's choice for vice president.[33]

The Republicans nominated Herbert Clark Hoover, the enterprising and imperious secretary of commerce under Harding and Coolidge. Hoover had been a prominent engineer, a successful businessman, and a noted humanitarian. His administration of relief efforts in post–world war Europe earned him universal applause for saving the lives of hungry millions. By the end of that effort, his reputation was such that Woodrow Wilson's assistant secretary of the navy, Franklin Roosevelt, coveted Hoover as the Democratic presidential candidate for 1920. Instead, Hoover became the leading force in the next two Republican administrations, earning him much of the credit for the economic successes of the 1920s and allowing him to dominate federal policies on everything from air travel to farm relief to radio broadcasting. All of this culminated with his coordination of recovery work in the wake of the catastrophic 1927 Mississippi River flood. By 1928, Hoover, like Smith, had emerged as his party's clear choice for the presidency.[34]

Officially Al Smith was running against Herbert Hoover, but in fact he was also running against the accumulated legacies of eight years of Republican rule. His acceptance address, delivered to a rain-soaked crowd in Albany as well as to a national radio audience on August 22, demonstrated that the Democrat intended to assault the status quo on progressive grounds:

> Dominant in the Republican Party today is the element which proclaims and executes the political theories against which the party liberals like Roosevelt and La Follette and their party insurgents have rebelled. This reactionary element seeks to validate the theory of benevolent oligarchy. It assumes that a material prosperity, the very existence of which is challenged, is an excuse for political inequality. It makes the concern of the government, not people, but material things. I have fought this spirit in my own State. I have had to fight it and to beat it, in order to place upon the statute books every one of the progressive, humane laws for whose enactment I assumed responsibility in my legislative and executive career. I shall know how to fight it in the nation.[35]

Smith critiqued Republican stewardship of the economy, calling the idea of general prosperity under the GOP a "myth": "When four million men, de-

sirous to work and support their families, are unable to secure employment
there is very little in the picture of prosperity to attract them and the millions
dependent upon them. . . . Specific industries are wholly prostrate and there
is widespread business difficulty. . . . Prosperity to the extent that we have it is
unduly concentrated and has not equitably touched the lives of the farmer,
the wage-earner and the individual business man."[36]

These sentiments contrasted sharply with those of Smith's opponent. Historians have long recognized in Hoover's ideology a tepid rebuff of free-market
orthodoxy; but as William Leuchtenburg points out, this was "much less germane than his rationalizations of the status quo."[37] As he began his campaign
for the White House, Hoover, who resigned his cabinet post in August, hoisted
the banner of Harding-Coolidge prosperity, promising that if elected he would
"go forward with the policies of the last eight years," and if "given this chance"
Republican economics would ensure that "poverty will be banished from this
nation." Hoover may once have declared that fairness "can only be obtained
by certain restrictions on the strong and the dominant," but by 1928 he appeared less a latter-day Wilson and more, in H. L. Mencken's phrase, a "fat
Coolidge."[38]

In his acceptance, Smith outlined a number of key differences between
himself and the GOP, including their policies on water power development,
farm relief, tariff policies, immigration restriction, Prohibition, and labor relations. The lines between the candidates' ideologies were sharply drawn,
and the Democrat intended to persist in this approach throughout the campaign. It was to be a national debate about issues of fundamental significance
to the American polity of 1928. Believing this, Smith revealed his national
strategy—the same popular approach to progressive reform he had employed
in New York:

> The people can and do grasp the problems of the government. . . . I have
> seen legislation won by the pressure of popular demand, exerted after
> the people had had an honest, frank and complete explanation of the
> issues. Great questions of finance, the issuance of millions of dollars of
> bonds for public projects, the complete reconstruction of the machin-
> ery of the State government, the institution of an executive budget, these
> are but a few of the complicated questions which I, myself, have taken
> to the electorate. Every citizen has thus learned the nature of the busi-
> ness in hand and appreciated that the State's business is his business.

In that spirit, the candidate proposed to continue "that direct contact with the
people . . . in this campaign."[39]

To the West

Having accepted the presidential nomination with a pledge to engage the public on issues of fundamental importance, Smith dedicated each campaign address to one or two major questions, outlining his views and attacking those of the Republican administration and the Republican nominee. For his first speech, Smith traveled to Omaha, Nebraska, and spoke on agriculture. Despite his urban background, it was fitting that the Democrat should commence his thematic critique of the incumbent party with agriculture, for a crash in commodities prices after the close of the Great War had left most farmers desperate for relief throughout the 1920s.[40] The Democrats called this "the most noteworthy flaw in our present prosperity."[41]

In 1927 and again in 1928, Congress had attempted to ease farm suffering through the McNary-Haugen bill, which called for the federal government to purchase agricultural surplus and sell it abroad at the world market price, segregating this crop from the domestic market (which would be protected by tariffs), thus boosting prices within the United States.[42] The cost to the government would be recovered by an "equalization fee" imposed on the agricultural commodities benefited. This program suffered the staunch opposition of Herbert Hoover, and President Coolidge followed his counsel to the order of two vetoes—each accompanied by a message the commerce secretary had helped compose.[43]

By 1928, "McNary-Haugenism" was dominating farm politics. Smith's urban advisers, led by Belle Moskowitz, were skeptical of the plan because it risked raising consumer prices; indeed, many observers believed that the program would inflate the cost of urban living, and this presented a conundrum for the Democrats; as Walter Lippmann noted, "The McNary-Haugen bill would, if it worked, cost the city people money."[44] Nevertheless, by September 18, when Smith delivered his Omaha address, the nominee was explicit in his approval of "the principle" of McNary-Haugenism.[45] Yet he would not commit to the equalization fee, a detail considered crucial by many in the Corn Belt but which Smith dismissed as a "mere matter of method."[46]

Smith's ambivalence over the equalization fee served to temper potential enthusiasm from farmers while earning him generations of scholarly scorn.[47] Nevertheless, the Democrat made significant inroads throughout the Corn and Wheat Belts in the weeks following his Nebraska visit and eventually secured the endorsements of two leading midwestern progressive Republican senators—Nebraska's George W. Norris and John J. Blaine of Wisconsin.[48] Blaine decried Hoover as "opposed to practically all of the policies of the great mass of progressive Republicans and independent forward-thinking people of

America," while Norris attributed the demise of Congress's farm relief proposals to Hoover's influence in the cabinet.[49] In contrast, "the farmers and those who depend on the farmers for their prosperity should support Mr. Smith," argued the Nebraskan. "His program, as he has announced in a number of his speeches . . . will give the farm sectors the relief they are so much in need of at the present. The Republicans offer nothing but a few kind words."[50] The Republican *Wall Street Journal* was aghast, speculating that Norris's "plate from his new Democratic friends is expected to consist of at least thirty pieces of silver"; while the *Hartford Courant* dismissively scoffed that "Senator Norris has but little more in common with the average rock-ribbed Republican than the late Henry Cabot Lodge had in common with the late Karl Marx."[51]

The agrarian drift toward Smith was broader still. Thousands of farmers in meetings across Iowa began extolling the Democrat.[52] In Wisconsin, the progressive revolt became so problematic for the GOP that Republican regulars were compelled to apply the "party boot" to "Young Bob" La Follette in order to thwart "the insurgent movement in the State."[53] Defying this crackdown, the *Madison Capital-Times*, "long known as the organ of the late Senator Robert M. La Follette and the voice of the western progressives," endorsed Smith in early October; while Michael K. Reilly, La Follette's Democratic challenger, withdrew from the Wisconsin race, suggesting that "Young Bob" was "just as in favor of the legislative program for which Gov. Smith stands as I am."[54]

In Montana, progressive Democratic senator Burton K. Wheeler, the elder La Follette's 1924 running mate, was observed "lining up the radicals of every ilk, in the endeavor to corral for Smith and himself the La Follette–Wheeler vote of four years ago," reviving "the old Nonpartisan League . . . to cast the farmer vote to Smith."[55] *Washington Star* columnist William Hard noted that along "the line from Chicago to Butte" Smith's campaign was developing a new "formidable alignment" to challenge Republican supremacy in the farm regions. This was so because the Democrat "has qualified, to La Follette and Farmer-Laborite eyes, as a 'Progressive.' He has qualified as a friend of the 'principle' of McNary-Haugenism and of the Northwestern farmer's own conception of his own salvation."[56]

Unlike Smith, his running mate, Joe Robinson, was of agrarian stock, and the Democrats sought to leverage this fact in the Corn Belt, romantically recalling the senator's childhood "on a farm in the Ozarks," where he was "reared among struggling farmers" and made "conversant with the problems of distribution and marketing."[57] Traveling to Lincoln, Nebraska, in October, Robinson charged that "there was never a time when reactionary influences were more dominant in the United States than at present," particularly given the Republican farm policy of "insincerity and indecision." The next day, at Sioux City, Iowa, the Arkansan took to the airwaves to denounce again the "reactionary" posture of Hoover and his running mate, Senator Charles Curtis of Kansas, in what the press interpreted as an attempt to "woo farm progressives."[58]

Yet Smith's agrarian appeal was limited. Despite Democratic entreaties, most farm politicians maintained either their Republican leanings or a Coolidge-like reticence.[59] Revealingly, even amid the open revolt of La Follette Republicans like John Blaine in Wisconsin, "Young Bob" never explicitly joined his fellow senator. La Follette stated that he had "disassociated" himself "from the Republican national ticket and platform throughout the campaign," and he lauded Smith's "public declarations and definite commitments which are in substantial accord with the Progressives' views on waterpower, farm relief, the injunction in labor disputes," and other key issues; yet despite Democratic implications to the contrary, he withheld any definite imprimatur from the New Yorker. While La Follette's words indicated even to Republicans that the progressive held a "slight preference" for Smith, his ambiguity allowed the Hoover-boosting *Los Angeles Times* to infer that "La Follette's 'Agin' Everyone."[60]

The Democratic effort in the midwestern granary was hampered by a reluctance to embrace the most aggressive agrarian remedies. Indeed, while Smith was praised by many western progressives for his "unequivocal endorsement" of McNary-Haugenism, he was less concrete on many of the details, and he continued to hedge on the specific question of the equalization fee. Smith's pledge to call a conference of experts to work out the problem comported with his progressive administrative style from New York State and seems to have been made in good faith; yet to suffering farmers, this promise to "talk things over later" must have appeared less like a firm stand and more like a flailing Charleston.[61]

Southward from Omaha, Smith trekked to Oklahoma City and delivered what has become the most celebrated address of his campaign—a fierce denunciation of intolerance coupled with an unapologetic defense of his gubernatorial record. Afterward, the Democrat traveled to Denver and made another tremendously important speech that suggested very real divergence between his views on the role of government in promoting public welfare and those of Hoover. For his Colorado address, Smith took up the subject of water power.

Harvard Law professor Felix Frankfurter wrote to Belle Moskowitz that Smith possessed "a trump card in water power. He knows about that issue at first hand; he has fought a fight on it, and . . . 'the interests' fear his stand on the issue. Hoover has extremely conservative views on it."[62] Smith's position did not change in any substantive way as he transformed from governor to presidential candidate. Referring to the nation's many rivers as "the property of all the people of the country and of the different States wherein they lie," Smith argued that where these resources were owned by a single state, they ought to remain the property of that state; where controlled by a group of states, those states should enter into a compact for developing the resource; and where nationally owned, the federal government should retain and develop the site. This may seem like a lot of qualification, but these nuances were the product of years of working through the intricacies of hydroelectric policy. A potential power site along the barge canal in New York should not be understood in the same way as the Boulder Dam project on the Colorado River, which affected seven states, or the project at Muscle Shoals, Alabama, which was on federal property. Yet despite these provisos, there was a unifying theme that differentiated Smith's position from that of the Republicans: the people's "absolute retention of the ownership of the power itself, by owning and controlling the site and the plant at the place of the generation." Smith continued to believe that "only in this way can the Government agency, State or Federal, as the case may be, find itself in a position to provide fair and reasonable rates to the ultimate consumer, and insist upon a fair and equal distribution of the power through contractual agreements with the distributing companies."[63]

This represented a stark departure from the status quo. The Republican Party also claimed to stand for public retention of power sites, but called for them to be leased to private developers for fifty-year intervals.[64] To Smith this was unacceptable, for "unless you provide for State or Federal development, there can be no control of the ultimate rates to the consumer and no control of the power site itself." Smith also contended that the Republican position was corrupted by the influence of big business. Hoover had not elaborated on the GOP platform—dodging the issue of public ownership during a speech at Los Angeles—and the party had maintained a firm commitment to inaction over the course of two presidential terms. "I will leave it to your imagination," the Democrat told his audience, but given the administration's quiescence and its fervent opposition to government development (manifested in Coolidge's pocket veto of a bill providing for federal operation at Muscle Shoals), they "must have been in sympathy" with the National Electric Light Association's push for private development and against public ownership. Indeed it did not take much imagination at all to make such connections, suggested Smith, when President Coolidge had just appointed as interior secretary Roy O. West, a figure with decades-long ties to the utilities industry.[65] According to Smith's notes, all of this indicated to the candidate "a spirit of unfriendliness, if not hostility, on the part of the Republican Party in the nation to those who stand for public ownership and control of the God-given resources of the nation" as well as "a leaning toward those seeking to exploit these resources for their own private gain and profit rather than in the interests of the people themselves."[66]

The question was a complex one, and Smith pledged to treat it as such. In the regionally relevant case of the Boulder Dam, Smith suggested deferring to expert opinion on whether control should be maintained by a multistate compact or the federal government. "But however this dam shall be constructed," he concluded, "one thing is sure: the site of the dam and the machinery generating this water power must be preserved in public ownership." Meanwhile, the hydroelectric potential at Muscle Shoals, which was already under federal control, ought to be developed by the national government.[67]

Smith presented this as a question of fundamental importance on which voters were offered a definite choice. He outlined both his record in New York and the record of his opponent, framing the issue as a manifestation of the progressive archetype "the people" versus "the interests." Producing further allure for western progressives, Smith avowed that he was "follow[ing] another Republican idea," quoting Theodore Roosevelt's warnings about the perils of uncontrolled hydroelectric development.[68]

The candidate spoke persistently on water power throughout the campaign. At Nashville, in the face of "considerable sentiment for private operation" at Muscle Shoals, Smith affirmed his commitment to government ownership and criticized Hoover's "evasion" of the issue.[69] The question received prominent consideration during speeches at Chicago, Boston, Baltimore, and Brooklyn.[70] Campaign literature hailed Smith's "consistent" advocacy as governor of "the absolute ownership and control by the State of water power resources."[71] At Reno, Nevada, Joe Robinson contrasted Coolidge's foot-dragging and Hoover's "vacillation" with Smith's promise to undertake work "promptly."[72] Days later, from Portland, Oregon, the Arkansan cautioned that "Republican victory will mean the triumph of a monopoly," while "the success of the Democratic ticket means protection of the people against extortionist rates. . . . It means conservation of the most valuable reserves remaining in the public ownership."[73] By November, *Time* declared: "Nominee Smith's stand for government control of water power is as well known as his first name."[74]

Historians have suggested that Smith's stand on power was an ambivalent one—not sufficiently assertive to render him a "progressive" on this national issue. David Burner, a leading exponent of this argument, cites Socialist presidential candidate Norman Thomas's statement that Smith's differences from Hoover on power were "comparatively insignificant."[75] This argument disintegrates in light of Smith's gubernatorial record, the clear demarcation between the two parties' proposals as enunciated by their nominees, and the national attention Smith's stand garnered from those interested in the question—including Senator Norris, the driving force behind the Muscle Shoals plan in Congress; Morris Cooke, director of Pennsylvania governor Gifford Pinchot's "giant power" survey; and Amos Pinchot, a leading progressive activist and brother of the conservationist governor.[76] Strong opponents of government control, such as *Barron's* magazine, which had warned of "creeping state ownership" in January 1928, also found Smith's statements "interesting," cautioning of the perils associated with transplanting the governor's "obstructionist" water power policies from Albany to Washington.[77] On both sides of the question, the New Yorker's ideas were in fact taken quite seriously.[78]

Indeed, it was based on the Democrat's water power stand, even more than on farm relief, that Senator Norris chose to campaign actively for Smith, whom he described as the "people's champion" against the "power trust . . . an octopus with slimy fingers that levies tribute at every fireside."[79] Smith operatives like Robert Moses had been entreating the Nebraska progressive for a cross-party endorsement based on the governor's espousal of public ownership from early in the campaign; yet Norris remained reluctant to support Smith in the opening months of the contest, because while the Democrat "went further and did better than Hoover in his speech of acceptance . . . still it was far from satisfactory."[80] In early September, Norris wrote Paul Anderson of the *St. Louis Post-Dispatch* that he feared that Smith's calls for "government control" might be manipulated by "the power trust representatives" to allow for privatization of Muscle Shoals. Instead, Smith "ought to have said . . . that he favored its ownership and 'operation' by the Government."[81] While recognizing that "many Progressives seemed to think that [Smith's] declaration was satisfactory and complete," Norris expressed doubts to Lewis S. Gannett of *The Nation*, reiterating the need for a commitment to "the word 'operation'" and concluding that Smith "may be alright, but . . . I hesitate to take the word of any man."[82] Perhaps this was all semantics, but Norris felt a deep obligation not "to mislead those who are placing their faith in me and my judgment" by prematurely endorsing the Democrat.[83] Eventually Smith would state unequivocally that the government should "own and build and operate the power house"; and in fact when he made this statement on October 31 at Newark, he was paraphrasing (he claimed to be quoting) what he had said a month earlier at Denver, which affirms the interpretation that the September 23 speech included an implicit call for government operation.[84]

Meanwhile, rank-and-file voters of the progressive persuasion took Smith's water power stand very seriously indeed, as revealed by the affluence of letters that inundated Senator Norris's office imploring him to support the Democrat. In June a realtor from Newark, responding to Norris's pronounced frustration with the Coolidge administration over Muscle Shoals, demanded that the only reasonable action now was for the Nebraskan to *"walk out of the convention and the party,"* goading the senator that "you men from the West, You, and Gov. McMullan [*sic*] and others talk a lot, but none of you seem to have the nerve to walk out. . . . Is there *no man in the West* who has the nerve of the Late Prs. Roosevelt?"[85] An attorney from Providence wrote in early September that "Governor Smith's declaration, which I have inclosed, stands foursquare with your own stand on this and other important issues and I suggest that you be as consistent in honesty now as you have been in the past, by advocating the election of the greatest humanitarian and statesman America has had since Lincoln."[86] A Georgist from Wichita declared Smith's Denver address "the high mark of all public utterances thus far by our Presidential candidates," concluding that as a La Follette voter he would be "ardently supporting" the Democrat.[87] A Washingtonian was also impressed by Smith's Denver address, sending Norris front-page coverage from the *Seattle Daily Times* and proclaiming: "Here comes the line of attack which Gov. Smith has opened on Hoover that wins his battle."[88]

These efforts were rewarded in late October. During an Omaha speech that was broadcast throughout the West, the maverick Nebraskan, speaking from a hall festooned with "huge portraits of Roosevelt, Robert La Follette, and Governor Smith," lauded the Democratic nominee on the power issue, declaring that "Governor Smith's attitude on this question places him side by side with that great father of national conservation, Theodore Roosevelt," and proclaiming to "those who have sympathized with and given support to the little group of Progressives in Congress in their terrible struggle to preserve for all the people the great water power resources of the nation, that it seems to me we are led . . . logically and inevitably to the support of Governor Smith."[89]

Norris' endorsement of Smith is astounding considering the daring it required to campaign for the wet, urban, Catholic candidate in his largely dry, rural, Protestant state. Outraged Nebraskans said as much: an attorney from Nelson wrote, "Personally, I pray to be forgiven for having supported you, for I now realize that you are not a Republican, but a moonshine Democrat, spiked with Socialism and boot-legged into the United States Senate under a Republican label"; while a telegram "deplor[ing] your recent course of action" was attributed to "we the undersigned former friends."[90] For the rest of his career,

"CARRY ON!"

—By Jerry Doyle.

FIGURE 5. The *Philadelphia Record*'s Jerry Doyle often tied Smith to the long progressive tradition. Jerry Doyle, "Carry On!" *Philadelphia Record*, October 29, 1928, 8.

Norris would be harassed by offended constituents, and during his 1930 reelection campaign, the Republican National Committee flooded Nebraska with charges that the incumbent was a drunkard and that his wife was a Catholic.[91] Historians rightly note Norris's initial reluctance to support Smith; but the larger story demonstrates the diligence of the senator's evaluation, the conviction behind his ultimate decision, and the serious consequences of his activities. As Norris himself wrote weeks after the election: "One thing seems clear to me, and that is that if I was right in supporting the so-called Progressive Senators regardless of politics, then, for the same reason, I was right in taking the attitude I did in favor of Governor Smith as against Mr. Hoover."[92]

Smith's position was sufficiently progressive—and unique from that of Herbert Hoover—to inspire such eventual boldness from George Norris. So too was Smith bold when challenged on his stand. Under scathing criticism from his occasional ally Charles Evans Hughes, Smith held firm and indeed sharpened his stance: "I believe the agency, whether it be State or [Federal] Government, should not only own the site, but should own and build and operate the powerhouse. It is the only way that you can guarantee equitable distribution of the power and fair and reasonable prices to the ultimate consumer. . . . The whole thing is contained in the sentence: the Government must keep its hands on the switch that turns on or off the power."[93]

Much of this occurred in the wake of the most scalding denunciation of Smith's water power policy—delivered by Herbert Hoover himself on October 22 at Madison Square Garden, where the Republican decried Smith's proposals as "State socialism." The assault centered on water power, farm relief, and Prohibition—issues on which Hoover claimed Smith had "confronted" citizens "with a huge program of government in business." Hoover asserted that wartime necessities had begotten an "organized despotism" under Wilson for purposes of national preservation: "To a large degree we regimented our whole people into a socialistic state." This may have been "justified in time of war," but "if continued in peace time it would destroy not only our American system but with it our progress and freedom as well." Recognition of this danger and the prompt return to normalcy under Harding and Coolidge—piloted in large part by Hoover—had spurred economic growth and averted the dangers of Bolshevism in the postwar period; but now the downfall of "American individualism" loomed again, in the ominous form of the Smith program:

> There has been revived in this campaign . . . a series of proposals which, if adopted, would be a long step toward the abandonment of our American system and a surrender to the destructive operation of governmental conduct of commercial business. Because the country is faced with difficulty and doubt over certain national problems—that is, prohibition, farm relief, and electrical power—our opponents propose that we must thrust government a long way into the businesses which give rise to these problems. In effect, they abandon the tenets of their own party and turn to State socialism as a solution for the difficulties presented by all three.

"Emphasiz[ing] the seriousness of these [Democratic] proposals," Hoover "submitted to the American people a question of fundamental principle. That is: shall we depart from the principles of our American political and economic system, upon which we have advanced beyond all the rest of the world, in order to adopt methods based on principles destructive of its very foundations?"[94]

Most Republicans enthusiastically accepted and repeatedly invoked Hoover's line of attack. When Smith attempted to respond, the *Los Angeles Times* announced: "Smith Defends His Socialism."[95] At Buffalo, Charles Evans Hughes affirmed his belief that the Democratic nominee's program was one of "State Socialism."[96] Of course, not all Republicans were as impressed—Hoover's speech provided the decisive nudge to Senator Norris: "How any progressive in America can support him now, after his Madison Square Garden address, in which he slapped every progressive-minded man and woman in America in the face, my God, I cannot conceive it."[97]

Not everyone took Hoover's remarks this seriously. The Socialist Jacob Panken, a former New York Municipal Court justice who had challenged Smith for governor in 1926, "ridiculed" the speech, deeming the assertion that Smith's policies were socialistic "absurd." "Hoover's attempt to pin the charge of socialism on Governor Smith is an illegitimate child which I wouldn't want placed on my doorstep," he scoffed. "The Democratic nominee wants the Government to develop Muscle Shoals and then to turn it over to private agencies for exploitation. That's not socialism. . . . We favor the development, ownership, and operation of our water power resources."[98] Here Panken was either disingenuous or obtuse, for Smith had quite literally called for "absolute retention of the ownership of the power itself, by owning and controlling the site and the plant at the place of the generation" during his Denver speech.[99] There were serious differences between Smith's plan and that of the Socialists: the Democrat would not necessarily have the government deliver power to consumers, instead favoring a system featuring government generation for sale to private distributors; moreover, Smith's calls for public ownership did not extend to sectors like railroads and mines in the manner of the Socialist platform.[100] Yet in spite of assertions by Norman Thomas, Jacob Panken, and others to the contrary, Smith's position on hydroelectricity was far different from that of Hoover, who opposed such government involvement as a matter of principle; and indeed upon comparison with the Republicans and Socialists, it is with the latter that differences in the Democrat's position on water power appear, using Thomas's phrase, "comparatively insignificant."

Many Socialists recognized this. In January, Thomas Duncan of Milwaukee, state assembly leader of Wisconsin's Socialist Party, lauded Smith, predicting that "he will get about half the Socialist vote because of his stand on the public utility question."[101] A socialist from Kansas wrote to George Norris that "Governor Smith's policies . . . are steps toward socialism & a possible ultimate solution to our economic woes."[102] Hoping to evaluate the virtues of the two left-leaning candidates, the Community Church on Park Avenue in New York City hosted a debate entitled "Smith or Thomas: Which Should Progressives Vote For?"[103] Moreover, on the same day that Hoover addressed Madison Square Garden, Norman Thomas himself implicitly acknowledged a genuine qualitative difference in the philosophies of Hoover and Smith. "Everything Hoover has said and done makes it clear that he will be on the side of special privilege. Contemplating this spectacle, some of our progressives are ready to throw their votes to the Democratic party." This was a fruitless venture not because of alleged conservatism on Smith's part but rather because "almost certainly they can't elect Smith . . . [or] rehabilitate the Democratic party."[104]

Hoover's remarks had served to exacerbate the confusion already clouding partisan alignments in the closing weeks of the 1928 election; the speech drew praise from conservatives and instigated panic among moderate Democrats, while antagonizing progressive Republicans—a number of whom defected to the Smith banner. In many ways, the address served to clarify real differences between the two candidates: Joe Robinson suggested that it provided any voter who "possesses sufficient intelligence" great insight into "the reactionary spirit which animates the Republican candidate for President."[105] Nevertheless, Smith was not a socialist, and he certainly was not running in a political atmosphere favorable toward socialistic proposals. For the Democrats, the Madison Square Garden speech could not be the last word. Hoover's criticism of Smith's "state socialism" compelled and drew a response—one which, when coupled with the Republican's remarks, clearly delineates the significant philosophical cleavage between the two contenders.

Economic Justice

The rejoinder came forty-eight hours later. From Boston, Smith famously denounced the "socialism" charge as "the cry of special interests" and as "subterfuge and camouflage" for "groups who either want to stop you or who want to get something for themselves." It was a familiar attack, claimed Smith— "the only argument in twenty-five years that they have been able to advance against the constructive policy of the Democratic Party" in New York.[106] As Oscar Handlin notes, the candidate "refused to hedge when Hoover charged that Smith was taking a road to socialism. In his reply in Boston, Al reaffirmed his conviction of the importance of his program and pointed out that the accusation of Communism was always an easy weapon in the hands of the enemies of progressive legislation."[107]

Democratic Party chair John Raskob denied Smith's interest in placing the "government in business," demanding that "if there ever was a candidate who was opposed to that principle it was Governor Smith."[108] Raskob's role in the party was administrative rather than visionary; he was an excellent fund-raiser whose importance to the 1928 campaign has been greatly exaggerated in the literature—a false prominence roundly debunked by Smith biographer Robert Slayton.[109] In fact, the General Motors vice president had been brought into the Democratic campaign specifically to mollify business, and his early assurances of Smith's soundness on economic matters had "caused such a flurry of buying that on Wall Street it was called a 'Smith Market.'"[110] While Smith had been "taken with Raskob, the kind of self-made successful man he admired," the chairman's comments, which also included a brief diatribe on states' rights, provide little insight into the beliefs of the nominee. It was not Raskob, but Belle Moskowitz who directed Smith's "personal campaign."[111] Indeed, Raskob was a relative newcomer to the Smith circle and had not witnessed his candidate fending off charges of socialism for a decade as governor—but then neither had most of the nation. For their benefit, Smith engaged the charge at Boston as it pertained not only to hydroelectricity but to his entire platform and indeed his entire career. The Democrat used Hoover's socialism offensive to broaden the debate, engaging his opponent in a wider ideological conflict over the role of government in American economic life.

Smith noted similar criticisms of his program for workmen's compensation and of "that great factory code in New York, designed to protect the health, the welfare and the well-being of men, women and children" before his Boston audience, which cramped an overcrowded arena and spilled out "for blocks around."[112] The governor rejected Republican charges that such programs constituted a socialist agenda. But he seconded Hoover's assertion that the campaign involved "a question of fundamental principle." While differing on the nomenclature, both candidates understood the conflict as one between the continuation of the Harding-Coolidge political economy and the development on a national scale of the progressive polity Smith had administered in New York and had touted throughout the campaign.

Of course, the election was not merely a referendum on New York's social welfare regime. Responding to Hoover's unflinching praise of the national economic status quo, Smith pointed out the struggles of certain sectors—most notably textiles—during his Boston address. Smith also criticized the Coolidge administration for its roseate view of employment and payroll statistics that the Democrat claimed masked profound suffering among many industrial laborers.[113] This was easy to do in New England, where the slump in textiles was causing great hardship for thousands of families. But Smith pursued this theme further the next week in Newark, renewing progressive calls for an unemployment survey. To remedy the accumulated ills of two terms of Republican dereliction, Smith proffered a program nearly identical to that proposed by Senator Wagner in March, calling on the Department of Labor to collect "accurate and comprehensive information on employment in important industries" and to formulate "a scientific plan whereby during periods of unemployment appropriations shall be made available for the construction of necessary public work." Turning his attention to those with jobs, Smith ridiculed the administration's Pollyannish interpretation of its own wage statistics, asserting that while the Republicans claimed that "everybody owns an automobile and everybody lives on chicken dinners," the Bureau of Labor Statistics had declared $2,000 the minimum livable annual income for a family of five while calculating that the average wage for a manufacturing worker was $1,280 a year.[114]

Smith partisans made similar arguments. At a Labor Day rally in Fort Hamilton, New York, John J. Manning of the American Federation of Labor "spoke of the necessity of caring for the 4,000,000 men . . . unable to secure employment."[115] In Elizabeth, New Jersey, Eleanor Roosevelt, head of the Democratic women's division, insisted that "there may be prosperity in spots, but it is not uniform. . . . Great groups of people are very badly off, including the farmers and the textile workers of New England."[116]

Working-class Americans were responsive to such assertions. In Newark, a voter named L. Mastriani wrote the *Evening News* what could easily have been an excerpt from a Democratic campaign speech:

> The spellbinders of the Republican party are making a desperate effort to garner the vote of the working-men in this year's campaign, and their chief stock in trade is stressing the prosperity issue. . . . They talk about great prosperity, regardless of the fact that, according to the Labor Department's Minimum Health and Decency Budget, a family of five should have an annual income of between $2,059.63 and $2,511.02, depending upon the locality, while the annual average earnings of all workers amounts to only $1,222. . . . Governor Smith has shown by his record in New York that he is in sympathy with the workers' struggle for improved conditions, and no attempt to frighten them about bad times if the Democrats are elected is going to swerve them from their purpose to help make him the next President of the United States.[117]

Smith and his supporters challenged the very notion of Republican prosperity, demanding that a truly universal public welfare required serious evaluation of the shortcomings of the U.S. economic order. They did not call for a massive overhaul of capitalism in the United States—such a demand from a mainstream candidate would have been anachronistic in the 1920s. But neither did they turn a blind eye to the failures of the American system, including the depression of certain sectors and rising unemployment. Smith proposed specific remedies, calling for scientific studies to inform state-run and state-funded solutions—an approach reminiscent of the progressive executive style he had administered over four terms as governor.

It was a nuanced point but one that mattered a great deal to many contemporary workers, if not to later historians. Allan Lichtman has written that Smith "neither articulated an alternative vision of America nor challenged the values represented by the candidacy of Herbert Hoover."[118] Robert Slayton has concluded that in 1928 there was "no substantial issue to differentiate the parties."[119] A number of other important works have shared in this assessment.[120] Smith's pronouncements were certainly tempered by the reality that he was running in a generally strong economy, and there is no evidence that he sought a profound remaking of the U.S. economic system. But this does not mean he did not question the efficacy of Republican policies and propose an alternative vision of a just society.

Indeed, the Democratic campaign, while in accord with the basic tenets of American capitalism, delivered mordant criticisms of Republican satisfaction with the economy. President Coolidge and Treasury Secretary Andrew Mellon were said to have "made some amazing tax reductions, amazing for the discrimination practiced for the benefit of the millionaire and profiteering classes as opposed to the interests of the great majority of taxpayers." The apparent prosperity of the 1920s was deemed "flawed"—not only because of the much commented upon struggles of agriculture and textiles, but also because of the "speculative" nature of the "unsound inflationary condition" which was being presented as prosperity. "As is usual under such circumstances, the 'insiders' have profited at the expense of the 'outsiders' and many small investors," lamented the Democratic campaign handbook. Much like Smith's speeches in Boston, Newark, and elsewhere, official campaign materials did not uncritically accept the economic assumptions of the 1920s in the way the historical literature suggests. "This is not prosperity at all, in a national sense, but a regrettable episode in our financial history. It has had its evil effects, not only upon the small trader and investor, but upon labor seeking employment, and upon legitimate business and the farmers, who need credit at reasonably low rates." Smith knew well from his tussles with Coolidge over hydroelectricity that the administration saw virtue in such conditions, but he and his campaign disagreed, assigning federal policy makers "some of the responsibility" for the "speculative inflation" that was deemed so harmful.[121]

Rank-and-file Smith boosters articulated their own renditions of these critiques, sometimes with comic effect. When an Iowan began harassing Charles Curtis "about tax reduction on the higher incomes" during a campaign stop in Spencer, the vice presidential nominee angrily scolded the elderly heckler, "I guess you are too damn dumb to understand it."[122] Indeed, Democratic assaults on Republican tax and fiscal policies were pointed enough that by late September, Senator Curtis assailed the "constant nagging" of the Smith campaign during a Denver speech praising the Coolidge administration's efforts "to restore conditions throughout the country."[123]

Speculative inflation and regressive taxation were not the only flaws Democrats identified within the apparently robust U.S. economy. They also decried a "shameful condition" whereby "in spite of the fact that the United States is now the richest country in the world . . . there are still large sections of the population whose incomes are so small or uncertain that they fall below the requirements for what would be recognized as a decent standard of life." The "most important cause of poverty and destitution" was unemployment, but campaign literature also pointed out that in spite of sustained growth, wages had failed to keep pace with productivity, just as employment had failed to parallel expansion.[124] Far from singing hosannas for the 1920s economy, Al Smith and his campaign were in fact beginning to point out what William Leuchtenburg would later describe so poignantly as "the rotten beams in the economic structure."[125]

Many in the contemporary press shared the view of subsequent historians that the candidates were indistinguishable. No less a Smith partisan than Walter Lippmann suggested just that in a piece for *Vanity Fair* in September. "My own personal opinion," he offered, "is . . . if Mr. Hoover and Mr. Smith met in a room to discuss any concrete national question purely on its merits, they would be so close together at the end you could not tell the difference between them."[126] Many progressive intellectuals felt this way: *The Nation* famously editorialized that during the campaign "the two older political parties" had become "as like as two peas."[127] Of course these were élite rather than popular perceptions; and the fact remains that despite widespread accolades for Republican economics, Smith partisans rejected the notion—however expedient—that their candidate was in accord with Hoover's proposals. Former Wyoming governor Nellie Tayloe Ross, addressing 500 fellow Democratic women at Rochester, New York, suggested that Republican leaders who sought "the aggrandizement of the carefully chosen few" trembled at the prospect of a Smith election, for they feared "the governor's progressive theories" and his talent for harnessing state power "in the interests of the rank and file of the people." There was "real conflict now," she insisted, "between the forces of conservatism and those of progressivism."[128]

Bronx congressman Anthony Griffin summarized this view for a crowd in Hamden, Connecticut: "It has become a custom today to make the frivolous generalization that there is no difference between the policies of the two great parties." But this was "vicious propaganda to lull the American people to sleep" because in fact the Republicans sought "to perpetuate the economic slavery of the American people" on behalf of "the aluminum trust, the coal trust and the . . . power trust." Against this backdrop, "the greatest imposition and the most outrageous insult to the intelligence of the American people is the effort of these minions of special privilege to circulate propaganda that prosperity now prevails and that it would be dangerous to trust the country's welfare to a Democratic administration." Citing Commerce Department figures with acknowledged irony, Griffin pointed to weakness in farming, textiles, and coal and called Republican optimism "tantamount to the cheering diagnosis of a Doctor, who tells his patient he is alright except that his heart is not working rightly, his lungs are [infected] and his skin is affected with dermatitis." Griffin adduced wage cuts in various industries, rampant strikes in textiles and in coal mining, and the desperate pleas for farm relief, to conclude: "No, all is not right in the land." A change of direction was needed, extricating the ruling Republicans who "truckle to the vested interests" and installing "Alfred E. Smith in the White House," so that "the common people can rely on having a friend at the seat of government."[129]

As Smith and his allies were touring the nation articulating the candidate's reformist vision and challenging aspects of the economic status quo, their vice presidential nominee was also strenuously campaigning on such questions. Joseph Robinson's campaign tour concentrated largely on the South and especially the West, where he focused on topics including agriculture and federal corruption.[130] Another recurring theme was the rights of labor. The Arkansan echoed the progressive sentiments of Smith's acceptance address during a speech at Dallas, condemning injunctions issued in "pretended emergencies," asserting Democratic support for "the principle of collective bargaining which implies that organized labor shall choose its own representatives without coercion or interference," and calling for "a scientific program for public works construction in times of unemployment." Most significantly, Robinson declared that "labor is not 'a commodity,'" but should be "exalted above the plane of mere things and given its proper recognition as a function of the human brain and hand."[131] In San Francisco, Robinson turned these arguments against Republican economic stewardship, demanding that while "the Democratic party recognizes the right of every individual to enjoy prosperity . . . it must be distributed among all who contribute to our national wealth." Thus he joined Smith in "condemn[ing] the system set up by the Republican Party whereby only a few enjoy real prosperity and the remainder are required, like Lazarus, to accept the crumbs which fall from the overladen tables of Dives."[132]

Both major-party candidates enjoyed support from organized labor—such as it was in the 1920s.[133] United Mine Workers president John L. Lewis declared over the radio that "from the standpoint of Organized Labor, as well as business and industry," it was imperative "that Herbert Hoover should be elected"; Lewis credited the secretary's economic vision with instigating "a new industrial revolution which has become the marvel of the civilized world."[134] American Federation of Labor president William Green lauded Hoover for his "announced opposition to any change in the quota and restriction provisions of existing immigration legislation," calling the policy "most welcome."[135] Meanwhile, George L. Berry, president of the International Printing Pressmen and Assistants Union (and chairman of the labor division of the Democratic National Committee) scourged Hoover as an enemy of labor, pointing out the Republican's consistent advocacy of "the open shop," a charge echoed by other unionists, including Chicago Federation of Labor president John Fitzpatrick and Frank E. Walsh, secretary of the Scranton Central Labor Union.[136]

Democrats meanwhile hailed their own candidate as a champion of labor. Voters were reminded that in 1925 Smith had asserted that "the labor of a human being is not a commodity or an article of commerce" and that the following year he had recommended hearings to circumscribe the judiciary's power to enjoin striking unions.[137] Teamsters president Daniel J. Tobin declared Smith "the best friend labor ever had"—a potent endorsement given that four years earlier Tobin had denounced the national Democrats under John W. Davis as "'just as reactionary' as the Republicans" in explaining labor support for Robert La Follette.[138]

The Republicans' favorite argument against Smith among workers was to criticize his opposition to immigration restriction. Smith's "plan to break down restriction would admit many more immigrants who immediately would become competitors with American labor," workers were warned. Since the Democrat was a Tammany man he was "bound to advocate the Tammany Hall idea on immigration—which is, MORE IMMIGRANTS." Nor should this surprise anyone, since "New York has the largest foreign-born population of any city in America," and the 1924 vote on restriction had come down to "Tammany Versus the Nation" with "New York City utterly opposed to the rest of America in the matter of restrictive immigration."[139]

Smith had indeed criticized the National Origins Act of 1924 for establishing discriminatory immigration quotas based on the 1890 census.[140] However, at St. Paul the Democrat attempted to assuage fears that he intended to "open up the flood gates and let Europe pour all over this country," which

Republicans warned would cause a glut in the labor market and depress American wages. While he had demanded a halt to the use of thirty-eight-year-old census data in the formulation of national origins quotas in his acceptance address, the candidate avoided calls for further changes, instead suggesting that there would be no difference in the number of immigrants admitted under a Democratic or a Republican administration.[141]

Even this was going too far for Smith's adversaries. In October, *Barron's* reminded their readers why quotas based on the 1890 census were imperative: "Nobody is opposed to Italians as such," the publishers explained, yet the United States had been "receiving the sweepings of the Mediterranean throughout the past twenty-five years."[142] Indeed, although some immigration historians have derided Smith's challenge to restriction policy as timorous and even duplicitous, it is noteworthy that the nominee maintained his opposition to the 1890 quota basis, many in his circle preferred retaining the status quo: Walter Lippmann and Felix Frankfurter repeatedly forwarded Smith messages from Harvard professor Calvert Magruder, who had convinced them of the wisdom of Hoover's call for retention of the existing quota and hoped to persuade Smith to adopt this perspective.[143]

While immigration restriction presented the GOP with an appeal to labor of specific usefulness against Al Smith, Republican advocacy of protective tariffs had long served to garner votes among industrial workers of native and foreign stock alike. In Louisville, Smith departed from party orthodoxy, gingerly suggesting that as president he would not necessarily abolish Republican protections for industry, instead calling for tariff formulation by a nonpartisan panel of experts and demanding that the benefits of the tariff be extended to agriculture.[144] Such a panel already existed, but Democrats, led by former tariff commissioner Edward P. Costigan, charged that it had been warped into a hotbed of partisanship and favoritism.[145] In fact, many progressives were frustrated with the decay of the Wilson-era tariff commission—"Young Bob" La Follette lamented that under Coolidge it had been "packed with men who were appointed . . . solely because they were subservient and ready to carry out the administration's will."[146] Indeed, reforms to the commission similar to those Smith was proposing had been suggested by a Senate select committee chaired by Joseph Robinson (and including La Follette) in the spring of 1928.[147]

While Smith's proposal showed hints of Wilsonianism in its reliance on detached experts and of Bryanism in its demand of equality for farmers, it unquestionably abandoned the traditional free-trade posture of the Democrats. Historians have concluded that this signaled a surrender to the contemporary popularity of Republican policies—Allan Lichtman has disparaged Smith's posture as "pusillanimous."[148] Yet if protectionist proposals broke faith with the populist left, free-trade policies had long cost the populist left the full support of organized labor. Diagnosing the ailments of the Democratic Party in late 1927, Walter Lippmann wrote in *Harper's Magazine* that "reduction of the tariff in the interest of the farmer might cost many workingmen their jobs. So while both farmers and workingmen may denounce Big Business, they do not have a common interest and they do not mean the same thing."[149] As high tariffs were an essential piece of labor's agenda, this change in direction is best understood as a strategic shift rather than a defeatist retreat; the Democrats were reaching out to urban workers who were convinced of the benefits of protectionism, seeking to neutralize the issue (as well as the question of immigration) and to differentiate themselves from the Republicans on other matters. Even so, on both questions Smith did suggest significant reforms in the execution of Republican policies, if not in the policies themselves.

In any case, Smith did find points of grievance with Republican economic policies, and in his Boston and Newark speeches he was particularly aggressive in distinguishing his posture from Hoover's. Some of this was explicit, such as his rejection of the notion of universal prosperity and his charges of rising unemployment. Other criticisms were more subtle; for example, the question of hydroelectricity was framed not merely as a moral clash over the disposal of public property but also as a struggle to determine which class should benefit from these resources—public water power projects were presented as a means for decreasing household expenses and therefore improving laborers' quality of life. Additionally, Smith's recapitulations of his record of industrial reforms and welfare initiatives in New York were always used to suggest that his administration would seek similarly to improve living and working conditions nationally—a case made even more explicitly by Smith's progressive labor surrogates.[150]

While Smith separated himself from Hoover on these issues of interest to both organized and unorganized laborers, he also sought to gain an advantage on the central concern of many unions: injunctions. While the Republican platform had noted an occasional abuse of the injunction, Smith exploited his position as challenger, asserting that Republican inaction was to blame for the perpetually high number of injunctions issued; legislation had been introduced, a commission had been called to study the problem (on which Hoover had served), and yet "what happened to it? Nothing."[151]

Democrats outlined specifics: picketing, a usual target of injunctions, was deemed "an essential activity for organized labor during a strike, and to forbid it is to place unions at a disadvantage as instruments for collective bargaining." While decrying violence or outright bullying of strikebreakers, the party claimed that "some forms of what courts have called intimidation . . . if one approves of unions and collective bargaining, may be legitimate and desirable expressions of group loyalty and social ethics." In order to promote this vision of liberated labor, the Smith campaign called for laws to regulate "the process by which courts may issue injunctions in industrial disputes," to control "the process by which guilt of constructive contempt may be determined and punishment meted out," and to exempt "organized labor from the antitrust laws." Furthermore, the party called for "a declaration of public policy in favor of collective bargaining, and the enumeration and definition, under that declaration, of the substantive rights of labor to perform legitimate acts necessary to further its interest. Such a guarantee of the rights of labor would have to be weighed by the courts against rights asserted for the employer. . . . It would permit emphasis upon the fact that, in most if not all cases, strikes are carried on, not as conspiracies to injure the employer, but as a part of the process of collective bargaining, to protect the interest of labor."[152]

In 1928, many American workers enjoyed relative comfort. This presented an obvious dilemma for a presidential candidate who sought to critique the economic ideology of the incumbent party. Yet while accepting many of the underlying principles of Republican policies—a tack that can only be seen as pragmatic given the apparently robust economy—Smith still challenged aspects of those policies on progressive terms crafted to attract the support of urban laborers.

Social Welfare

If Smith partisans proposed to challenge aspects of the Harding-Coolidge-Hoover polity, their alternatives could be found in the Smith governorship. Not only did the Democrat seek the presidency on the merits of his gubernatorial résumé; he also submitted that résumé to the American voters as a means for divining his executive temperament and policy intentions.[153] The candidate said as much on the campaign trail repeatedly.[154] While Smith himself made these assertions, some of the most important iterations of this argument came from the very group that had been central to crafting and implementing his particular style of progressivism over the course of two decades in New York State: social work women.

Eleanor Roosevelt, whose husband had nominated Smith at the Democratic National Convention in Houston, spearheaded the women's division of the campaign, utilizing existing contacts to propagate campaign information.[155]

The division coordinated the work of numerous activists—including Molly Dewson, president of the New York Consumers' League and former secretary of the Massachusetts State Minimum Wage Commission. Dewson would rise to national prominence as a leading Democratic partisan during the Franklin Roosevelt years, but she was already an active Democrat by 1928—serving as a campaign vice chair and director of women's activities for the central United States. During a radio speech from St. Louis, Dewson explained why she had chosen to campaign for Smith: "My own interests are in the field of education and social economics. It is natural, therefore[,] that my attention should have been early called to the man who has been unceasingly active as the chief executive of New York in making real for the people through the channels of government those opportunities and services about which most of us can only theorize." Dewson proceeded to outline Smith's progressive record on public education, health care, and factory legislation.[156]

Unsurprisingly, one of the most active Smith partisans was New York State Industrial Board chairperson Frances Perkins, a central architect of the governor's expansive welfare regime. Perkins made a number of speeches for her fellow Democrat, and in all of them she emphasized his progressive record, particularly as an advocate for the social work agenda. In a September speech in Boston, Perkins stressed Smith's "social service record" and admonished her audience that it was "the duty of social worker[s] to press for their social conception as controlling political policies" by voting for the Democrat.[157] Perkins reiterated this point in a radio address from New York on September 24, proclaiming: "Governor Alfred Smith has stood by us, has put the women's social welfare problems into effect, has listened with sympathy, with knowledge and understanding, to the aspirations of working women for leisure, for fair wages, for a good life. . . . Will they recognize their duty to be loyal, not only to the man and his service, but to the program of industrial progress and of social welfare, of equality of women, and the protection of the weak, which he represents and on which his public career rests today?"[158] Perkins was not the only social welfare progressive to demand that loyalty compelled a vote for the Democrat: Mary Van Kleeck, who chaired a national committee of social workers supporting the New Yorker, reportedly stated "emphatically that any working woman who failed to support Smith is almost guilty of treason."[159]

Returning to Boston in October, Perkins predicted that Smith would garner tremendous support within the social work community, "because he is the one outstanding personality in American political life who has translated into reality and made effective the social welfare programs which social workers have formulated and have dreamed of throughout this country for the last generation."[160] Furthermore, this was not simply one aspect of Smith's political sensibilities; rather, he was "the first politician who has built his political career on the practical expression in legislation and in government of this passion for social justice."[161] Before these audiences, Perkins outlined Smith's park and playground initiatives, his "strengthening the work of the State Health Department," his "increase of nurses for maternity care," his development of "traveling child health clinics throughout the state," his work "to secure suitable widows' pensions," and his "leadership in the movement for better factory and labor laws." Indeed, suggested Perkins, Smith's was "a program of social welfare legislation which might have been written by the National Social Workers' Association."[162]

Many social workers longed for a Smith presidency because of his record—the essence of which Perkins captured neatly at Boston: "He understands these problems and talks about them as a social worker. The greatest contribution perhaps to the whole program of making a better life for the plain people in New York State, has been his political leadership."[163] Smith's governorship had advanced social welfare through both progressive policies and artful politics, and this was ample reason to promote him to the nation's highest office.

After the Boston speech, during which she had "got a great hand," Frances Perkins recalled feeling that the 1928 "campaign, whether it elected Al Smith or not, would *plant the seed of a set of ideas all over the country.*" Perkins gave similar speeches in Pittsburgh, Chicago, Buffalo, and Detroit—each time arguing that Smith was the social welfare candidate.[164] To Perkins and many other social welfare progressives, the 1928 campaign was not only about electing Al Smith; it was, at its core, a drive to broaden an entire agenda—the articulation for the first time on the national stage of a set of progressive values that they had promoted at the state level and hoped to implement in Washington under the presidency of their strongest political patron.

Another Smith supporter, Lillian Wald, took a much different approach. Fellow settlement house leader Jane Addams, a Hoover supporter, had written Smith adviser Henry Moskowitz that she would not speak on the Republican's behalf; and so in a sort of gentlewomen's agreement, Wald acted in kind. Yet Wald was "working all the time" for the Democrat.[165] She penned dozens of letters to fellow social workers on behalf of the campaign, assuring colleagues that Smith possessed a "tender sympathy for humanity" rivaled in American political history only by Abraham Lincoln.[166] To justify this appraisal, she directed correspondents to "the record of his unique and able administration of the affairs of New York State."[167] Wald implored one Chicago settlement activist to "ask . . . the doctors who know his programs for hospitalization, and the

New York child labor committee who know his comprehension of children's needs. Ask the housing people and the people who understand his great program for conserving the water power for the benefit of the people." In these letters Wald praised not only Smith's progressive policies but also the efficacy of his political methodology: "Time and time again when the opposition has [blocked] measures that the Governor thought important for the welfare and happiness of the people, he has gone before the voters directly, explaining as only Theodore Roosevelt ever did."[168]

Transcending personal appeals, Wald reached an even wider audience with an open letter to her charitable colleagues. The document, coauthored by John L. Elliott of New York's Hudson Guild Settlement and mailed to social workers across the nation, proclaimed that Smith had "done more to promote human welfare and social justice in New York than any other man in public life throughout the history of the State." Citing accomplishments including the $50 million hospital bond, "financial assistance to mothers of dependent children," the creation of a commission on child welfare, "efforts to promote the building of low priced houses and to improve housing conditions generally," the forty-eight-hour work week for women, and administrative reorganization, Wald and Elliott determined that "social workers and the socially minded generally may find great satisfaction in Governor Smith's record of transforming hopes for social reform into the realities of legislation and efficient administration." Readers were reminded also of Smith's ability to make "an appeal to the people" and to achieve "victories of popular government." Once again, in making the case for Smith's candidacy, social welfare advocates were describing his unique qualifications for the presidency by precisely defining his specific brand of progressivism: "His record of legislative achievement in social work and his rare qualities as a public leader, displayed in dealing with the social problems of the State, have fitted him in an unusual way for national leadership."[169]

As Perkins spoke and Wald wrote on Al Smith's behalf, Belle Moskowitz crafted political strategy for the campaign. In fact, Moskowitz had for years been the central figure maneuvering on Smith's behalf behind the scenes, and her position was strengthened as the election season dawned. According to Elisabeth Perry, Moskowitz "could almost be said to dominate" the leadership of the Smith campaign, meeting regularly with "a smaller, more intimate group within the War Board." Bolstered by a decade of assiduous recordkeeping, as well as by a vast national network of correspondents and political allies, Moskowitz was probably the only indispensable person within the Smith circle. She did not always get her way: Moskowitz had opposed Smith's selection of Raskob as party chair, and like many women within the party she was disgruntled when female members of the Democratic National Committee (who constituted precisely half of the membership) were excluded from the process of selecting vice chairs for the campaign by a rump session of male committee members.[170] Nevertheless, Moskowitz, along with Smith's other longtime advisers, Joseph Proskauer and Robert Moses, sat atop what Robert Slayton has deemed "the *real* flowchart" of power within the campaign.[171] As a member of the party's executive committee and head of the publicity bureau, Moskowitz was charged with "the selling of Al Smith": coordinating materials for the press, directing research, and preparing campaign literature. It was she who compiled the party's campaign handbook, shaping an image of the candidate and his credentials that reflected her conception of his "best points." Thus campaign publicity stressed Smith's progressive achievements as governor of New York, his attachment to the progressive tradition, and his personal virtues.[172] While Moskowitz molded Smith's official public image, she also distributed talking points to speakers and approved advertisements for publication.[173] With direct authority over the Social Work, Public Health, and Education Committee and the Women's Activities Committee, she was further empowered to promote Smith's social welfare credentials.[174] While many progressive women played important parts in the Smith campaign, Belle Moskowitz had enjoyed, in Rexford Tugwell's words, an "elevation to the role of President-maker."[175]

One branch of the campaign that fell under Moskowitz's jurisdiction was the Public Health Workers for Smith, a group formed to promote the Democrat's candidacy among social welfare progressives on the key issue of health care.[176] In an effusive letter to their colleagues, the committee declared: "No man in public life in New York State has contributed as much in terms of constructive legislation, and in the support of adequate appropriations for the development of the state's modern public health facilities." The development of county health units and generous state funding for local health work were praised, as was the governor's understanding that "the health of the people is one of the State's most precious assets." Moreover, these programs would be nationalized under a Smith presidency: "Those of us who subscribe to this letter believe that he would bring to the complex public health problems of the nation, the same intelligent and sympathetic understanding that has marked his leadership in New York State."[177]

These activists understood Smith's gubernatorial achievements and his platform for the nation as manifestations of their social welfare agenda. Moreover, in Smith they saw not merely a politician playing the part of reformer, but rather a coworker who shared genuinely in their progressive vision. Smith made much of this clear in his campaign speeches, and women like Molly Dewson and Frances Perkins made the case more explicitly and in greater detail in addresses of their own. Unsurprisingly, their sentiments comported with Smith's own defense of his program during his Boston rejoinder to Hoover's "socialism" charge—after all, wrote Lillian Wald, "most of us are for what Hoover designates as 'Smith's state socialism.'"[178]

Not all progressive women rallied to Smith. One group that roundly rejected his platform was female progressives who might be dubbed "equal rights feminists." During the 1910s, as the historian Nancy Cott has written, "the suffrage coalition temporarily concealed" fundamental divisions among progressive women; by the 1920s there was a clear gulf between women interested in social welfare and labor legislation and those who prioritized women's absolute political, legal, and economic equality.[179] The latter coalesced around groups like Alice Paul's National Woman's Party and pressed for an Equal Rights Amendment to the Constitution. These feminists, in contrast with the social work progressives, frowned upon welfare and labor legislation that presupposed sex differences. Simultaneously, those who supported the social welfare agenda tended staunchly to oppose the Equal Rights Amendment because its adoption would render the lion's share of their progressive labor statutes unconstitutional.

Given this background, it is not surprising that the National Woman's Party—which Smith derided as an "interesting sidelight" in his notes—endorsed Herbert Hoover, citing Charles Curtis's support for the Equal Rights Amendment and chastising the Democratic candidate for "refusing to put their ideas into effect in New York State."[180] Walter Lippmann cabled Smith that this presented an "admirable opportunity" to enunciate his social welfare vision, since "what is meant by equal opportunity is the destruction not only of laws unfavorable to women but laws specially designed to protect them."[181] The *Fall River Globe*, which supported the Democratic nominee, bluntly shared this assessment: "An organization exerting itself for the interests of the sweatshop is something that could not properly find a place for itself under the Smith banner."[182] The candidate himself addressed the question directly the following month at Newark: "When it comes to women's legal status, when it comes to the custody of children, when it comes to property rights, I will go as far as anybody in the world to maintain the equality between women and men. But what I will never do is consent to an amendment to the Federal Constitution that will prohibit the States from enacting legislation to promote the health, the comfort and the happiness of women who are compelled to work in factories."[183]

Even among progressive women who prioritized social welfare there was nothing approaching unanimity. Jane Addams, like many social work progressives, supported Hoover largely based on the Republican's own progressive credentials, particularly his humanitarian efforts at the close of the world war. Hoover, she believed, was "the one American connected with the Great War that should have been distinguished not for his military services but for 'conservation of tender lives menaced by war's starvation.'"[184] A social worker from Minneapolis concluded that despite her own preference for Al Smith, she saw "little to choose between the social service record of the two men," for Hoover, like Smith, had proved a great humanitarian.[185]

Many others opposed Smith because of his stance on Prohibition. As had been the case among some agrarian reformers, Smith's openly questioning the efficacy of the Volstead Act had earned him mistrust from many social welfare progressives—both male and female. Responding to Lillian Wald's entreaties, Irving Fisher, a noted Yale economist and social reformer, wrote that despite Smith's "great vision in Public Health measures, educational and labor measures," he was compelled to support Hoover because "Prohibition in the hands of its enemies could never succeed."[186] A social worker from Kalamazoo, Michigan, expressed similar ambivalence: "I am sorry, for Governor Smith fills my imagination and I would have liked to vote for him but I believe a victory for Mr. Hoover at the present time would settle the question of the Eighteenth Amendment."[187] Meanwhile, rumors of "the number of highballs and cocktails which the Governor is in the habit of imbibing daily" swirled throughout the autumn.[188] An anonymous "progressive" woman attacked Eleanor Roosevelt for supporting Smith, suggesting, "You must have seen him at some time or another at some of his public appearances in a condition which you as a supporter of the Volstead Act would disdain."[189] In most cases, however, it did not require legends of gubernatorial debauchery to convince such voters. "I am for prohibition," concluded a correspondent of Lillian Wald, "and I am therefore compelled to vote against Governor Smith."[190]

Another demerit for Smith in the eyes of some social workers was his lack of a formal education. The fact that the governor had sedulously educated himself to a par with any of his colleagues, to the point that he was correcting fellow assemblymen's grammar during debate, was less renowned than his famous boast that his only degree was from the Fulton Fish Market.[191] This was an obvious liability when courting professionals in a field founded by college graduates on principles of social scientific expertise. A correspondent of Lillian Wald's from Pittsburgh pointed this out, demanding: "Do you social workers, belonging to a group that is stressing so much these days the importance of training for the job—do you not think the presidency is the biggest job there is and cannot have a man too well educated and trained?"[192] This suggested an education gap in the opinion of the executive secretary of the

Massachusetts Child Labor Committee, who pointed out that Hoover "has had the best training for president of any man we have had."[193] A social worker from St. Louis was less charitable, admonishing Wald for "trying to 'go down the line' for a man whom you would otherwise call illiterate, just because he favored a few good things for suffering humanity"; while another, from Hartford, deemed the reputedly unlettered Democrat "ill fitted to fill the position which he is seeking."[194]

Hoover's progressive credentials, Prohibition, and the education gap all served to divert much of the social work vote, a particularly influential bloc among progressive women, away from Smith. In spite of these failures, the New Yorker attracted the support of many female progressives, and it was these women who gave voice (and in the case of Belle Moskowitz, direction) to the most fundamental aspirations of Smith's progressive agenda. Prohibitionists or not, many important progressive women worked tirelessly on behalf of the Democrat; for they could not easily set aside their hope that with Governor Smith in the White House they might be able to accomplish a few more "good things for suffering humanity."

From Albany to Washington

Other issues received expansive treatment during Smith's speaking tour. Prohibition, which cost the Democrat dearly among progressive farmers and social workers, was the focus of Smith's speech in the beer capital Milwaukee, Wisconsin, where "no more popular subject could have been chosen for an audience," according to the *Brooklyn Eagle*, since "a large proportion of [the residents] are Germans or of German extraction."[195] The topic also received prominent comment in Newark and Philadelphia, as well as in Chicago—dubbed six years earlier "the town that Billy Sunday could not shut down" by the songwriter Fred Fisher.[196] In these speeches, Smith defended his plan to allow states to decide how to handle the question as "nothing more nor less than the simple application of the good old Jeffersonian democratic theory of States' rights."[197] While he often discussed the topic, Smith shared the opinion of a group of forty Harvard professors who had suggested in endorsing the Democrat that Prohibition "should not be allowed to overshadow other matters."[198] Indeed, when asked directly in Omaha, "Do you believe that liquor is the great issue in this campaign?" he responded tersely, "I certainly do not."[199]

Controversial as it was, Smith's position was little more than a nationalization of the stance he had taken throughout his tenure as governor, during which he signed an act repealing the Mullan-Gage Law, which had provided for Prohibition enforcement in New York.[200] Based on this record of what the journalist Frederick Lewis Allen dubbed "unterrified wetness," no one should have been surprised by the New Yorker's antipathy toward the Eighteenth Amendment.[201] Yet his handling of the issue left much to be desired. Walter Lippmann, who approved of Smith's position as "wise, courageous and fine," nevertheless disapproved of the Democrat's reticence on the question prior to the primaries and the party convention, demanding that "good faith requires you to serve notice on the convention as to the *line* you intend to take on a matter of such importance."[202] Publicly, Lippmann suggested in *Harper's* that Prohibition was emerging as the most important issue of the pending campaign, and that Smith was being muzzled by his advisers for fear of alienating dry Democrats.[203] Smith chose a different course. As former secretary of the navy Josephus Daniels, a North Carolina delegate and committed Prohibitionist, would later recall: "At Houston . . . the only fight was in the Committee on Platform where the drys had a small number of determined men who were opposed to a plank demanding the repeal of national prohibition. Such men . . . told the Smith forces that if they insisted on an outright repeal declaration we would offer a minority report and carry the debate to the floor of the Convention. The Smith forces wished to avoid that if possible for fear of its effect on the election."[204]

Thus, hoping to avoid an intraparty rift, Smith evaded the sort of outright declaration urged by Lippmann—until after the nomination and the platform were finalized. Then, he abruptly broke his silence and sent a telegram to the delegates at Houston declaring his intent to stand by the platform but simultaneously reiterating his belief in the need for "fundamental changes" in Prohibition. Evidently, Smith acquiesced to Lippmann's exhortations—Franklin Roosevelt would later blame this "fool telegram" on Lippmann and the *New York World*.[205]

The dilatory tactics of Smith's representatives may have kept the major actions of the convention amicable, but the telegram did indeed alienate many dry delegates and cause serious problems throughout the campaign.[206] A league of New York Bryanites, organized in 1900, announced their defection to the party of McKinley after seven presidential campaigns, largely on the question of Prohibition—speculating quite plausibly that if the Great Commoner "were living he would do the same."[207] Yet despite such faulty strategy, the Smith forces remained relatively disciplined on the alcohol question, avoiding outright calls for repeal while focusing on the "Jeffersonian" nature of Smith's position as New York governor; and so while many Prohibitionist

Democrats were antagonized, figures like Josephus Daniels were given ample cover to remain within the partisan fold.

Another issue on which Smith proposed New York policy writ large was government efficiency—a question of greater consequence in New York but lesser comment in 1928. In a major speech at the Missouri State Fairgrounds in Sedalia, Smith mocked Republican claims of "economy in government" as petty compared to what he considered the grotesque waste overseen by the Coolidge administration. He ridiculed Republican boasts about government employees "going through the wastepaper baskets every night and picking out the pins and the paperclips and the short stubs of pencils and saving them all," and "the Consul General at Curacao . . . [who] saved $14 in one year by turning off the electric lights early at night." Concurrently, the Democrat skewered federal officials for failing to allocate funds to develop government properties across the country—leading to millions of dollars in unnecessary expenditures for rent; and generally depicted Republican frugality as miserly and pernicious—blaming federal haggling with the states for delays in Mississippi River flood controls and lambasting poor funding within the Department of the Interior that had resulted in horrible neglect of American Indians living on reservations.[208]

As he had in New York, Smith proposed that such austerity did not constitute real economy; instead, the adoption of businesslike management and wise investments (such as a robust construction program to eliminate the long-term cost of rent) could enable the federal government to provide for the people's welfare while promoting more efficient administration. The Democratic campaign suggested that "there are endless anomalies, often serious as well as humorous, in the grouping of activities within departments. . . . The lack of coherence in the departments . . . is accompanied by a scattering of the same kinds of work among numerous, unconnected branches of the administration." The party's official campaign book tartly juxtaposed Smith's position on government economy with that of the Republicans: "The real friends of departmental reorganization are not these cheese-paring sticklers for an economy that is merely negative. Rather they are those who view government in positive terms, seeing what effective governmental service can mean in the lives of ordinary people. It is not accidental, therefore, that the last two administrations should have seemed so lacking in real seriousness and should have been so demonstrably unable or unwilling to put driving force behind its lip-service to the ideal of reorganized administration."[209] It is unsurprising that this national rationale paralleled so closely the case Smith had made against miserly government and in favor of positive reorganization as governor, for the person charged with compiling these arguments was Belle Moskowitz.[210]

After the nominee articulated all of this in Missouri, the *Wall Street Journal* expressed indignation at Smith's "cheap" attempt to "ridicule . . . economy in government." Not content with this rebuff of the Democrat, the *Journal* then objurgated Smith in one of the most patronizing paragraphs of the campaign: "All of us think the more of him that he rose from humble surroundings and made himself a genuine success in politics. . . . But if Mr. Smith rose in the world in so creditable a way, he took a less worthy part of his original sur- roundings with him. Just as your maid-servant or your office boy sees no sense in economy and nothing reprehensible in waste, each believing that your income is far greater than any needs they can imagine, so the politician of the Smith type views the public purse."[211]

Equally critical was Secretary of the Treasury Andrew Mellon, who believed that the Democrat "undertook to challenge my good faith and to accuse me of presenting a false picture of the nation." Referencing the "scorn and ridi- cule" Smith had offered to "examples of minor savings," Mellon queried: "Doesn't he realize that these . . . are simply proof that the example set by the President at the top has reached down until it has permeated the whole civil service and revolutionized their attitude toward the expenditure of public funds?" Mellon concluded that "Governor Smith has been led to draw rash conclusions from insufficient data and inadequate study."[212] Smith's alterna- tive executive philosophy revealed yet another fundamental difference between his view of federal administration and responsibility and that of the incum- bents; Republicans like Mellon demanded that this divergence illustrated the imperative of preserving the policies of Calvin Coolidge.

In January 1928, after Al Smith's eighth and final annual report to the New York State legislature, labor leader Mary Dreier noted the potency of the gov- ernor's approach to progressive politics: expressing "delight" over Smith's ad- vocacy of labor regulations and social legislation, Dreier concluded that the report "gives such an opportunity for the citizens of our State to become lib- erally educated in the methods of government, that I must thank you heartily for it."[213] That fall, throughout his campaign for the presidency, Smith again assumed the role of political pedagogue, deploying this talent in behalf of his robust reform program. The *New Orleans Times-Picayune* detected the signifi- cance of Smith's popular progressivism: "Had the colorless Hoover been op- posed by an equally colorless Cox or Davis this year, again America would have experienced one of those dull campaigns where issues would have been left largely to professionals. . . . Al Smith was the type of man required to arouse the nation and to bring back to every voter a realization of his part in the nation's economy." A "new self-determination" had been "awakened in the people by the Al Smith school of political thought and action."[214]

Meanwhile, Herbert Hoover staunchly championed the Harding-Coolidge status quo; the erstwhile independent and sometimes progressive was now the foremost exponent of conservative normalcy—leading the great cowboy-philosopher Will Rogers to query, "Did you ever see a man become more thoroughly Republicanized?"[215] Smith delivered a reformist critique of the political economy of the 1920s; Hoover defended that political economy and censured Smith's alternatives as folly at best—Bolshevism at worst.

Smith's popular approach to reform, combined with the stark programmatic divergence between the two major candidates, meant that voters were presented with a clear choice in 1928. This would unleash a dramatic surge in rank-and-file political activity and instigate an important electoral realignment. Voters responded enthusiastically to the conflicting entreaties of the presidential combatants, aroused by *both* class *and* culture.

CHAPTER 4

The People's Verdict

Not only were there serious policy disputes between the candidates and among their lieutenants; these debates also transcended the realm of élite politics and were taken up in the nation's press and by rank-and-file citizens. Al Smith and Herbert Hoover offered contrasting visions of the state's role in promoting a just society, and these distinctions were taken seriously by press and public. Indeed, far from drowning out the other issues of the campaign, the infamous controversies surrounding Smith's religion and the broader debates that ensued over sundry cultural questions served to invigorate all sides of the contest and to awaken many quiescent citizens to the importance of national affairs. For those voters who were initially attracted to Smith because of his faith or his friendliness toward drink there became evident a robust agenda that spoke to their isolation from mainstream American society on cultural *and* economic levels. For these voters as well as those who cast a skeptical eye on Smith's famous brown derby, such questions added another layer of complexity to a labyrinthine political-economic landscape that exhibited very real challenges to which the candidates proposed very different remedies.

The Religious Question as Entering Wedge

The malignant calumnies swirling darkly in the American atmosphere over Smith's religion cast a perpetual shadow on the many serious policy debates of 1928. The governor recognized this, and so he decided to devote much of his September 20 address at Oklahoma City to opposition to his candidacy on the basis of his Catholicism. A somewhat naïve confidence that the American voter would instinctively ponder a candidate's qualifications rather than their ethnicity or religion had always been part of Smith's worldview. He had dismissed the Ku Klux Klan's taunts in New York, and this posture had been justified by electoral success.[1] Even in 1928, the nominee tried literally to laugh off the issue. As his campaign locomotive crept into Oklahoma, Smith and Joseph Proskauer gazed out their window at the fiery crosses that had been erected on a hillside near the tracks in anticipation of the Catholic candidate's arrival. Rather than take the display to heart, he brushed it aside with humor, turning to the Jewish Proskauer and inquiring, "Joe, how did they know you were on this train?"[2]

Nevertheless, the Democrat took an uncompromising stand against such bigotry during the second speech of his campaign tour. At Oklahoma City he declared that it was not immigrants or racial or religious minorities who were un-American, but rather the Klansman and his ilk who were "totally ignorant of the history and tradition of this country and its institutions." Addressing a series of documents circulating in Kentucky to defame his morals, the governor grew angry, declaring that the "set of men responsible for the publication of that wicked libel, in my opinion, do not believe in Christ."[3]

Smith believed that addressing the religious question would inoculate him against inevitable future attacks, refocusing public debate on his reform agenda: "The wicked motive of religious intolerance has driven bigots to attempt to inject these slanders into a political campaign. I here and now drag them into the open and denounce them as a treasonable attack upon the very foundations of American liberty. . . . Let the people of this country decide this election upon the great and real issues and upon nothing else." Thus, Smith hoped to move permanently beyond the religious issue, which he believed had no place in political debate—stating that if this happened he could be "confident of the outcome in November."[4]

In fact, the candidate's cheerfulness reflected a gross misjudgment of the political and cultural climate. As early as 1926, Ku Klux Klan imperial wizard Hiram W. Evans had promised: "We will march in 1928, chanting a funeral dirge, carrying a coffin on which will be inscribed: 'Here lie the political remains of Al Smith.'"[5] Like-minded Americans did not disappoint the wizard. Reminiscing on 1928, Eleanor Roosevelt recalled that "if I needed anything to show me what prejudice can do to the intelligence of human beings, that campaign was the best lesson I could have had."[6]

In 1928, Alabama Democrat Thomas Heflin, who had already denounced Smith and the pope on the floor of the U.S. Senate, embarked on a nationwide speaking tour, partially funded by the KKK.[7] North Carolina's fifth-term Democratic senator, Furnifold Simmons, was similarly cheered by enthusiastic pledges of support from Klansmen after proclaiming his own opposition to his party's presidential nominee.[8] The Klan periodical *Fellowship Forum* "regularly . . . devoted eight of its ten pages to violent, blatant and inaccurate attacks on Al Smith, the Pope and rum," featuring headlines like "Drunk Negro Boosting Smith" and "Kissing Pope's Ring Insult to Flag." *Time* magazine calculated that during the campaign, *Fellowship Forum* "won more circulation and showed a greater increase in gross revenue than any other U.S. publication."[9] By October, the Democratic National Committee had established a "Chamber of Horrors" at its Manhattan headquarters to display for the public the Klan's prodigious production of pernicious propaganda.[10] While the Klan's zenith had occurred earlier in the decade, 1928 provided the hooded order with its blazing last hurrah.[11]

Nor did one need to be a Klansman to be troubled by the notion of a Catholic in the White House. Governor Angus McLean of North Carolina lamented that local opposition to Smith was "based on the fact that he is a Roman Catholic," while in Arkansas, the president of Central College had his school's funding discontinued by "the bigoted leaders of my church in Arkansas—the Baptist Church," as retribution for his active support of the Catholic Smith.[12] The Anti-Saloon League characteristically conflated religion and rum in literature that not only alleged that Smith drank "from four to eight 'cocktails' a day," but also described the looming threat of "THE DOWNFALL OF CHRISTIAN CIVILIZATION" and the opposition to the Democrat by "Evangelical Churches."[13]

A flyer entitled "Appointments Made by Gov. Al. Smith" circulated nationally, falsely asserting that of twenty-one judicial appointments made by Smith, "ONLY 21 Were Roman Catholics."[14] As a result, Smith's campaign was inundated with letters requesting "a *certified* list of appointees" and verification of the religious affiliations of each Smith hire.[15] Nor was reality gratifying for many of these inquisitors, who were appalled by the heavy Hebrew presence within the Smith circle: "Neither Bismarck nor Gladstone had to get a Jewess to edit their speeches to make them grammatical," went one journal's sneering reference to Belle Moskowitz.[16]

These concerns were not quarantined among anonymous bigots or public clowns like Thomas Heflin. In March 1927, after a discussion with Idaho

Republican senator William Borah, Walter Lippmann alerted Al Smith that "there has been a very strong development in the last few months, of fear, on the part of progressive and on the whole tolerant-minded people about the political power of the Catholic Church."[17] Hostility over the candidate's faith and related cultural questions was evident even among social welfare progressives. One letter to Eleanor Roosevelt identified a complex of cultural objections to Smith, attacking the Democrat's position on immigration and criticizing "those men whose names appear on your stationery . . . For the most part they are Catholics and Jews, who would at any time, it is evident, support one of Smith's type . . . for the sake of opposing what to them is anathema, the 'Old Americans' of the United States."[18] A welfare advocate from New Orleans fretted to Lillian Wald that "even among social workers, who ought to know better, Smith's remarkable record in social legislation, and his unquestioned ability, courage and honesty, seem to go for naught as against his church affiliation."[19] Wald herself aired similar frustrations—and with good reason: one social worker had attacked her for supporting the Democrat since "wherever the Catholic Church rules, there is darkness, superstition, and deterioration," while another, who called Smith "a cheap politician," accused her of "prostitut[ing]" herself on his behalf.[20]

These shameful episodes and others like them have led scholars to conclude that Smith's faith instigated a backlash that bifurcated the electorate, Catholic against Protestant, and produced a result neatly understood through religious affiliation. Such a framework may be convenient, but it is also far too simplistic to account for the realities of the contest. The first hint of this is contained in the speech renowned for Smith's denunciation of the Klan. At Oklahoma City, the candidate spent nearly as many pages dealing with his progressive record as he did decrying intolerance. Of equal significance, the issues that he chose to demonstrate his executive credentials—water power, administrative reorganization, labor reforms, social welfare—were those on which he was seeking to differentiate himself from Herbert Hoover. Indeed, the Oklahoma City address demonstrates the multifaceted nature of Smith's campaign in a way that challenges the literature's singular focus on religion. It is clear that Smith's denomination cost him votes—and that it helped attract other votes. But reviewing the positive side of this equation—examining those voters who were drawn to Smith because of his Catholicism—demonstrates just how complicated the issues of the election really were and invites a more profound consideration of the complex motives of American voters.

As the conventional narrative goes, Smith, a working-class urbanite and grandson of immigrants who was the first Roman Catholic to secure a major-party nomination for the presidency, became himself the central issue of the campaign. Formerly loyal Democrats, especially in the South, turned away from this representative of the "new Americans," while many of those new Americans became enthusiastic supporters of the New York governor. While this traditional history contains many elements of truth, it masks the authentic, discernible ideological differences between Smith and Hoover. It also obscures the fact that the new Democrats of 1928, the urban ethnic workers who were voting as a bloc for Alfred E. Smith, were fully aware of his progressive approach to economic and social welfare issues, and that these voters supported Smith based not only on their biographical similarities but also on an emerging political ideology. The implications of this point are profound: if urban ethnic workers were voting for Smith based not exclusively on ethnocultural issues but also on economic and social concerns, then the 1928 election should be viewed as one in which a new coalition began to develop around principles that would inform the New Deal and provide the basis of Democratic policy for decades. It would certainly be going too far to say that New Deal liberalism per se was forged in the battles of 1928. More appropriately, it must be acknowledged that in the midst of the cultural struggles of that year, the Smith campaign would, as Frances Perkins prophesied, "plant the seed of a set of ideas all over the country."[21]

Importantly, those antagonized by the 1920s march toward "one-hundred percent Americanism" were themselves diverse. Southern and eastern European Jews and Catholics, Irish-Catholics, and African Americans had very little in common besides their enemies. While these groups were often bitter toward one another, they did harbor similar resentments toward a society that seemed intent on excluding them from the mainstream.[22]

Nevertheless, there is nothing to suggest that by the late 1920s there was any sort of alliance on the horizon. There were no obvious signs that these diverse groups would coalesce behind Alfred E. Smith. And yet that is precisely what occurred. The Democracy's opening wedge with these voters was the cultural assault being leveled against their nominee, and the party's allies in the press made the most of this line of attack.

One favored theme of pro-Smith newspapers was the opposition to their candidate by the Ku Klux Klan. This was reiterated time and again to urban ethnic audiences—as when readers of the rabidly Democratic *New York World*, a leading paper among that city's working classes, were told of a thwarted Klan plot to march on the Democratic convention at Houston in a desperate attempt to deny Smith the nomination.[23] Meanwhile, Smith's speeches denouncing the Klan, particularly those delivered at Oklahoma City and Baltimore, were lauded in front-page tributes and reprinted in full.[24]

THE THREE MUSKETEERS

FIGURE 6. Anti-Hoover cartoon from the *New York World* by Rollin Kirby, encouraging readers to associate the GOP with anti-Smith bigotry. Rollin Kirby, "The Three Musketeers," *New York World*, November 4, 1928. By permission of the Estate of Rollin Kirby Post.

Some articles went further, asserting that Hoover's reticence regarding the Klan, as well as the antics of Hoover lieutenants like Assistant Attorney General Mabel Walker Willebrandt—allegedly tied to scurrilous anti-Smith propaganda—demonstrated that the Republicans and perhaps even their nominee were party to the "whispering campaign."[25] Numerous political cartoons made the same point. One that appeared on the front page of the *Baltimore Afro-American*, entitled "Where They Roost," represented Smith as a bird nesting with "Religious Freedom" and "Personal Liberty," while Hoover nested with "Bigotry," "Race Prejudice," and the "Ku Klux Klan."[26]

Democratic propaganda encouraged such connections. A Democratic ad appearing in Marcus Garvey's *Negro World* admonished readers: "Smash Republican Deal with the Ku Klux Klan Vote Right This Year."[27] A full-page advertisement that ran in several cities pictured the tomb of the Unknown Soldier and queried: "Who Asked His Religion?" As if this icon were not enough, the ad included an excerpt from a speech in which New York mayor Jimmy Walker suggested to a Newark crowd with righteous indignation that "no one knew what color he was, and no one knew where he went to church." "Beau James" also took aim at Hoover, slyly remarking that he did not "feel like charging the Republican candidate with the responsibility of the whispering, bigoted campaign that is carried in contradiction of the Declaration of Independence, but there are men in this country who would refuse to be President if they got it with that kind of vote."[28] The Unknown Soldier was also invoked by Democrats in Boston, where once and future mayor James Michael Curley displayed an image of the monument with the sardonic caption: "What a tragedy if we should learn he was a Jew, Catholic or a Negro."[29]

It is significant that the Democrats' rhetoric incorporated black citizens into their hypothetical constellation of American outsiders and that similar advertisements and cartoons appeared in African American newspapers. The nebulous community that began to materialize in 1928 in response to Smith's candidacy and the constricted view of Americanism espoused by his detractors was not restricted to the specific religion and ethnicity of the Democratic nominee. Rather, in a crucial development, recent immigrants, Catholics, Jews, and many African Americans began to see each other as similarly under assault and thus discovered an impetus for alliance. The important development of 1928 was not that minority groups realized they were threatened by a movement to homogenize American society under Anglo-Saxon hegemony—this had been understood for generations; what mattered was that these groups all recognized within the Democratic candidate's struggles against bigotry an analogy to their own cultural battles, and with encouragement from the Democrats and their allies in the press they developed an incipient sense of coalition.

When the *Baltimore Afro-American* announced in a banner headline that "Religious Intolerance Is Biggest Campaign Issue," it followed with the hopeful declaration, "Race Question Is Next" and reprinted an editorial from the *Kansas City Call* that held Smith's denunciation of the Ku Klux Klan at Oklahoma City "as momentous as Lincoln's question to Stephen A. Douglas."[30] Similarly, the *Chicago Defender* supported Smith, in part, because the Catholic candidate, like blacks, was an enemy of the Klan.[31] In fact, at least eighteen typically Republican black newspapers, including leading national publications like the *Defender* and the *Afro-American*, endorsed Al Smith.[32]

Not only black publications, but their readers, responding on the editorial pages, pronounced notions of a community of interest among ethnic, religious, and racial minorities. One reader from St. Louis wrote to the *Afro-American* that "the Ku Klux Klan has put us with the Catholics and they will have to defend us if things go on as they have. . . . Please do all you can to help elect Smith."[33] A Harrisburg, Pennsylvania, man reminded fellow readers that the "Preamble to the Constitution does not say 'We The Protestants'" and that "Catholics are people."[34] The ambivalent *St. Louis Argus* editorialized that "the Klan is opposed to the Catholics, Jews or Negroes holding public office. Let the real Americans rise up and down such a doctrine."[35]

Similarly, many Jewish leaders and publications began to adopt a coalitionist posture in the midst of the 1928 struggle. At a New York luncheon featuring Democratic gubernatorial nominee Franklin Delano Roosevelt, Rabbi Stephen S. Wise called for "a great uprising of the American people to smite the bigots and fanatics who dare to say to 20,000,000 loyal American citizens, 'Not one of you is fit and qualified, not one of you shall be trusted by us to be President of the United States of America!'"[36] Rabbi Wise played a prominent role in boosting Smith on such terms within Jewish America—for example, a sermon he delivered against the Republican campaign at Carnegie Hall was reprinted in the Cincinnati *American Israelite* and accounted for the most prominent election coverage of the entire season in that publication.[37] Adopting a similar line, the Chicago *Jewish Courier* scolded Herbert Hoover for not condemning those who invoked religion against the Catholic candidate.[38]

Jewish and African American citizens began to see assaults on Smith's Catholicism as analogous to their own disadvantaged social position. Outsiders who aspired to mainstream acceptance could relate naturally to the Democrat's travails. The historian Oscar Handlin, thirteen at the time, later recalled of Smith: "I heard a lot of talk about the religious issue, and I knew his middle name was Emanuel—I thought he was Jewish."[39]

Meanwhile, Catholic ethnic groups began reaching out to these non-Catholic minorities in order to cultivate a sense of shared purpose. In New York, where many Democrats had already embraced such pluralism, Smith campaign events reflected this diversity. Brooklyn's largest Columbus Day celebration, hosted by the deputy street cleaning commissioner, Michael Laura, erupted into a Smith-for-President rally, prompted by speeches from a heterogeneous set of dignitaries, including Monsignor Alfonso Arcese, a prominent Italian-Catholic priest; John McCooey, the Irish head of the Kings County Democratic machine; Frank Ferrari, president of Manhattan's

Italian Hospital; and Herbert Lehman, the Jewish Democratic nominee for lieutenant governor of New York.[40] A Democratic rally for "up-town Italians" held at New York's Central Opera House featured Irish, Italian, and Jewish speakers and even included an Anglo-Dutch Protestant for good measure— Franklin Roosevelt.[41]

Nationally, coalitionist sentiment was encouraged by the Democratic Party and facilitated by the Democratic press. But if ethnic and religious questions were an effective opening wedge, they were insufficient to establish a durable coalition among this polyglot confederacy of the culturally disfranchised. Tirades against Yankee snobbery, southern racism, and Protestant fanaticism only told these groups what they were against; recognition of their similar position in American economic life facilitated an affirmative sense of community among these diverse members of the nation's working class.

In September, the *Brooklyn Eagle* reminded its readers that Herbert Hoover, whose fortune was "shrouded in mystery," would be the first millionaire president should he achieve victory.[42] Contrastingly, the Democratic *Philadelphia Record* described how Smith was beloved by even the domestic workers at the New York governor's mansion, where his ascent to prominence had apparently not diminished his working-class humanity.[43] This thesis was confirmed in the *Record* through the findings of a psychologist who deemed Smith the American politician with the closest affinity to the common man since Abraham Lincoln, while Hoover was found to be "out of touch."[44] The *Negro World* repeatedly reminded the public that Smith was "a man from the people" and beckoned its readers "to the polls for 'the Happy Warrior,' the truckman's son!"[45]

Such strategically placed biographical morsels held a narrow currency in a decade when the cult of wealth had taken deep root in U.S. society—they were of use only within a specific community: among the working class. The constant invocation of such background information uncloaks the Democratic alliance-building strategy. More significantly, the relentless cataloguing of Smith's social welfare and labor achievements in New York, as well as his similar agenda for the nation, both by the Democratic campaign and their allies in the media, demonstrates that economic justice, along with cultural pluralism, would undergird this nascent coalition.

Democratic oratory—especially Smith's own speeches—often focused on the concerns of the working class; and such rhetoric was disseminated to workers by the Democratic press, which vigorously extolled Smith's positions on labor issues. Hoover meanwhile was painted as an enemy of the labor movement and of workers more broadly—a disgusted *Philadelphia Record*, for example, angrily alerted its readers that "brushing aside a custom of Presidential candidates declaring their views of labor [on Labor Day], Herbert Hoover rested again today in the quiet of his home."[46] Claims of Republican prosperity were challenged in political cartoons that highlighted the plight of textile workers, miners, and farmers in a manner paralleling the arguments of Smith and other Democrats.[47]

Democratic newspapers emphasized Smith's support for government-owned and -operated hydroelectric plants to demonstrate their candidate's kinship with workers and his sympathy with their daily struggles; public power was framed as a proposal that would profoundly benefit workers—and one that clearly distinguished the Democrat from his Republican rival.[48] The *Brooklyn Eagle* declared this "the first time since 1912 that a great economic issue has been seriously debated in a national campaign," and publications left no ambiguity as to what was at stake for workers.[49] "Billions" would be saved by rank-and-file consumers under the Smith plan, Philadelphians were told.[50] "Hoover is for the power trust," the *Negro World* summarized; "Smith has renounced this giant economic threat to the poor man in terms which none may misunderstand."[51] Democratic newspapers went wild when George Norris endorsed Smith and his power plan and were aroused further by Smith's caustic rejoinder to Hoover's "state socialism" charge, reprinting the Boston address verbatim and dismissing the Republican critique as a ridiculous "straw man."[52]

Smith's social welfare record was routinely lauded. While Democrats reached out to Jews and African Americans by emphasizing Smith's appeals for tolerance, his gubernatorial achievements were also highlighted—adding an important class dynamic to these cultural entreaties. Why should Philadelphia's Jews support the Democratic nominee? asked one advertisement. "Because he stands for (1) Constructive, broad, social service legislation as evidenced by his splendid record of achievement as Governor of New York State," and "(2) Absolute elimination of the spirit of bigotry, intolerance and snobbishness."[53] Similarly, an ad by the Smith for President Democratic Colored League of Maryland appearing in the *Afro-American* listed seven reasons "why New York Negroes favor Al Smith," including his housing program, his dramatic increase in appropriations for public education, his widow's pension program, and his advocacy of minimum wages and employment standards for women and children.[54] The *Negro World* saw these policies as proof that Smith was a man of "broad humanitarian sympathies" and dubbed him "the symbol of liberalism and Christian charity."[55] On election eve, a front-page editorial in that paper proclaimed: "Hoover believes in millions for the few and crumbs for the millions; Smith believes that a competence is the right of the humblest of the nation's citizens."[56] The cartoon in the *Afro-American* that

WHERE THEY ROOST

FIGURE 7. The *Baltimore Afro-American* assigned Smith's campaign both cultural and economic significance. By permission of the *Baltimore Afro-American*.

had placed Al Smith alongside freedom and liberty included another bird in his roost: "industrial democracy."

These genuine policy differences on economic questions such as labor rights, public power, and social welfare helped feed the broader argument of the Democrats and their allies that, as Marcus Garvey contended, because "Smith is a man who has sprung from the common people, he knows their wants and their heart-beats and their pulse. Hoover has been pampered by the monopolist class; he is himself a millionaire; he can only see American politics and American power from the capitalist point of view."[57] The *Afro-American* noted that "the Fords, Chevrolets, and used cars, etc., are for Al Smith. The Studebakers, Packards, Lincolns, etc. are for Hoover. But, there are more Fords, etc., than Studebakers and Packards, etc."[58]

This sharp class dichotomy was not merely implied by speeches given by Democrats and articles published by their allies in the press; it was often absorbed by workers. A report about the behavior of a rowdy group of Smith supporters published in the *Philadelphia Record* demonstrates both the success of this class-based community-building strategy and the manifestation of that strategy in the presentation of news. In a scene "reminiscent of Hallowe'en or New Year's Nights," a mob of several thousand milled about the Bellevue-Stratford Hotel in Philadelphia, hoping to catch a glimpse of their political hero. These "ebullient Smith rooters tooted raucously on horns, cried out and cheered every passing automobile that bore a Smith tag." But as the evening progressed, "a hundred lusty-lunged Smith followers let out an uproarious 'Hooey!' as an expensive limousine with a Hoover placard behind rolled by. . . . The occupants, two men and a woman in evening clothes, stared frigidly."[59] This shamelessly partisan journalism demonstrates the success of the Democratic strategy—these ordinary, probably working-class Smith supporters were aroused but apparently not surprised by a passing group of élite Hoover voters. Simultaneously, the story is a blatant attempt to perpetuate this class politics with its meticulous attention to the fancy attire and fine automobile that are implied to be typical of Republicans.

The Democratic press successfully imbued portions of the working class with a sense of shared values under the auspices of the Smith presidential campaign. In response, urban ethnic working-class citizens exhibited unprecedented enthusiasm for Smith's candidacy. Tales of individual initiative on behalf of the New Yorker abounded. Thomas De Mayo of the Bronx, an Italian immigrant and musician, was "not content merely to cast his vote for Gov. Alfred E. Smith" and "dedicated his latest composition, a campaign march, to the Democratic nominee."[60] Francis J. McGuire, a truck driver from Manhattan, drove to Democratic headquarters and donated $25 of his $42 wages to the Smith cause, exclaiming, "I can't afford to give this much money, but the Governor has been a hero of mine for years. I want to see him President."[61] John F. Donohue, a former hobo from Idaho now working as a carpenter in Philadelphia and supporting a family of seven, sketched a charcoal portrait of Smith for publication in the *Record*.[62] Even children got involved: three-year-old William James McKay of Camden, New Jersey, "had been saving his pennies for months only to decide that he would spend them for flowers when he heard Governor Smith was coming."[63]

While these episodes demonstrated grassroots initiative, they also provided instructional tales for other potential Democrats, and so Smith-friendly newspapers covered such human interest stories in depth. At times they strained credulity, like the saga of James Joseph Buriage, a seven-year-old Baltimore boy who was struck by a car and according to his doctors was saved by a packet of Smith placards he was carrying under his shirt, which "had broken the blow and protected the boy's heart and lung jacket." (As an inspiring footnote, readers were informed that the brave lad's nurses had "assented to his appeal and displayed the twenty-five pictures about the room.")[64]

Meanwhile, readers were reminded of the sinister tactics that unscrupulous Republican operatives were willing to employ to thwart these enthusiastic Democrats. Stories were told of a Republican scheme to disenfranchise tens of thousands of voters in Hudson and Essex Counties in New Jersey in "an effort to defeat Governor Smith."[65] New Yorkers learned of a Republican plot in Columbus, Ohio, to deny the franchise to nuns.[66] Philadelphians were informed with outrage by the *Record* that the city's Republican machine had terminated a tax collector for supporting Smith with the brazen proclamation "This is a Republican office."[67]

Local passion translated into enthusiastic receptions for Smith at campaign stops nationwide. Welcomes for the Democrat in cities like Omaha were compared favorably to the only similarly triumphal display of unbridled effusion in recent memory: welcome parades for aviator Charles Lindbergh.[68] Eastern journalists noted the "uproarious and spontaneous outpouring of enthusiasm" for Smith by an audience of 12,000 in St. Paul, where it was reported that the Democrat had been greeted by "25 miles of humanity-lined streets."[69] Writers described the "riot" over Smith in Chicago, where a "huge crowd gathered" at the train station to "thunder" their approval of the New Yorker.[70] A "gay tumult" greeted the Democrat in Baltimore; and in Richmond enthusiastic bands blasted "The Sidewalks of New York" along with "Dixie."[71] Boston provided particularly potent fodder for the Democratic press. The *Brooklyn Eagle* described Smith's reception there as "without exaggeration, the most overwhelming that a candidate for President—or for that matter a President of the United States—has ever had. . . . It was a combination of the most turbulent, riotous and wild elements of Armistice night and the return of Lindbergh." As the Happy Warrior departed the city that had granted him this fantastic popular endorsement, the "vociferous reception [was] repeated as a goodbye," as crowds stormed the railroad tracks to bid farewell to the Democrat, delaying his train. Indeed, enthusiasm for Smith in industrial New England was such that it spurred "hope of winning the east."[72]

After this triumph, Smith journeyed to Republican Philadelphia. There, the *Record* used the "eager, welcoming crowds of Boston" to instruct residents on how to greet the nominee in the City of Brotherly Love.[73] Publishing a photograph of the "greatest crowd Boston ever saw . . . hail[ing] Democracy's leader," the editors implored, "Will Philadelphia duplicate this welcome to Al Smith Today?"[74] They were not disappointed: "Hundreds of thousands jam[med] sidewalks . . . cheering like a tidal wave" as Smith made his way to deliver "his striking speech before a wildly enthusiastic crowd."[75] Smith was the first Democratic candidate even to campaign in Philadelphia in twenty years, and the response was deemed the "greatest political triumph in city annals."[76] *Negro World* reporter S. A. Hayes described "a roaring, cheering, maddened throng of 12,000 souls within, and 20,000 more outside upon the ramparts. . . . What a mob!" he exclaimed, "What an ovation! Folks, you really ought to be here to join in the revelry."[77]

New Yorkers responded to these developments with a clamorous reception of their own. A crowd of 45,000 approached delirium during Smith's speech in Brooklyn, while "23,000 yelling voices" granted Smith the "biggest ovation of his campaign" at Madison Square Garden.[78] Outside the halls, two million citizens feverishly greeted their governor as he paraded triumphantly down the streets of his home town to conclude his campaign.[79] After nearly three decades of decline, popular interest in politics had been revived.[80]

An Ambiguous Rout

Alfred E. Smith lost the 1928 presidential election in a landslide. The Democrat carried only eight states, while Herbert Hoover won the Electoral College 444 to 87 and attracted almost 60 percent of the popular vote.[81] In the process, the Republican sundered the "Solid South"—Florida, North Carolina, and Virginia voted Republican for the first time since Reconstruction; Texas did so for the first time in its history.[82]

The result was a rout; yet simultaneously Smith had received more votes than any previous Democratic candidate—the 15 million ballots marked for the Happy Warrior were more than 5.8 million greater than the second-largest total for a nominee from his party.[83] Because Smith was able to attract so many new voters to the Democratic cause despite being defeated so soundly, many scholars have recognized within this ostensible fiasco the beginnings of a significant electoral shift.[84] The boldest of these, political scientist V. O. Key, labeled the contest a "critical election," asserting that "the Roosevelt revolution of 1932 was in large measure an Al Smith revolution of 1928."[85]

This "revolution" was found in the impressive gains Smith made in areas dominated by working-class ethnic citizens, producing substantial inroads for the Democratic Party among recent-immigrant, Catholic, and Jewish laborers

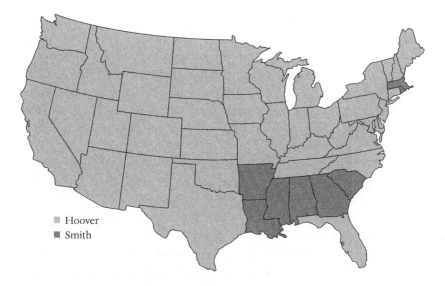

FIGURE 8.   Presidential results by state, 1928.

across the Northeast and the Midwest. Of the nineteen cities with a population over 250,000 that had ethnic (either immigrant or child-of-immigrant) majorities at the time of the 1930 census, all nineteen had given strong majorities to Harding in 1920. In 1928, Smith won seven of these cities; and in each of the nineteen, his tally represented a Democratic increase of over 100 percent.[86]

Smith attracted the support of these diverse voters in large part because his background embodied their own struggles for respect—for ethnic equality, religious tolerance, and social acceptance. Smith's career was a metaphor for all of these things, as well as for the rise of the city and its newest inhabitants to prominence in American life. But the governor offered more than hopeful metaphors. His campaign, like his career, spoke effectively to these voters' desire for household security and reliable, dignified employment. Americans who flocked to the Democratic banner in 1928 were often those hungriest for such assurances—those to whom accolades for Republican prosperity seemed increasingly preposterous. As tens of thousands of these anxious citizens cheered Al Smith at speeches and rallies, he and his allies promised them dignity—something that entailed both social acceptance *and* economic security.

In fact, Smith's appeal to those voters least enamored with the 1920s political economy transcended urban environs and traditional minorities, influencing the rural vote perceptibly. Despite his ultimate defeat in the region, Smith showed marked improvement over recent Democratic performances in the struggling Corn and Wheat Belts of the upper Midwest—including in "predominantly Protestant" counties and especially among farmers who had backed the progressive insurgencies of Theodore Roosevelt in 1912 and Robert La Follette in 1924.[87] In the formerly solid South, Smith was most successful in holding struggling farm regions and suffered his greatest defeats in the booming industrial towns of the "New South."[88] The midwestern granary and the Cotton Belt, like the ethnic enclaves of the industrial North, harbored many of those citizens most disaffected by 1920s economic realities; and while ethnocultural factors (and in the Midwest, long-standing partisan loyalties) meant that farmers exhibited more hesitancy toward Smith's message than many city-dwellers, the Democrat nevertheless appealed to both groups' desire for stability, with each responding in tangible ways.[89]

Al Smith's 1928 presidential campaign featured the nationalization of the particular progressivism he had exercised as governor of New York. There were places in both the Cotton South and the Corn Belt Midwest where Smith's articulation of progressive solutions to agrarian challenges earned him strong support among pockets of struggling farmers. Yet whether due to substance or style, this politics did not captivate rural voters in an electorally powerful way. Even noting the Democrat's successes among some farmers, it is clear that the population for whom his progressivism had been formulated was to be found elsewhere. It is no surprise, then, that Smith's greatest triumphs came among those who toiled not in the fields, but in the factories.

Under Smith, the Democrats unleashed an electoral incursion among ethnic workers in the nation's great manufacturing centers. Across urban Massachusetts, new-immigrant groups flocked to the polls on behalf of the Democrat.[90] In Chicago, throughout the 1920s ethnic voters "could be confidently labeled neither Democratic nor Republican in presidential voting," but "from 1928 on, they were clearly Democratic," with tremendous gains for Smith among Poles, Italians, Germans, Czechs, Slavs, and African Americans.[91] In Pittsburgh and environs, Smith's appeal to the region's growing new-stock electorate launched the Democratic percentage of the Allegheny County presidential vote from John W. Davis's paltry 9 percent to a robust 48 percent, with unprecedented wins in ethnic working-class communities, including Homestead, Rankin, and Braddock.[92] In Philadelphia, sections of the city with heavy concentrations of Germans, Poles, Irish, and Italians gave Smith 64 percent of their vote—a dramatic upsurge from the combined 21 percent these same neighborhoods granted the Democrat Davis and the Progressive La Follette in 1924.[93] Across Wisconsin, many Catholic Germans, Czechs, Belgians, and Poles, who had "left the Democratic Party in the 1920s," overwhelmingly supported Smith in 1928; in Milwaukee the Polish vote was

86 percent for the Happy Warrior, lifting him to victory in the Cream City.[94] Shifts in Jewish voting patterns were similarly dramatic: in Philadelphia, the Jewish vote for Smith was twenty-one points higher than the combined Davis / La Follette tally; Jewish Chicago voted 60 percent for Al Smith, a forty-one-point Democratic improvement.[95] Across the country, histori- cally Republican or independent Jewish enclaves voted heavily for Smith.[96]

The profusion of such evidence notwithstanding, the "Al Smith Revolution" thesis has remained contentious.[97] Indeed, the particularly forceful historian Allan Lichtman has furnished extensive statistical analysis suggesting that the Smith-Hoover contest was simply an "aberrant election that had little impact on later patterns of politics."[98] Anecdotal evidence of the increasingly working- class, ethnic, and urban nature of the Democratic Party in this period, how- ever voluminous, can only be inoculated against charges of impressionism quantitatively. To affirm the importance of 1928, it must be demonstrated that the Democratic vote became more urban and working-class in that year, and that it remained so during the Roosevelt era.

Smith lost in 1928; Roosevelt won four years later. Therefore, a meaningful measure of the connections between the two Democratic candidacies is not to chart winning and losing but to track jurisdictions' *relative importance to the party's state electoral coalition.*[99] Dividing a county's percentage of the state Demo- cratic vote by its percentage of the state turnout provides a useful metric: if this "Democratic Quotient" (DQ) is under 1.0 for a given county, then that jurisdic- tion was not a source of relative Democratic strength. Tracking changes in the DQs of urban counties across the presidential elections from 1896 through 1944 demonstrates that in many important instances, the 1928 election dramati- cally altered the urban/rural balance of state Democratic voting coalitions and did so in a way that would be reinforced during the Roosevelt years.

Counties containing Philadelphia, Brooklyn, Chicago, Cleveland, Detroit, and Pittsburgh, as well as the independent cities of St. Louis and Baltimore, present an important pattern. These cities showed consistently low DQs from 1896 through 1924. In 1928, all of the scores underwent a precipitous rise, to a level well above 1.0, indicating that the cities had suddenly become a rela- tively rich source of Democratic votes in their states. These new higher ur- ban DQs often declined slightly in 1932 and 1936 because of the landslide nature of those elections, in which most jurisdictions in many states were strongly Democratic, and thus the relative significance of any specific juris- diction was tempered; but the rates would not decline to their pre-1928 levels, and ultimately rebounded to nearer the 1928 figures in the later Roosevelt elec- tions, when FDR's political appeal was less universal. Therefore, an important

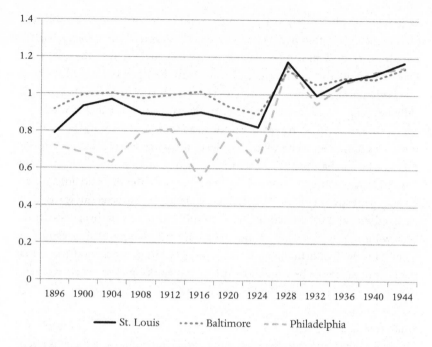

FIGURE 9. Democratic quotients (DQs) for St. Louis, Baltimore, and Philadelphia, 1896–1944. These cities provide representative samples of the pattern of DQ change over time revealed in many midwestern and northeastern cities.

trend becomes evident in these cities, many of which were not previously Democratic strongholds: the jurisdiction's relative importance to the state Democratic coalition rose—in most cases quite remarkably—in 1928, and then straddled this plateau for the entirety of the Roosevelt era.

These patterns were far from universal. In some states, especially in New England, the largest cities had already been centers of Democratic strength; and divergent patterns also emerged for midsized metropolises.[100] From the national perspective, it was the largest cities that propelled the shifts in the electorate. Indeed, totaling the voting results for the counties containing the twenty largest cities from the 1930 census and tracking their combined DQ within the national popular vote reveals a pattern similar to that produced at the state level by Philadelphia, Baltimore, St. Louis, and other great metropolises.[101]

In these urban locales, the Smith campaign improved Democratic percentages drastically over those of the preceding two elections and often set new high marks for the party; in places like Milwaukee and St. Louis the Democrat even achieved majorities. These relative successes, coupled with decreased rural Democratic percentages, shifted the DQs in the northeastern and mid-

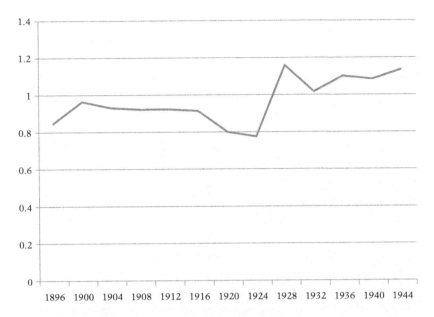

FIGURE 10.   DQ of the twenty largest cities according to the 1930 census, 1896–1944.

western states to reflect increasingly urban coalitions—a quantifiable change with profound qualitative significance. Moreover, Democrats would build on these successes during the New Deal era, crystallizing the realignment initiated in 1928. Ultimately, Roosevelt was able to transform new areas of *relative Democratic strength* into sources of *statewide Democratic majorities*. Thus, even in states where Smith lost badly—such as Michigan, where he received 28.9 percent of the vote and did not carry a single county; or Pennsylvania, where he won only three counties and 33.9 percent of the vote—his campaign had shaken old patterns of political behavior and replaced them with the foundations of a new system.

These quantifiable developments suggest one conclusion and one hypothesis. First, the 1928 election was in fact "critical," insofar as it heralded the elevation of the great urban centers to prominence within the Democratic Party on the national level, establishing a new pattern that would persist throughout the Roosevelt years. Second—and more controversially—this process, completed nationally by the Great Depression and by Franklin Roosevelt's New Deal, came to maturation four years earlier in southern New England, making that region worthy of particular scrutiny as a case study in the dynamics relating the 1928 campaign to those of the 1930s.

Indeed, auguries of the new system could already be observed in 1928 in places where Al Smith actually won. Unlike in the mid-Atlantic and midwestern states, Smith was able to achieve victories in Massachusetts and Rhode Island. There he improved on the relative Democratic strength that had already been established in large cities like Boston and Providence, where Irish Democrats were firmly ensconced power brokers. This had been reflected in the high DQs of these cities prior to 1928 but had never translated into sustainable statewide majorities. In 1932, Roosevelt would construct durable coalitions on the urban Democratic foundations established in 1928 by rallying broader, more committed support in the face of economic depression; similarly, Smith built on and broadened existing urban Democratic strength in southern New England in 1928 with a campaign that spoke directly to the social and economic grievances of ethnic workers in the context of a regional industrial downturn. In the midst of economic calamity, the national Democratic Party, fueled by the activation of urban, ethnic, working-class voters, achieved majority status in Massachusetts and Rhode Island. It was the confluence of cultural grievances with economic despair that set New England apart and enabled Al Smith to capture the loyalties of millions for his political vision of progressive government action on behalf of his conception of social and economic justice.

From its origins in 1910s New York, Smith's progressivism had always spoken to multiple layers of human experience, pragmatically recognizing that people have both cultural and economic needs. By articulating his particular progressive agenda throughout the national campaign, Smith had presented his formula for fulfilling those needs. In the great cities, where urban, ethnic, working-class voters heard a major-party presidential nominee speaking to these questions in a relatable fashion for the first time, portents of the looming Roosevelt Revolution became manifest. In New England, where the longing for dignity and respect and industrial democracy was coupled more often than in other manufacturing regions with desperate uncertainty as to the stability of one's job or how to provide meals or pay rent, Smith's progressivism attracted majorities. In that region, there was unquestionably an Al Smith Revolution. In order therefore to understand the dynamics of 1928 at the grass roots level, to elucidate the motivations of rank-and-file Smith voters, and to determine the kindred qualitative phenomena linking the idiomatic Smith Revolution of 1928 and the more universal Roosevelt Revolution of 1932, attention must be turned in greater specificity to southern New England, where the hardships of the Depression and the liberal embrace of cultural pluralism had conflated to produce Democratic upheaval four years early.

CHAPTER 5

The Revolution before the New Deal

— he does not discuss the issue raised by Douglas Craig in a the [?] [?], that while Smith [?] [?] open registration, FDR in 1932 [?] both registration — [?] in [?] voted for Smith the not the party

Herbert Hoover's landslide victory over Al Smith marked both an affirmation of the Republican economic policies of the 1920s and a rejection of the new, urban, pluralistic United States represented by the Democrat. Yet Smith ran strong in Republican New England, scoring unprecedented victories in Massachusetts and Rhode Island. There, anti-Catholic sentiment and prohibitionist harangues failed to resonate as they had nationally; rather, urban, ethnic, "wet" voters were rallied to the Democratic cause by these ethnocultural controversies. Moreover, Smith's criticisms of Republican economics also found a receptive audience in New England, a region languishing through a decade of industrial decline. Smith was successful in New England because his particular progressivism appealed idiomatically to the region's ethnic working class on both cultural *and* economic levels. Therefore, the Democrat was able to construct a new and durable coalition in this depressed region—a realignment that foreshadowed New Deal voting patterns and has rightly been dubbed an "Al Smith revolution."[1]

Smith's success in southern New England, punctuated by his victories in Massachusetts and Rhode Island, was not "revolutionary" because of a pair of relatively narrow state-level wins. What makes Smith's New England success noteworthy is that it revealed the electoral potentialities of the Democrat's particular focus on social welfare, labor rights, and cultural pluralism—given the right political and economic atmospherics. In the 1930s, such conditions were widespread; but in 1928, they were quarantined to pockets of economic decline and social frustration.

Thorough exploration of the world in which these new Democratic voters lived and labored elucidates their complex political motivations, disclosing that the cultural and economic elements of Smith's appeal were inextricably intertwined from the perspective of new-stock workers. In 1928, New England's ethnic working class was striving for both economic security and social acceptance; they had been battered by regional decline as well as by religious and ethnic prejudice; they longed for good pay in decent conditions and for a glass of beer. Shepherding these long-quiescent, politically disorganized masses into an electoral majority would require a candidate who addressed their varying motivations. Smith criticized Republican economics while standing, both symbolically and rhetorically, against cultural condescension. By necessity, Al Smith's New England victory was a holistic revolution.

The Happy Warrior in New England

Portents of the coming upheaval could be discerned in late October when Al Smith arrived in New England. As he departed the familiar environs of the Empire State and crossed eastward into the Republican citadel of Massachusetts, ardent mobs in the tens of thousands hailed their guest with "tremendous demonstrations" at every stop along the line.[2] When the visitor arrived at Boston, he was met by three-quarters of a million effusive allies, who engulfed the Hub in an unprecedented exhibition of political passion.[3]

As Smith traveled from Boston to Providence, he abandoned his train in favor of an automobile tour "through the mill towns of the Blackstone Valley," which were "traditionally Republican, French-Canadian, wet and Roman Catholic." As he did, "mill hands left their piece work, ran to big windows and yelled," forcing "numerous mills to shut down from five minutes to an hour."[4] Smith toured Woonsocket, Manville, Central Falls, Pawtucket—greeted all along the way by the shouts and cheers of mill families who formed "one unbroken line of howling humanity . . . all the way down the historic valley."[5] Arriving in Providence, Smith encountered a "frenzy of mobs" that "cheered him lustily."[6] In Hartford, "five miles of packed humans jammed the streets, through which police fought a slow way for the Candidate's car," and in this "pandemonium," Smith's famous brown derby seemed more like "a magician's wand" able "literally to conjure cheers" from the 200,000 who thronged to catch a glimpse of the Democratic nominee. In Bridgeport, Smith's train was greeted by 20,000, who "roared a welcome" as "red torches flared."[7]

Republicans insisted that New Englanders remained in their camp—particularly on economic matters—and that the enthusiasm for the Happy Warrior was less a political display than excitement over the arrival of a celebrity. The *Woonsocket Call* declared the Smith visit "a non-partisan event," for "a cheering crowd will always turn out to welcome any prominent figure in the life of the nation," concluding that "crowds and cheers are seldom an indication as to just how the political wind is blowing."[8] Similarly, the *Providence Journal* explained that "Governor Smith may be pardoned if he concluded, after his enthusiastic reception, that he is destined to carry Rhode Island, but he will receive more definite information on that score the night of November 6"; while the *Hartford Courant* clarified that "as the one and only 'Al' Smith, he was enthusiastically received by fellow Democrats, while those of a different political faith, who admire the Governor but who will not vote for him for president, joined in the greetings."[9]

It was likely the case that the majority had come to see the champion of religious liberty and of liberation from Volsteadism, while many others were there to witness a national star waving his iconic hat. A group in Providence probably articulated the motivations of many as they traipsed about the confetti-laden streets carrying a large banner that read: "Remember November sixth—beer!"[10] But as these New Englanders listened to Smith's Boston address at the auditorium or on their radios, as they read his words in their local newspapers or heard regional politicians expound on the Democratic agenda, a more complete picture emerged. With purpose, Smith had chosen New England as the setting for his most vigorous response to Hoover's consistent praise of the economic status quo—which was said by Republicans to have "filled the workingman's dinner pail and his gasoline tank besides" and "placed the whole nation in the silk-stocking class," allowing the GOP to invoke the promise of "a chicken for every pot."[11] Smith called attention to those neglected by this "Republican Prosperity." The Democrat elicited laughter from his Boston audience by asking them to "picture a man at $17.30 a week going out to a chicken dinner in his own automobile, with silk socks on." The crowd was amused, but the issue was no joke to Smith—and certainly it was not a throwaway to thousands of struggling New England workers, most notably those employed in the slumping textile sector. "In one manufacturing city in this State the number of wage earners in industry dropped from 33,300 in 1921 to 24,800 in 1927, a loss of work for 8,500 men and women, particularly in the woolen and cotton mills," he reported solemnly. "In that same period the amount of wages earned in a year had fallen from $36,904,884 to $28,961,874, or a loss of $8,000,000 a year."[12]

Dissenting from popular accolades for Republican economics, Smith presented a serious consideration of the thousands of jobs lost in New England textiles and suggested that the interests of workers were being disregarded in favor of rich, powerful forces.[13] Furthermore, he suggested an alternative policy approach, rooted in his record of progressive social welfare and labor reforms in New York. Smith campaigners constantly invoked his gubernatorial record and argued that the Democrat would bring a similarly dynamic and compassionate posture to the White House. Indeed, for the hundreds of thousands who had flocked to hear the Boston address, Smith presented a vigorous defense of his social welfare record and of his ambitions to mobilize the federal government to assuage the condition of American workers.[14]

Progressive Smith allies like Frances Perkins were particularly active in espousing the governor's program in New England.[15] Social welfare and labor activists promoted Smith's cause in the industrial Northeast by trumpeting his progressive accomplishments and by insisting that such a humanitarian agenda was the key to remedying the injustices of 1920s America. New Jersey congresswoman Mary T. Norton took to the region's airwaves to celebrate the New Yorker's "humane record," including struggles to limit women's working hours, end child labor, provide aid for infant and maternal welfare, extend generous funding for public health services, and mandate equal pay for female teachers.[16] In New England such efforts were buttressed by local initiative. In the closing weeks of the campaign, a group of Massachusetts trade union women barnstormed the Bay State for Smith, setting out for "every factory city and town in Massachusetts."[17] Smith's progressive backers did their utmost to notify New Englanders of their candidate's reform agenda, and the public proved responsive.

Political historians have long sought to categorize voters and their motivations, and in the case of 1928 the most assertive studies have concluded that cultural issues were absolutely dominant. Yet political motivations often defy neat classification. This is so because the vast majority of human beings defy such classification. Most of the actors in working-class New England, aside from the most conservative priests or the most myopic Marxists, lived their lives with multiple layers of interests covering varying categories of analysis. People are complex—their lives and their problems and their hopes are complex, and it has been as superficial for historians to neglect this basic reality as it has been for them to dismiss Al Smith's strenuous challenge to the political-economic status quo. Granting serious consideration to both Smith and his constituents demonstrates that prior to the national onset of the Great Depression and the national ascent of Franklin Delano Roosevelt, a Democratic revolution was under way in New England, fueled both by changing demographics and by industrial turmoil, and led by a working-class Irish-Catholic social welfare progressive from "the sidewalks of New York."

Ethnic New England

Angelo Bizzozero was a notable figure among the Italians of Quincy, Massachusetts. A veteran of the Great War, Bizzozero was on the honor roll of the West Quincy Knights of Columbus and had been repeatedly elected as a Republican to the city council during the 1920s.[18] By 1928, the councilman was prominent enough in the Fourteenth Congressional District that the Massachusetts Republican Party nominated him to stand for Herbert Hoover at the Electoral College should their candidate carry the Bay State as predicted.[19] This was done without the knowledge of the nominee, however, and three days later Bizzozero formally declined. "I cannot on election day go and vote for Alfred E. Smith and permit my name to be used as Presidential elector for Herbert C. Hoover. . . . I would be unworthy of the trust which has been placed in me by the voters if I was false to myself in voting and appearing on the ballot in another way." This vignette was but a minor episode—noteworthy more for the "amusement" it brought Democrats than for any profound electoral influence.[20] Yet it is indicative of a tremendously important phenomenon that occurred across New England during the 1928 election: the shift in the ethnic vote away from neutrality and even Republicanism, and into the Democratic fold.

In 1928, the "ethnic vote"—nebulously understood as the political preferences of communities dominated by second-wave immigrants and their progeny—underwent transitions that alone make that election momentous, for these voters were to become the core of Roosevelt's Democratic majority.[21] While the bulk of second-wave immigrants had remained electorally aloof until the late 1920s, the leadership of these communities had been quite active politically, purporting to speak for their ethnic brethren. These élites supported Republicans at least as often as Democrats. The behavior of such ethnic political pioneers mattered, for their influence at the local level would help direct the partisan preferences of their cohorts as they entered into the franchise. Some Republican ethnic notables dug in during the 1928 campaign; but there were enough Angelo Bizzozeros in New England and elsewhere to alter significantly the political dynamics of many communities.

It did not have to be this way. The Democrats were not predestined to become the party of pluralism. The dual processes of converting Republican ethnic communities and mobilizing naturalized citizens and their children were a vital phase—perhaps *the* vital phase—in developing the foundation for Roosevelt's Democratic majority. It was not until the 1928 Smith campaign that these new voters were firmly established as Democrats.

On October 14, 1920, Democratic presidential nominee James Cox delivered an address at Memorial Hall in Columbus, Ohio, in which he denounced a "motley array of questionable groups and influences" that he believed were propelling the candidacy of Republican Warren G. Harding. Many of these groups were identified as "reactionaries" who sought low wages, suppression of "progressive thought," and "martial law" as "a solvent for all industrial disputes." This populist rhetoric, particularly as it appealed to the apprehensions of the working class in a period of uneasy economic adjustment to peacetime conditions, could have bolstered the Democrat among urban ethnic laborers. Yet this was hardly the overriding theme of the speech. Cox identified such "selfish" blocs as "the pro-German party," "the Italian party," "the Greek party and the Bulgarian party," and the "Afro-American party" as some of the "racial groups" bolstering the Republicans.[22]

However noble Cox's intention to carry on Wilson's quixotic pursuit of the League of Nations, his speech became memorable for its denunciation of "hyphenated" Americans.[23] While the African American vote was already overwhelmingly Republican, this rejection of ethnic-group cohesion hastened the Democratic Party's alienation of recent-immigrant voters—a process well under way by the close of the Wilson years. Many Irish and German citizens had opposed U.S. participation in the Great War from the outset; other groups were dismayed as the shape of the postwar world became clear—most notably Italians, whose motherland's claims to the Adriatic port of Fiume had been scuttled at Versailles by the U.S. president.[24] Nationwide, including in the ethnic enclaves of America's great cities, Cox and the Democrats were trounced.

In fact, this was only the latest setback in the turbulent Democratic courtship of immigrant voters in the Northeast. The lure of the "full dinner pail" and promises of higher wages through Republican protectionism had entranced urban workers of immigrant and native stock alike since the Gilded Age. Meanwhile, the Democrats embodied much that repelled immigrants. There was the undiluted agrarianism of the party's populist western wing; the domination of the national party by the South and of the regional party by the Irish; the homiletic declarations of Bryan and, to a lesser extent, Wilson; all of these Democratic hallmarks had served to repulse ethnic voters.[25]

This was particularly true in New England. There, high-tariff shibboleths beckoned mill workers into the Grand Old Party, while resentment against monopolization of the Democratic Party and the Roman Catholic hierarchy by the Irish tempered any potential for cross-ethnic cooperation in an anti-Yankee alliance.[26] The Irish themselves were dismayed by the alleged Anglophilia of Wilson's internationalism—despite Governor Cox's intentional exclusion of

Hibernians from his catalogue of malignant hyphenators.[27] While conditions were more complex at the local level, in the 1920s, French Canadians, Italians, Poles, Portuguese, and other New England ethnic groups whose electoral strength had been steadily increasing since the turn of the century were deeply skeptical of the Democratic Party. In federal and especially presidential voting this reality was particularly consequential to the electoral calculus in places like Massachusetts and Rhode Island, where such groups held the balance of power between Yankee Republicans and Irish Democrats.[28]

For decades the Irish had dominated the Democratic organizations of many American cities, among them Boston, New Haven, and Providence.[29] But in contrast to the evolving ethnic pragmatism of Tammany Hall, New England's Irish Democrats clung to power through exclusionary tactics—monopolizing political offices and patronage and in turn isolating other ethnic groups. In response, recent immigrants often aligned themselves with the Republican Party in Massachusetts, Rhode Island, and Connecticut, producing a counter-intuitive coalition that set Italian, Polish, Portuguese, Jewish, and especially French Canadian voters alongside old-stock Yankee Protestants.

Within the Democracy, Irish hegemony remained strong in 1928. In Boston, a cacophonous quartet of Smith organizations materialized that fall, headed by former mayor James Michael Curley, former fire commissioner Theodore Glynn, Schoolhouse Commission chair Francis Slattery, and former mayor Andrew Peters—three Irishmen and a Yankee. Moreover, the list of speakers for Commissioner Glynn's "Smith Flying Wedge" was 80 percent Irish—with a dusting of English and Scottish orators, as well as a single Italian. There were no French, Polish, or other recent-immigrant names listed.[30] These groups fared only slightly better in Hartford, where the executive committee named to make preparations for Smith's October 25 visit was dominated by Irish Democrats, with a strong English presence. Meanwhile, Italians made up just under 7 percent of the sixty-member board, and Poles represented slightly over 3 percent of the body.[31]

As Irish dominance of New England's Democratic organizations persisted into the 1928 campaign, élites from other ethnic groups—especially fellow Roman Catholics—continued to stoke resentment at their exclusion from power. During a Republican rally at a Sons of Italy hall in Newport, Rhode Island, lodge venerable Luigi Cipolla reminded his brethren that "the Democratic party in the nation and the state has always discriminated against the Italians."[32] In the same state, one Franco-American leader claimed that his community "had been persecuted by the Irish for over fifty years."[33] Indeed, while prevalent across New England, these internecine antagonisms were especially bitter among Rhode Island's Catholics—largely due to lingering animosity between the Irish and the region's sizable French Canadian community, which held its greatest force in the Ocean State.

The political significance of this animosity was well established by 1928. Throughout New England, the French Canadian vote had been a source of Republican strength since the late nineteenth century, by virtue of these citizens' rivalries with the Irish as well as their general support for the economic doctrines of the GOP.[34] In Rhode Island, Republicans had amplified their advantage with this crucial bloc through recognition at nomination time. By 1908, the party had elected a French Canadian governor, Aram Pothier, who served five terms and was followed after a six-year Yankee interlude by another French Canadian, Emery San Souci, who was elected in 1920.[35] Pothier was himself restored to the governorship in 1924, reelected in 1926, and died as governor in January 1928.[36]

That fall, there was little reason for Republicans to doubt the security of the French vote—particularly in Rhode Island. There, an ongoing feud between Bishop William Hickey, the Irish American prelate of Providence, and an outspoken group of French Canadians who had been excommunicated the previous year during a quarrel over school funding seemed destined to inflame Franco-Irish enmity. One of the rebels, Elphege Daigneault of Woonsocket, did his part to exaggerate this wedge, penning a screed for the French-language *La Verité* in which he both exalted Herbert Hoover and denounced Bishop Hickey.[37]

Further boosting their prospects, the Republicans nominated Felix Hebert, a prominent French Canadian jurist from West Warwick, to challenge Democrat Peter Gerry for the U.S. Senate. Republicans emblazoned this nomination as "the greatest honor ever conferred on the Franco-American element" in ads featuring Hoover and Hebert. Gerry himself faltered in his attempts to court the French vote, condescendingly centering his pitch on the Volstead Act and allowing Hebert to charge that the senator "meant the only interest the French had in the election was prohibition."[38] Rhode Island's French Canadians were persuaded to their countryman's cause, and Gerry was ousted in favor of the Republican.

Yet 1928 proved pivotal for French Canadian politics in Rhode Island. While these voters had occasionally entered the Democratic ranks, such alliances had always proved ephemeral. In 1928, the French Canadian vote went strongly for Al Smith, departing from precedent; and the patterns established in that year would persist for decades. On the strength of this vote, Smith carried communities such as Central Falls and the French wards of Pawtucket. The great French enclave of Woonsocket went to Al Smith by a margin of nearly two to one—this despite the ongoing battle between members of the French community and the Catholic hierarchy and despite decades of mistrust between the French and both the Irish and the Democratic Party. In several of the city's most heavily French districts, Smith won by margins of eight and even ten to one—and his appeal in these communities was so strong that Peter Gerry rode Smith's coattails to a narrow defeat of Felix Hebert in French Woonsocket.[39]

The Democrats enjoyed similar success among French Canadians across New England, the result of momentum established in the closing weeks of the campaign.[40] In Lowell, Massachusetts, Democrats were compelled by requests "from numerous French-American voters of the city" to begin organizing a local French American Smith club.[41] A few days later, former Fall River mayor Edmund Talbot, head of the Massachusetts French-American Smith League, began sending agents into the region to coordinate a registration drive.[42] In short order bilingual meetings were held to organize local French American women interested in the cause.[43] All of this was an official reaction to the initiative of French Canadians in Lowell who found the Democratic nominee attractive and sought aid in mobilizing their community politically.

The case of Hartford provides a sense for the vitality the Democratic campaign enjoyed in French New England in the crucial final weeks. In October, the city's French-American Al Smith Club was formed by a mere thirty-five people at St. Ann's Hall, with bilingual mass meetings scheduled through Election Day. By election eve, the club drew a "demonstrative" crowd of 600 to a rally featuring congressional nominee Herman Kopplemann.[44]

Smith's success with Italian New England was equally dramatic. In September, the Smith Italian-American League of Massachusetts was formed, touted by the *Boston Globe* as "the first movement of its kind to band the Italo-American voters of this State for a presidential candidate."[45] By October 1, local clubs had been founded in twenty-five municipalities, with ambitions to organize "in every city and town where there are Italian-American residents." These organizations were always headed by Italians themselves—Tony Garofino in Lynn, Silvio Bernardini in Lowell, George Costanza in Boston.[46] In short order, a state women's division was launched, while local groups simultaneously established their own women's auxiliaries.[47] Statewide, Smith forces had clearly captured the enthusiasm of the Italian community: an Italian American Smith rally in Springfield drew more than 4,000 citizens; a few nights earlier, an Italian meeting for Hoover in the same city had attracted 42.[48]

In Hartford, local Italians organized on Smith's behalf in early September, founding a nonpartisan "Italian-American Smith-for-President Club" for the purpose of "educating the voters" and entering "whole-heartedly" into the presidential campaign. The Hartford club was part of a national movement among Italians that had emerged outside the purview of the Democratic

Party—the organization elected several Republicans to its executive committee and declined an offer of quarters at the Democratic regional offices. Moreover, women served alongside men on prominent committees, and the club elected a female vice president, Rose D'Esposo.[49] While the Connecticut effort remained ostensibly independent, and in Massachusetts the Italian Leagues operated outside the old party machinery, New England Democrats also courted the Italian vote with vigor: Italian partisans served prominently on the local Smith committees, while New Britain mayor Angelo Paonessa refused the Democratic nomination for lieutenant governor "so that he might have complete freedom in leading an Italian campaign" for Smith.[50]

Local circumstances encouraged this new enthusiasm for the Democrats, just as local conflicts had previously foreclosed such possibilities. In Connecticut, Francis A. Pallotti had been elected secretary of state as a Republican in 1922 and had come to be regarded by Italians as "one of the outstanding citizens of their race in the State." However, Pallotti's ambitions for higher office were thwarted in 1928, when his bid for the Republican nomination for lieutenant governor was rejected at the party's convention. In response, thirty-eight Pallotti clubs "changed their names to Al Smith-for-President clubs and . . . indicated that they would give their whole-hearted support to the candidacy of Governor Smith." Mayor Paonessa sought to capitalize on the "dissatisfaction" that he detected sprouting from the incident, and in fact the Pallotti controversy helped many Italian Democrats transform the presidential election into a campaign against the political denigration of their community—a microcosm of what many ethnic groups saw as Smith's national battle against racial, ethnic, and religious bigotry.[51] "We shall respect those who have shown respect for us," declared George DiCenzo, toastmaster at a rally of 800 Italian Americans in New Haven.[52] At a Hartford rally for 1,200 on the Sunday before the election, editor Giovanni Lizzi warned the crowd in Italian that "they would set back the cause of the Italian-Americans at least 25 years unless they voted to carry the State and the United States for the Democratic party."[53] By late October a *Boston Globe* analyst declared that in next-door Rhode Island, "the Italians are almost solid for Smith."[54]

Poles were another source of traditional Republican strength in New England, and the party did what it could to maintain the community's favor in 1928. On October 20, when 250 members of the Polish Political Organization gathered for a banquet in Hartford, they were met by John Trumbull, Connecticut's Republican governor. Trumbull noted that his party had "always had loyal support from the Polish citizens of this state," expressing confidence that 1928 would witness the continuance of this happy tradition. Indeed, the banqueters were treated to a procession of Republican luminaries, each of whom shared the governor's self-assurance. All of this was capped by the surprise appearance of Herbert Hoover's running mate, Charles Curtis, who pithily beckoned his hearers to the support of the national ticket with his "warm and contagious smile" and a bonhomous "God bless you all!"[55]

Other Republicans were more explicit in rallying Poles to the party banner. "You, of all people, should vote for the man who made the new Poland possible," insisted State Senator Frederic Walcott, the party's choice for U.S. Senate. "We are on the verge of an industrial era of prosperity, and we want men in office like Senator Curtis," proclaimed Governor Trumbull.[56] These three themes—traditional ethnic Republicanism, Polish nationalism, and Republican prosperity—constituted the bulk of the Hoover pitch to Polish New England.

Republican spellbinders deemed their nominee's work in feeding postwar Europe, including millions of desperate Poles, a particularly powerful argument for his elevation to the presidency. A Hartford attorney instructed a Polish gathering at Meriden, Connecticut, that "Herbert Hoover did much for Poland during the dark days of the World War. He fed and clothed the Polish people and he did not ask their faith."[57] Suzanne Farnam, a veteran of Hoover's Belgian relief efforts, reminded a group of Hartford Poles gathered at White Eagle Hall of the Republican's postwar humanitarianism.[58] Farther north along the Connecticut River, a "Polish Citizen" wrote the *Springfield Daily News* that Poles "owe a personal debt of gratitude to Herbert Hoover" for feeding Polish children after the war.[59]

Smith Poles also drew on cultural motifs to promote their candidate. Unsurprisingly, the Democrats relied heavily on the twin issues of Prohibition and Catholicism. Connecticut Democratic senatorial nominee Augustine Lonergan told a Polish group in Bridgeport that Prohibition was a "sham," and ventured that "if Smith is elected, it will insure new hope in every mother's breast and will again prove to the world that in America a lowly birth or any membership in the Catholic church is no bar to the presidency."[60] On November 4, Herman Kopplemann warned separate Hartford rallies for French, Polish, and Lithuanian voters that the Anti-Saloon League was "playing a major part in the campaign for Mr. Hoover" and that anti-tobacco legislation loomed in the event of a Republican triumph.[61]

While projecting superficial confidence in the security of the Polish vote, Republican speeches betrayed a fear that these cultural issues threatened their viability with this usually reliable bloc. Hoover campaigners frequently felt compelled to dismiss Prohibition.[62] Moreover, when addressing Smith's Catholicism before ethnic audiences, New England Hoover Republicans often sounded like national Smith Democrats: "I believe that politics and religion are two distinct subjects that should never be mentioned at the same time, much less mixed," was the sermon from Joseph Kulaf, a Hartford lawyer.[63] "There is no religious issue in this campaign," Suzanne Farnam assured Connecticut's Poles.[64]

Affirming these arguments, especially those regarding Hoover's good deeds for the old country, New England's Polish élite maintained their customary Republicanism—as was the case in other American Polish enclaves.[65] When the Republican nominee visited Boston, the president of the Massachusetts Polish State Club thanked him personally for his relief work and pledged the support of "Bay State Poles" during a reception for "the spokesmen of the foreign groups" hosted by Republican governor Alvan Tufts Fuller.[66] Nationalist gratitude toward Hoover was even articulated by Poland's legendary pianist-patriot Ignacy Jan Paderewski, who spoke warmly of the Republican nominee during the campaign.[67] Predictably, the Polish Federated Political Clubs of New England endorsed Hoover in October. Yet observers soon noted indications of "a sizable reaction among the Poles in this vicinity" against the endorsement: in Chicopee, an officer of the federation responded to the endorsement by resigning, "with the frank statement that he is unreservedly for Smith." Others went further, immediately forming a Polish Democratic Club for Chicopee. In Holyoke, an existing club "expressed strong dissatisfaction with the course of the New England federation."[68] In New Bedford, the endorsement had been preempted when Stanley Sieczkowski had declared in late September that the Polish-American Bristol County Club was for Smith.[69] Republican rallies for Poles in several Massachusetts towns were canceled "because of sparse attendance."[70]

By November, it was predicted from Springfield that "a heavy vote for Smith is certain among the Polish people of this city, Chicopee and Holyoke as a result of an intensive campaign that has been carried out in each neighborhood," and on Election Day this prophecy came to fruition.[71] Indeed, in 1928 Al Smith captured new-immigrant loyalties for the Democratic Party— permanently—and thus swung the balance of power in southern New England away from its traditional Republicanism. Shifts in the French Canadian vote, although most impressive in Rhode Island, were not confined to the Ocean State. In Massachusetts, the *Boston Globe* noted that many French voters "who had hitherto supported Republican candidates voted for Gov Smith."[72] In Fitchburg, Smith improved the Democratic vote by 4.6 percentage points in the old-stock ward; in the French ward, he was up an astounding 20.1 points. In Lowell, Smith topped 65 percent in the two majority-French wards; in Chicopee, the French ward gave Smith 71.5 percent; in Holyoke it was 84.1 percent.[73] Similarly, Smith carried 79 percent of the vote in the Italian sections of Providence.[74] In Boston, Smith topped 80 percent in Wards One and Three, both with sizable Italian populations; and in the precincts encompassing the Italian-dominated North End, Smith received 2,325 votes to Hoover's 134.[75] In cities with large Italian populations, such as Waterbury, Connecticut—which was about one-quarter Italian—turnout surged and buoyed Democratic totals; Smith carried the Brass City with 58 percent, and the Democratic ticket was swept to victory there as a result.[76] Massachusetts voting analysis by the historian J. Joseph Huthmacher has revealed similar Smith successes in the Polish wards of Chicopee and Haverhill as well as Portuguese New Bedford, Greek Haverhill, and Jewish wards in Boston, Chelsea, and Malden.[77]

These developments helped fuel a broader Democratic explosion in the region. The precipitous increase in Democratic voting among Poles and French Canadians in Chicopee, Holyoke, and Springfield helped Hamden County, Massachusetts, return a Democratic presidential majority for the first time in the twentieth century.[78] In Chicopee, Smith carried over 70 percent of the vote; in the previous two elections, Democrats had averaged just under 28 percent, and since 1896 the party had won the city only twice—each time by slim majorities. In nearby Holyoke, Democrats such as Bryan and Wilson had sometimes gained small majorities (the best performance was Wilson's 56.3 percent in 1916), but the party's presidential nominees in 1920 and 1924 had achieved 35.5 and 32.3 percent, respectively. Al Smith carried the Paper City with 66.5 percent of the vote in 1928.[79] In neighboring Hampshire County, Smith achieved a majority of 54.3 percent in heavily Polish Northampton—making him the first Democrat to win the Meadow City in the twentieth century.[80] Southward in the Connecticut River valley, other large ethnic enclaves propelled similar transitions. In both Hartford and New Britain, with large concentrations of Polish and Italian voters, the wards with the largest first- or second-generation immigrant populations delivered the strongest Democratic totals; Smith carried both cities, and his 46 percent of Hartford County's presidential tally was a substantial improvement over the 31.2 percent that had been averaged by Cox and Davis.[81]

All of this occurred despite the long-standing Republicanism of ethnic New England and in contravention of the ethnic élite's avowed preference for Hoover. Much of this popular dissent was based on hostility toward Prohibition and on membership in the Catholic Church—both of which the vocal majority of Polish, Italian, and French Canadian New Englanders shared with the Democratic nominee. A Polish American baker from Hartford noted how his community had mobilized on their co-communicant's behalf—and that as a result pro-Hoover Poles had been shunned. "With the opening of the present Presidential campaign I naturally continued my Republican activities. . . . Yet because of my course some of my friends have ostracized me and some of my customers have withdrawn their trade," reported John Winialski. The baker's erstwhile friends and patrons admonished him that he had a duty "to support Governor Smith because his religious faith is the same as mine."[82]

In fact, chronicling Democratic attempts to mobilize rank-and-file Polish, Italian, and French Canadian New Englanders does much to commend the literature's traditional focus on cultural conflict. In East Hartford, Angelo Paonessa labeled federal Prohibition agents "a bunch of grafters" and denounced the Eighteenth Amendment as "a curse to this country."[83] In New Haven, Democratic gubernatorial nominee Charles Morris deplored "the injection of the religious question into the campaign" before that city's Italian Smith club.[84] A Yale divinity student rallied his French audience in Hartford by promising that a Smith victory would settle with finality "the question of a man's religious faith as a test for public office."[85] Along with Prohibition and religious bigotry, speakers before these groups often denounced Republican-sponsored immigration quotas—"perfectly insane" was the assessment of Herman Kopplemann at an Italian rally in Hartford.[86]

Religion, Prohibition, and immigration restriction are the well-known troika of ethnic rallying points from 1928, and they have achieved this prominence with justice, for they were all employed enthusiastically by Democrats before new-stock audiences. Shifts in the ethnic vote during the 1928 election help affirm the importance of these ethnocultural concerns. However, this was only one facet of the reasoning employed by such voters in their flight to the Democratic Party. Among the many Polish Americans who were stirred to rebellion by élite Polonia's support for the Republican nominee was Alexander Bielski of Chicopee, who wrote to the *Springfield Daily News* that "so-called" Polish leaders, "drunk with their own powers of intimidation and coercion," had attempted to deliver the Polish vote to Hoover; but rank-and-file Poles would mobilize to defeat this "clique." The reason, according to Bielski, was not so much ethnocultural as it was economic: "For the past seven and one-half years, our government has been of the type which has furthered, protected, and fostered the special interests of a certain few against the common interests of the many."[87] Another Pole wrote to the Republican *Springfield Union* in even more explicit terms that reveal the connections between class and culture: "Capital governs the Republican party and influences the people to vote for Hoover, who thus far favors prohibition. It is said that after a workman performs his daily task and refreshes himself with a glass of beer or wine he becomes unable to maintain his efficiencies. . . . Alfred Smith . . . holds that should the laborer, the farmer and the small business man prosper, money will be in more free circulation and the country will prosper. . . . It is the duty and obligation of every free-minded Polish citizen to cast his vote for Alfred E. Smith."[88]

These attitudes were not confined to Hamden County, nor were they limited to Polonia. Indeed, while Smith's unprecedented electoral success among new-stock New Englanders demonstrates his quantifiable appeal within those communities, the actual words of such voters help to establish that this attraction was based on a complex of cultural *and* economic factors through which the Democratic campaign spoke directly to the trepidations and aspirations of the ethnic working class.

A letter from one Italian American Rhode Islander to the *Westerly Sun* forcefully articulates the multifactorial nature of ethnic New Englanders' political preferences. The Republican *Sun* had lamented in an editorial that Italians could be expected to vote for Al Smith because of their desire to restore the saloon.[89] One reader, V. Gentile, became indignant at this superficial analysis, composing a corrective letter to the editor that incorporated economic reckoning reminiscent of the Democratic campaign handbook: "The deplorable existing conditions and partiality and favoritism that the Republican party has been showing to the manufacturer and powerful combines with their poor records during the eight years and with the uniform and despicable tactics that they are using against Gov. Smith is the reason why he is going to be our next president."[90] The "deplorable" state of New England's working class was just as significant as the "despicable" cultural conflicts of the 1920s in shaping the views of such voters.

Indeed, such denunciations of Republican economics rang painfully true for many living in New England's ethnic enclaves, adding a strong class dynamic to these voters' interest in Al Smith's Democratic Party. For the region's working class, Herbert Hoover's confidence in the policies of the previous eight years demonstrated a favoritism of capitalist over laborer, especially when compared to the Smith campaign's regular probing of the weaknesses of the Coolidge economy. Hoover's contentment with the status quo suggested to the *Springfield Daily News* that the Republican approved of what many New Englanders perceived as sharpening economic inequality: "He has been content to hide behind a mass of evasions and irrelevancies, which is ever the way of conservative elements who live by the rule that 'them that has gets.'"[91]

Industrial New England

A chorus of Republicans responded to these critiques by reiterating their party's support for high tariffs as a tonic for low wages and unemployment. Visiting Swampscott, Massachusetts, Speaker of the House Nicholas Longworth of Ohio presented a stark choice: "No Republican protective tariff ever closed a factory, mortgaged a farm, or caused an American man or woman to lose their jobs. No Democratic tariff law ever failed to do all three." "It would be suicide for Massachusetts to turn the country over to the Democrats," agreed A. Piatt Andrew, a member of Longworth's caucus from Massachusetts who spoke at the same meeting. "The depression in the industries of New England" was the result of cheap foreign goods undermining domestic manufacturing and imperiling "the future of those industries and of the hundreds of thousands of persons employed therein." The congressman concluded that "a continuance of the policy of protection," under prudent Republican administration, was the only way to assure an industrial revival.[92]

Andrew's acknowledgment of the languid state of New England textiles reveals a unique dimension of the economic stance of regional Republicans. National figures like Longworth could invoke widespread prosperity and allude only in passing to localized blemishes; New England Republicans had no such luxury. At Whitinsville, Massachusetts, on October 5, Loring Young, the Republican challenger to Senator David Ignatius Walsh, encapsulated his party's response to the regional recession: "Bad as conditions now are in the textile industry, they would be even worse today if Senator Walsh and his southern associates had written the tariff law."[93]

For their part, Democratic speakers in New England sought to distance themselves and their presidential nominee from the party's traditional free-trade posture. Democratic National Committeeman Thomas Spellacy assured New Haven's Italian-American Smith Club that the governor's "attitude on the tariff is one of absolute protection," a position that was reinforced by Augustine Lonergan at the same rally.[94] The nominee himself bolstered these claims on October 13 with his Louisville speech, criticizing Coolidge's tariff commission but also suggesting that his election would not foredoom protectionism.[95] New England Democrats were cheered by this articulation of a new Democratic trade policy—the *Lowell Sun* called Smith's Louisville address "probably the best he has yet delivered."[96] Herman Kopplemann buttressed Smith's point at a Hartford labor hall, declaring that "he, together with all other Democratic congressmen, would favor a high protective tariff."[97]

Smith affirmed these arguments with a note he handed to Angelo Paonessa during a visit to New Britain in late October. Emerging from a private meeting with the nominee, the mayor revealed a signed statement promising Connecticut laborers that Smith "will do nothing to bring about tariff legislation which will so injure the industries of their cities as to reduce their earning powers one penny."[98] In the closing weeks of the campaign, the *Hartford Cou-*

rant, for years an advocate of high tariffs and of Republican leadership, would mockingly announce that "we are all protectionists now."[99]

New Jersey's Franklin Fort summarized Republican skepticism toward Smith's conversion. In Boston, the congressman contemplated, "How can we turn over the Government to a party which changes its views as it changes its shirts or socks?"[100] The *Courant* was similarly incredulous, citing the New Yorker's past denunciations of the Fordney-McCumber Tariff and other protectionist policies and concluding that if Smith "were elected the policy of protection which he now espouses would not weigh heavily on his conscience."[101]

With few exceptions, the region's leading capitalists were broadly in accord with their traditional Republican allies in looking askance at the Democrat's economic policies; and so, as usual, New England industrialists rallied to the Republican banner.[102] The Boston Wool Trade Association held an important public meeting in support of "the election of all candidates on the Republican ticket in Massachusetts" that featured Frank G. Allen, the party's nominee for governor (and a member of the association).[103] DeWitt Page, president of the New Departure Manufacturing Company and a vice president with General Motors, lauded "the policies that have made for the prosperity of the country over a considerable number of years," remarking from Bristol, Connecticut, after his nomination as a Republican presidential elector, "I must support the party that has served the best interests of our own and other industries during the past two decades."[104] As Hoover departed Boston after an October 15 speech, his tour through textile country was greeted with the enthusiasm of mill owners, who "turned their steam on for Candidate Hoover . . . [and] kept every whistle at full toot as long as he was in hearing."[105] Republican newspaper advertisements implored workers to preserve prosperity: "Let's keep what we've got!"[106] Horace Greeley Knowles, a lawyer and retired diplomat, warned that "within a very few weeks after the election, should Smith be successful, lack of confidence, doubt and uncertainty as to the effect of the change of administration . . . would develop into a panic, would result in many thousands and probably millions of men and women being thrown out of work."[107]

Simultaneously, manufacturers inundated those on their payrolls with similar predictions about the catastrophic consequences of a Smith victory. On October 16, responding to Smith's Louisville address on tariff policy, Brigadier General Charles Cole, Democratic nominee for governor of Massachusetts, had gloated that "no longer will the mill overseer stand by the gate and assure the men that their job and pay envelope depends upon so-called republican protection."[108] In fact, Smith's candidacy only served to exacerbate such activities. Republican-aligned industrialists doggedly promoted Hoover among those who toiled in the textile mills and machine works of New England. One large Connecticut manufacturer posted signage: "Hoover and Curtis—If these men are elected your jobs are safe."[109] Pictures of the Republican nominee were "conspicuously" placed at the doors of the New Bedford Spinning Company.[110] The Bigelow-Hartford Carpet Company cautioned millworkers, "Hoover and prosperity—save your job."[111] From Lowell came reports that Massachusetts workers were "receiving in their pay envelopes little folders showing the home of a working man protected by a tariff wall which the democrats are pictured as tearing down."[112]

Smith alluded to these tactics during his labor speech at Newark, claiming that this national phenomenon was bankrolled by the Republican National Committee.[113] Responding to the Democrat, the *Lowell Sun* testified that "such coercion . . . is nothing new," for "in past years" Massachusetts Republicans had employed "the old tariff bogey" to "intimidate labor" into voting the GOP ticket.[114] Indeed, the scale may have been novel, but by 1928 Republican propaganda extolling high tariffs was an autumn tradition in New England. What was quite new, however, was how the region's workers responded to these entreaties.

While some New England laborers were stirred by the Republican economic argument, as they had been since the nineteenth century, many were now unmoved by such boilerplate.[115] "We get a lot of prosperity hash, with here and there something about the full dinner pail," went a letter to the *Hartford Courant*, "but working men are reading up a little these days and the old dinner pail argument is getting to be more of an insult than an incentive."[116] A voter from Northampton dismissed Republican claims of prosperity as "a myth": "Prosperity in New England just is not. The McCallum Hosiery Company, the Cutlery, the Corticelli mills in Northampton have slashed salaries and let help go. The Northampton Hosiery Company has failed. A community in this condition cannot feel there is prosperity simply because Mr. [Charles Evans] Hughes says so."[117] A writer from Glastonbury, Connecticut, agreed, protesting, "Our prosperity is not anything to brag about and has been that way for the last three years. Far too many people are jobless and the number is increasing."[118] In letter after letter, New England workers articulated their frustration with Republican economic policies in language that paralleled the rhetoric of the Democratic presidential nominee.

In fact, the lived experiences of tens of thousands of working-class New Englanders belied Republican satisfaction with Coolidge prosperity. A pseudonymous "Breadwinner" from Springfield noted an increase in panhandling, sardonically suggesting that "perhaps it would be best after all to elect Mr. Hoover, with his wide experience in feeding the hungry in other lands and let him direct the 'Prosperity Breadlines' in America."[119] A former Republican from Holyoke agreed that there was a perceptible decline in the region's economic fortunes: "Our closed industrial plants, comprising textile, shoe, paper and those producing from iron and steel does not uphold the Republican slogan, Prosperity! New England's thousands of industries that operate from four days to 12 days per month; the hundreds of thousands of idle and part-time idle workers is a refutation of the statements made by the ballyhoo speakers of the Republican Party."[120] A writer from Westfield, Massachusetts, emphasized that in the unbalanced economy of the 1920s, these questions were ultimately a matter of perspective: "Yes, there is prosperity, but not with the poor, the struggling tradesman or the farmer. But the rich are prospered, the bloated bondholder, the manipulator in stocks and the politically high up."[121]

Democratic politicians perceived this discontent, joining both New England workers and their party's presidential nominee to challenge the very notion of Republican prosperity. Speaking before 3,500 in Lowell, James Michael Curley uncorked some of his characteristic ethnocultural appeals— denouncing the Klan, lauding the Americanism of those who had fought in the Great War "regardless of race or creed," and amusing Irish listeners by adopting a cockney accent to mock "'Erbie 'Oover" and his ties to England. But the "Purple Shamrock" also engaged in a lengthy dissertation on the worsening lot of New England workers. "Where is the prosperity?" he queried. "Where is the protection the Republicans talk about? . . . It is too bad Hoover couldn't have stayed in this state a few days and seen the bread lines in New Bedford. They are timid of talking about prosperity here—with 2300 homes unoccupied in Lawrence, 3000 here, 2000 in New Bedford and the same number in other textile cities. What have the republicans done for the people of this state?"[122]

At Ansonia, Connecticut, Augustine Lonergan speculated whether the state's closed mills were indications of Republican prosperity.[123] In Manchester, Connecticut, Herman Kopplemann wondered which workers were receiving the supposed "luxury wages" Speaker Longworth had claimed resulted from GOP policies.[124] Prosperity was unbalanced, asserted Senator Walsh at a Massachusetts mill town—"centered on a preferred class of men, namely big business."[125] Bronx congressman Anthony Griffin agreed during a visit to Hamden, Connecticut: "Every one concedes that the big fellows are doing well, with plenty of money in the bank—the thing now to do is to give the little fellows a show and an opportunity to earn a living."[126]

New England Textiles

During the Hamden speech, Congressman Griffin centered much of his critique on "the strike in the textile industries of a neighboring State—a strike which lasted for 25 weeks and was only settled by the starving workmen at last consenting to accept a reduction of 5% in their meager wages."[127] This was the New Bedford textile strike of 1928, a conflict that began on April 16 as a response by both union craftsmen and hastily organized unskilled workers to a 10 percent wage cut that had been announced by mill owners on April 9—Easter Monday. The strike had involved more than 20,000 mill hands and, as noted by Griffin, did not end until ragged, exhausted workers voted on October 6 to concede a 5 percent reduction.[128] For Smith and his allies, the New Bedford episode exemplified the perils of Republican economics: the administration, in this view, had been too swollen with its own sense of accomplishment to address the struggles of certain sectors—in this case, textiles—and as a result the working class was forced to absorb the consequences of regional misfortune. Thus, to Griffin and other Smith Democrats in New England, bromides on the nation's flourishing economy were ludicrous.

Across the region, the New Bedford crisis and that of textiles generally furnished Smith's forces with a potent rebuttal for Republican warnings about Democratic recklessness. At Lowell, Curley pointed bitterly to the irony of the strike: "When the country was supposed to be prosperous, there were soup kitchens in New Bedford."[129] In the same city, the Smith-boosting *Lowell Sun* scoffed at the suggestion that workers should retain Republican administration to rehabilitate the textile sector. "The continuance of present conditions would threaten the extinction of what remains of this industry. The republican party has been in control of the government since 1920, and it is safe to say that the textile industry never experienced any period of such intense depression as during that time."[130] The next day, the editors continued on this theme: "The people of Massachusetts, and particularly in the textile cities, realize how absurd is the claim that general prosperity abounds."[131]

About twenty miles to the southwest, in the shoemaking hub of Marlborough, Massachusetts, Senator Walsh "doubted the glowing stories of the country's prosperity when strike conditions exist" in cities like New Bedford—a theme he reiterated in towns across the state.[132] General Cole joined Walsh in Ludlow, Massachusetts, just east of Chicopee, to review the influence of Republican policies on local workers: "You people here have nothing to thank the Republican party for. You know how many families have had to leave Ludlow in the past few years because there is no work here. . . . Republican talk of raising the tariff wall to restore the textile industry will not fool the people in Ludlow any more than it will fool the people in Lowell, in New Bedford, in Fall River, where the mills have under the Republican party written their own tariff schedules."[133] In struggling manufacturing communities this rhetoric had resonance: two weeks later, Al Smith carried Ludlow with 54.9 percent of the vote—the first Democrat to win the town in the twentieth century.[134]

Responsiveness to Democratic derision of Republican prosperity was not limited to small mill towns like Ludlow. The great Massachusetts textile cities of Fall River, Lawrence, Lowell, and New Bedford all voted heavily for Al Smith in 1928. Of these, only Lawrence had produced multiple Democratic majorities since the realignment of 1896—in 1900 and 1916. In the latter election Lawrence had been joined by Lowell and Fall River, each of which produced their lone pre-Smith Democratic majority. New Bedford never delivered a Democratic majority or even plurality in this period, and during the 1920s none of these cities had a Democratic presidential percentage above the mid-30s. Put simply: New England textile cities were Republican in presidential voting. In 1928, Smith took 71.6 percent in Lawrence, 64.8 percent in Fall River, 64.1 percent in Lowell, and 55.8 percent in New Bedford.[135] Traditionally Republican textile centers helped propel Smith to a statewide victory in Massachusetts, as they did in neighboring Rhode Island, where the New Yorker became the first Democrat to win since Woodrow Wilson in 1912—and the first to gain a majority in the Ocean State since Franklin Pierce. In both Massachusetts and Rhode Island, this new Democratic strength in the textile regions would be fortified during the New Deal era.

Of course, the mill workers who voted for Al Smith in droves in 1928 were also largely Catholic and heavily immigrant. In 1926, Lawrence was 72.4 percent Roman Catholic. In other textile centers this figure was even higher: in New Bedford, as well as in Pawtucket and Cranston in Rhode Island, Catholics constituted more than 73 percent of the religious population. In Lowell, the figure was 79.8 percent. Woonsocket, Rhode Island, was an astoundingly homogeneous 89.8 percent Roman Catholic.[136]

It is clear that such citizens were aroused by the cultural conflicts of the day, and this likely influenced many votes. In Fall River, for example, wards with large concentrations of first- and second-generation Americans were particularly supportive of the Massachusetts referendum calling on the state's U.S. senators to repeal the Eighteenth Amendment. Fall River was 78.4 percent immigrant or child of immigrant and 78.8 percent Roman Catholic; its voters favored repeal by a healthy 70.7 percent, and also gave 74.7 percent to a separate referendum to lift the state ban on Sunday sports. This was the archetypical Smith stronghold, and the Democrat carried the city with nearly 65 percent of the vote.[137]

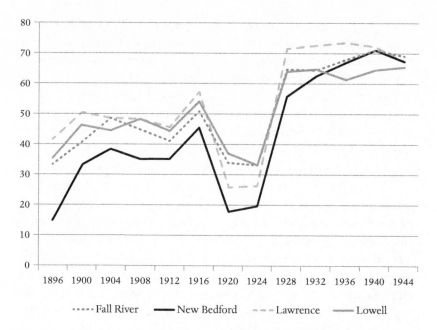

FIGURE 11. Democratic percentages in four Massachusetts textile cities, 1896–1944. Note the precipitous increase in the Democratic vote in these major textile cities in 1928.

Yet this is an incomplete profile of the city—and of Smith's supporters. Fall River was also a textile center, and by 1928 it was in the doldrums of industrial depression. On January 30, 1928, 30,000 of the city's laborers in thirty of its thirty-two mills acquiesced through their frail union to a 10 percent wage reduction. This was in the wake of an identical cut in Lawrence, and shortly in advance of the 10 percent cut that would precipitate mass strikes less than fifteen miles to the east in New Bedford.[138]

The political mobilization of New England's working class behind Al Smith and the Democrats in 1928 can only be understood within the broader context of the decade-long decline in textiles. In Bristol County, Massachusetts, home of both Fall River and New Bedford, the 1920s were a disastrous time. Due to plummeting cloth prices after the close of the Great War, New Bedford's mills were shuttered for several months beginning in late 1920, and in February 1921, a shrunken workforce returned to the mills for 20 percent less pay. In early 1922, some workers in Fall River, which had followed a similar trajectory, were complaining that since resuming operations their salaries had been halved. By 1927, New Bedford mill hands were paid 15 percent less than even their reduced 1921 salaries.[139]

Moreover, conditions were even worse elsewhere in the region. As 1922 began, a wave of industrial austerity swept irresistibly northward from Connecticut and Rhode Island across southeastern New England.[140] Layoffs and wage cuts were rife; workers in Lawrence, Fitchburg, Pawtucket, and elsewhere erupted in protest; and by Valentine's Day 1922, there were more than 50,000 New Englanders out on strike against a ubiquitous 20 percent pay cut—as well as against a parallel campaign to "restore" the fifty-four-hour work week.[141] The situation in Rhode Island's Blackstone and Pawtuxet valleys was especially volatile, witnessing riots at factories, soldiers patrolling the streets of textile towns, mass evictions from company housing, and the storming of the statehouse in Providence by an army of 2,000 desperate mill hands.[142]

By September 1924, as investors questioned the viability of New England textiles, Rhode Island manufacturers were heralding another round of wage cuts.[143] That winter, one after another, the dominoes fell. A week before Christmas, mills in Lowell announced 10 percent wage reductions.[144] On January 3, 1925—after a year of operating at half capacity—Fall River manufacturers announced their own 10 percent cut affecting 25,000 workers.[145] United Textile Workers president Thomas F. McMahon did a great deal of foot-stomping—lambasting the Fall River and Rhode Island reductions as an "outrage" and a "steal"—but his unions acquiesced within four days.[146] Neighboring New Bedford made the call on January 9.[147] Mills in Lawrence and in Willimantic, Connecticut, soon followed.[148] The 1925 "adjustment" in labor costs was not the last word—in the years following this burst of parsimony, wage cuts continued across the region.[149]

Nor did such cuts prove the salvation of New England textiles. Throughout the 1920s, mills halted operations for extended periods due to poor business.[150] Often factories were closed altogether. Some mills were simply liquidated, while many others were relocated to the South in search of cheap labor and lax regulations. Indeed, a 1925 survey by social worker Mary Van Kleeck found a tremendous disparity in the prevailing work weeks of Massachusetts and North Carolina: in Massachusetts, 93.2 percent of cotton factories operated with a work week of forty-eight hours or less; in North Carolina, that figure was 0.2 percent—and 51.1 percent of Tar Heel State cotton mills were operating at a sixty-hour week.[151] Such conditions were nothing new, and this exodus had been ongoing since the late nineteenth century; yet in some cases regional wage and regulatory differentials had actually sharpened in the 1920s.[152] In the face of such disadvantages, New England was hemorrhaging manufacturing jobs by mid-decade.[153]

In 1928, the Lowell Sun, gazing downstream along the Merrimack to Lawrence, lamented that the city's workers had lost "$8,000,000 as compared with the amount earned in 1921." Moreover, thousands had been laid off, "these having been mainly employed in the woolen, worsted and cotton mills."[154] The next week, the *Sun* turned its focus inward, noting sharp declines in the total value of cotton and woolen goods manufactured in Lowell and an alarming drop in cotton textile employment in the City of Spindles. The ongoing "slump in Lowell" held broader social implications, "seen in the total property valuation," which had declined by over $9 million since 1926.[155]

Across New England, throughout the decade, mill workers endured this incessant barrage of pay cuts, layoffs, and shutdowns. In 1919, before the textile slump began in earnest, there were 122,499 people employed in cotton textiles in Massachusetts and 53,869 employed in woolens; by 1930, these numbers had plummeted to 73,404 for cotton and 48,401 for wool—reductions of 40.1 percent and 10.2 percent, respectively. In Rhode Island the employment rolls went from 31,404 to 18,427 in cotton and from 24,393 to 20,861 in woolens; in Connecticut, employment declined from 15,647 to 10,711 in cotton and from 7,798 to 6,747 in woolens; in New Hampshire, from 21,183 to 12,691 in cotton and from 9,772 to 5,265 in woolens.[156] From 1919 to 1930, these four states lost 15 percent of their woolen textile jobs and 40 percent of their cotton textile jobs. In Massachusetts, these 1920s losses alone would have accounted for 3 percent of all Bay State employment in 1930.

The ubiquity of such conditions renders comprehension of their social influence critical for interpreting the region's working-class politics. Indeed, from the macro perspective the considerable economic motivation behind the political mobilization of New England workers becomes compelling; and to the workers themselves these were not numbers merely, but a threat to their very survival. Even in good times life had been a bitter struggle for the unskilled immigrant laborers who ran New England's mills. They dutifully continued their tasks out of desperation, but also out of a nebulous sense of promise: there was a vague spirit of progression—grindingly slow, yes, but improvement nonetheless—that seemed to fuel the aspirations of mill workers despite reality's daily assaults on hope itself. That vision of eventual progress, along with traditional elements including culture, family, and religion, sustained these New Englanders against abominable circumstances.[157] In the 1920s, their culture and their religion were under attack, and this affected working-class politics. Statistically it is obvious that hopes of progression as a reward for years and even generations of faithful toil were also under siege. This too had a profound influence on the political outlook of these workers. The upheaval of the 1920s undermined the conviction many had held that, however bad things might be, they could get better with hard work—or at the very least, one might expect to maintain the status quo. Now there was regression, and an already tenuous existence appeared unsustainable.[158]

Mill Life

Meanwhile, there were real human actors living through these paroxysms of industrial recalibration. Their world was fraught with many of the same baneful Gilded Age excesses that Al Smith's social welfare regime had been constructed to ameliorate in the first place—perilous working conditions, truncated childhood, insalubrious housing, indifference to public health, creeping dehumanization. It is instructive briefly to explore the quotidian experiences of the people whose electoral response to economic calamity is in question—to transcend the regional perspective to trace personal travails; for that world, along with the celebrated cultural conflicts of the Roaring Twenties, was the context for the Al Smith Revolution in New England.

The mill hands' very schedules provide immediate insight into the astonishing centrality of work life to their broader outlook—as a New Bedford labor activist put it, work had become "the main vein of their existence."[159] In Pontiac, Rhode Island, bells rang nightly at nine o'clock to clear the streets and then rang again at five in the morning to awaken workers in preparation for the six o'clock factory opening. Thus began the twelve-hour six-to-six shift at the Pontiac mill Monday through Saturday.[160] Bleachers at the nearby Cranston Print Works put in an eighty-four-hour week in 1926, toiling from 7:00 a.m. to 10:00 p.m. for $40 weekly.[161] These marathon shifts affected children as well as adults, for family life was severely restricted. Remembering Lowell's twelve-hour shifts in the 1910s, a son of one worker would remark that the mills "kidnapped your parents. You never saw them."[162]

Nor was this the only way in which the factories touched these children's lives. Teens in textile families usually went to work in the mills as soon as it was legal to do so—often earlier.[163] Although for most of this period the minimum age for textile employment was fourteen, parents' scant wages meant that even young children needed to help support the household. Schoolchildren scavenged for wood, boxes—anything combustible for winter heating. One Massachusetts mill hand's daughter recalled the simple reason she had taken up selling newspapers in the streets of Brockton at an early age: "After all I was a worker's kid."[164] Indeed, "if you had a large family, everyone went to work. There was no question"—and this meant that there was "no chance" that a child attending school "was allowed to continue after 14."[165]

Because of Progressive Era restrictions on children's work hours, New England's most youthful mill hands were often limited to forty-hour weeks until age sixteen, and then to nine-hour shifts on weekdays, plus some morning work on Saturday, adding up to a robust forty-eight-hour week. For investors, this represented a frustrating intrusion into mill management and a motivation for southerly exodus. For teenagers from Lowell to New Bedford to Peace Dale, Rhode Island, it meant working from 7:00 a.m. to 5:00 p.m. with an hour for dinner and some work on Saturday mornings.[166] The specifics varied, but the recurring theme in textiles during the 1910s and 1920s was labor less appropriately described as work than as a daily test of human endurance.

It was an unpleasant atmosphere, lacking even the most rudimentary comforts. In many plants, sitting was forbidden, and most departments had no chairs or stools.[167] Drinking water was often "ladled out of a pail" or provided in an unsanitary barrel that was shared by all of the hands. In summer, workers were given ice to cool the water they drew from the barrel—at a 25 cent charge.[168]

The carding room—where laps of mixed cotton fibers still containing debris were cleaned, combed, and straightened in preparation for spinning—featured particularly disagreeable conditions.[169] As a nine-year-old boy, Joseph Figuerido would walk from school to visit his mother, an immigrant from the Azores, at her New Bedford mill during lunch. "I used to get very upset. . . . She would be sitting on a box of bobbins, cotton all over her eyebrows and around her ears," adhering to her face with sweat. Even "when the machinery was shut down there was still cotton in the air." Throughout the mills but particularly in the card room, "workers used to breathe a lot of cotton dust," and "a lot of workers in those days . . . got tubercular effects."[170] Especially in the winter, workers breathed a great deal of the lint that was constantly "flying around" the work area, since the windows were shuttered with the cold. "I always had a feeling that wasn't good for your lungs," recalled a doffer from Lowell.[171]

The machinery itself could be quite hazardous. Lena O'Brien, who began working at the Little Scholl mill in Tiverton, Rhode Island, after turning fourteen in 1918, once caught her dress in the spinning machinery and was spared catastrophe only by a quick-thinking coworker cutting her free. O'Brien was less fortunate on another occasion, when her hair was caught in the machinery and "yanked . . . right off!"[172] Such accidents were an occasional spectacle: at one Lowell mill, horrified employees witnessed a long-haired girl become "caught in the pulley and she went up with the strap"; coworkers "heard the screech" of the girl as the machinery "pulled a lot of hair out"—a sound that would haunt witnesses for life. The victim soon died.[173] Blanche Graham, whose mother was also scalped in a Lowell mill when her hair became ensnarled in a belt, suffered through a less traumatic accident herself when her finger was "squashed" by the gears of a twister.[174]

In general, mill work was arduous and dangerous.[175] Many positions required teenage girls to lift heavy bobbins—leading Martha Doherty to rupture her appendix in a Lowell spinning room. She recalled, "I was out about two months and almost died."[176] Joseph Figuerido recalled that his father had also suffered internal injuries from working conditions—a boiler attendant in New Bedford's Hathaway mill, Thomas Figuerido, a Portuguese immigrant, died of a work-related bladder condition when his son was only four years old. The reality was that "in those days there was little concern on the part of mill owners of any safety conditions. . . . Everything was geared to satisfy production."[177]

When Doherty's appendix burst, the mill beneficently paid for her surgery. This was an act of charity, for there was no compensation coverage for such occurrences.[178] Certainly there was nothing resembling a "safety net" for these workers, despite the dangerous nature of their jobs. One mill hand from Rhode Island recalled that "if a fella lost a finger in a mill or was taken ill, he'd never get anything. There was no workmen's compensation." Most cities had some sort of municipal charity by the 1920s, but there was "no such animal" as social welfare in the mill villages; instead, "each town had a poor farm." These institutions were each run by "a political appointee who had the opportunity to run the poor farm as a money-making proposition and it was just pitiful." Likewise, there was "no retirement. There was nothing. If he worked 50 years, they'd give him a gold watch. . . . But there was nothing. If a fella quit work, that was it. It was a pitiful situation. . . . So far as helping a disabled workman who worked in the plant, no matter how many years, they never did a thing for him."[179]

All of this took an exceptional toll on mill women, many of whom "had large families and they had to take care of their children, take care of their family life . . . and they thought of themselves last. . . . When they used to leave their mills to go home, you would look at their faces and they were the faces of people that were worn out."[180] Valentine Chartrand continued working at the mills through each of her five pregnancies. Only two of her babies survived. "I worked until I was ready to go," she recalled, noting that many women did the same. "I was in the Boott Mill and they had to take me to First Aid and they called the ambulance. I thought I was going to have her in the ambulance."[181]

There was rarely respite for these workers, and when rest did come, it did not take place in anything resembling comfortable—even healthful—conditions. Even with the entire household contributing, life for mill families was "very meager." Houses, while proudly kept, were "rather barren," with "little in the form of actual comfort."[182] By the 1920s, mill hands in larger centers like New Bedford and Fall River typically obtained housing from independent landlords, but in many of the smaller towns workers still rented from their employers.[183] In Pontiac, company housing featured "a kitchen and the pantry and the bedrooms," with "four families and one entrance." Cranston village consisted of multifamily duplexes with "no indoor plumbing" and "no central heating system." In such communities, "if you wanted water, you had to go to the village pump in the center of the town, and bring a galvanized bucket along."[184]

These homes, heated only by the kitchen stove, were especially susceptible to harsh New England winters. Put bluntly, residents "froze sometimes in the cold, going to bed."[185] "You wake up in the morning and you could draw pictures on the frost on the windows."[186] Preparing for the long day at the mill became complicated under such conditions, for "in the winter, without having central heat, the first thing you would have to do before you could wash your face was to break the ice in the bucket."[187]

Water and warmth were not the only rudiments usually wanting. In a bitter irony, these textile workers often went without the most elementary of their own products. For some unskilled New Bedford hands, towels proved a luxury. Likewise, "sheeting was a commodity," and thus families made their own—usually not large enough to provide full coverage or comfort.[188]

Strenuous, often noxious working conditions and an impoverished home life left workers prone to disease. "You'd have epidemics of scarlet fever, stuff like that. You'd take up the red card on your door and your father wouldn't come home," since, in most mills, "if you were sick, there was no pay."[189] In New Bedford, rates of "children's deaths from gastric, respiratory and intestinal diseases" ranked "among the highest in the country."[190] In the 1910s in Lawrence, a third of mill hands died within their first decade on the job, and the average worker lived to age thirty-nine—nineteen years less than the typical mill boss.[191]

Considering the Dickensian circumstances in which they lived and labored, these New Englanders were remarkably resilient. Often workers thought themselves fortunate to have what so many described as "good jobs."[192] "Good" is of course a relative term; but it is clear that most of these mill hands were doing what was necessary to survive, embracing whatever small felicities they encountered along the way. One Lowell woman concluded that textile employment "was very difficult work, but . . . one didn't have a lot of choices available to them. And you made the best of what you could."[193] Treacherous though it was, mill work at least provided the means of self-preservation, and this source of security was something worthy of thanksgiving. This was a perfectly sensible posture to assume in such a precarious world, and this attitude helped the workers maintain a measure of dignity and a vague glimmer of optimism. In the 1920s, struggling manufacturers began increasing workloads, cutting pay, raising rents, and issuing layoffs. In the process they sapped their workers' ability to provide themselves with a sense of dignity and robbed them of the lingering hope that life would someday brighten through faithful service in the mills.

Anton Huettel, an immigrant from Russian Poland who went to work at the Ever-Lastic factory in Pawtucket in 1918 at age fourteen, recalled that being a weaver "to begin with . . . wasn't so bad." But "as the years went on, they wanted more production—they'd speed up the machinery to the limit without giving you an increase in pay."[194] Speed-ups and layoffs, instituted in earnest during the 1920s, chafed mill workers. Many believed that "the mill owners were making a lot of money but they were obviously never satisfied. . . . They always wanted to make more, and the way they could do that is by taking it off the hides of workers by increasing their production with less workers." In real terms, this meant "giving the workers more machines to operate, more looms for the weavers or more spinning frames for the spinners and so on down the line."[195] Victor Signorelli, who worked at a mill in Peace Dale, concluded that management "wanted new machinery so they could . . . cut down the help. It was 200 laborers in there, just the weave shop. All they run is one loom." But with automation came efficiency, and what this meant from Signorelli's perspective was more work for fewer workers. "There would be three weavers, instead they only had one. They put two people out of work. They was always figuring how to throw people out of a job." By 1928 in Peace Dale, each worker operated six looms.[196]

In the mid-1920s, Theophile Brien observed similar changes at the Weybosset mills in Rhode Island, where he worked as a twister, like his father before him. His plant had once run 1,200 looms, with fifty workers per shift. Then management introduced "a bobbin-combing knotting machine. . . . They were using 2 men on each shift to replace 40 men." Management was not satisfied with even this substantial reduction in labor costs, because foremen began to notice that many of the remaining workers, eager to preserve their tenuous employment, were running more looms than they had been assigned. "When the foremen seen that they said these guys can run 4 looms, so we'll give them 4 looms [to work] for the same price as 3 looms."[197]

Mill workers had endured a great deal, often maintaining a surprisingly cheerful disposition in the face of grueling hours, paupers' wages, and deplorable conditions at the plants and in their homes. In the 1920s, mill owners began seeking to economize by slashing wages and cutting payrolls, effectively robbing workers of their only motivation for industrial cooperation—the vague hope that hard work would pay off. As confidence waned, resentment built: "The workers were angry about this," recalled Figuerido. Yet the actions of owners only occasionally provoked rebellion, for while workers were frustrated, "at the same time they were kind of influenced in terms of job security."[198] Indeed, even when conflicts did flare, they were often about security. Looking back on the 1920s, one Rhode Island worker agreed with the premise that "the people went out on strike not because they were trying to make one man work three looms, but because people were losing their jobs"; in this view, the purpose of the labor activism of the 1920s was the modest goal of preventing the company from arbitrarily throwing people out of work.[199] Wage cuts exercised a similarly devastating influence on workers whose original income had scarcely been adequate—these too threatened the security of mill families and instigated further turmoil.[200] "They were treading water," recalled one New Bedford worker, "and no one could see how they could make 'ends meet' with a 10% cut."[201] All of these actions, especially the wage cuts, precipitated a series of strikes; but they also primed New England's ethnic working classes for a dramatic shift in political sensibilities.

The final requisite ingredient for such a political shift was a candidate who understood both the social and the economic needs of these potential voters. This of course had been the precise formula of Alfred E. Smith's political success in New York State. Smith was the first major national candidate to embody the cultural aspirations of ethnic workers. His denunciations of religious and ethnic prejudice, his opposition to Prohibition, his very biography—all seemed to affirm ethnic workers' vision of their place in America. Simultaneously, the economic dimensions of that vision—increased security, livable conditions, and dignified, rewarding labor—were addressed in Smith's acknowledgment of the weaknesses of the 1920s economy and the progressive agenda he proposed in response. The frenzied reception New England granted the Happy Warrior in 1928 resulted largely from the arrival of a candidate who espoused ethnic workers' holistic vision of a just society.

A Tale of Two Cities and One Town

Three Massachusetts manufacturing centers reveal how profoundly the intersection of this human drama and the convulsions of industrial decline affected electoral politics. The personal, economic, and political collided across New England to produce the Democratic revolution of 1928. The textile city of New Bedford, the mill town of Ware, and the factory city of Chicopee each provide instructive cases.

The alternating despondency and outrage provoked by wage cuts, speed-ups, and layoffs, the desire for comprehensive solutions to economic and social grievances, and the resultant attraction to Smith's particular progressivism could all be seen in New Bedford—a major textile center that voted for a Democratic presidential nominee for the first time in 1928.[202] There, the strikes against the 10 percent wage cut that raged through most of 1928 and ended in October were followed within a month by an Al Smith victory at the local polls. The complicated demarcations within the Whaling City—by ethnicity, class, and craft—and the ultimate political conclusions to which these conditions led demonstrate the importance of the accumulated social and labor grievances of New England's ethnic workers to political outcomes in 1928 and beyond.

A complicating feature of New Bedford's ordeal was the existence of dueling labor organizations: the Textile Council, a well-established craft union, and the Textile Mill Committees (TMC), the first real effort to organize New Bedford's unskilled immigrant workers.[203] The former group was affiliated with the United Textile Workers and through that organization the American Federation of Labor, while the latter was directed by Communist veterans of such episodes as the 1926 textile strike in Passaic, New Jersey.[204]

The Textile Council was focused narrowly on averting the wage cut—indeed, earlier in the decade they had acceded to speed-ups in order to maintain their salaries. The TMC had a more ambitious agenda, owing to both its leftist heritage and its constituency among New Bedford's unskilled Polish, French, and especially Portuguese American workers: they called for a forty-hour week, an end to child labor, a reversal of speed-ups, equal pay for women, and a 20 percent raise.[205] Their radicalism and aggressive tactics drew the ire of institutional forces in the city who also opposed the cut, including the Textile Council, Democratic mayor Charles Ashley, and the city's three daily newspapers.[206] But when the Textile Council began denouncing the TMC as "reds," few were swayed—because the craft union lacked grassroots credibility.[207] A Portuguese worker captured this antagonism as he catalogued his cohorts' accrued grievances in the opening weeks of the strike: "One south end mill with 144 twisters had from 16 to 20 tying-in men. The same mill now with 168 twisters has but six to eight tying-in men with no wage increase. . . . Same mill same department—two doffers and piecer for eighteen frames. Now the same three men doff from 50 to 60 frames. . . . This department is 100 per cent union. Is the secretary of this union asleep? . . . What's the matter with the union?"[208]

Part of the matter with the union was that for years it had been conspiring with management to buttress the pay of organized craftsmen by cutting the salaries of unskilled workers. Moreover, divides between skilled and unskilled employees were notoriously coterminous with divides between national groups; and so the recent-immigrant laborers were also the workers operating under the worst conditions with the least security for the lowest wages.[209] In New Bedford, "it was clear that there was a discriminatory policy in effect in terms of hiring and in terms of promotions . . . [because] among the skilled workers the predominant group would be among the English." French Canadians, Poles, and Portuguese were left to the lesser positions, while Cape Verdeans, the only major "black" immigrant group in New England textiles, were "relegated finally to the card room which was the dirtiest, unhealthiest department."[210]

As a result of this cliquishness, Portuguese workers constituted "the backbone" of the TMC. For Jack Rubenstein, one of the radical organizers, this was unsurprising. "You didn't have to go very far to tell these people that they were down-trodden, when kids made thirteen cents an hour and they got a ten percent cut."[211] The prospect of checking declines in labor conditions and pay at all skill levels while asserting their own social worth fueled unskilled workers' enthusiasm for the TMC. These workers, who sang Portuguese folk songs with "no strike ideology whatsoever" on the picket lines, were not as interested in the TMC's dialectic as they were in its willingness to mobilize the unorganized and treat them with a respect their skilled coworkers had always withheld.[212] Thus did the Textile Council's anticommunist screeds fall on indifferent ears; as the economist Daniel Georgianna has noted, workers "knew the difference between a labor strike for higher wages and a political revolution to overthrow the government. . . . For them, the TMC was fighting for higher wages and equality with other workers, principles easily identified with American democracy."[213]

The TMC treated Polish and Portuguese workers, who "knew that they [were] really getting the raw deal in terms of equal opportunity," with dignity, and pursued a platform that essentially sought to provide the security that events in the 1920s had revoked.[214] Yet this did not lead to a surge in ethnic support for radical politics. Socialist Party presidential nominee Norman Thomas donated $500 to aid the strikers and addressed a rally of 3,000 unionists in New Bedford during the conflict.[215] In November, this support earned Thomas 510 New Bedford votes—just under 1.6 percent of the city's presidential ballots.[216]

Communist candidates, whose ideology more closely aligned with that of the TMC, fared even worse. Workers Party presidential nominee William Z. Foster carried 0.4 percent of the New Bedford vote, while the Socialist Labor Party's Verne L. Reynolds achieved 0.07 percent. None of these figures represented a substantial increase from the previous presidential election.[217] These results partially confirmed the observations of organizers like Jack Rubenstein, who saw TMC success as a testament to the group's frank embrace of workers' basic economic needs rather than as a portent of revolution. They also confirm the reflections of one Portuguese mill hand, who lamented the Communists' hostility toward workers' cultural and especially religious traditions. "This was one of their main issues—the religious question. That isolated them. It made them ineffective because most of them saw religion as the opiate of the people and we did not share that concept at all."[218]

For his part, Al Smith showed phenomenal improvement in New Bedford, and his victory in the Whaling City was facilitated by shifts among textile workers. As Huthmacher has noted, "Traditionally Republican precincts populated with old-stock English textile workers were listed in the Democratic column." Even more revelatory was Smith's performance in Ward Five—the most heavily Portuguese and Cape Verdean district—where he won 51.1 percent of the vote (Democrat Davis and Progressive La Follette had managed to combine for a mere 18.9 percent there in 1924).[219]

Smith achieved a similar Democratic breakthrough in the small textile town of Ware, whose economic and political tale exemplifies a motif found in scores of communities scattered along dozens of rivers across New England. On the eve of Thanksgiving 1926, the Otis Company announced that its stockholders would be voting to move operations from Ware (where they had been located since 1835 and employed almost 20 percent of the population) to Lee, Alabama—a decision bound to affect "nearly every family in town."[220] Along Main Street, shopkeepers "sadly discussed the future," as wistful mill hands talked openly of "going to the almshouse." Merchants were left with bloated stock as Thanksgiving inventories sat untouched on shelves and buyers reneged on orders made in happier times. Town leaders feared that Ware would share the fate of nearby Thorndike—a community similarly dependent on a single mill that had closed earlier in the year, leading the town to "suffer disastrously."[221]

Ware, however, was more fortunate. In December, the board of the Otis Company voted to postpone action, causing the townspeople to "rejoice."[222] An anonymous Associated Press reporter captured the prevailing mood: "Just as to the man in the death cell any stay of execution is an augury of good holding out infinite possibilities, so to the mill worker" the delay was "an omen of good that holds out hope—none too strong, to be sure—that the town may not be called upon to face a readjustment so basic as to [en]gender a feeling almost of despondency."[223] Otis stockholders granted Ware clemency the next day, voting to remain "indefinitely" and "brighten[ing] the Christmas outlook," according to Governor Fuller, who informed Otis that "you may consider us entirely at your service" as the company began to dictate the terms of its continued residence in Massachusetts.[224] These included "relief from excessive State and town taxation and an amendment to the law limiting the hours of daily operations." Stockholders denounced "social legislation, particularly the law forbidding women to work after 6 pm, even when they so desire."[225] As Massachusetts contemplated these demands, Ware moved to become more hospitable to business; that winter, the town meeting voted to cut over $20,000 from the municipal budget, "in an effort to keep the Otis Mills here by materially reducing the taxation on property."[226]

In the meantime, Otis did what it could to maintain profitability. On Christmas Eve, those living in company housing "received notice that an increase in rentals will be effective for the future, probably averaging about 25 percent."[227] Two weeks later, a "wage readjustment" was declared.[228] The price of keeping the mills had been a substantial reduction in household incomes—but then, netting less was better than netting nothing at all. Through all of this "cooperation," the mills were saved—for the present—"with the understanding that should their future operation prove unprofitable they would eventually be closed."[229] Spared the fate of Thorndike, the people of Ware toiled on at the mills—now for less pay and always with the sword of Damocles dangling overhead.

Politically, these laborers were left to ponder their new reality until the following year's presidential election, when the plight of industrial New England became a centerpiece of Al Smith's pitch to working-class America. They did not turn in that year to radical third parties—although Ware had a history of doing so (Eugene Debs had routinely polled 5 percent there and in one election had carried 13 percent, while in 1924, Robert La Follette had carried nearly 17 percent of the town's vote); in 1928 the combined tally for Thomas, Foster, and Reynolds was six votes. Nor did these workers vote to affirm the Republicans who had brokered their apparent industrial salvation—although the town was historically Republican. Instead, Ware, like many textile towns, be-

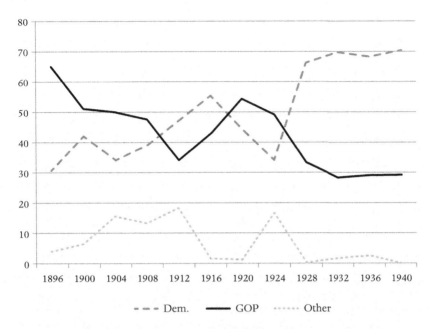

FIGURE 12.   Presidential voting in Ware, Massachusetts, 1896–1940.

came a Democratic stronghold—granting Smith an unprecedented two-thirds of its presidential vote and setting a pattern for the Roosevelt years.[230]

Even in Chicopee, where "contrary to the trend . . . employment and payroll figures indicated an actual improvement in the economic situation compared with 1926 and 1927," Smith's success involved a confluence of economic and cultural factors, for workers did not suddenly perceive economic anguish in 1928 and therefore precipitously mobilize as Democrats.[231] Rather, years, decades, even generations of accumulated degradation left these populations poised for activation by the right political leader. Poverty and prosperity are not short-term conditions. Nor are they purely quantitative. Small, recent improvements in household incomes were insufficient to provide a sense of security to workers who had long suffered physically and socially from their economic position and lived within a regional context of industrial instability.

Chicopee in fact provides an outstanding example of all of this. The city had lost a number of important manufacturers during the 1920s.[232] The Chicopee Manufacturing Company, a textile concern purchased in 1916 by Johnson and Johnson, saw many of its operations shipped in 1927 to a new mill town that had been built in Georgia by the New Jersey firm. Enunciating a now-familiar trope, Johnson and Johnson treasurer Charles A. McCormick cited the Peach State's "sane policy of taxation" in justifying the move. As a final insult, the new town was named for the textile company around which it was constructed—it was called Chicopee, Georgia.[233] By far the worst blow to Chicopee, Massachusetts, was delivered by another textile firm, the Dwight Manufacturing Company, which ceased all operations there in 1927, shifting production to Alabama and throwing around 2,000 people out of work.[234]

In fact, what mattered most about Chicopee's economy was not that wages improved slightly in 1928 but that the opulence of the Roaring Twenties never arrived in this factory city to begin with. Like so many ethnic industrial communities, Chicopee lacked any real middle class from the 1890s forward, and its working class saw few prospects for upward mobility. In 1929, a mere 979 of Chicopee's 43,930 residents met the income threshold to pay federal taxes.[235]

Chicopee was compelled to abstain from the consumption boom of the Coolidge years, and this influenced the working class profoundly. Per capita annual food sales were $112 in 1929—far lower than comparable Bay State industrial cities. A 1934 study identified "a large factory population living on a lower food standard than is usual in communities which have a larger middle class element."[236] This in turn affected the health and welfare of Chicopee's working families. The city's infant mortality rate (IMR) in 1921 was a horrific 105 per 1,000 live births. In 1928, the IMR was reduced, but it remained an appallingly high 88 per 1,000 live births. These reductions over the decade paralleled those made across the commonwealth and across the nation; but parallel declines, while indicative of progress, do not suggest a satisfactory improvement in local infant and maternal health care, since Chicopee's IMR in 1921 was 38 percent higher than that of Massachusetts as a whole. In fact, in only one year between 1921 and 1928 was Chicopee's IMR less than 20 percent higher than the Massachusetts rate—which itself was usually slightly above the national rate. In 1928, Chicopee's IMR remained 35.4 percent higher than the figure for all of Massachusetts. Among all municipalities in the state with a population greater than 15,000, Chicopee had the second-highest IMR in 1928—behind only nearby West Springfield, a small industrial town with large Italian and French Canadian populations. A child born in Chicopee in 1928 was 2.5 percent less likely to survive its first year than a child born elsewhere in the state. This damnable condition could be observed to a lesser degree in many of the ethnic industrial cities of Massachusetts: Fall River, New Bedford, Lowell, and Holyoke all had above-average IMRs throughout the 1920s. Chicopee was not unique—it simply had things even worse.[237]

So while Chicopee's wages and employment rolls remained relatively stable on the eve of the Great Depression, other measures of quality of life—consumption, social mobility, nutrition, infant mortality—remained unacceptably steady. Voters in Chicopee did not necessarily experience a sudden economic shock in 1928 that primed them for political activation. Rather, encroaching economic insecurities and years devoid of progress, along with a profound yearning for ethnocultural affirmation, had readied these citizens for mobilization by a candidate who acknowledged both their cultural and economic plight. In 1928, those citizens, who had provided slim Democratic majorities in 1900 and 1916 and had otherwise been reliable Republicans, voted 71 percent for Smith—with a turnout that smashed the previous city record by 54 percent.[238]

Successful political mobilization of New England's ethnic workers could neglect neither their cultural nor their economic desires. There was indeed an appetite for change, and there existed among these laborers the sheer numbers to fuel a dramatic political realignment. But such an upheaval would require sensitivity to the complex realities of those workers, while proposed solutions must be crafted in terms acceptable to the workers themselves.

Solutions

Republicans were at a disadvantage on both economics and culture. In New England, they attempted to neutralize the latter challenge—openly rejecting Klan attacks on Smith, denouncing the notion of a "religious test" for political office, and downplaying Prohibition. On economics, Republicans were cursed with incumbency in a region suffering industrial decline. They sought to check this by appealing to their traditional strength with New England workers—proposing to amplify customary prescriptions such as protective tariffs and reduced regulation. For many workers these were familiar, even comfortable remedies; but their plunging economic fortunes now complicated once-reliable solutions.

For their part, the Democrats ardently embraced the cultural aspirations of the majority of ethnic workers—fiercely condemning Prohibition and demanding that Smith's election would strike a blow for tolerance. Smith himself provided both rhetorical and symbolic material for this narrative. The Democrats attempted to leverage regional economic discontent by insistently linking industrial woes to Republican stewardship. Ironically, these challengers also sought to negate traditional Republican strength among industrial workers by adopting a friendlier posture toward protectionism.

All of this shuffling did not minimize important differences between the remedies proffered by the two major parties. For New England businessmen and many Republican politicians, the solution was reductions in taxation and regulation. "The return of New England's manufacturing resources to a position of parity with those of the South," reported the Boston Chamber of Commerce in 1926, demanded "the elimination of legislative inequalities," and so officials were admonished to reestablish "equal competitive opportunities with the South with respect to labor legislation."[239] Massachusetts officials had themselves noted this as early as 1923, when Republican governor Channing Cox's commissioner of labor and industries had identified a number of industrial disadvantages suffered by the Bay State—among them high wages, the forty-eight-hour week, and, "worst" of all, the prohibition against women's night work.[240]

Regulatory repeal had yet to gain traction; but the business-government cooperation proposed by Governor Fuller and others in response to crises like that in Ware meant reductions in state and local taxes. This approach was of course shared by national Republicans, who consistently decried governmental burdens on business and extolled tax cuts. At the state and municipal levels, tax cuts meant budget cuts, and these were already well under way by 1928—with tangible results. In Ware, the $20,000 budget reduction in February 1926 came mostly from the town's snow removal fund.[241] In early 1928 in New Bedford, as wage reductions struck nearby Fall River, aldermen debated a 10 percent tax cut—and concomitant municipal layoffs—in order to avert similar adjustments to pay scales in the city's mills.[242] The layoffs were rejected, but the budget was slashed by $162,000, with the "bulk of reductions" coming at the "expense of children" as "no new teachers" would be hired that fall.[243] After the mills decided to reduce wages anyway, the city health board, also struggling at "living within the amount given us by the City council," decided to "concentrate our resources on the work that is required by law," and terminated its program of dental clinics for school children.[244]

Furthermore, in order to keep factories in New England, some Republicans were indeed contemplating rolling back labor protections. Cooperation with business would therefore mean acceding to corporate demands for reversals in Progressive Era industrial codes. Announcing their 10 percent wage cut for New Bedford, textile manufacturers made a representative statement, complaining that "New Bedford manufacturers, paying the old wage scale, limited to a 48-hour week and restricted as to night work, must be doing business under a serious handicap."[245] The message was clear: state and local politicians must seriously reconsider labor regulations if they desired to retain the mills.

Frank P. Walsh, the leader of the Smith Progressive League who had served under Woodrow Wilson as chairman of the United States Commission on Industrial Relations, connected these demands to Hoover himself during a fiery address at Weavers Hall in Fall River on October 18, censuring the Republican nominee as "the open-shopper of open-shoppers." Textile workers ought to support Smith, Walsh demanded, because of the New Yorker's endorsement of public power projects and his record of reforms in New York State; but also because Hoover opposed eight-hour laws and had called instead for "cooperation" among management, labor, and the state.[246] For New England workers, "cooperation" meant surrendering to wage readjustments or rolling back industrial reforms in order to assuage business.

Smith Democrats never entertained these options, instead suggesting that industrial conditions were worsening precisely because business interests dominated the Republican Party and were manipulating the regional response to the downturn. In Medway, General Cole charged that "prominent Republicans who are raising funds and urging the election of Hoover" had demanded that "Massachusetts mills be removed to Texas or other Southern States because of lower wages and longer working hours."[247] A week later he asserted that "'the big business' interests prefer to obtain the larger dividends paid by mills in States where the protection afforded employes is less rigorous."[248] These politicians—and most of the workers whose votes they sought—insisted that the mills were profitable but that their owners were either insatiable or incompetent: Gilded Age labor conditions in the South were an attractive alternative for avaricious Massachusetts industrialists who had grown weary of encumbrances like wage and hours regulations or unionized employees; while failing mills were victims of inept businessmen who mulishly retained outdated marketing practices or foolishly expanded beyond their means.[249]

Like most of his New England allies, Al Smith was in many ways vague on solutions, focusing instead on criticizing the shortcomings of Republican governmental administration. While there is within such a critique an implicit agenda of policy reversal, this was not the Democrat's lone contribution to the debate. Rather, what mattered most about Smith was his record as governor of New York and his promise to bring to Washington the agenda and approach he had employed at Albany. Often the connections were obvious, as between the Muscle Shoals controversy and the ongoing debates over resource conservation and power development in New York. What was most pertinent in New England, aside from Smith's pledge to protect industry and to rework tax and tariff policies to end what Democrats considered inequitable distribution of national prosperity, was the governor's record regarding social welfare and labor legislation.

While Smith never explicated with precision a proposed set of federal labor regulations, the public reception of his candidacy is more politically germane—and what mattered to workers in New England was the fact that he had championed such measures in New York and that he had unabashedly defended the principles behind such laws during his national campaign. This allowed

Smith's supporters to invoke the governor's record for solutions to New England's industrial woes that presented a remarkable alternative to Republican calls for deregulation and dissolution of the welfare state. "New York State has labor laws on its books even more progressive than those of Massachusetts," noted the Smith-boosting *Fall River Herald News*, and "practically all of these laws have been enacted since Alfred E. Smith became governor." Textile workers in Fall River and elsewhere ought to place their hope in Smith, to improve "the situation in the south . . . giving the women and children who toil there the same protection," and thus removing manufacturers' incentive to abandon the North. "Isn't it obvious?"[250]

Indeed, Smith's progressive supporters insisted that his election would "make social justice a national issue." A group of prominent social workers, including Lillian Wald, Mary Van Kleeck, Mary Simkhovitch, and Harry Hopkins, judged Smith "unique among our statesmen for his contribution to social progress." Since they believed that "all the problems of the nation have their roots in the needs of the people and . . . can best be solved by one who has not only faith in social progress but skill in bringing the resources of government to bear upon it," these progressives enthusiastically promoted the ambitions of Al Smith, who would nationalize the progressive policies and administrative tactics he had established in New York State.[251]

Campaign surrogates often referred specifically to Smith's successful—and, for those living in places like Chicopee, highly relevant—push to bring the Sheppard-Towner maternal health program to the Empire State. Smith had made Sheppard-Towner an election issue in 1922, and it helped him oust Republican Nathan Miller, who had blockaded New York's participation in the program. Miller's party brethren to the East enjoyed greater longevity: boasting that Connecticut was "a state that begs no favors," Senator Hiram Bingham and other Republicans had held the Nutmeg State out of Sheppard-Towner, and their Massachusetts neighbors followed suit—placing the two Yankee stalwarts among only three states never to accept Sheppard-Towner funds.[252] Once again, New England Republicans and Smith Democrats provided starkly contrasting views of the role of government—including the federal government—in promoting health and welfare. Within the context of the dangerous, unhealthful conditions experienced in New England's manufacturing cities—conditions that sometimes manifested themselves in inflated rates of disease and nearly always were reflected in abnormally high infant mortality rates—it is understandable that Smith's progressive social welfare agenda resonated with working-class voters.

Indeed, such language, employed nationally, was especially compelling in battered New England. While regional business interests were demanding that states abrogate social welfare programs and labor regulations, Smith Democrats were boasting of the New Yorker's activist record in the Empire State and suggesting that this would be a central facet of his national regime.[253] At Quincy, during a speech skewering Republican leaders for their handling of the textile crisis, Senator Walsh explained that "more than all else [Smith] has a heartfelt realization of the problem of the common man. . . . He has shown this in the great program of social welfare legislation which he put into effect in the State of New York."[254] Other New Englanders invoked Smith's achievements specifically to challenge the wisdom of retrenchment. A Connecticut Democrat suggested in Southington that her state should not celebrate its record of austerity, since Smith's more aggressive spending had yielded manifold benefits to the people of New York.[255] Massachusetts state senator John W. Mc-Cormack, running for Congress in Boston's Twelfth District, concluded that Smith "typifies the progressive leadership America needs and demands," adding that "the people . . . appreciate the straightforward manner in which he has stated . . . his position on the great issues of the day."[256]

Indeed, Smith was straightforward enough so that everyone, including his political foes, recognized that he sought to pursue his progressive gubernatorial policies at the federal level. Republicans criticized both the record and its national implications. Of course there were the famous denunciations of Smith's proposals as "state socialism"—articulated by everyone from Secretary Hoover to Congressman Fort, who alerted a Boston audience that Smith was committed to "the broadest policy of Government in business ever proposed to the people of any Nation except Russia." Supplementing such castigation were critiques of Smith's liberal spending as governor. Massachusetts state representative Henry Shattuck warned the same rally of Smith's "extravagant" outlays in the Empire State.[257] The *Hartford Courant* ridiculed Democratic rebukes of President Coolidge's spending policies, given their nominee's prodigality at Albany.[258] In a radio address contrasting Smith's New York record with his own sober stewardship of Connecticut, Governor Trumbull claimed that the interest payments on New York's bonded debt "would run every department and institution of Connecticut for three quarters of a year."[259] From Torrington, a Connecticut writer questioned whether voters were "willing to have [their] taxes increased over 100 percent" as a result of "Governor Smith's free and easy spending," admonishing readers to "remember that they are the ones who must pay for extravagance."[260] Given the Democrat's propensity for lavish state programs, Senator Bingham suggested that the Happy Warrior might more accurately be called "the Happy Spender."[261]

Despite these denunciations, Smith's social welfare policies and his support for expansive labor protections bolstered his cause in struggling industrial cities like New Bedford, where economic insecurity and reductions in welfare services were rampant. They also held obvious relevance in depressed New England mill towns, where families living in premodern shacks raised children to begin working forty-eight-hour weeks at age fourteen while harried parents toiled without interruption until they were laid off, maimed, or became too old or sick to work and were sent off to the dreaded "poor farm." Much like New Bedford, Fall River, Lawrence, and Lowell, Massachusetts mill towns such as Clinton, Easthampton, Ludlow, and Ware delivered unprecedented Democratic presidential majorities. Palmer, Massachusetts, which contained the struggling textile village of Thorndike, voted Democratic for the first time in the twentieth century, while in Easthampton, Smith's 53.6 percent made him the first Democrat to avoid losing the city by at least 25 points since Grover Cleveland.[262]

Many New England laborers were beginning to understand their struggles within a broader national political context, and the 1928 Smith campaign hastened this development. As Smith and his local allies promoted social welfare reforms, labor protections, economic progressivism, and cultural tolerance, rank-and-file ethnic workers registered as Democrats, organized Smith Clubs, delivered speeches, and opined in local newspapers. Their words and actions reveal that the inspiration for this initiative came from their own life experiences, stimulated at last by the arrival of a candidate who both symbolized their view of social progress and articulated their concept of economic justice.

While workers' enthusiasm for Smith may have originated with admiration for his humble roots or their shared religious affiliation, his record of achievement in New York—and the promise of a similarly progressive administration in Washington—was also especially attractive to these voters. An address delivered on the Democrat's behalf in Springfield, Massachusetts, in October 1928 captured these sentiments:

> Why is Alfred E. Smith, a graduate of the city streets, the political idol and the political hope of so many of his country-men? Because he possesses leadership, honesty, human interests and the executive ability necessary for presidency. . . . His strongest opponent has recognized his achievement in the total reorganization of the government, in the business-like management of state finance. Through his leadership he was able to show the quality of interest in humanity. On the enactment of a legislative program, he has been able to protect the man, woman, and child engaged in industry, he has improved the public health and he has attained the finest standard of public service. This interest in

humanity could only be attained with his leadership. . . . The Governor has proved during his eight years as Governor of New York his desire and his power to make the people as interested in the government as he is himself. . . . Governor Smith senses [the needs] of the people because he has [been] through hardships himself. Between him and the people is that bond which makes them trust him with their loyalty and love.[263]

This could easily have come from the notes of Frances Perkins or Molly Dewson, but these particular lines were not delivered by one of the legions of social workers trekking the nation espousing Smith's credentials. Nor were they delivered by a visiting Democratic luminary, a state-ticket candidate, or even a local Springfield politician, community leader, or labor activist. The speech was given by Katherine Cofski, a Polish American high school senior from Springfield, during a school debate on the presidential campaign. Smith's ideas and achievements and the entire reform narrative associated with his campaign were successfully diffused among receptive New Englanders.[264]

The battles of 1928 established durable electoral coalitions in New England, determining party allegiances and setting the parameters for regional politics in the ensuing decades. In many ways, those nascent coalitions were personified by the combatants in another high school debate, in Hartford. Arguing for Smith were James Clancy and Stanley Straska; for Hoover, Allen Hyde and Robert Crandall—Irish and Polish for Smith; English and Scottish for Hoover.[265]

Yet ethnocultural analyses render only partial explanations. Democrats had often tried to leverage such issues, and these efforts had repeatedly failed. In his 1924 campaign for governor of Massachusetts, James Michael Curley ran a flamboyantly urban and Irish operation, denouncing religious intolerance and making attacks on the Ku Klux Klan a centerpiece of his movement—to the extent that multiple historians have joined Curley's Republican opponent in accusing the Democrats of staging cross burnings in order to arouse their ethnic base.[266] Yet while Curley showed strength in some of the working-class ethnic areas that would fuel Smith's 1928 victory, he did not gain enough support in such locations to achieve a statewide majority; as one biographer noted, "The Klan as an issue was not enough."[267] Indeed, Curley garnered a paltry 38.6 percent of the vote in New Bedford, despite that city's tremendous Catholic majority.[268] The same year, Connecticut's Democratic Party "decided to wage its campaign on the Klan issue"; this proved ineffective, and the election was a "one-sided" Republican romp. It was only with the rounded campaign of 1928 that Connecticut Republicans would be forced to admit that "Smith had pulled the Italian and Polish vote from the GOP."[269] Similarly, Rhode

Island Democrats chose to stress cultural issues in 1924 and ultimately sur-
rendered the modest gains they had made with Italian and French Canadian
voters during the labor troubles of the early 1920s; Democratic strength with
these groups was crystallized only when Al Smith carried the Ocean State
with a holistic platform embracing both the cultural and economic aspirations of these voters.[270]

New England's ethnic working-class voters were clearly offended by anti-
Catholic bigotry and sanctimonious prohibitionism. But in many cases, economic desperation was also a defining characteristic of these workers' outlook.
Tellingly, when Victor Signorelli, an Italian immigrant who began working in a
Peace Dale textile mill at fifteen, recalled "one time during the depression" in
an interview decades later, he was referring not to the 1930s but to events that
occurred in 1927 and 1928.[271] Religion and Prohibition were important, but so
were labor and welfare, and it was the confluence of these factors that produced the upheavals of 1928.

In New England, the Smith campaign ran blatantly contrary to national
policy assumptions—the Democrats were almost iconoclastic in their open
rejection of the widely held faith in Republican economics. "Smith Raps
G.O.P. Prosperity" went a representative headline.[272] Meanwhile, New England
Republicans maintained that only the preservation of their party's administration with a renewed commitment to orthodoxy could ameliorate the woes
of regional manufacturing. Thus, Republicans presented the election as a clearly
defined contest pitting the sober continuance of Coolidge's pro-business policies against the experimentation of myopic critics too focused on lingering regional complications to appreciate the architecture of the robust national
economy. The *Hartford Courant* summarized this position:

> Hoover says: "You have been travelling along this road. You know where
> it leads to. There are no uncertainties about it. Your progress has been
> pleasant thus far. The next four years of the journey will be like the last
> four, not tedious and painful, but marked all along the way by agree-
> able experiences." Mr. Smith says: "The road you have just passed over
> was full of all sorts of pitfalls which perhaps you didn't notice. You
> thought you had a comfortable journey, but that was because you sim-
> ply do not know what real comfort means. Go along with me on the
> next lap, pursue the course that I and my associates have charted, and
> you may be sure that no evil will befall you."[273]

Speaking on Smith's behalf at Mechanics Hall in Boston on October 12,
Franklin Roosevelt concurred that the election was a question of continuity
versus change: "The Republican candidate for President will appeal to those

in New England who are satisfied with things as they are, who are content to have no change even though it be a change for the better. The Democratic candidate and his party are appealing to New England because they believe New England wants and needs a change, that conditions today are bad, and that they will be doing everything that lies in their power to bring a more fundamental and general prosperity not only to New England, but to all of the United States."[274]

FIGURE 13. Rollin Kirby, "A Great Army," 1928. By permission of the Estate of Rollin Kirby Post. Credit: Rollin Kirby (1875–1952) / Museum of the City of New York.43.366.136.

Thus the lines were drawn in bold relief for New England voters. Republicans hoped to leverage their economic credentials to retain the loyalties of workers despite Smith's appealingly familiar profile; Democrats hoped to employ that profile to secure a forum for leveling their broad critique of the status quo. This made many people's decisions very complicated. On October 26, Hartford's Republican mayor, Walter E. Batterson, praised Judge John L. Bonee's steadfast loyalty to the party cause. Bonee, the Republican nominee for state senate from the Third District, was a Roman Catholic but had unequivocally endorsed Herbert Hoover in what Batterson deemed "one of the finest demonstrations of tolerance any man could give." The judge's reckoning was commendably frank—he "asserted that prosperity was the principal matter in which individuals should be interested."[275] A Catholic, an Italian, and a Republican, Bonee understood the stakes for New England in the 1928 presidential contest, and he exhorted his fellow ethnic citizens to consider their economic welfare when casting their ballots.[276] They did—and they voted overwhelmingly for Al Smith.

Conclusion
The Happy Warriors

> The future of the Democracy lies in following the
> furrow plowed by Al.
>
> —H. L. Mencken, November 12, 1928

Why did urban ethnic working-class voters flock
to Alfred E. Smith in 1928? What did they hear from the candidate and his campaign? How did they respond?

After almost two decades of development in New York State, Smith's particular brand of progressivism had been presented to the nation in a coordinated fashion by the nominee and his Democratic allies. In the urban, industrial
North—particularly in New England and in many of the nation's great cities—
this amalgam of social welfare, labor progressivism, and cultural pluralism
had been popularized by the nominee and fueled unprecedented Democratic
successes. Smith's avid supporters in those regions were activated by the arrival of a candidate who spoke to working-class realities and embodied their
vision of social progress. Yet, faced in 1928 with the nation's prevailing economic and cultural conservatism, Al Smith and his ideas went down to defeat.

The story is more complex, however, for though Smith was vanquished, the
Republican landslide of 1928 did not halt the momentum that the New Yorker's candidacy had lent the forces of change. In September of that year, columnist Mark Sullivan had noted the increasingly urban cast of the Democratic
Party, discussing the influx of ethnic city-dwellers into politics and the consequent influence this would exert on debates over Prohibition and immigration.
He concluded that irrespective of Smith's fortunes, this was to be a permanent transformation: "In the new Democratic party, the bulk of the votes

are going to come from the wets in the big cities and the new wet leadership will keep control." Sullivan's headline blared his conclusion: "New Democratic Party Is Born."[1] Following Smith's defeat, John W. McCormack, congressman-elect from Massachusetts, insisted that his chosen candidate had exerted a transformational effect on U.S. politics. When Representative John Box, a Texas Democrat, composed an open letter urging his party to abandon the course Smith had pursued in 1928, the precocious freshman retorted that the party's future "rested north of the so-called solid South."[2]

In fact, a substantive metamorphosis of the Democratic Party had been set in motion by Smith's national campaign. In its wake, an increasingly influential faction within the party began to insist both that their voices be recognized and that their proposals be enacted. During the 1930s, the idiomatic progressivism championed by Al Smith and embraced by his urban ethnic working-class constituents would form a considerable portion of the liberal Democratic program.

Father of the New Deal?

While remarkable and even revolutionary, the subtleties of this development must be acknowledged in order to define the precise role Smith's progressive priorities (and the ambitions of his adherents) played in shaping Franklin Roosevelt's New Deal. There has been an understandable tendency to overstate Al Smith's significance as the inspiration or even the progenitor of the liberal program of the 1930s. A particularly strong exponent of this position, the historian Paula Eldot, identified Smith as "an important source of the New Deal" in her thorough examination of his governorship. Eldot, who rightly identified Smith's gubernatorial program as that of a progressive reformer, pointed to a "continuity of policy" between Smith and Roosevelt in areas including administrative reorganization, conservation, housing, labor, and water power, to affirm the thesis—set forth by Frances Perkins—that the Happy Warrior ought to be remembered as "the forerunner of the New Deal."[3] Eldot was not the first author to make such observations. Before her death, Perkins herself had commenced a study of Smith's career, alerting her publishers that "her purpose was to show Alfred Smith as a great Governor whose social reforms in New York State were the forerunners of the New Deal."[4] The Perkins project was inherited by Matthew and Hannah Josephson, who asserted in 1969 that under Smith, "in New York you could find the beginnings of the Welfare State which was to reach full bloom later in its federal form under the New Deal Administration of Franklin D. Roosevelt."[5] Moreover, this view has commanded remarkable staying power: in 1986, the *New York Times* recalled how "what began in Albany under Governor Smith had been honed and expanded into the New Deal by President Roosevelt"; while in 2011, *Salon* editor-in-chief Joan Walsh went as far as to dub Al Smith "the real father of the New Deal."[6]

Many studies have presented a far different view of the Happy Warrior. William Leuchtenburg suggested that the New Yorker had been a moderate reformer who was "from the first fundamentally conservative" and who "never questioned the assumptions of capitalist society, certainly not the profit motive or the virtue of success," pointing out that "the notion of a planned society was as repugnant to [Smith] as to Hoover."[7] Similarly, Arthur M. Schlesinger Jr. determined that "Smith stood for a social welfare liberalism, indifferent to the concentration of wealth, uninterested in basic change, but concerned with protecting the individual against the hazards of industrial society."[8]

Both positions spring from essential truths, yet each errs in its basic premise. Historians are correct to recognize the significance of Smith's governorship to the development of a social welfare regime prior to the onset of the Great Depression and the consequent establishment of the New Deal state. However, Smith's reformism must not be extracted from the world in which it was exercised. Each facet of his gubernatorial agenda was a programmatic manifestation of his progressivism—variously applied in diverse contexts based on specific problems and crafted each time to succeed within a unique political environment. To the extent that Governor and then President Roosevelt faced many of the same challenges that Smith had combated at Albany, precedents had been established by the elder Democrat for robust governmental intervention to promote social welfare. Moreover, figures who had helped to develop Smith's progressive approach to state governance—most notably Frances Perkins and Robert Wagner—would play central roles in formulating FDR's solutions to many of the challenges of the Great Depression. Because of the singularity—in breadth, scale, and success—of Smith's progressivism during the 1920s, and because of the intimate connections between the two New York Democrats, it is only logical to perceive a line of development running through Smith to Roosevelt and the New Deal. Yet Smith never faced the Great Depression as an executive; nor did he ever have to deal with national problems as anything more than a candidate. Smith's progressive administration set precedents on which Roosevelt would build and established a strong social welfare tradition from which Roosevelt would draw; but Al Smith's progressivism *did not* constitute the genesis of the New Deal—the origins of which were far too complex, diverse, and situational for any theory of direct lineage to be anything but an oversimplification.

On the other side, there is truth to the argument that Al Smith was not particularly interested in establishing a "planned society," especially at the national level. But Smith's gubernatorial record belies the notion that he instinctively found such planning "repugnant." Similarly, while he was no populist crusader or visceral maligner of the rich, Smith's record demonstrates a willingness to deploy such rhetoric in situations where this was a useful political technique for promoting his vision of social justice. Indeed, the very notion that social justice ought to be established—and that this usually meant an active government promoting the interests of the poor and working classes while infringing on the prerogatives of the wealthy and powerful—was a central tenet of Smith's progressivism, which runs counter to the declarations of Schlesinger and Leuchtenburg. From the perspective of the social workers and machine politicians who had initially aligned to develop this reform agenda, and most importantly from the perspective of the urban workers on whose behalf that agenda was pursued, the assertion that "protecting the individual against the hazards of industrial society" did not constitute "basic change" would have been absurd.

The flaw of both positions is their attempt to understand Smith's program through the prism of the New Deal era. One looks back to the 1920s and discovers that many of the social welfare battles won by New Dealers had earlier been joined by Al Smith; the other scours Smith's progressivism and finds an absence of Tugwellian planning and a lack of class rhetoric in the manner of the 1936 Democratic campaign. What emerges in both cases is a narrative that necessarily discounts the subtleties of Smith's progressivism and risks projecting unique contextual elements such as the Great Depression and the Roosevelt landslides into the political reality of the 1920s, thus utilizing anachronistic standards for "progressivism," "conservatism," "liberalism," and other concepts that were themselves redefined by the upheavals of the 1930s. Eldot is absolutely correct that Smith was a progressive governor and that many of his achievements can be seen at least to have foreshadowed elements of the New Deal; and Leuchtenburg and Schlesinger are equally correct that Smith's progressivism was not New Deal liberalism. Here J. Joseph Huthmacher's nomenclature is the most precise: many New Deal programs were *"akin* to those [Smith] had espoused at Albany."[9]

In fact, Al Smith's career did contribute fundamentally to the broader evolution from progressivism to New Deal liberalism, both in policy and politics. In New York, Smith and his allies reconciled and then synthesized the social work and urban Democratic traditions; they politicized the resulting ideology as a partisan agenda, institutionalized that agenda as a comprehensive program for New York State, and nationalized their program during the 1928 presidential campaign. Simultaneously, Al Smith's presidential bid precipitated an electoral revolution in key regions—especially the urban Northeast—and the powerful voting bloc that emerged would in turn prove an essential component of the Roosevelt coalition.

While cultural factors like religion and Prohibition clearly bolstered Smith's cause among parched voters from the ethnic working class, the candidate's progressivism, articulated throughout the campaign by the nominee and his partisans, also resonated with those being neglected by Republican economics. Historians widely accept that, irrespective of the cultural controversies surrounding Smith's candidacy, Republican success in 1928 was foreordained by the prosperity being enjoyed by much of the nation.[10] In fact, this argument is even stronger than its proponents have acknowledged, for rather than adopting *tout court* a "me too" posture toward Republican policies, Smith articulated his alternative vision of a robust social welfare regime at a time when economic conditions left most Americans disinterested in such matters.[11]

Yet this program was not universally repulsive. As the case of industrial New England reveals, the experiences of urban ethnic workers left these voters eager to embrace Smith's policies, and therefore responsive to his party's entreaties. The 1928 campaign strengthened ties between such voters and the Democratic Party, setting in motion a fundamental transformation of the party itself. As urban ethnic voters became an increasingly significant Democratic bloc, they became increasingly assertive. In Smith's wake, these voters and their elected leaders became forceful advocates within the Democracy for social welfare and labor reforms. Before 1928, noted Frances Perkins, this "program of social justice" had been at most a marginal priority for Democratic presidential aspirants; but the voters who were initiated into the party by Smith's candidacy would prioritize such questions, altering the parameters of serious public policy debate.[12]

The tumult of the Depression catapulted Franklin Roosevelt into the White House just as these voters attained prominence within the Democratic Party. Simultaneously, their representatives began to assert their particular progressive priorities with increasing force and urgency, and did so within a new economic context that opened possibilities for novel proposals. Thus, specific facets of the New Deal would be imbued with the distinctive progressive agenda that had been nationalized by Smith and embraced by his admirers.

Those who entered the 1930s espousing such an agenda were in many ways satiated. With the New Deal, the engaged state envisioned by social workers and their political allies was firmly established. The 1935 Social Security Act restored expired Sheppard-Towner–era maternal and infant health initiatives, provided for disabled and neglected children, and nationalized mothers' pensions, while laying the foundation for the modern welfare state—developments that Molly Dewson and other social work progressives found "just dazzling."[13] Housing, the herculean challenge with which social workers had been contending since the Gilded Age and which had become a focus of state policy under Smith's Reconstruction Commission, became a federal question in 1933 when the New Deal began refinancing mortgages through the Home Owners' Loan Corporation; the following year, the Federal Housing Administration was created to encourage widespread homeownership by insuring mortgages. By 1937, an even more active federal role had been established through the Wagner-Steagall Act, which created the United States Housing Authority and helped finance slum clearance and public housing developments.[14]

Specific national problems that had been identified during the Smith campaign and that gained more urgent notice with the onset of the Great Depression were often met through amplified, nationalized formulations of earlier progressive proposals. Through New Deal agencies including the Civilian Conservation Corps, the Public Works Administration (PWA), the Civil Works Administration, and the Works Progress Administration (WPA), great projects were initiated to alleviate unemployment and modernize the national estate in a manner reminiscent of Wagner and Smith's 1928 proposals. Meanwhile, Senator Norris's Tennessee Valley Authority (TVA) settled the heated debate from 1928 over the disposition of Muscle Shoals by unequivocally establishing federal control.[15]

Industrial life, the evils of which had provided the original impetus for the New York progressive alliance of social workers and Tammany men, became the focus of serious federal regulation. As Leuchtenburg notes, by codifying labor practices for major industries, the National Recovery Administration (NRA) "wiped out sweatshops, ended various forms of exploitation, and removed some 150,000 child laborers from factories."[16] Workers were also provided with the means of self-advocacy. Section 7(a) of the National Industrial Recovery Act (NIRA) set the precedent for federal protection of collective bargaining rights; and while this would evaporate with the Supreme Court's 1935 decision in *Schechter Poultry Corp. v. United States* and the resulting demolition of the floundering NRA, even stronger and more durable union protections would be established in the wake of the ruling. The National Labor Relations Act of 1935, known colloquially as the Wagner Act after the New Yorker who sponsored the bill in the Senate, guaranteed collective bargaining rights; legalized strikes and boycotts; outlawed company unions, yellow-dog contracts, and blacklists; and formed a National Labor Relations Board empowered to supervise union elections and adjudicate labor grievances. As a result of these protections, industrial union membership nearly quadrupled from 1933 to 1941. Moreover, in the tradition of the state-level labor progressivism of the 1910s and 1920s, the federal government established minimum wages and maximum hours and sought to improve workplace conditions through such legislation as the 1936 Walsh-Healey Act and the 1938 Fair Labor Standards Act.[17]

Indeed, the urban ethnic workers who were brought into the Democratic column beginning in 1928 could fairly consider the New Deal *their* deal. They had gained labor protections, unemployment relief, and at least a modicum of financial security. Perhaps as meaningfully for these groups, the New Dealers had inherited from the Smith Democrats a distaste for social policies based on proscriptions on personal behavior and élitist drives for old-stock cultural hegemony. As Leuchtenburg characterized the change: "Reform in the 1930's meant *economic* reform; it departed from the Methodist-parsonage morality of many of the earlier Progressives, in part because much of the New Deal support, and many of its leaders, derived from urban immigrant groups hostile to the old Sabbatarianism."[18]

On March 22, 1933, less than a month into his presidency, Franklin Roosevelt signed legislation amending the Volstead Act to legalize beer with an alcoholic content of up to 3.2 percent. By December, the Twenty-First Amendment, which had passed both houses of Congress prior to FDR's inauguration, had been ratified. Prohibition was over.[19]

The Happy Warriors

Of course, FDR had not ascended to the presidency intent on nationalizing social welfare progressivism or with a stated goal of instituting the proposals of Alfred E. Smith. His mission was much more straightforward: defeat the Depression. Constitutionally, many others shared this responsibility with the new president, and so Roosevelt and his "Brains Trust" were compelled to work with Congress in restoring the economy and ameliorating the suffering of the American people.

Often, Roosevelt enjoyed the support of a cooperative—in the early days, sometimes even pliant—Democratic caucus, which dominated both houses of Congress for his first six years in office and held majorities for his entire tenure. Yet, just as often congressional forces insisted on promoting their own agendas, and this legislative volition helped shape the course of the New Deal.[20] Such was certainly the case with the newest major bloc inside the motley Democratic caucus: representatives of the urban, ethnic working classes—

especially those from the Northeast and other areas where Al Smith had made tremendous inroads for Roosevelt's party.

In general, these northeastern urban Democrats were among the most loyal supporters of New Deal legislation. In his study *Congressional Conservatism and the New Deal*, the historian James T. Patterson found that of the seventy-seven most conservative House Democrats from 1933 to 1939, eighteen were from the Northeast or the Midwest, and of these, only ten were from "urban" districts. Significantly, only four of the seventy-seven conservative Democrats were from urban districts in either southern New England or the New York metropolitan region. Only one of these conservatives was from New York City; there were none from Boston or northern New Jersey, nor were there any from Connecticut or Rhode Island.[21]

Put more positively, the Democratic delegations from New York, New Jersey, and New England were important congressional partners in much of Roosevelt's program.[22] In 1933, these representatives unanimously supported the Federal Emergency Relief Administration and the NRA; they gave 85 percent support to the Agricultural Adjustment Act and 87 percent support to the TVA conference report.[23] In 1935, they unanimously backed the Social Security Act and the conference report creating the WPA; and later initiatives including housing legislation (1937 and 1939) and the Fair Labor Standards Act (1938) also attracted unanimous support.[24]

As with any collection of politicians, this bloc could be fickle. There was regular dissent among these representatives, for example, on matters of corporate regulation and taxation. Nearly one in five of these northeasterners opposed creating the Securities and Exchange Commission in 1934.[25] Similarly, 14 percent opposed the conference report on the so-called soak the rich Revenue Act in 1935 (with another 27 percent either abstaining or voting present), and only 80 percent backed the undistributed profits tax the following year, marking the northeasterners as relatively tepid Democratic supporters of the administration's more populist ambitions.[26] Certainly this was the case when two-thirds of the northeastern representatives voted to replace the Senate's public utilities holding company "death sentence" provision with a milder House substitute in 1935. Indeed, only 55 percent ultimately supported the conference report on that bill.[27]

Conversely, northeastern congressional Democrats sometimes bucked the administration in ways that hardly marked them as conservatives. The first and most noteworthy instance was with the Economy Act. Intent on restoring business confidence and moving toward a balanced budget, Roosevelt called for federal retrenchment nearly immediately after tackling the banking crisis, on

March 10, 1933. House Democrats initially rebelled, with some portraying the move as a tribute to the investing classes and others as simply coldhearted; yet Leuchtenburg notes that such appeals "made little headway against the power of the President in a time of crisis. . . . Under the leadership of Franklin Roosevelt, the budget balancers had won a victory for orthodox finance that had not been possible under Hoover."[28] Despite the strong support Roosevelt had gained for this fiscal maneuver (the bill passed the House 266 to 139), the northeastern bloc proved implacable, with only 45 percent of the region's Democrats supporting the bill.[29] Similarly, 86 percent of these Democrats voted in 1936 to override Roosevelt's veto of a bill to distribute bonuses to world war veterans.[30] In this case they were joined by overwhelming majorities in both houses of Congress, but, as with the Economy Act, the bonus question demonstrated the delegation's willingness to defy Roosevelt and promote prodigality—a temperament that was more often manifested in strong *support* for New Deal proposals reflecting similar goals, including the $1.425 billion deficiency appropriation of 1936 and Roosevelt's "pump-priming" program in 1938.[31]

When such initiatives were attacked by Republicans as "socialistic"—as during an August 1935 debate over the president's proposed tax increases, urban Democrats responded with rhetoric reminiscent of Al Smith, who had always countered such criticisms with a two-pronged retort both belittling the merits of the charge and extolling his own record. The tax bill would effectuate "a socialistic condition," warned New York Republican Bertrand Snell. In response, Chicago Democrat Adolph Sabath presented a seventeen-point recitation of the economic and social welfare achievements of 1933 and 1934, exalting Roosevelt as "the first and only President of the United States who has ever insisted upon feeding the hungry and furnishing clothing and shelter to the needy." Next, John J. O'Connor of New York asserted that "the people of this country from 1929 to 1933 suffered such distress and privation under Republicanism that, if a solution to their problems did mean socialism, they would welcome it rather than go back to Republicanism." Some of this was a product of the ebullient liberalism of Roosevelt's "Second Hundred Days" of 1935, while much of it represented political histrionics—O'Connor displayed the latter when he identified Snell as "a candidate for president."[32]

Yet it was also part of a broader pattern of programmatic preferences. As a rule, the agenda of the urban liberals reflected national priorities that their constituents had begun to express in 1928 with their embrace of Al Smith's progressivism: insistent promotion of social welfare measures—no matter the cost—and enthusiastic support for labor protections. The other ingredient to this progressive formula was a pluralistic vision of Americanism. Predictably, therefore, these representatives were also staunch advocates of the panoramic Americanism that had been championed by Smith and his allies—and which, when fused with issues of economic security and social welfare, had drawn urban ethnic workers into the Democratic Party.

This advocacy occurred irrespective of the Roosevelt administration's wishes; indeed, the 1930s were not a period of great federal activity on such issues. However, when presented with the opportunity, the heirs of Smith's version of progressivism were unanimous backers of pluralism. The most famous instance was the Beer Bill, backed by the president and approved overwhelmingly in both houses of Congress.[33] This was passed with total support from the Democrats of the "wet" Northeast—and indeed largely at their instigation.

Much more serious—and ultimately less fruitful—was the fight for federal antilynching legislation. Bills granting federal authorities legal powers to compel local sheriffs to investigate lynching had been introduced repeatedly in the past and had always failed to survive the machinations of filibustering southern senators. Previously, these bills had come from Republicans—providing Southern Democrats with invaluable campaign fodder. By the 1930s, however, New York Democrats had taken the lead. Robert F. Wagner repeatedly pursued antilynching legislation in the Senate; from 1934 to 1937 this went nowhere, but in 1938, reintroduction of the bill spurred a filibuster that tied up the Senate from January 6 through February 21. As Wagner's biographer gloomily concluded, "The Senate's first major civil rights debate of the New Deal era" had "ended in defeat for the proponents of racial justice."[34]

This was not the case in the House of Representatives, where filibusters were not available to racial reactionaries. There, companion legislation was introduced in the spring of 1937 by Joseph Gavagan, a New York City Democrat. Lacking the dilatory powers of their Senate brethren, southern representatives resorted to virulent race-baiting in their efforts to defeat the Gavagan bill. While the proposal passed the House by a wide margin (277 to 120, including 100 percent of the northeastern Democrats), the floor debate exposed a major ideological rift between Democratic congressmen representing the old "Solid South" and those who had been elected from the new Democratic strongholds in the urban industrial North.

Some southerners denigrated the plan as a political ploy by Tammany Hall. After all, the Irish Gavagan's Twenty-First Congressional District included large swaths of Harlem; thus, many snickered that the proposal ought to be entitled "a bill to make Harlem safe for Tammany." Mississippi's John E. Rankin went a step further: "I think it should be called 'A bill to encourage rape.' "[35]

Worse, from Rankin's perspective, was the fact that the bill fit into a broader pattern of northern Democratic assaults on long-standing racial mores. "We are told that this is just the beginning of a series of drives to destroy the color line and try to force race amalgamation on the American people," he reported. "One member from Connecticut [Herman Kopplemann], I understand, has already introduced a bill to wipe out segregation in the District of Columbia. . . . Mr. O'Connor of New York stated on the floor that he favored such a measure and hoped the gentleman from Connecticut would pursue it."[36]

North Carolina's Alfred Lee Bulwinkle, among others, agreed. Southern Democrats had been promoting party interests in Congress for decades—and now these Yankee upstarts were shattering partisan traditions and seeking to transform the very nature of the Democracy. Edward Leo O'Neill, a New Jersey freshman representing parts of Newark, retorted that northern Democrats had been hampered in their own electoral sorties by the kind of rhetoric being employed against the Gavagan bill—rhetoric that had discredited Democrats in the North and had cost candidates African American votes. When Bulwinkle then demanded to know if O'Neill meant that "the Negro vote [sent] him here," the Garden State congressman presented a basic articulation of the new, moderate Democratic position on racial inclusion. While hardly a righteous sermon from a bold civil rights pioneer, O'Neill's rejoinder was nevertheless a challenge to old Democratic attitudes—a challenge that started from the straightforward, egalitarian premises of Smith's pluralistic progressivism and pressed them toward a more just, more inclusive posture: "Lynching is a heinous crime against American concepts and as such alone should it be treated. The gentleman from North Carolina wishes to know whether I represent a Negro district. I represent a number of Negroes, and I am grateful for the suffrage of those who voted to send me here, and I intend to represent them as vigorously as I would any other person in the district. I made such a statement during my campaign, not to an audience of Negroes but to an audience of whites."[37] This speech by a relatively obscure Democratic freshman (O'Neill would not be reelected) reflected the mounting intrapartisan challenge to long-held positions on race and inclusion. The party was beginning to fulfill Al Smith's private 1928 pledge to the NAACP's Walter White, that "the old Democratic Party, ruled entirely by the South, is on its way out, and that we Northern Democrats have a totally different approach to the Negro."[38]

The historian Jordan Schwarz has argued that during the Great Depression, certain élite business and legal actors pursued "permanent improvements of

America's capital structure and its standard of living" independent of democratic whims; their "timely opportunism" was so influential that the New Deal and its enduring legacies were shaped by figures with agendas that only occasionally overlapped with the relief, recovery, and reform initiatives radiating from the White House.[39] Others, including Lizabeth Cohen, have demonstrated how rank-and-file workers began collectively to assert themselves to define the course of labor and welfare policies in the 1930s.[40] Somewhere between the power players of finance and politics and the increasingly class-conscious working masses operated the middle ranks of the New Deal Revolution: legislators who advocated in Washington on behalf of their increasingly assertive urban ethnic working-class constituents and who often pushed the Roosevelt administration toward stronger positions on the rights of labor and the government's responsibility to promote social welfare.

These figures did not "make" the New Deal, for while they supported a diverse set of initiatives, their focus remained on the problems of their home districts. But they did help to *shape* the New Deal, advocating from within Roosevelt's coalition on behalf of the pro-labor, social welfare, pluralistic progressive agenda their constituents had adopted as their own. Over the course of the 1930s and 1940s, the popularity of many New Deal initiatives, as well as Roosevelt's personal appeal to urban workers, would transform these citizens from nebulously defined self-advocates into New Deal Democrats; and since FDR had embraced the lion's share of their agenda, it was a relatively small step for these voters to evolve from Smith-era progressives into what Huthmacher has called "modern, urban liberals." The "middle-men" (and women) in this process were Smith's erstwhile allies in Congress—those legislators who represented the interests of urban workers specifically and who helped shift the focus of the New Deal increasingly toward their own constituents.

While there can be no ideal type for these urban liberal legislators, several cases are instructive in understanding their motives and their influence. A lesser-known but illustrative figure was Herman Kopplemann, a Jewish immigrant from Ukraine who became a leading Hartford Democrat and was elected to Congress in 1932 after his fellow Democrat, Congressman Augustine Lonergan, opted for a senatorial bid. Before ascending to Congress, Kopplemann had been an advocate of social welfare initiatives: as a state senator in the late 1910s, his "most notable" achievement was his sponsorship of a "widows' aid and children's dependent act."[41] During the 1928 campaign, he had been a strong supporter of Al Smith on both cultural and economic issues, and his positions on these questions remained progressive into the Depression. Once in Washington, Kopplemann consistently favored New Deal social welfare and labor programs, and indeed the congressman was a reliable Roosevelt supporter. Although he produced little legislation of note, three proposals he repeatedly introduced were an antilynching bill, a bill to promote industrial employment by enhancing the loaning power of the Reconstruction Finance Corporation, and a bill to cover emergency medical costs of war veterans whose expenses had been left unpaid after Roosevelt initiated his early drive for federal austerity.[42]

The unheralded Congressman Kopplemann is indicative of how the progressive tradition embodied by Smith in 1928 became influential with the rise of a congressional bloc of urban, working-class Democrats in the 1930s—both in his background (he was of recent-immigrant stock, represented an urban district, and had a history of support for social welfare generally and Al Smith specifically) and in his activities during the New Deal (he compiled a fairly liberal voting record, particularly on questions relating to social welfare, labor rights, and cultural pluralism). Understanding the backgrounds and agendas of some of the more noteworthy members of the urban liberal bloc helps furnish a useful profile. Like Kopplemann, they had come to Congress as advocates of labor or of social welfare; they had been strong supporters of Al Smith in 1928 and usually in 1932 as well; and they were the most strident proponents of labor and welfare legislation in the New Deal era. In their biographies and priorities, and usually in their dispositions, these were the "happy warriors" of the 1930s.

In his 1953 autobiography *You Never Leave Brooklyn*, Congressman Emanuel Celler identified the fundamental element that marked the unique perspective of these urban liberal legislators within the New Deal coalition. During Roosevelt's first months in office, Celler recalled, "I voted as the other Members of Congress did in those days of honeymoon between the Executive and Legislative branches of the Government. There was this difference though: I was not voting to remedy the new and different onslaught of economic distress which seemed suddenly to have descended upon us. I had come from a little bit of [the] world where economic distress had, it seemed, always been a part of life." Indeed, Celler realized: "What I had known, what I had seen in Brownsville, Pitkin Avenue, in the Bushwick section of Brooklyn, in the Park Places of Brooklyn, in the markets of Brooklyn, had now become the generalized commonplace experience. I had known people hungry, cold, homeless, afraid, insecure. I was not talking and voting about anything new. I represented a district that had never known leisure, had never known freedom from want and freedom from fear."[43]

Moreover, "I had now made a discovery about myself. For the first ten years of my life in Congress, I had been timid. I had been too timid to tell the truth as I saw it. In a way I had betrayed my trust." While he had fought immigration restriction, battled Prohibition, sought to establish "a Negro industrial commission," opposed "monopoly power," and "introduced a few civil rights bills," ultimately the congressman "had driven back all the emotion that rose from the Brooklyn streets, so that I could belong unobtrusively to the exclusive club of Congress." The Depression, however, "loosened my inhibitions against being different. For the first time in ten years I could be myself."[44] Conditions now permitted representatives with such an outlook to present their agenda within a more accommodating social context and under a sympathetic executive. Thus it would be legislators from districts like Celler's, with experiences and agendas similar to his, who would be the strongest forces behind most of the social welfare and labor legislation of the New Deal Congress— Celler himself was a steadfast New Deal liberal.

The most obvious figure through whom the urban liberal agenda influenced the course of the New Deal was Robert F. Wagner—one of the early architects of that agenda. Wagner's legislative prolificity as the sponsor or co-sponsor of New Deal staples including the National Industrial Recovery Act, the National Labor Relations Act, the Social Security Act, and the National Housing Act, among many other bills, is well known. Significantly, Wagner was actively pursuing this agenda prior to Roosevelt's "Hundred Days." At the time of FDR's inauguration, the New York senator had proposals pending in Congress for a federal-state employment exchange, unemployment insurance, railroad retirement insurance, investigations of conditions among African Americans working on the Mississippi River flood control project, and the legalization of beer and wine. Indeed, notes Huthmacher: "All these Wagner proposals were forerunners of the New Deal . . . and they were indicative of the groups that would benefit from New Deal policies—the destitute, the unemployed, businessmen shorn of orders and customers, the elderly, exploited minority groups, and yes, even those who yearned to take a legal drink."[45]

Wagner's experiences in New York imbued his entire agenda with such progressive principles. In fact, social welfare advocates who had worked with Wagner recognized that his background would help guide his response to the Depression and prompt him to direct the New Deal beyond recovery and toward an emphasis on economic justice. In October 1932, Lillian Wald confidently wrote her senator: "When Mr. Roosevelt enters the White House, your position in Washington and in the Senate will make many measures possible. . . . And I feel that . . . courageous men like you who have training and the sense of values will push us on."[46]

Robert Wagner is rightly remembered as the progenitor of key New Deal initiatives. His lesser-known partner in many of those initiatives, particularly

the National Labor Relations Act, was William Patrick Connery Jr., a Democratic congressman from Lynn, Massachusetts—another legislator whose
career reflected the trajectory and priorities of Smith's earlier progressivism
and its significance in shaping key features of the New Deal. After seeing combat in the world war, Connery returned to Massachusetts, where he took
work in a General Electric plant, providing him with experiences "as a laboring man" that "were to echo and re-echo throughout the land in years to
come." Connery, whose mother was an Irish immigrant and whose father
had been elected mayor of Lynn in 1912, entered political life himself in
1922—running for Congress on the pledge that "when I get there I am never
going to forget my life's work. And that life's work is to gain for every man
and woman in this country a decent living wage."[47] During the Coolidge years
he plodded away in the minority on the House Labor Committee; by the end
of the decade his efforts had already gained him recognition as "a reliable Progressive and a good friend of labor" by the *Machinists' Monthly Journal*.[48]

Connery's background among the urban working class consistently shaped
his response to the Depression, which in 1930 and 1931 included a series of
unsuccessful proposals for relief programs and labor reforms.[49] "When Billy
Connery thinks of the depression," wrote Washington reporter Bulkley
Griffin in 1931, "he does not think so much of banks or railroads as of
people. . . . When Connery thinks of the depression he sees hungry children
and men with their shoes worn through, and gaunt women." Informed by
this perspective, "When he hears the word dole and direct relief . . . he asks if
people shall starve because of a phrase."[50]

In 1932, campaigning for reelection as well as for Al Smith's presidential
nomination, Connery continued to focus on the human suffering wrought by
the Depression. "There are thousands of little children all over the United
States . . . who have not Grade A milk to drink and need it; who have no stock-
ings and who need them; who have no clothing and need it; who are starving
to death," he reported, promising to fight such conditions as long as he could.[51]
With the dawning of the Roosevelt administration, the prospects of successfully undertaking such efforts improved drastically, and several facets of
Connery's 1930 labor proposal—including "outlawing the yellow-dog con-
tract, outlawing child labor," and "insuring labor the right to organize and
the right . . . to bargain collectively"—were incorporated into the NIRA.[52]
When the NRA was dismantled in 1935, labor legislation introduced in Congress to entrench those advances (legislation that had initially received a chilly
response from the White House) became more pressing; and so the National
Labor Relations Act, sponsored in the House by Connery as chair of the Labor
Committee, was enacted that summer. Given the Massachusetts Democrat's

FIGURE 14. Representative William P. Connery (D-MA, left) and Senator Robert F. Wagner (D-NY, right), 1937. "Awaiting Decision on Labor Relations Act," April 5, 1937. Harris & Ewing Collection, Library of Congress, Washington, DC

centrality in drafting and passing the legislation, the Wagner Act "should really be known as the Wagner-Connery Act," reflected International Union of Electrical, Radio, and Machine Workers president Paul Jennings in 1965.[53]

Undeterred by any lack of recognition, the congressman sought reelection in 1936 with the motto "100 per cent for labor, 100 per cent for the veteran, and 100 per cent for social justice for all."[54] These priorities, a reflection of the Democrat's working-class background and of his constituency among the laborers of Lynn and Lawrence, sometimes placed Connery at odds with the broader priorities of Franklin Roosevelt. Thus was Connery among the leading voices against FDR's Economy Act in 1933. He similarly helped marshal the forces that overrode the president's veto of the veterans' bonus bill in 1936.[55] The nature of Connery's occasional opposition to Roosevelt serves to buttress the conclusions drawn from his customary support for the administration: he was primarily interested in guaranteeing the rights of labor and promoting social welfare. To that end, he next set out in pursuit of legislation to develop federal standards on wages, hours, and working conditions. He would not live to see his victory. Billy Connery died on June 15, 1937, at age forty-eight, in the midst of hearings on his legislation, which would eventually become the Fair Labor Standards Act.[56]

It was left to Connery's successor as chair of the Labor Committee to complete the codification of federal labor standards. As it turned out, she was no less an exemplar than Connery of the urban, ethnic, working-class, northeastern tinge of the new welfare- and labor-oriented Democrats now exerting profound influence over New Deal policy making. A representative from Jersey City, Mary Teresa Norton embodied this brand of progressivism as completely as any member of Congress.

Norton had lost her only child in infancy in 1910 and became active in social welfare work, spending many years as president of the Day Nursery Association of Jersey City. Following a trajectory strikingly similar to that of New York social workers like Frances Perkins and Belle Moskowitz, Norton's activities gained the attention of Jersey City Democratic boss Frank Hague, who in 1920 presciently suggested that Norton might make a good representative of Hudson County women on the State Democratic Committee. In 1923, she became the first Democratic woman elected as a freeholder in New Jersey, and in this capacity she leveraged her political connections to pursue her welfare agenda—gaining notoriety with her successful push to construct a state-of-the-art maternity hospital for Hudson County.[57]

Norton was elected to Congress with Boss Hague's backing the following year. She quickly gained prominence within the national party and campaigned actively across the nation for Al Smith in 1928, thrashing Prohibition and Republican administration more broadly while lauding Smith's record "on legislation for the protection of women and children."[58] With the coming of the New Deal, Norton obtained the opportunity to support such reforms, and did so consistently—her voting record reveals particular enthusiasm for bills promoting social welfare, protecting labor rights, and halting Prohibition. Upon the death of Billy Connery in 1937, Congresswoman Norton inherited the chair of the House Labor Committee, and would play a crucial role in piloting the Fair Labor Standards Act to passage in 1938.[59]

Like Wagner, Connery, and Norton, numerous members of Congress from similar urban working-class districts who had been participants in the Smith campaign and who espoused the ideals of Smith's progressivism were key figures in crafting and passing significant pieces of New Deal legislation affecting labor and social welfare. One was Arthur D. Healey of Somerville, Massachusetts, who had made a series of unsuccessful runs for political office in the 1920s, including a bid for Congress on the Smith ticket in 1928, which he lost to the incumbent Republican by 643 votes out of over 100,000 cast.[60]

Successful in 1932, Healey entered Congress with a mission to pursue specific goals of the urban working class. In the long New England tradition, this sometimes meant advocating protectionism.[61] More often it meant work in labor and housing.

While still a congressional freshman, Healey coauthored legislation establishing the Federal Housing Administration in 1934.[62] Reelected that fall, Healey continued to espouse federal aid to housing—for private home owners with attempts to fund the Home Owners Loan Corporation more robustly; for renters with the Healey-Russell Bill of 1936, which authorized "the Federal Government to pay service charges in lieu of taxes on its low-cost housing projects" to keep rents low without undermining local taxpayers.[63]

Healey was similarly active in promoting labor protections. In early 1936 he was point man in the House Judiciary Committee for the Walsh-Tobey Bill—a minimum wage compact between Massachusetts and New Hampshire (and including signatories from Connecticut, Maine, New York, Pennsylvania, and Rhode Island).[64] Later that year, he was coauthor and House sponsor of the Public Contracts Act (or Walsh-Healey Act). This law articulated minimum labor standards required of any firm doing business with the federal government, threatening to "deprive corporations of government contracts" if they failed to comply.[65] Both pieces of legislation were pragmatic, piecemeal forerunners of the Fair Labor Standards Act.

The records of Healey and Connery fuse with that of Boston's John W. McCormack, whom voters had promoted from the Massachusetts State Senate to Congress on the Smith ticket in 1928, to produce a useful profile of the priorities of Bay State Democrats in this period. McCormack helped draft the Social Security Act as well as the "soak the rich" tax of 1935, and his votes on questions of housing, work relief, and labor standards marked him as a strong administration ally on these key issues. Like his fellow northeastern Democrats, McCormack strongly opposed immigration restriction and was a committed wet. As with so many in this emerging cohort of urban liberals, moreover, McCormack's understanding of the problems of the Depression grew from personal experience. As one biographer asserted, because McCormack was "born to poverty and forced to work at age thirteen to support his widowed mother and two younger brothers," his "strong support of the New Deal came not from his sudden conversion to Roosevelt politics nor merely from party loyalty, but was rather a product of his South Boston boyhood."[66]

John J. O'Connor, a quarrelsome congressman from Manhattan who was the brother of Franklin Roosevelt's law partner Basil O'Connor, is the exception that proves the rule. He was a consistent supporter of the early New Deal, and his voting record even into 1935 and 1936 certifies him at least superficially as a party regular; yet as chairman of the House Rules Committee, O'Connor wielded great power to sidetrack New Deal priorities, which he did with increasing zeal as his indignation over presidential infringements of congressional prerogatives devolved into a churlish territoriality. This earned the chairman the political wrath of the White House and, ultimately, the dubious distinction of being the lone target of Roosevelt's 1938 "purge" to be defeated in that year's Democratic primaries.[67] O'Connor's flailing demise is instructive—he insisted before Tammany gatherings that "his record as a New Dealer was identical to that of Senator Robert F. Wagner" while also attacking "self-styled liberals" and radical labor before Republicans; he was rejected by the people of his district and replaced with a fellow Catholic Tammany Democrat who, like the bulk of his constituents, was more supportive of the New Deal.[68] When Roosevelt attempted to dislodge conservative Democrats in the South and West, he suffered political embarrassment; when he focused on the urban Northeast and targeted a Tammanyite whom Republicans denounced as "a more than 90 percent New Dealer," the president—and liberalism—carried the day.[69]

All of these figures represent particular cases in the broader story of northeastern urban liberals who pursued an agenda reminiscent of Smith's progressivism during the 1930s, and who did this in a way that profoundly influenced the course of the New Deal. There were dozens of such figures, and many, like Herman Kopplemann, did not have a great deal of major legislation to their name. Indeed while some—like Wagner—have rightly gone down in history as crucial architects of important aspects of the New Deal, and others—like Connery—ought to be remembered in a similar way, many of these figures were particularly unremarkable members of Congress. Yet besides their geographic roots in the urban Northeast and their political support among the ethnic working classes of the region, these legislators also engaged in a common, discernible pattern of support for labor and welfare legislation and did so at the behest of their constituents.

One other political characteristic that most of these Democrats shared was their strident support for Alfred E. Smith's presidential ambitions—in 1928 and usually also in 1932. The activities of many of these figures during the 1928 presidential campaign have already been noted. Interestingly, many of these same figures remained loyal to the Smith cause in the early stages of the 1932 contest. In February, Congressman Connery promised that should Smith run, his "friends, who were always loyal, will now work zealously for him not only in Massachusetts but in the New England states." Congressman McCormack was similarly "pleased" to hear of Smith's interest in another race.[70] In April, an all-star slate of Massachusetts politicos described by the *Boston Globe* as "the 'heavy artillery' of the Smith campaign" began a bombardment in support of the New Yorker's nomination. Connery and McCormack joined other important figures to tour greater Boston on Smith's behalf. At an April 24 Smith rally at Boston's Hotel Statler, a crowd of 3,500 women heard Congresswoman Norton denounce anti-Smith Democrats as "political chameleons and charlatans" and "an unprincipled band of political Judases."[71] Nor were these merely the vituperations of "stop Roosevelt" conservatives or machine pawns.[72] In a rousing address at Lawrence, Congressman Connery called for inflationary policies, generous and speedy payment of war bonuses, a lowering of the pension age from seventy to sixty-five, and the maintenance of current pay rates for federal employees, concluding that "as for Billy Connery, I am for Smith to the finish."[73]

Eventually, of course, all of these figures became New Deal Democrats and Roosevelt supporters. But their loyalty to Smith had been an accurate reflection of their constituents' preferences—at least in the spring of 1932.[74] At a rally of 500 in Quincy, Massachusetts, on April 24 (featuring, among others, Somerville attorney Arthur Healey), Dr. Joseph Santosuosso had declared the Italian vote "100 percent for Smith."[75] At least in the urban Northeast, this proved true not only of Italians but among most urban workers. On April 27, Smith swamped Roosevelt three to one in the Massachusetts primary, winning all thirty-nine Bay State cities and even sweeping Boston, where Mayor Curley had sided with FDR.[76] Indeed, Huthmacher has argued that in Massachusetts the 1932 primary "boiled down to a contest between Al Smith and James Michael Curley"; the results "demonstrated just how strong a hold the 1928 candidate retained."[77]

With a note of irony, Walter Lippmann suggested that Smith's ability to "overwhelm the Curley machine in Boston itself is clear proof that the 'forgotten men' intervened in the contest."[78] The same week, in Connecticut's Democratic caucuses, Smith defeated Roosevelt in "virtually all the large cities"; he won 75 percent of Hartford County delegates (many of the other 25 percent simply remained unpledged); and he captured 375 delegates statewide—to Roosevelt's 51.[79] Smith went on to wins in New Jersey and Rhode Island, and received strong support among the urban workers of Pennsylvania.[80]

This was a temporary condition, however, and it had little influence on the eventual nomination. When Roosevelt emerged victorious, Democrats feared that they might alienate the northeasterners whom Smith had attracted into the party—especially in New England. In what would prove a final episode of partisan loyalty, Smith spoke on the nominee's behalf at a major rally in Boston on October 27, abandoning the "lukewarmness" of his previous Roosevelt speeches and adopting a vigor reminiscent of his own campaigns.[81] En route to the event, Smith made several stops in Connecticut, attracting fervent crowds, as he had in 1928, and remarking, "I feel like I'm running again."[82] Elected to the Senate from the Nutmeg State on Roosevelt's ticket, Augustine Lonergan would reflect that "it was [Smith's] personal magnetism and leadership that brought many thousands of votes to the polls on election day allowing the majority of the Democratic candidates to win."[83] Among the Democrats who did not win in Connecticut that year was Franklin Roosevelt; but by 1936 he too would carry the state, adding it to the Smith strongholds of Massachusetts and Rhode Island, which he had retained in 1932.

As the New Deal took hold and Roosevelt's agenda became increasingly palpable, the urban ethnic workers who had embraced Al Smith's progressivism became the most enthusiastic of New Deal Democrats.[84] Smith himself would not participate in this movement. Instead, the man once known as the Happy Warrior, increasingly bitter and increasingly isolated from his old world, launched himself in a strange and discordant new direction, hopelessly battling the unstoppable forces that he himself had helped to unleash.

Quantum Mutatus ab Illo

If Alfred E. Smith's peculiar progressivism provided fundamental inspiration for key New Deal initiatives, then how does one account for his strident 1930s conservatism? After 1928, Smith was alarmed to find his state and national profile abruptly eclipsed by that of his successor; he was increasingly perturbed by his fading political prospects and increasingly affected by new, conservative voices. Out of office, he was detached from the travails of his erstwhile constituents. Most of his progressive collaborators had remained engaged policy makers while Smith, divorced from such concerns, became subsumed in the business world and consumed by a business perspective. Tracking Smith's story through the New Deal era illuminates two important points: first, his 1930s conservatism was a fundamental break with his 1920s progressivism; second, his rightward shift, while an interesting biographical curiosity, influenced virtually nothing.

The ignominy of Smith's national landslide defeat was made bitterer still by his heartbreaking loss of New York State.[85] Simultaneously, his hand-picked inheritor of the governorship had won by a slim margin. With the ascent of Franklin Roosevelt, Smith anticipated a new role as the Empire State's éminence grise—to the point of renting an apartment at Albany's DeWitt Clinton

Hotel "to be close to Roosevelt at all times." Yet FDR "was determined to go it on his own," remaining "completely divorced from Smith's influence"— which meant not only that Robert Moses and Belle Moskowitz would not be retained by the new governor and that Smith would grow "offended" by his dismissive treatment, but also that for the first time in nearly three decades, Smith was compelled to find a new calling.[86]

Shortly after Al Smith's defeat, a longtime ally contacted him to propose a real estate investment. On November 20, 1928, Lillian Wald wrote Smith, entreating him to come home to the Lower East Side. "It would be glorious if you and your family would return," she pleaded. "It would fire the imagination of a people, and our real trouble is the lack of imagination." Moreover, Wald had identified "a lovely site . . . where the river bends at Corlears Point." Warning that "if we do not look out, the millionaires will capture it," the social work icon envisaged that "upon this site could be built a place dignified and great for you—a home that would become a shrine as Thomas Jefferson's home."[87] Smith's urban Monticello never came to be.[88] Rather than return to the Fourth Ward, Al Smith began to drift uptown.

Except for a brief, successful stint as head of a trucking firm during 1921 and 1922, Smith had spent his entire adult life in the public sector, and absent the marauding administrative techniques of his more notorious Tammany forebears, this was not a lucrative career path. This meant that financial anxieties plagued Smith throughout his life. Nevertheless, during his time in the corporate world he had forged lifelong connections with New York businessmen—most of them self-made Irishmen who shared Smith's background and his affinity for Tammany Hall. His increasingly opulent social circle, along with four terms in the executive mansion, left Smith with a taste for the high life: "After I left Albany, after living in a mansion for six years I couldn't see First Avenue very well, so I went over on Fifth Avenue." The Smiths settled in a $10,000 a year apartment on Fifth Avenue at Sixty-Third Street, from which the former governor was taxied about town in a limousine. His new, lavish lifestyle was financed through investment help from John Raskob and eventually through Smith's appointment (again by Raskob and his associate Pierre Du Pont) as president of the Empire State Building Corporation at an annual salary of $50,000.[89]

Yet Smith's timing was abysmal. If he had run for president four years too soon, he had arrived in the real estate business four years too late. The coming of the Great Depression made corporate office rentals a tough sell; thus, when the Empire State Building opened in 1931, it was three-quarters vacant. Meanwhile, his investments evaporated with everyone else's beginning in October 1929, and in the early 1930s he was "in an extremely bad position" financially, managing dutifully to maintain a façade of solvency as he continued his work beseeching struggling businessmen to lease space in his empty skyscraper.[90]

Like most Americans, Smith had real problems during the Depression. Because he was employed, housed, fed, and clothed, the former governor did not face challenges nearly as severe as those confronting many of his countrymen. Yet, having chosen Fifth Avenue over Oliver Street, Smith viewed the Depression not from the perspective of the urban workers to whom he had devoted most of his life but rather through the eyes of a businessman. His understanding of the crisis was increasingly constricted by his own experiences, for he was no longer working every day to understand and conquer the problems of ordinary citizens. Smith's new challenge was to kick-start a business intimately dependent on the good fortunes of corporate America.

This myopia was exacerbated by Smith's dramatic change in associations in the years after he departed Albany. To the end of Smith's life, Bob Wagner remained one of his closest friends—throughout the 1930s, their Sunday evening poker games descended into "hotter and hotter" political arguments, but "liquid spirits plus the good spirits invoked by reminiscences of times past invariably restored amicability as the two old cronies, arm in arm, made their unsteady exit."[91] Yet despite enduring cordiality with figures like Wagner, Frances Perkins, Eleanor Roosevelt, and others, Smith was increasingly detached from their struggles with public policy. In January 1933, the most prominent of the old voices was silenced when Belle Moskowitz died of an embolism while recovering from a bad fall.[92] Smith's views were increasingly shaped not by social workers or even Tammany precinct captains but by the businessmen with whom he maintained regular professional and social contact. As H. L. Mencken would later conclude, Smith had been "ruined by associating with rich men."[93] Arthur Schlesinger proposed a similar, albeit haughtily constructed thesis: "Plunged into a world of business against which he had no intellectual defense, he rapidly absorbed the Raskob point of view."[94]

This shift in perspective meant that Smith's 1932 bid for the Democratic nomination was not the encore of 1928 that voters in Boston, Hartford, or Scranton—not to mention a good many of their political leaders—were anticipating. Smith's ill-fated 1932 campaign was a conservative affair. It is true that he called for a federal public works program (Schlesinger called this "a last fling for the old Al Smith") and steadfastly maintained his commitment to "government ownership and control of all electrical power developed" from federal or state holdings.[95] But the heart of his program involved calls for retrenchment, budget balancing, and cuts in business taxes—to be offset by a sales tax. While it is not accurate to say that Smith's bid was simply a "stop Roosevelt" campaign—he clearly believed he deserved another chance at the nomination—it is certainly the case that Smith was the candidate of conservatives like Raskob and his Bourbon sidekick Jouett Shouse, and that most of his efforts were devoted to thwarting the ambitions of his gubernatorial successor. Indeed, Smith's 1932 campaign is best remembered for his vitriolic denunciation of FDR's "forgotten man" speech ("I will take off my coat and fight to the end against any candidate who persists in any demagogic appeal to the masses of the working people of this country to destroy themselves by setting class against class and rich against poor").[96]

His ambitions frustrated at the party convention in Chicago, Smith grudgingly settled into the role of party elder during the fall contest. This did not mean that he had accepted Roosevelt's ideas: "We should stop talking about the Forgotten Man and about class distinctions," Smith counseled in October; instead, the party should advocate fiscal prudence.[97] Nor were his views moderated with the conclusion of the campaign: in mid-November, as desperate soldiers continued demanding bonus payments, Smith complained coldly that "the veterans were imposing on the taxpayer without real justice for their claims."[98]

Smith's conservatism of 1932, even his rage against the "forgotten man" speech, was but a temperate preview of the unrestrained fury soon to be unleashed by the former governor. As an editorialist in the New Outlook, Smith became increasingly critical of the New Deal throughout 1933, decrying its "baloney dollars" and "alphabet soup." He emerged as the "most vehement" among conservative Democratic critics of the Roosevelt program, denouncing centralization, mocking administration by "inexperienced young college professors," and skewering by name New Dealers such as Donald Richberg, Harold Ickes, Henry Wallace, Harry Hopkins, and Rexford Tugwell. When Raskob and Shouse began organizing prominent businessmen into a "non-partisan" organization to "preserve the Constitution" and "safeguard Jeffersonian government" against the machinations of New Deal bureaucrats, Al Smith was among the charter members of this "American Liberty League."[99]

Under the auspices of the Liberty League, Smith delivered his most inflammatory speech on January 25, 1936, from Washington. The Democratic agenda was indistinguishable from a Socialist platform, he fumed. In fact, communism was threatening representative democracy, for the New Dealers were not Democrats at all, but rather Marxist ideologues with the temerity to "march under the banner of Jefferson, Jackson, [and] Cleveland."[100]

At this point it may have been possible that Smith had forgotten what he had once advocated; but others had not. PWA information director Mike Straus, for one, recalled Smith's 1928 Boston speech defending his own program from Herbert Hoover's similar red-baiting, reminding his boss, Secretary of the Interior Harold Ickes, that "in his reply Smith had said that the cry of socialism had always been raised by powerful interests that desired to put a damper upon progressive legislation. It was raised, according to him, by reactionary elements in the Republican party and he had fought it for twenty-five years." The next day, before the Washington press corps, Ickes had Kentucky senator Alben Barkley question him about Smith's anti-administration tirade. In a prepared response, Ickes was able to refute Smith's contemporary attacks by quoting the latter's 1928 remarks verbatim. The irony was too much— the exchange "brought down the house."[101]

Smith's 1928 running mate found it all quite distressing. Joe Robinson, still in the Senate representing Arkansas, concluded that Smith was now "the unhappy warrior," a sadly diminished sellout. "The brown derby has been discarded for the high hat; he has turned away from the East Side with those little shops and fish markets, and now his gaze rests fondly upon the gilded towers and palaces of Park Avenue." Robinson, who believed that Smith had once stood for much of what was being instituted through the New Deal, regretfully lectured the former nominee in absentia that "it was as difficult to conceive of you at the Liberty League banquet as it would be to imagine George Washington waving a cheery good-bye to the ragged and bleeding band at Valley Forge while he rode forth to dine in sumptuous luxury with smug and sanctimonious Tories in near-by Philadelphia."[102]

The president himself was bemused by the reactionary positions of his erstwhile ally, famously lamenting to Frances Perkins, "I just can't understand it. . . . Practically all the things we've done in the Federal Government are like things Al Smith did as Governor of New York. They're things he would have done if he had been President of the United States. What in the world is the matter? Why can't Al see this is the program he ought to be for?"[103]

A number of scholars have struggled admirably to determine the precise reasons Smith had taken this course.[104] Ultimately, such explanations are less meaningful than the obvious conclusion that there had in fact been a pronounced transformation—that these new positions were a departure from the old Al Smith. The Happy Warrior—jaundiced and resentful—had chosen a new, reactionary path. But his legions of political followers were reluctant to join him. Indeed, the motivations behind Smith's conversion do not matter much beyond biographical interest, because the shift affected so few people. When Smith helped author a Liberty League manifesto demanding that the Democrats dump Roosevelt and cabled it to the party's 1936 convention in Philadelphia, the document stirred conversations—but the party simply chose not to respond. The public reaction was similar to that of Congressman O'Connor, who dismissed the Smith telegram as "an impertinence."[105] In October, after Smith delivered a radio address for Republican presidential nominee Alfred M. Landon, there was no outpouring of urban support for the challenger from Kansas; instead, a Democratic club on Second Avenue in Manhattan took Smith's portrait down from their wall.[106] The next month, when Smith formally took his "walk" out of the party to which he had devoted his life and into a booth to vote Republican for the first time, no one followed. The working-class, ethnic cities that he had secured for the Democracy in 1928 became *more* Democratic in 1936.

Smith's greatest influence on the politics of the 1930s had been exerted the preceding decade. As a presidential nominee, the Happy Warrior had welcomed millions into his party with a straightforward articulation of his

FIGURE 15. President Franklin Delano Roosevelt (center) joins Congressman Herman Kopplemann (D-CT, center-right) at a campaign stop in 1940. Herman Kopplemann Collection, Jewish Historical Society of Greater Hartford, West Hartford, Connecticut.

progressive vision for humanitarian government. Smith had always pictured the Democratic Party as the vehicle that would transport "the people" toward a just society, and so he had ushered his enthusiastic followers aboard the Democracy for a drive to an America marked by cultural tolerance and a strong concern for social welfare. During a national campaign that centered on this particular progressive platform, he helped urban ethnic working-class Democrats articulate an agenda based on their own definition of progress. As the Great Depression struck and these Smith voters became an increasingly powerful bloc within the Democratic coalition, their drive began to pick up momentum: they were able to influence the directions in which Roosevelt would steer his New Deal, leveraging their electoral clout and mobilizing their vibrant cohort of political representatives. In this way, working-class urban ethnic Democrats wielded their newfound power and institutionalized the most important facets of Smith's progressivism within the emerging liberal order.

Al Smith had been a hero to many of these voters. For over a decade he had been their foremost champion. Now their agenda was building steam; but the old conductor refused to remain on board. This baffled many admirers and broke many hearts—to her death, Lillian Wald kept a clipping of a 1936 article from the New York *Sunday News* that pondered Smith's renunciation of his former ideals.[107] Among urban Democrats still struggling to reshape the nation to reflect their conception of social justice, the vanquished warrior was reluctantly relegated to irrelevance. While the working masses continued to board the refashioned Democracy in search of a better life in a more equitable nation, Smith disembarked—a sad, bitter, increasingly disregarded figure. As the New Deal steamed irrepressibly toward the future, Alfred E. Smith was left at the station, a surly old man shaking his fist angrily from the platform as history passed him by.

NOTES

Introduction

1. "Cloudy Fall Weather for Smith Visit Here," *Boston Globe* (hereafter *BG*), October 24, 1928, 1; "The Weather," *BG*, October 24, 1928, 1; quoted from "The Weather," *BG*, October 25, 1928, 1.

2. M. E. Hennessy, "Crowds Greet Train at All of Its Stops," *BG*, October 25, 1928, 21; "10,000 Hail Smith Party Going through Pittsfield," *BG*, October 25, 1928, 21; "Thousands Greet Governor Smith at Springfield," *Holyoke Daily Transcript*, October 24, 1928, 1; "30,000 People Cheer Gov Smith as He Halts Here on Way to Boston," *Springfield Daily News*, October 24, 1928, 1; "Worcester Crowd Comes Early to See Governor," *BG*, October 25, 1928, 21; "Greeting Gov. Smith on His Way to Win the Atlantic Seaboard," *New York World* (hereafter *NYW*), October 25, 1928, 4; "150,000 Hail Smith on Boston Common," *BG*, October 25, 1928, 1, 24; John D. Merrill, "Smith Issues Reply to Hoover at Arena," *BG*, October 25, 1928, 1, 24; Louis M. Lyons, "Boston Gives Heart to Candidate Smith, Greeting Breaks All Records," *BG*, October 25, 1928, 1, 23; "Overflow Meetings Almost Miss Smith," *BG*, October 25, 1928, 22; "Battle of the Atlantic," *Time*, November 5, 1928; "Arena Crowd Twice Breaks Police Lines," *BG*, October 25, 1928, 1, 24; Charles Michelson, "Boston's Greeting to Smith Outdoes One for Lindbergh," *NYW*, October 25, 1928, 1; Charles Michelson, "Smith Smites Hoover for Cry of 'Socialism'; Boston Wild over Him," *NYW*, October 25, 1928, 1; U.S. Department of Commerce, Bureau of the Census, *Fourteenth Census of the United States, Taken in the Year 1920: Population 1920—Number and Distribution of Inhabitants* (Washington, DC: Government Printing Office, 1921), 229.

3. First quote from "A Conversation with Robert Moses," 1973, Columbia Oral History Research Office, Columbia University, New York (hereafter Columbia Oral History), 14; second quote from Alfred E. Smith, "Address of Acceptance, Albany," in Democratic National Committee, *Campaign Addresses of Governor Alfred E. Smith, Democratic Candidate for President, 1928* (Washington, DC: Democratic National Committee, 1929) (hereafter *Campaign Addresses*), 1–26, quote from 1–2.

4. "Text of Hoover's Speech on Relation of Government to Industry," *New York Times* (hereafter *NYT*), October 23, 1928, 2.

5. William E. Leuchtenburg, *Herbert Hoover* (New York: Henry Holt, 2009), 72; "Calls Hoover Better Fitted," *BG*, October 24, 1928, 1.

6. Quoted in "Stenographic Report of Smith's Boston Speech Answering Hoover on 'State Socialism,'" *NYT*, October 25, 1928, 2; Alfred E. Smith, "Boston," in *Campaign Addresses*, 203–218; Michelson, "Smith Smites Hoover for Cry of 'Socialism,'" 1.

7. "Text of Hoover's Speech on Relation of Government to Industry," 2.

8. "Stenographic Report of Smith's Boston Speech Answering Hoover," 2.

9. Thomas F. McGrath to George W. Norris, September 30, 1928, George W. Norris Papers, Library of Congress, Washington, DC (hereafter Norris Papers), box 4, folder 15—1928 Presidential Campaign (Smith).

10. "Stepping Out," *Brooklyn Eagle* (hereafter *BE*), August 28, 1928, 8.

11. L. Mastriani, letter to the editor, *Newark Evening News*, October 30, 1928, 13; "Luke Warm," letter to the editor, *Hartford Courant* (hereafter *HC*), September 30, 1928, A2; Alexander Bielski, letter to the editor, *Springfield Daily News*, November 1, 1928, 8; V. Gentile, letter to the editor, *Westerly Sun*, October 7, 1928, 4.

12. See, for example, Robert A. Slayton, *Empire Statesman: The Rise and Redemption of Al Smith* (New York: Free Press, 2001), 125–233; Oscar Handlin, *Al Smith and His America* (Boston: Little, Brown, 1958), 90–111; Elisabeth Israels Perry, *Belle Moskowitz: Feminine Politics and the Exercise of Power in the Age of Alfred E. Smith* (Boston: Northeastern University Press, 1992), 122–183; Paula Eldot, *Governor Alfred E. Smith: The Politician as Reformer* (New York: Garland, 1983).

13. Eldot, *Governor Alfred E. Smith*, 399.

14. David Burner, *The Politics of Provincialism: The Democratic Party in Transition, 1918–1932* (New York: Knopf, 1968), 194–197. In *Anxious Decades*, Michael Parrish declares that "Smith ran an ideologically conservative campaign." William E. Leuchtenburg's *The Perils of Prosperity* suggests that Smith was either unable or unwilling "to establish a progressive position sharply different from Hoover's," while Arthur M. Schlesinger's *The Crisis of the Old Order* portrays Smith's campaign as an ambivalent one, "too liberal for the business community . . . too mild for the more ardent reformers." Donald McCoy classified Smith's stance on issues as "an amalgam . . . designed to appeal to both economic liberals and conservatives." Michael E. Parrish, *Anxious Decades: America in Prosperity and Depression, 1920–1941* (New York: Norton, 1992), 213; William E. Leuchtenburg, *The Perils of Prosperity: 1914–32* (Chicago: University of Chicago Press, 1958), 234; Arthur M. Schlesinger Jr., *The Crisis of the Old Order: 1919–1933*, vol. 1 of *The Age of Roosevelt* (Boston: Houghton Mifflin, 2002), 128; Donald R. McCoy, *Coming of Age: The United States during the 1920's and 1930's* (New York: Penguin, 1973), 146–150.

15. Slayton, *Empire Statesman*, 275. See also Allan J. Lichtman, *Prejudice and the Old Politics: The Presidential Election of 1928* (Chapel Hill: University of North Carolina Press, 1979), 5.

16. Parrish, *Anxious Decades*, 209.

17. "The Best People" editorial, *Beatrice Daily Sun*, October 7, 1928, 10.

18. Translated by Smith's office. Nazzareno Marconi to Alfred E. Smith, May 21, 1928, George Graves Papers, New York State Archives, Albany, New York (hereafter Graves Papers), box 44, folder MAR.

19. Joseph F. Nolan, letter to the editor, *Newark Evening News*, November 3, 1928, 13.

20. Walter Lippmann, "The Sick Donkey: Democratic Prospects for 1928," *Harper's Magazine* 155 (September 1927): 415–421, quote from 418.

21. Handlin, *Al Smith*, 6–8.

22. Slayton, *Empire Statesman*, 16; Handlin, *Al Smith*, 12; Emily Smith Warner, with Hawthorne Daniel, *The Happy Warrior: The Story of My Father, Alfred E. Smith* (Garden City, NY: Doubleday, 1956), 26.

23. Research by Frances Perkins has shown that Smith was in fact of mixed Irish, Italian, English, and German extraction. While this is a fascinating biographical point, there is no evidence Smith knew it; indeed, Smith's lineage is not as significant to this study as his *professed* heritage, which was, according to one grandson, "100% Irish." Slayton, *Empire Statesman*, 9–13; Matthew Josephson and Hannah Josephson, *Al Smith: Hero of the Cities; A Political Portrait Drawing on the Papers of Frances Perkins* (Boston: Houghton Mifflin, 1969), 8–18.

24. Handlin, *Al Smith*, 12.

25. Ibid.; "National Affairs: The Brown Derby," *Time*, April 30, 1928, 9–11.

26. "Tribute Given to Alfred E. Smith at School Dedication," *NYT*, December 13, 1966, 51.

27. Arthur Mann, introduction to *Plunkitt of Tammany Hall: A Series of Very Plain Talks on Very Practical Politics*, ed. William L. Riordan (New York: Dutton, 1963), vii–xxii, x; Terry Golway, *Machine Made: Tammany Hall and the Creation of Modern American Politics* (New York: Liveright, 2014), 60–87, 290–301.

28. Riordan, *Plunkitt of Tammany Hall*, 27–28, 37.

29. See, for example, James J. Connolly, *An Elusive Unity: Urban Democracy and Machine Politics in Industrializing America* (Ithaca, NY: Cornell University Press, 2010), 31; Clifton K. Yearley, *The Money Machines: The Breakdown and Reform of Governmental and Party Finance in the North, 1860–1920* (Albany: State University of New York Press, 1970), 105–118; and Riordan, *Plunkitt of Tammany Hall*, 3–6.

30. Handlin, *Al Smith*, 20–21.

31. "National Affairs: The Brown Derby," 10.

32. Warner, *The Happy Warrior*, 40–41; Handlin, *Al Smith*, 12–17.

33. Handlin, *Al Smith*, 26–27.

34. Robert A. Caro, *The Power Broker: Robert Moses and the Fall of New York* (New York: Vintage, 1975), 118.

35. Handlin, *Al Smith*, 27.

36. Ibid., 27; Caro, *The Power Broker*, 118–120, 122.

37. Julian E. Zelizer, *Governing America: The Revival of Political History* (Princeton: Princeton University Press, 2012), 6. See also: *America at the Ballot Box: Elections and Political History* ed. Gareth Davies and Julian E. Zelizer (Philadelphia: University of Pennsylvania Press, 2015), 1–6.

1. The Making of a Progressive

1. For example, Arthur S. Link, "What Happened to the Progressive Movement in the 1920's?," *American Historical Review* 64, no. 4 (July, 1959): 833–851. Other scholars who have noted progressive elements surviving into the 1920s include Clarke Chambers and Robyn Muncy, whose works are discussed below.

2. For example, Gary Gerstle, "The Protean Character of American Liberalism," *American Historical Review* 99, no. 4 (October 1994): 1043–1073, quote from 1051. On the status revolution: Richard Hofstadter, *The Age of Reform: From Bryan to F.D.R.* (New York: Vintage, 1955); bureaucratization: Robert H. Wiebe, *The Search for Order, 1877–1920* (New York: Hill and Wang, 1967); social control: Michael E. McGerr, *A Fierce Discontent: The Rise and Fall of the Progressive Movement in America, 1870–1920* (New York:

Free Press, 2003); European connections: Daniel T. Rodgers, *Atlantic Crossings: Social Politics in a Progressive Age* (Cambridge, MA: Belknap Press of Harvard University Press, 1998); James T. Kloppenberg, *Uncertain Victory: Social Democracy and Progressivism in European and American Thought, 1870–1920* (New York: Oxford University Press, 1986); public interest: Thomas R. Pegram, *Partisans and Progressives: Private Interest and Public Policy in Illinois, 1870–1922* (Urbana: University of Illinois Press, 1992); Shelton Stromquist, *Reinventing "the People": The Progressive Movement, the Class Problem, and the Origins of Modern Liberalism* (Urbana: University of Illinois Press, 2006).

3. Mugwumps: Hofstadter, *The Age of Reform*; new middle class: Wiebe, *The Search for Order*; McGerr, *A Fierce Discontent*; worldly reformers: Rodgers, *Atlantic Crossings*; settlement house workers: Kathryn Kish Sklar, *Florence Kelley and the Nation's Work: The Rise of Women's Political Culture, 1830–1900* (New Haven, CT: Yale University Press, 1995); machine politicians: John D. Buenker, *Urban Liberalism and Progressive Reform* (New York: Norton, 1973).

4. Peter G. Filene, "An Obituary for 'The Progressive Movement,'" *American Quarterly* 22, no. 1 (Spring 1970): 20–34; Daniel T. Rodgers, "In Search of Progressivism," *Reviews in American History* 10, no. 4 (December 1982): 113–132, quote from 123.

5. For example, James J. Connolly, *The Triumph of Ethnic Progressivism: Urban Political Culture in Boston, 1900–1925* (Cambridge, MA: Harvard University Press, 1998).

6. Arthur S. Link and Richard L. McCormick, *Progressivism* (Wheeling, IL: Harlan Davidson, 1983), 2.

7. For example: Buenker, *Urban Liberalism*; John D. Buenker, "The Mahatma and Progressive Reform: Martin Lomasney as Lawmaker, 1911–1917," *New England Quarterly* 44, no. 3 (September 1971): 397–419; J. Joseph Huthmacher, "Urban Liberalism and the Age of Reform," *Mississippi Valley Historical Review* 49, no. 2 (September 1962): 231–241; J. Joseph Huthmacher, *Senator Robert F. Wagner and the Rise of Urban Liberalism* (New York: Atheneum, 1968); Robert F. Wesser, *A Response to Progressivism: The Democratic Party and New York Politics, 1902–1918* (New York: New York University Press, 1986).

8. J. Joseph Huthmacher, "Charles Evans Hughes and Charles Francis Murphy: The Metamorphosis of Progressivism," *New York History* 46, no. 1 (January 1965): 25–40.

9. Richard B. Sherman, "The Status Revolution and Massachusetts Progressive Leadership," *Political Science Quarterly* 78, no. 1 (March 1963): 59–65, quote from 59.

10. John D. Buenker, "Sovereign Individuals and Organic Networks: Political Cultures in Conflict during the Progressive Era," *American Quarterly* 40, no. 2 (June 1988): 187–204, quote from 188.

11. Ibid., 198–199; John D. Buenker, "The Urban Political Machine and the Seventeenth Amendment," *Journal of American History* 56, no. 2 (September 1969): 305–322.

12. Otis Graham Jr., *An Encore for Reform: The Old Progressives and the New Deal* (New York: Oxford University Press, 1967), 38; Clarke A. Chambers, *Seedtime of Reform: American Social Service and Social Action, 1918–1933* (Minneapolis: University of Minnesota Press, 1963).

13. Robyn Muncy, *Creating a Female Dominion in American Reform: 1890–1935* (New York: Oxford University Press, 1991), 36–37; Susan Ware, *Partner and I: Molly Dewson, Feminism, and New Deal Politics* (New Haven, CT: Yale University Press, 1987), 33.

14. Muncy, *Creating a Female Dominion*, 3–37, quote from 3; Sklar, *Florence Kelley*, 171–316.

15. Linda Gordon, *Pitied but Not Entitled: Single Mothers and the History of Welfare* (Cambridge, MA: Harvard University Press, 1994), 55; Molly Ladd-Taylor, *Mother-Work: Women, Child Welfare, and the State, 1890–1930* (Urbana: University of Illinois Press, 1994), 75; Patrick Wilkinson, "The Selfless and the Helpless: Maternalist Origins of the U.S. Welfare State," *Feminist Studies* 25, no. 3 (Autumn 1999): 571–597; Gwendolyn Mink, *The Wages of Motherhood: Inequality and the Welfare State, 1917–1942* (Ithaca, NY: Cornell University Press, 1995); Eileen Boris and S. J. Kleinberg, "Mothers and Other Workers: (Re)Conceiving Labor, Maternalism, and the State," *Journal of Women's History* 15, no. 3 (Autumn 2003): 90–117; Joanne L. Goodwin, *Gender and the Politics of Welfare Reform: Mothers' Pensions in Chicago, 1911–1929* (Chicago: University of Chicago Press, 1997); Kathryn Kish Sklar, "The Historical Foundations of Women's Power in the Creation of the American Welfare State, 1830–1930," in *Mothers of a New World: Maternalist Politics and the Origins of Welfare States*, ed. Seth Koven and Sonya Michel (New York: Routledge, 1993), 43–93; John McGuire, "From the Courts to the State Legislatures: Social Justice Feminism, Labor Legislation, and the 1920s," *Labor History* 45, no. 2 (May 2004): 225–246.

16. Corruption: Joseph F. Dinneen, *The Purple Shamrock: The Hon. James Michael Curley of Boston* (New York: Norton, 1949), 50–61, 299–313; John M. Allswang, *Bosses, Machines, and Urban Voters* (Baltimore: Johns Hopkins University Press, 1977), 36–90; Arthur Mann, *La Guardia Comes to Power, 1933* (Chicago: University of Chicago Press, 1965), 51–62; Caro, *The Power Broker*, 324–325; William L. Riordan, ed., *Plunkitt of Tammany Hall: A Series of Very Plain Talks on Very Practical Politics* (New York: Dutton, 1963), 3–6; 17–20. Power: Wesser, *A Response to Progressivism*, esp. 218–219. Lomasney is quoted in Buenker, "The Mahatma and Progressive Reform," 412.

17. For example: Gordon, *Pitied but Not Entitled*, 74; Connolly, *An Elusive Unity*, 122, 168–170; Linda Gordon, *Heroes of Their Own Lives: The Politics and History of Family Violence* (New York: Penguin, 1988), 14–16, 297; McGerr, *A Fierce Discontent*, 77–117; Mink, *The Wages of Motherhood*, 3–26, 77–79; Perry, *Belle Moskowitz*, 41–57; Stromquist, *Re-inventing "the People,"* 9; Gayle Gullett, "Women Progressives and the Politics of Americanization in California, 1915–1920," *Pacific Historical Review* 64, no. 1 (February 1995): 71–94.

18. Frances Perkins Oral History, Oral History Research Office, Columbia University, New York, NY (hereafter Perkins Oral History), book 2, 260–263. In fairness to Smith, Perkins, a devout Protestant, agreed with this assessment. Ibid., 260, 263.

19. Since labor protections were a key element of Smith's progressivism, it is conceivable that a third political tradition, organized labor, influenced his outlook. A number of important works have noted the contributions of the labor movement to the creation of modern political liberalism: Richard Schneirov has demonstrated that in Gilded Age Chicago, labor helped convene a reassessment of the prime tenets of liberalism, driven by "a new type of reform intellectual allied with working people in the name of social harmony and social justice," and with an especially prominent role for women. Richard Schneirov, *Labor and Urban Politics: Class Conflict and the Origins of Modern Liberalism in Chicago, 1864–97* (Urbana: University of Illinois Press, 1998), 289. The coalition described by Schneirov between urban workers and settlement house reformers is strikingly similar to the New York phenomenon described herein, and to the extent that this provided electoral power to the first Carter Harrison's Democratic

coalition, it also contained important political dynamics; however, in New York the new reform alliance took permanent command of the Democratic Party, whereas in Chicago this did not yet manifest itself in a durable transformation of a major political party. In another pertinent work, Julie Greene has shown that beginning with the 1908 presidential campaign, Samuel Gompers and the American Federation of Labor embraced partisanship and became key members of an evolving progressive Democratic coalition. Yet labor's political ambivalence in the 1920s reveals the transitory nature of the Wilsonian alliance; more significantly, the priorities of élite organized labor differentiate this phenomenon from Smith's New York, for the AF of L certainly did not embrace the sort of pluralistic politics described below, nor did the craftsmen of that organization show particular sympathy for the unskilled ethnic laborers who would form the backbone of the Smith coalition in 1928 (see chapter 5). Julie Greene, *Pure and Simple Politics: The American Federation of Labor and Political Activism, 1881–1917* (New York: Cambridge University Press, 1998), 142–214. See also Joseph A. McCartin, *Labor's Great War: The Struggle for Industrial Democracy and the Origins of Modern American Labor Relations, 1912–1921* (Chapel Hill: University of North Carolina Press, 1997), esp. 12–37, 199–227.

20. Handlin, *Al Smith*, 21–26.

21. Perkins Oral History, book 1, 238, 241, 417, 428.

22. Perry, *Belle Moskowitz*, 122; Caro, *The Power Broker*, 119–122.

23. "The Reminiscences of Joseph M. Proskauer," 1962, Oral History Research Office, Columbia University, 98.

24. Huthmacher, "Charles Evans Hughes and Charles Francis Murphy," 30–32.

25. Henry F. Pringle, *Alfred E. Smith: A Critical Study* (New York: Macy-Masius, 1927), 142; Huthmacher, *Senator Robert F. Wagner*, 19.

26. "The Reminiscences of Robert F. Wagner, Jr.," Oral History Research Office, Columbia University, 12. According to Robert Wagner Jr., the boy died in infancy.

27. George Martin, *Madam Secretary: Frances Perkins* (Boston: Houghton Mifflin, 1976), 85; Perry, *Belle Moskowitz*, 79.

28. Perry, *Belle Moskowitz*, 83.

29. Perkins Oral History, book 1, 140.

30. Ibid., 142–143; Alfred E. Smith, *Up to Now* (New York: Viking, 1929), 91; Martin, *Madam Secretary*, 76–90.

31. Perkins Oral History, book 1, 143.

32. Frances Perkins, *The Roosevelt I Knew* (New York: Viking, 1946), 22.

33. Huthmacher, *Senator Robert F. Wagner*, 10–11.

34. Perkins Oral History, book 1, 162.

35. Ibid., 169.

36. Perry, *Belle Moskowitz*, 83.

37. Perkins Oral History, book 1, 170–172.

38. Calculated by the author from data published in the annual editions of the *New York State Legislative Record and Index* (Albany, NY: Legislative Index Publishing Group, various years): *1910*, 277–278, 290; *1911*, 352, 368; *1912*, 303, 316–317; *1913*, 448–449; *1914*, 322–323. See also Caro, *The Power Broker*, 124.

39. Perkins Oral History, book 1, 93.

40. Robert F. Wagner, untitled speech, 1912, Robert F. Wagner Papers, Georgetown University, Washington, DC (hereafter Wagner Papers), box 327, folder 7.

41. Richard F. Welch, *King of the Bowery: Big Tim Sullivan, Tammany Hall, and New York City from the Gilded Age to the Progressive Era* (Albany: State University of New York Press, 2008), 157–161.

42. Wesser, *A Response to Progressivism*, 95–96, 197. See also Annelise Orleck, *Common Sense and a Little Fire: Women and Working-Class Politics in the United States, 1900–1965* (Chapel Hill: University of North Carolina Press, 1995), 15–86.

43. Henry Moskowitz, "New York's East Side as a Political Barometer," *Outlook*, February 27, 1918, 325–327, quote from 326.

44. Wesser, *A Response to Progressivism*, 153–156, 213–214; Moskowitz, "New York's East Side as a Political Barometer," 326; Buenker, *Urban Liberalism*, 11; Thomas M. Henderson, *Tammany Hall and the New Immigrants: The Progressive Years* (New York: Arno, 1976), 266.

45. Moskowitz, "New York's East Side as a Political Barometer," 326–327.

46. Ibid., 326.

47. John Buenker has noted a similar evolution among bosses in many large northern cities. Buenker, *Urban Liberalism*, 31.

48. Riordan, *Plunkitt of Tammany Hall*, 33; Perkins Oral History, book 1, 85–95, 106. See also Golway, *Machine Made*, 197.

49. Moskowitz, "New York's East Side as a Political Barometer," 325; Buenker, *Urban Liberalism*, 32.

50. Perkins Oral History, book 2, 21, 36. Emphasis added.

51. Rebecca Edwards has challenged this widely held understanding of women's political independence in the Progressive Era, noting that that in the Gilded Age, women—especially suffragists—"sought their victories largely by partisan means," and that the ideology accompanying political realignment in the 1890s made "certain female political roles, recognized by men in Gilded Age campaigns . . . temporarily unavailable in the first decade of the twentieth century." Rebecca Edwards, *Angels in the Machinery: Gender in American Party Politics from the Civil War to the Progressive Era* (New York: Oxford University Press, 1997), 9–10.

52. Perkins Oral History, book 1, 211–212.

53. Ibid., book 2, 39–42.

54. Ibid., 43.

55. Ibid., 44, 46–47. In fact, beginning in 1918, Smith aggressively encouraged women to register as Democrats. "Candidate Smith Talks to Women," *New York Times*, September 21, 1918, 8.

56. Frances Perkins, "Outline Used at Rainy Day Club, New York, 1911," Frances Perkins Papers, Columbia University (hereafter Perkins Papers), box 42, 1. See also Frances Perkins, "Notes for Report to Consumers' League, 4/7/11," Perkins Papers, box 42.

57. Frances Perkins, "Notes for Report to Consumers' League, 10/6/11," Perkins Papers, box 42, 1. Emphasis in original.

58. Frances Perkins, "Notes for Address on the McManus Bill, Albany, 1/1912," Perkins Papers, box 42, 1; Frances Perkins, "Notes for Lecture: 'Remedies for Unemployment,' Adelphi College, Garden City, NY, 3/5/12," Perkins Papers, box 42, 2–3.

59. Perkins biographer Kirstin Downey notes that Smith "chided" a reluctant Perkins: "If you girls are going to get what you want through legislation, there better not be any separation between social workers and the government." Kirstin Downey, *The Woman behind the New Deal: The Life of Frances Perkins, FDR's Labor Secretary and His Moral Conscience* (New York: Nan A. Talese, 2009), 77.

60. For example, Hull-House activists had won labor legislation in Illinois as early as the 1890s. Jane Addams, *Twenty Years at Hull-House* (Boston: Bedford / St. Martin's, 1999), 122–136.

61. McGuire, "From the Courts to the State Legislatures," 226.

62. Sklar, *Florence Kelley*, 236–264; Muncy, *Creating a Female Dominion*, 48.

63. See Allen F. Davis, "Settlement Workers in Politics, 1890–1914," *Review of Politics* 26, no. 4 (October 1964): 505–517.

64. Connolly, *An Elusive Unity*, 115, 118–122; Davis, "Settlement Workers in Politics, 1890–1914," 509; Harold Platt, "Jane Addams and the Ward Boss Revisited: Class, Politics, and Public Health in Chicago, 1890–1930," *Environmental History* 5, no. 2 (April 2000): 194–222; Allen F. Davis, "The Settlement Worker versus the Ward Boss," in *Urban Bosses, Machines, and Progressive Reformers*, ed. Bruce M. Stave (Lexington, MA: D. C. Heath, 1972), 102–117.

65. Davis, "Settlement Workers in Politics, 1890–1914," 516. Roosevelt biographer John Morton Blum notes that "it was a party with only three assets, all transitory: enthusiasm, money, and a Presidential candidate." John Morton Blum, *The Republican Roosevelt* (New York: Atheneum, 1967), 150. See also Arthur S. Link, *Woodrow Wilson: A Brief Biography* (Chicago: Quadrangle Books, 1972), 58.

66. Mary Simkhovitch, "Are Social-Settlers De-barred from Political Work?" Mary Simkhovitch Papers, Schlesinger Library, Radcliffe College, Harvard University, Cambridge, MA, box 3, folder 61, 3–4. This item is undated, but appears to have been written in the aftermath of World War I because it speaks of "reconstruction" programs—the popular nomenclature for assorted welfare initiatives of that period.

67. For example: Frances Perkins, "Notes for Campaign Address, for Al Smith, NY, 1920"; "Notes for Campaign Speech for Al Smith, Troy, NY, 11/3/22"; "Campaign Speech for Governor Alfred E. Smith, NY, 10/15/24"; "Notes for Campaign Speech, to Reelect Gov. Smith and to Elect Senator Wagner, Troy, NY, 10/29/26," Perkins Papers, box 43.

68. James Malcolm, ed., *The New York Red Book: An Illustrated Legislative Manual of the State* (Albany, NY: J. B. Lyon, 1928), 165.

69. Perkins Oral History, book 2, 574.

70. For example, Lillian Wald to Alfred E. Smith, May 20, 1911, Lillian Wald Papers, New York Public Library, New York, NY (hereafter Wald Papers), reel 1. Indeed, Wald had been active in electoral politics, fighting against Tammany as a member of the Woman's Municipal League of New York City. S. Sara Monoson, "The Lady and the Tiger: Women's Electoral Activism in New York City before Suffrage," *Journal of Women's History* 2, no. 2 (Fall 1990): 100–135, esp. 100.

71. Lillian Wald to Mrs. E. Broden Harriman, August 12, 1912, Wald Papers, reel 1.

72. Lillian Wald to Mrs. E. Broden Harriman, telegram, August 10, 1912, Wald Papers, reel 1.

73. The evolving attitudes of Smith and other Tammany politicians toward women's political participation in this period are noteworthy. In the early teens, Smith and the Democrats had helped defeat women's suffrage amendments in the legislature, and Tammany opposition led to the "decisive defeat" of a statewide suffrage referendum by New York City voters in 1915. However, in 1917, the machine had adopted a position of "true neutrality," and the referendum carried the metropolis as well as the state; and in 1919, Governor Smith "called the Legislature in special session . . . in order to record New York among the first of the States to ratify the woman suffrage amendment"; by 1928, Democratic literature could accurately boast of his *relatively* enlightened attitude toward women, praising his "appointment of women to high State offices," his struggle to "secure equal pay for women for equal work in the teaching profession," and his achievement of "equal representation for women in party affairs." Democratic National Committee, *What Everybody Wants to Know about Alfred E. Smith* (New York: Democratic National Committee, 1928), 13–14. The definitive article on this process is John D. Buenker, "The Urban Political Machine and Woman Suffrage: A Study in Political Adaptability," *The Historian* 33, no. 2 (February 1971): 264–279, quotes from 267, 269.

74. The Wald Papers contain no correspondence pertaining to her opinions on the 1918 campaign, although letters written after the fact strongly imply support for Smith. Lillian Wald to Alfred E. Smith, December 28, 1918, Wald Papers, reel 2.

75. Lillian Wald to Alfred E. Smith, January 9, 1920, Wald Papers, reel 2.

76. Alfred E. Smith to Lillian Wald, January 13, 1920; Wald to Smith, January 15, 1920, Wald Papers, reel 2.

77. Lillian Wald to Joseph Proskauer, October 5, 1920; Wald to Proskauer, October 8, 1920; Secretary to Miss Wald to Proskauer, October 18, 1920, Wald Papers, reel 2.

78. Lillian Wald to Alfred E. Smith, September 12, 1923, Wald Papers, reel 2.

79. Secretary to Miss Wald to Mrs. Henry Moskowitz, August 15, 1923, Wald Papers, reel 2.

80. Both Proskauer and Lehman were also noted progressives, and Lehman had spent time working at the Henry Street Settlement. Nevertheless, Wald was involved in Democratic politics on behalf of these progressive candidates, demonstrating a commitment to partisan action beyond a personal attachment to Al Smith. Secretary to Miss Wald to "Campaign Committee for Justice Joseph M. Proskauer," October 24, 1923; Lillian Wald to Franklin D. Roosevelt, October 16, 1925, Wald Papers, reel 2.

81. Perry, *Belle Moskowitz*, 41–57, 74, 98, 102, 114–117, quote from 58.

82. Ibid., 117, 121, 115–160, 161–213.

83. "Woman Smith's Colonel House," *Charlotte Observer*, July 1, 1928, 1; Robert Stone, "The Woman behind Alfred E. Smith: A Sketch of Mrs. Henry Moskowitz," *Jewish Criterion*, July 6, 1928, 3.

84. Anthony Griffin, "Speech: 'Ideals. National and International,' delivered before Women's State Democratic Forum at the Hotel Astor," November 22, 1917, Anthony Griffin Papers, New York Public Library, New York, NY (hereafter Griffin Papers), box 14, 1–2.

85. Ibid., 5.

86. Anthony Griffin, "Speech: Woman's Democratic Party," December 10, 1917, Griffin Papers, box 14.

87. Perry, *Belle Moskowitz*, 117.

88. "The Reminiscences of Robert F. Wagner, Jr.," 13; Huthmacher, "Charles Evans Hughes and Charles Francis Murphy," 32; Caro, *The Power Broker*, 128; Buenker, *Urban Liberalism*, 33.

89. Indeed, Moskowitz had been part of a reform group that attacked New York City's Sunday drinking ban in pragmatic terms in 1913. Perry, *Belle Moskowitz*, 72.

90. "Child Labor Laws Enacted since 1915," Alfred E. Smith Papers, New York State Library, Albany, NY (hereafter Smith Papers), box 2, folder 31, 2.

91. Mary E. Dreier to Alfred E. Smith, telegram, March 23, 1927, Graves Papers, box 18, folder "Dreier, Mary E."

92. Mary E. Dreier to Alfred E. Smith, December 24, 1922, Mary Dreier Papers, Schlesinger Library, Radcliffe College, Harvard University, Cambridge, MA (hereafter Dreier Papers), box 9, folder 161; "Annual Report of the Consumers' League of New York 1926–1927," Consumers' League of Massachusetts Papers, Schlesinger Library, Radcliffe College, Harvard University, Cambridge, MA, box 16, folder 264; Mary E. Dreier to Alfred E. Smith, March 31, 1925; Smith to Dreier, April 2, 1925, Graves Papers, box 18, folder "Dreier, Mary E."

93. Alfred E. Smith to Mary E. Dreier, March 25, 1927, Graves Papers, box 18, folder "Dreier, Mary E."

94. Alfred E. Smith, "Radio Address at Carnegie Hall, November 5, 1928," in Democratic National Committee, *Campaign Addresses*, 309–316, quote from 315.

95. Alfred E. Smith, "Speech at Oneonta, NY," October 14, 1924, Smith Papers, box 27, folder 274, 5.

96. Robert Moses, "Suggested Statement by the Governor regarding Results of 1920 Legislative Session and Need of a Special Session," May 28, 1920, Robert Moses Papers, New York Public Library, New York, NY (hereafter Moses Papers), box 5, folder: "Citizens Committee on Reorganization in the State Government," 2.

97. Norman Hapgood and Henry Moskowitz, *Up from the City Streets: Alfred E. Smith* (New York: Grosset and Dunlap, 1927), 239; Moses, "Suggested Statement by the Governor regarding Results of 1920 Legislative Session," 2; Perry, *Belle Moskowitz*, 132.

98. "Governor Smith's Record on Conservation: Parks and Recreation in New York State," Smith Papers, box 3, folder 43, 2–7; "Governor Smith's Record on Conservation: Forest Protection, Wildlife, and the Saratoga Reservation," Smith Papers, box 3, folder 43, 1; Caro, *The Power Broker*, 143–157.

99. Alfred E. Smith, "Speech at Flushing," October 28, 1926, Moses Papers, box 6, folder "Governor's Speeches," 1; Thomas K. McCraw, *TVA and the Power Fight, 1933–1939* (Philadelphia: J.B. Lippincott, 1971), 29.

100. On Smith and education, see Robert Chiles, "School Reform as Progressive Statecraft: Education Policy in New York under Governor Alfred E. Smith, 1919–1928," *Journal of the Gilded Age and Progressive Era*, 15, no. 4 (October, 2016): 379–398.

101. Moses, "Suggested Statement by the Governor regarding Results of 1920 Legislative Session," 2; Perry, *Belle Moskowitz*, 129, 133; J. Stanley Lemons, "The Sheppard-Towner Act: Progressivism in the 1920s," *Journal of American History* 55, no. 4 (March 1969): 776–786, esp. 782; "The Reminiscences of Charles Poletti," 1978, Oral History Research Office, Columbia University, 193; "Report on Governor Smith's

Health Program," Smith Papers, box 13, folder 158, 1, 5; "The Reminiscences of Robert F. Wagner, Jr.," 84–85.

102. Golway, *Machine Made*, 160–163, 251.

103. Slayton, *Empire Statesman*, 177–179; Michael L. Goldstein, "Black Power and the Rise of Bureaucratic Autonomy in New York City Politics: The Case of Harlem Hospital, 1917–1931," *Phylon* 41, no. 2 (2nd Quarter 1980): 187–201, esp. 189.

104. Huthmacher, *Senator Robert F. Wagner*, 13.

105. Welch, *King of the Bowery*, 132.

106. Louis Eisenstein and Elliot Rosenberg, *A Stripe of Tammany's Tiger* (New York: Robert Speller and Sons, 1966), 8–10.

107. Sol Bloom, *The Autobiography of Sol Bloom* (New York: G. P. Putnam's Sons, 1948), 10, 200.

108. Thomas M. Henderson, "Immigrant Politician: Salvatore Cotillo, Progressive Ethnic," *International Migration Review* 13, no. 1 (Spring 1979): 81–102, quotes from 82, 84–85; Alfred E. Smith, introduction to *A New American: From the Life Story of Salvatore A. Cotillo, Supreme Court Justice, State of New York*, by Nat J. Ferber (New York: Farrar and Rinehart, 1938), v–viii.

109. Allswang, *Bosses, Machines, and Urban Voters*, 91–116; Buenker, *Urban Liberalism*, 11, 19.

110. Steven P. Erie, *Rainbow's End: Irish-Americans and the Dilemmas of Urban Machine Politics, 1840–1985* (Berkeley: University of California Press, 1988), 22, 100–102; J. Joseph Huthmacher, *Massachusetts People and Politics, 1919–1933: The Transition from Republican to Democratic Dominance and Its Implications* (New York: Atheneum, 1973), 15; Evelyn Savidge Sterne, *Ballots and Bibles: Ethnic Politics and the Catholic Church in Providence* (Ithaca, NY: Cornell University Press, 2004), 46, 51, 84; Buenker, *Urban Liberalism*, 17.

111. Eisenstein and Rosenberg, *A Stripe of Tammany's Tiger*, 49.

112. Riordan, *Plunkitt of Tammany Hall*, 77–79; Welch, *King of the Bowery*, 50.

113. Slayton, *Empire Statesman*, 193, 197.

114. Welch, *King of the Bowery*, 50.

115. Riordan, *Plunkitt of Tammany Hall*, 79.

116. Slayton, *Empire Statesman*, 196–199.

117. Oscar Handlin, *The Uprooted: The Epic Story of the Great Migrations That Made the American People* (Boston: Little, Brown, 1952), 201–226; Robert King Merton, *Social Theory and Social Structure* (Glencoe, IL: Free Press, 1963), 74. The functionalist interpretation employed by Merton and Handlin (as well as Richard Hofstadter), while widely accepted, has been problematized by the historian Terrence McDonald, who views it as a reflection of Cold War liberal pluralism rather than rigorous intellectual investigation. Terrence J. McDonald, "The Problem of the Political in Recent American Urban History: Liberal Pluralism and the Rise of Functionalism," *Social History* 10, no. 3 (October 1985): 323–345, esp. 328–338. Moreover, McDonald has argued that in the case of San Francisco, machine politicians were fiscal conservatives and "did not campaign for the expansion of the public sector or use it to aid the needy, hire immigrants, or mobilize new groups into the electorate." Terrence J. McDonald, *The Parameters of Urban Fiscal Policy: Socioeconomic Change and Political Culture in San Francisco, 1860–1906* (Berkeley: University of California Press, 1986), 18. Meanwhile, Steven

Erie has countered that by the opening decades of the twentieth century, many machines were marked by fiscal extravagance. Erie, *Rainbow's End*, 79–85. A thoughtful defense of the functionalist school, sensitive to McDonald's revisionism, is provided by John M. Allswang in Bruce M. Stave, John M. Allswang, Terrence J. McDonald, and Jon C. Teaford, "A Reassessment of the Urban Political Boss: An Exchange of Views," *History Teacher* 21, no. 3 (May 1988): 293–312, esp. 295–299.

118. Robert F. Wagner, "Speech Delivered by Senator Robert F. Wagner in State Senate on a Resolution Introduced by Him, Petitioning Congress Not to Pass Literacy Test Bill," 1917, Wagner Papers, box 401, folder 1.

119. "Memorandum Emanuel Celler," September 21, 1928, Smith Papers, box 9, folder 104.

120. Meyer Jacobstein, "Memorandum re: Governor Smith's Position on Immigration," Smith Papers, box 9, folder 104.

121. For example, Slayton, *Empire Statesman*, 204.

122. "Memorandum Emanuel Celler," Smith Papers, box 9, folder 104. Emphasis added.

123. Mary E. Dreier to Warren G. Harding, telegram, April 20, 1921, Dreier Papers, box 9, folder 161.

124. Robert F. Wagner, press release, Address of Acceptance, October 8, 1926, Wagner Papers, box 401, folder 2.

2. Progressive Governor

1. For an excellent treatment of the broad social welfare agenda of Smith's Reconstruction Commission, see Perry, *Belle Moskowitz*, 115–139.

2. Alfred E. Smith, "Inaugural Address, 1919," in *Progressive Democracy: Addresses and State Papers of Alfred E. Smith*, ed. Henry Moskowitz (New York: Harcourt, Brace, 1928) (hereafter Moskowitz, *Progressive Democracy*), 71–74, quote from 73.

3. Democratic State Committee, "Agriculture under Alfred E. Smith as Governor," 1920, Smith Papers, box 1, folder 1, 8.

4. "Report of Governor Smith's Public Health Program," Smith Papers, box 13, folder 158, 1.

5. "Governor Smith Takes Office amid Crowds' Acclaim," *New York Times* (hereafter *NYT*), January 2, 1919, 1–4, quote from 4.

6. S. S. Goldwater, "To the Editor of the *New York Times*," *NYT*, January 27, 1916, 10; "Health Insurance for New York's Workers," *NYT*, January 30, 1916, SM8; Irving Fisher, "The Money Value of Human Beings," *NYT*, March 19, 1916, 18; Beatrix Hoffman, *The Wages of Sickness: The Politics of Health Insurance in Progressive America* (Chapel Hill: University of North Carolina Press, 2001), 27. See also Rodgers, *Atlantic Crossings*, 209–235.

7. Milton Terris, "National Health Insurance in the United States: A Drama in Too Many Acts," *Journal of Public Health Policy* 20, no. 1 (1999): 13–35, quote from 13.

8. Hoffman, *The Wages of Sickness*, 29, 33.

9. "Health Insurance for Workers Asked," *NYT*, January 24, 1916, 20; "Study Health Insurance," *NYT*, April 18, 1916, 22; Terris, "National Health Insurance in the United States," 13–14.

10. For a comprehensive history of the standard bill and the political battles surrounding it, with a focus on New York but with no examination of Governor Smith, see Hoffman, *The Wages of Sickness.*

11. Malcolm, *New York Red Book, 1928,* 278.

12. *New York State Legislative Record and Index* (Albany, NY: Legislative Index Publishing Group, various years): *1919,* 10; *1917,* 10.

13. "Health Insurance Measure Amended," *NYT,* March 17, 1919, 20.

14. "Insured against Illness," *NYT,* March 12, 1920, 12.

15. "Health Insurance Measure Amended," 20.

16. From the beginning, the New York bill explicitly excluded agricultural workers, domestic servants, and government employees from the program. Hoffman, *The Wages of Sickness,* 29–32; "Health Insurance Measure Amended," 20.

17. "Unite in Attack on Health Insurance," *NYT,* March 20, 1919, 5.

18. "New York Bar Finds Bad Bills in Albany," *NYT,* February 21, 1919, 8; "Wants Coal Men United," *NYT,* February 28, 1919, 13; "Health Insurance Measure Amended," 20; "Unite in Attack on Health Insurance," 5; "Move to Conserve Health," *NYT,* May 27, 1919, 17.

19. "Senators Defy Albany Leaders," *NYT,* April 2, 1919, 1, 5; "Barely Retain Assembly Control," *NYT,* April 17, 1919, 4; "Republicans Agree on Graduated Plan for Income Tax," *NYT,* April 18, 1919, 1, 7; Terris, "National Health Insurance in the United States," 14.

20. "Legislature Noted for Little It Did," *NYT,* April 20, 1919, 10.

21. "Smith Says State Neglects Health," *NYT,* August 28, 1919, 14.

22. Quoted in Hoffman, *The Wages of Sickness,* 34; see also 115–136.

23. "Governor Calls for a Referendum on Dry Amendment," *NYT,* January 8, 1920, 1–2, quote from 2.

24. Lillian Wald to Alfred E. Smith, January 9, 1920, Wald Papers, reel 2.

25. "Insured against Illness," 12.

26. "Republican Women in Tilt with Sweet," *NYT,* April 8, 1920, 11.

27. Ibid.

28. On the relationship between the Red Scare and Smith's broader agenda, see David R. Colburn, "Governor Alfred E. Smith and the Red Scare, 1919–20," *Political Science Quarterly* 88, no. 3 (September 1973): 423–444.

29. "To Extend Health Work," *NYT,* March 26, 1920, 12; Democratic State Committee, "Agriculture under Alfred E. Smith as Governor," 8; "Child Welfare," Smith Papers, box 2, folder 31, 1; "Report of Governor Smith's Public Health Program," 1; "Health Centres Bill Indorsed," *NYT,* April 2, 1920, 11.

30. Hoffman, *The Wages of Sickness,* 18–21.

31. Democratic State Committee, "Agriculture under Alfred E. Smith as Governor," 8.

32. "Assembly Buries Governor's Bills by Caucus Order," *NYT,* April 24, 1920, 1; "Legislative Record of the 1920 Session," *NYT,* April 26, 1920, 3.

33. "22 Madmen Die in Ward's Island Fire; 3 Attendants Perish in Rescue Work; Fire Apparatus Ancient and Inadequate," *NYT,* February 19, 1923, 1; "Six Inquiries Begin into Hospital Fire," *NYT,* February 19, 1923, 1–2; "War Veterans Lost Lives in the Fire," *NYT,* February 19, 1923, 2; "More Death Traps Bared by Inquiry into Ward's Island

Fire," *NYT*, February 20, 1923, 1; "Ward's Island Fire Not Due to Wiring," *NYT*, February 21, 1923, 19.

34. "Warned by Former Fires in Hospital," *NYT*, February 19, 1923, 2; "Six Inquiries Begin into Hospital Fire," 1–2; "The Ward's Island Tragedy," *NYT*, February 20, 1923, 16.

35. "Grand Jury Calls Hospital Firetrap," *NYT*, June 1, 1923, 40.

36. "Governor at Work on Fire at Hospital," *NYT*, February 20, 1923, 2.

37. Alfred E. Smith, *Progress of Public Improvements: A Report to the People of the State of New York* (Albany, NY: J.B. Lyon, 1927), 6–7.

38. "More Death Traps Bared by Inquiry into Ward's Island Fire," 1.

39. "Asks $50,000,000 for New Hospitals," *NYT*, February 22, 1923, 1, 5, quote from 1.

40. "Ward's Island Loss Laid to Crowding," *NYT*, March 14, 1923, 3.

41. "Governor Gets Plan for Safe Hospitals," *NYT*, April 28, 1923, 4.

42. "Speech by Governor Alfred E. Smith Delivered at Yonkers, October 11, 1923," Smith Papers, box 27, folder 271, 3.

43. "Memo re: Ages of State Hospitals," February 19, 1923, Smith Papers, box 1, folder 19, 1–2.

44. "Speech by Governor Alfred E. Smith Delivered at Yonkers, October 11, 1923," 4; Smith, *Progress of Public Improvements*, 7.

45. "Memorandum No. 4. Draft of paragraphs in re. Bond Issue for the Governor," Smith Papers, box 1, folder 18, 1–2.

46. Belle Moskowitz, "Memorandum for Governor Smith on Bond Issues," December 17, 1925, Belle L. Moskowitz Correspondences, New York State Archives, Albany, NY, folder 4, 1; "Allotment of Funds Derived from the Bond Issue," Belle L. Moskowitz Correspondences, folder 4, 1–3.

47. Smith, *Progress of Public Improvements*, 17.

48. Moskowitz, "Memorandum for Governor Smith on Bond Issues," 1–2.

49. "Debate between Governor Smith and Former Governor Miller on State Bond Issue," July 9, 1925, Smith Papers, box 28, folder 295, 7, 15, 16, 18, 28; "Constitution of the State of New York," in Malcolm, *New York Red Book, 1928*, 534–591, quote from 572.

50. Smith, *Progress of Public Improvements*, 119–120.

51. "Child Welfare," Smith Papers, 1.

52. "Report of Governor Smith's Public Health Program," 1.

53. "Governor Smith's Record in Relation to Public Health, Medicine and Public Welfare," Smith Papers, box 13, folder 158, 3; "Report of Governor Smith's Public Health Program," 2; "Asks More Rural Doctors," *NYT*, February 14, 1923, 4.

54. "Report of Governor Smith's Public Health Program," 2.

55. "Against a Subsidy for Rural Doctors," *NYT*, March 19, 1923, 19.

56. Alfred E. Smith, *Legislative Document No. 87, Message from the Governor Relative to Public Health in Rural Districts and Narcotic Drug Evil* (Albany, NY: J. B. Lyon, 1923), Wald Papers, reel 33, 3.

57. Ibid., 4; "Smith Asks for Act to Meet Drug Evil," *NYT*, April 12, 1923, 4.

58. "Governor Smith Gives Legislative Chart of His Proposals and the Action Taken," *NYT*, May 7, 1923, 2.

59. "Report of Governor Smith's Public Health Program," 3; "Text of Gov. Smith's Annual Message to the Legislature Detailing His Policies," *NYT*, January 8, 1925, 20.

60. "Governor Smith's Record in Relation to Public Health," 3.

61. Lemons, "The Sheppard-Towner Act," 782.

62. "Text of Gov. Smith's Annual Message to the Legislature Detailing His Policies," 20.

63. "State Aid to Counties," 1927, Smith Papers, box 13, folder 157, 1–2.

64. "Report of Governor Smith's Public Health Program," 6.

65. "State Aid to Counties," 3.

66. "Report of Governor Smith's Public Health Program," 6.

67. "Report of the Department of Mental Hygiene for the Calendar Year, 1927," Alfred E. Smith Subject and Correspondence Files, New York State Archives, Albany, NY (hereafter Smith Correspondences), reel 45, 16.

68. "Report of the Governor's Public Health Program," 6; "Report of the Department of Mental Hygiene for the Calendar Year, 1927," 16.

69. "Full Text of Governor Smith's Message to the Legislature, Setting Forth His Policies," *NYT*, January 6, 1927, 22; U.S. Department of Commerce, Bureau of Foreign and Domestic Commerce, *Statistical Abstract of the United States* (Washington, DC: U.S. Government Printing Office, various years), *1920*, 84; *1925*, 81; *1930*, 80, 88; *1933*, 79, 87.

70. "Text of Gov. Smith's Annual Message to the Legislature Detailing His Policies," 20; "Complete Text of Annual Message Read by Gov. Smith to the Legislature," *NYT*, January 7, 1926, 10; "Full Text of Governor Smith's Message to the Legislature, Setting Forth His Policies," 22; "Smith Urges Clinics to Insure Health," *NYT*, October 17, 1931, 1.

71. "Text of Gov. Smith's Annual Message to the Legislature Detailing His Policies," 20.

72. Portions of this section appear in Robert Chiles, "Working-Class Conservationism in New York: Governor Alfred E. Smith and 'The Property of the People of the State,'" *Environmental History* 18, no. 1 (January 2013): 157–183.

73. The classic text on progressives and conservation is Samuel P. Hays, *Conservation and the Gospel of Efficiency: The Progressive Conservation Movement, 1890–1920* (Cambridge, MA: Harvard University Press, 1959). See also Thomas R. Wellock, *Preserving the Nation: The Conservation and Environmental Movements, 1870–2000* (Wheeling, IL: Harlan Davidson, 2007), 13–74; Keith W. Olson, *Biography of a Progressive: Franklin K. Lane, 1864–1921* (Westport, CT: Greenwood Press, 1979), 47–119. On progressive conservation in New York, see David Stradling, *The Nature of New York: An Environmental History of the Empire State* (Ithaca, NY: Cornell University Press, 2010), 138–172.

74. "Governor Smith's Record on Conservation Parks and Recreation in New York State, Part I: 'Parks,'" Smith Papers, box 3, folder 43 (hereafter "Parks"), 1, 3; "Asks $15,000,000 to Aid State Parks," *NYT*, April 19, 1923, 4.

75. "Parks," 3–4; "Asks $15,000,000 to Aid State Parks," 4; "Constitution of the State of New York," in Malcolm, *New York Red Book, 1928*, 572.

76. State Council of Parks et al., "What the State Park Bond Issue, to Be voted on at the November Election, Will Do for You," Smith Correspondences, reel 88, 2–6.

77. "Parks," 1.

78. "What the State Park Bond Issue," 2.

79. "Parks," 4–5.

80. "Governor Smith's Comment on Action of Legislative Leaders on the State Park Program on Long Island," August 16, 1928, 1–3, Smith Correspondences, reel 88; "Parks," 5–18.

81. The Long Island story has been masterfully rendered by Robert Caro in his biography of Robert Moses, the architect of much of Smith's parks program, who would later serve the governor as secretary of state; the story need only be reviewed here insofar as it elucidates Smith's ideology on the question. Caro, *The Power Broker*, 143–240.

82. "Parks," 8, 10.

83. "Minutes for the Second Hearing . . . on the Estimates and Maps Submitted by the State Council of Parks in Accordance with the Provisions of Chapter 16 of the Laws of 1926," 1, Smith Correspondences, reel 88; "Parks," 11–13.

84. "Speech of Governor Smith to the People of the State on the Park Situation Delivered over the Radio, Thursday, June 11th, 10:00 P.M.," Smith Papers, box 28, folder 293, 10.

85. Ibid., 10–11.

86. Ibid., 11, 15.

87. It is worth completing the story of Long Island. Because the legislature held firm in June, there was no money to purchase the Taylor Estate. This might have ended in victory for the golf club had it not been for the donation of $262,000 by the philanthropist August Heckscher to the state for the purpose of purchasing the property. In 1928, Smith announced that the property, originally called Deer Range State Park after the large herd of white-tailed deer residing in the area, would be renamed Heckscher State Park in honor of its benefactor. "Parks," 15–16; "Smith Back Rested, Eager for Battle," *NYT*, August 2, 1928; "Governor Smith's Comment on Action of Legislative Leaders on the State Park Program on Long Island," August 16, 1928, 1–3.

88. "Parks," 18.

89. "Address of Hon. Alfred E. Smith at Staten Island Coliseum, October 27, 1925," Smith Papers, box 28, folder 286, 13; "Governor Smith's Primer on the Constitutional Amendments—1, 2 & 3—Public Improvement Bond Issue," Smith Papers, box 1, folder 19, 5; Smith, *Progress of Public Improvements*, 8–9.

90. "Speech of Acceptance Delivered by Governor Alfred E. Smith at Schenectady, NY, October 4, 1924," 5, Smith Papers, box 27, folder 274.

91. Smith, *Progress of Public Improvements*, 6.

92. "Speech by Governor Alfred E. Smith at Carnegie Hall," Smith Papers, box 27, folder 274, 3.

93. "Address of Governor Alfred E. Smith at Vielmeister Hall, Stapleton, S.I., on Tuesday Evening, Oct. 26, 1926," Smith Papers, box 29, folder 301, 12.

94. "Governor Smith's Record on Conservation Parks and Recreation in New York State, Part II," 1, 4.

95. Ibid., 4.

96. Ibid., 2, 7–8.

97. Melville Rosch to Alfred E. Smith, Graves Papers, box 62, folder "ROS"; T. J. McLaughlin to Smith, December 3, 1927; James S. Cawley to Smith, March 24, 1926, Smith Correspondences, reel 88.

98. Cawley to Smith, March 24, 1926; E. Cooperman to Smith, May 8, 1926; Florence G. Downs to Smith, September 12, 1923, Smith Correspondences, reel 88.

99. "Speech of Alfred E. Smith at Troy, NY, October 16, 1922," Smith Papers, box 26, folder 258, 3; "Speech of Governor Alfred E. Smith, Rochester," October 20, 1924, 4–5, Smith Papers, box 27, folder 274; "Governor Smith's Record on Conservation Parks and Recreation in New York State, Part III: 'Water Power'" (hereafter "Governor Smith's Record: Water Power"), 2.

100. Alfred E. Smith, "Water Power and Its Social Uses," *Survey Graphic* 10, no. 4 (January 1927): 421–425, esp. 421–422; "Speech of Alfred E. Smith at Troy, NY," 4.

101. "Speech of Alfred E. Smith at Troy, NY," 5.

102. "Speech of Governor Alfred E. Smith, Rochester," 7; "Governor Smith's Record: Water Power," 2.

103. "Speech of Alfred E. Smith at Troy, NY," 5; "Governor Smith's Speech at Lexington Opera House, Saturday, November 4, 1922," Smith Papers, box 26, folder 258, 5; "Governor Smith's Record: Water Power," 2.

104. Alfred E. Smith, "Speech at Elmira, NY, October 14, 1920," Smith Papers, box 26, folder 255, 3.

105. "Says Miller Avoids Water Power Issue," *NYT*, October 21, 1920, 14. Smith often repeated the argument that water power ought to be, but was not, cheaper than coal. For example, "Address of Governor Alfred E. Smith at the Town Hall, Saturday Evening, November 3, 1923, at the Closing Session of the School of Democracy of the Women's Democratic Club," Smith Papers, box 26, folder 269, 25.

106. "10,000 Hail Smith as Next Governor as He Hits Miller," *NYT*, October 31, 1920, 1, 19, quote from 19.

107. "Smith Denounces Miller as Servant of 'Big Interests,'" *NYT*, October 6, 1922, 1.

108. "Governor Smith's Record: Water Power," 3.

109. "Smith Says Miller Stifled Home Rule," *NYT*, October 17, 1922, 8; "Governor Smith's Speech at Lexington Opera House," 6.

110. Malcolm, *New York Red Book, 1928*, 376.

111. Constitution of the State of New York (1894), Art. VII, § 7, reproduced in Robert Moses, *Manual for the Use of the Legislature of the State of New York, 1928* (Albany: J. B. Lyon, 1928), 85–175, esp. 148; Malcolm, *New York Red Book, 1928*, 279; "Governor Fights Adirondacks 'Raid,'" *NYT*, September 15, 1923, 20.

112. "Fires a Broadside on Adirondack 'Raid,'" *NYT*, September 16, 1923, E1.

113. "Governor Fights Adirondacks 'Raid,'" 20.

114. "The Adirondack 'Raid,'" editorial, *NYT*, September 15, 1923, 14; "Governor Fights Adirondacks 'Raid,'" 20; "Vote No," editorial, *NYT*, October 25, 1923, 18.

115. "Assails Power Interests," *NYT*, September 22, 1923, 7; "Asks Voters to Aid Two Amendments," *NYT*, October 14, 1923, E2; F. A. Huebner, letter to the editor, *NYT*, October 27, 1923, 12; "Sees Conspiracy by 'Power Trust,'" *NYT*, October 30, 1923, 18.

116. Governor Fights Adirondacks 'Raid,'" 20.

117. Alfred E. Smith, Yonkers, October 11, 1923, Smith Papers, box 27, folder 271, 1–2; "Governor Smith's Record: Water Power," 3–4.

118. Alfred E. Smith, "Power," December 22, 1923, Smith Papers, box 22, folder 226, 1–4.

119. "Speech of Alfred E. Smith at Troy, NY," 6.

120. Smith, "Power," December 22, 1923, 4–5.

121. "Conference on Water Power Development," Smith Papers, box 23, folder 228, 17.

122. Ibid., 18, 21.

123. "Governor Smith's Record: Water Power," 4–6. "Address of Governor Alfred E. Smith Delivered at Rochester, New York, October 18th, 1926," 1.

124. Alfred E. Smith, "For Release in the Morning Papers of Monday March 15 1926," March 13, 1926, Smith Papers, box 22, folder 226, 2.

125. Alfred E. Smith, "Water Power," in Moskowitz, *Progressive Democracy*, 315–327, 318–319.

126. For example: "I have recognized that transportation, light, heat and power are necessary services to the life, health, comfort, convenience and industry of our great cities. I have held that where they are monopolies they should be public monopolies, especially where they offer a service of universal use." "Address by Governor Alfred E. Smith, Accepting Renomination as Governor," September 24, 1920, 4, Smith Papers, box 26, folder 269. On "decommodification," see Rodgers, *Atlantic Crossings*, 30.

127. "Address of Governor Alfred E. Smith Delivered at Rochester, New York, October 18th, 1926," 9.

128. "Address of Governor Alfred E. Smith at Vielmeister Hall," 16.

129. Samuel Untermyer, "Why Ogden L. Mills Is Unqualified to Be Governor of New York," November 1, 1926, Smith Papers, box 22, folder 225, 8–9.

130. Alfred E. Smith, "Speech at Flushing," October 28, 1926, Moses Papers, box 6, folder "Governor's Speeches."

131. For example, "Mills Is Linked in Power Combine," *New York World*, October 20, 1926.

132. "Use Schools to Beat Smith's Power Plan," *NYT*, May 29, 1928, 1, 10.

133. Smith, "Water Power and Its Social Uses," 422, 424.

134. Ibid., 425.

135. On the widespread contemporary national interest in hydropower: Walter H. Voskuil, "Water-Power Situation in the United States," *Journal of Land and Public Utility Economics* 1, no. 1 (January 1925): 89–101, 89. See also Samuel Gompers, "The Future of Giant Power: Tyrant-Servant or Coordinator," August 1924; Gompers, "Giant Power—Its Possibilities, Potentialities and Its Administration," December 1923; "Resolution Adopted by 1923 Convention, American Federation of Labor, Portland, Oregon," all in Smith Papers, box 22, folder 224.

136. As Thomas McCraw notes of the water power potential at Muscle Shoals, Alabama, "The presence of government structures capable of producing vendible items such as electricity . . . offended the Harding administration's sensibilities about government in business. Harding and the two Republican presidents who followed him strove to sell or lease the project to private entrepreneurs." McCraw, *TVA and the Power Fight*, 1–2.

137. "Governor Rejects Appeal by Pinchot," *NYT*, March 16, 1923.

138. "Governor Smith's Record: Water Power," 9.

139. "Smith Assails Rival on Economy Pledge," *NYT*, October 28, 1924, 1, 4, quoted on 4; Alfred E. Smith, "Speech at Mt. Vernon, NY, on Economy, October 27, 1924," Smith Papers, box 27, folder 274, 4.

140. J.H.C., "Memorandum for Governor Smith Showing How the Federal Government Regards Public Regulation," December 22, 1926, Smith Papers, box 22, folder 227, 1.

141. Ibid., 3–4. Emphasis in original.

142. Ibid., 4.

143. Julius Henry Cohen to Samuel Untermyer, October 11, 1927, Smith Papers, box 23, folder 228.

144. "Smith Assails Rival on Economy Pledge," 1; Smith, "Speech at Mt. Vernon," 2.

145. "Ex-Gov. Smith's Speech Nominating Gov. Roosevelt," NYT, October 1, 1930, 22; "Both Parties Back $50 Million Bonds," NYT, November 2, 1930, N3; "Clergy Join in Plea for State Bond Issue," NYT, November 2, 1930, N4; "Makes Final Plea for Welfare Bonds," NYT, November 3, 1930, 30; "State Bond Issue Wins by Huge Vote," NYT, November 5, 1930, 3; "City Gives Governor Greatest Plurality," NYT, November 5, 1930, 1.

146. Perry, Belle Moskowitz, 135; Eldot, Governor Alfred E. Smith, 76.

147. Perry, Belle Moskowitz, 122, 125, 134–135; Caro, The Power Broker, 100.

148. "Legislature Noted for Little It Did," 10.

149. Alfred E. Smith, "Campaign Speech at Poughkeepsie, October 19, 1920," Smith Papers, box 26, folder 255.

150. Perry, Belle Moskowitz, 129, 132, 134; Caro, The Power Broker, 181–206.

151. Elihu Root, "Invisible Government," in Addresses on Government and Citizenship (Freeport, NY: Books for Libraries Press, 1969), 191–206; Alfred E. Smith, "Personal Notes on Reorganization," Smith Papers, box 14, folder 167.

152. F. C. Crawford, "Legislative Notes and Reviews: New York State Reorganization," American Political Science Review 20, no. 1 (February 1926): 76–79; Elihu Root, "A Study of the Proposed Constitution," in Addresses on Government and Citizenship, 213–225, quotes from 217–218.

153. Slayton, Empire Statesman, 110.

154. F. C. Crawford, "Legislative Notes and Reviews: New York State Reorganization," 77.

155. Caro, The Power Broker, 111.

156. "Reorganization of the State Government," NYT, February 11, 1920, 10.

157. Alfred E. Smith, "Campaign Speech at Brooklyn, October 26, 1920," Smith Papers, box 26, folder 255.

158. Ibid.

159. Caro, The Power Broker, 111.

160. "City's Vote Goes to Harding and Smith," NYT, November 3, 1920, 1.

161. "Smith Defeated by About 74,000," NYT, November 4, 1920, 1; "Miller Lead, 64,014, 107 Dists. to Come," NYT, November 5, 1920, 2.

162. Caro, The Power Broker, 111.

163. Smith, "Responsive and Responsible Government," 83–85, 87–89; Alfred E. Smith, "Campaign Speech at Lexington Opera House, November 4, 1922," Smith Papers, box 26, folder 258; Malcolm, New York Red Book, 1928, 372.

164. Alfred E. Smith, "Inaugural Address: 1923," in Moskowitz, Progressive Democracy, 74–75, esp. 75.

165. Alfred E. Smith, "The Difference between the Republican and Democratic Parties in New York State," in Moskowitz, Progressive Democracy, 43–51, esp. 46.

166. Minutes kept by Robert Moses demonstrate that reorganization was usually the first item on the agenda in this period. Calendars of the Governor's Meetings, February, March 1923, Moses Papers, box 4, folder "Cabinet."

167. "Full Text of the Annual Message of Governor Smith to the State Legislature," *NYT*, January 3, 1924, 10.

168. Ibid.

169. Awaiting repassage by the senate, since the lower house had already passed the bill twice. "Text of Gov. Smith's Address," *NYT*, October 5, 1924, 2.

170. For example, according to Perry, in April 1924 "the club sent every Assembly member an appeal to pass the executive budget and also four-year term bills." Perry, *Belle Moskowitz*, 165.

171. Ibid.; Caro, *The Power Broker*, 124.

172. M.W.D. (Molly Dewson), untitled document, Mary W. Dewson Papers, Franklin D. Roosevelt Library, Hyde Park, NY (hereafter Dewson Papers), container 4, folder "Smith, Alfred E., Correspondence re 1928 Campaign"; Perry, *Belle Moskowitz*, 165.

173. Quoted in Perry, *Belle Moskowitz*, 165; "Governor Cheered, Lowman Is Hissed in Budget Debate," *NYT*, March 8, 1925, 1, 23.

174. "Governor Cheered, Lowman Is Hissed in Budget Debate," 1.

175. Ibid., 23.

176. Alfred E. Smith, "Speech at the Economic Club of New York, May 18, 1925," Smith Papers, box 28, folder 294.

177. Alfred E. Smith, "Speech at Carnegie Hall, July 9, 1925," Smith Papers, box 28, folder 295.

178. Yearley, *The Money Machines*, 168.

179. Draft of letter to the editor, Elihu Root and Henry Stimson, Smith Papers, box 2, folder 25; press release, Democratic Publicity Committee, 1925, Smith Papers, box 2, folder 25; Richard S. Childs and William P. Burr, "Executive Leadership in a Democracy: Discussion," *Proceedings of the Academy of Political Science in the City of New York* 8, no. 1 (1918): 54–55.

180. F. C. Crawford, "New York State Reorganization: Legislative Notes and Reviews," 76; Finla G. Crawford, "Administrative Reorganization in New York State," *American Political Science Review* 21, no. 2 (May 1927): 349–359, quote from 350; "Hughes in Message Calls for Reforms," *NYT*, January 6, 1910, 3.

181. Merlo J. Pusey, *Charles Evans Hughes* (New York: Macmillan, 1951), quote from 215, see also 191–215; Robert F. Wesser, *Charles Evans Hughes: Politics and Reform in New York, 1905–1910* (Ithaca, NY: Cornell University Press, 1967), 124–145; Charles Evans Hughes, "Administrative Efficiency," in *Conditions of Progress in Democratic Government* (New Haven, CT: Yale University Press, 1910), 32–58, esp. 32–41, 55.

182. Alfred E. Smith to Henry L. Stimson, December 7, 1925; Stimson to Smith, December 9, 1925, Smith Correspondences, reel 86.

183. Pussey, *Charles Evans Hughes*, 623.

184. Richard S. Childs to Charles Evans Hughes, July 1, 1925; Robert Moses to Alfred E. Smith, July 8, 1925; Hughes to Childs, July 6, 1925; Childs to Hughes, July 1, 1925, Moses Papers, box 4, folder "Alfred E. Smith–George Graves Correspondence"; Pussey, *Charles Evans Hughes*, 624; Handlin, *Al Smith*, 96.

185. F. G. Crawford, "Administrative Reorganization in New York State," 350; Handlin, *Al Smith*, 96; Childs to Hughes, July 1, 1925.

186. "Text of the Hughes Report on the Consolidation of State Departments," *NYT*, March 2, 1926, 13; Malcolm, *New York Red Book, 1928*, 598.

187. "Text of the Hughes Report," 13; Pussey, *Charles Evans Hughes*, 624.

188. "Text of the Hughes Report," 13.

189. Smith, "Responsive and Responsible Government," 84–86; "Text of the Hughes Report," 13.

190. F. C. Crawford, "Legislative Notes and Reviews: New York State Reorganization," 78–79.

191. Alfred E. Smith, "A Typical Financial Accounting to the People," in Moskowitz, *Progressive Democracy*, 116–131, quote from 122.

192. Ibid., 13.

193. Ibid.

194. Pussey, *Charles Evans Hughes*, 624.

195. Malcolm, *New York Red Book, 1928*, 598.

196. Thomas E. Dewey, in *A Tribute to Governor Smith*, ed. Robert Moses (New York: Simon and Schuster, 1962), 9–10, esp. 9.

197. For example, from 1926 to 1929, the state budget increased by over $8 million *more* annually in the first three years after reorganization. Moreover, while some redundant entities were eliminated, many others were placed under the control of the sixteen new departments—which promoted better organization and established a clear chain of command with authority vested in the governor but did not necessarily reduce the size or complexity of government. Smith's heir Franklin Roosevelt's 1929 budget was longer than any previous budget in state history. Alfred E. Smith, *The Citizen and His Government* (New York: Harper, 1935), 225; "Smith Avoids New Taxes in Budget of $229,269,065, Reducing the Levy on Realty," *NYT*, January 17, 1928, 1, 16; "Text of Governor Roosevelt's First Budget Message, the Longest on Record," *NYT*, January 29, 1929, 14–15; Caro, *The Power Broker*, 98. A 1980 study showed that this experience was not anomalous: "Of 16 reorganized states, only three showed a statistically significant long-term decline in employment, while none showed a significant short-term decrease. None of the short- or long-term reductions in expenditures were statistically significant." Kenneth J. Meier, "Executive Reorganization of Government: Impact on Employment and Expenditures," *American Journal of Political Science* 24, no. 3 (August 1980): 396–412, esp. 410.

198. Alfred E. Smith, "Campaign Speech at Brooklyn," October 26, 1920, Smith Papers, box 26, folder 255.

199. Under Smith's immediate successor, budget-making authority quickly proved crucial to the executive's ability to promote social welfare. By the end of Franklin Roosevelt's first year in office, the nation was embroiled in the Great Depression; the executive budget gave him "some flexibility in initiating . . . programs," and so Roosevelt was able to mobilize the state in response to the economic catastrophe. Allan M. Winkler, *Franklin D. Roosevelt and the Making of Modern America* (New York: Pearson, 2006), 49–51.

200. Yearley, *The Money Machines*, 147.

201. Quoted in McGerr, *A Fierce Discontent*, 164.

202. Mary Kingsbury Simkhovitch, *The City Worker's World in America* (New York: Macmillan, 1917), 199.

203. "A Conversation with Robert Moses," 1973, Oral History Research Office, Columbia University, 14.

204. "The Reminiscences of Robert F. Wagner, Jr.," Oral History Research Office, Columbia University, 99; "The Reminiscences of Charles Poletti," Oral History Research Office, Columbia University, 189.

205. Franklin D. Roosevelt, *The Happy Warrior, Alfred E. Smith: A Study of a Public Servant* (Boston: Houghton Mifflin, 1928), 16.

3. The Campaign of the Decade

1. Allan J. Lichtman, "Critical Election Theory and the Reality of American Presidential Politics, 1916–40," *American Historical Review* 81, no. 2 (April 1976): 317–351, quote from 340. Indeed, many historians argue that Smith's campaign was essentially conservative. One fundamentally influential work is David Burner's *The Politics of Provincialism*, which presents Smith as conservative and Hoover as the more progressive candidate (a view shared by Hoover biographer Joan Hoff Wilson). Greatly affected by Burner, Matthew and Hannah Josephson's Smith biography downplays the governor's progressivism during the 1928 election, despite the consistent assertions of their major source, Frances Perkins, that Smith's was a progressive campaign. Given the central place of Burner's work in the historiography, it is necessary to address several misconceptions on which the author bases these claims. First, he states that "Hoover was . . . the more explicitly progressive candidate—enough so that Coolidge's Secretary of the Treasury Andrew Mellon fiercely opposed his presidential candidacy." Not so: while Mellon had initially opposed his cabinet colleague's nomination, he ultimately endorsed Hoover and gave an important national radio address on his behalf, during which he declared that Hoover's election would be tantamount to ensuring four more years of Coolidge. Indeed, according to Hoover (who after his victory retained Mellon's services at the Treasury), "Mr. Mellon telephoned me from [the Republican National Convention at] Kansas City that the Pennsylvania delegation would meet the following morning, and 'I am going to recommend that they vote for you on the first ballot.'" Burner also notes the opposition to Smith among many social workers contacted by Lillian Wald, the role of John Raskob, and Smith's alleged weakness on the issue of water power—these questions will all be addressed presently. Burner, *The Politics of Provincialism*, 194–197; Joan Hoff Wilson, *Herbert Hoover: Forgotten Progressive* (Boston: Little, Brown, 1975), 132; Josephson and Josephson, *Al Smith: Hero of the Cities*, 371; Parrish, *Anxious Decades*, 213; "Mellon over Radio Makes Last Appeal to Elect Hoover," *New York Times* (hereafter *NYT*), October 30, 1928, 1, 22; "Mellon Says Hoover Will Make No Change," *Atlanta Constitution*, November 5, 1928, 6; Herbert Hoover, *The Memoirs of Herbert Hoover: The Cabinet and the Presidency, 1920–1933* (New York: Macmillan, 1952), 194.

2. "Storm over Klan Menacing," *NYT*, June 28, 1924, 1; Elmer Davis, "Georgia Beats Klan Plank," *NYT*, June 29, 1924, 1, 5; "Georgian Says Band Insulted Delegation," *NYT*, July 1, 1924, 1. See also Slayton, *Empire Statesman*, 209–213; Burner, *The Politics of Provincialism*, 114–121.

3. Slayton, *Empire Statesman*, 208; Burner, *The Politics of Provincialism*, 107–109.

4. Quoted in Davis, "Georgia Beats Klan Plank," 1, 5.

5. Slayton, *Empire Statesman*, 216.

6. John Vincent Donahue to Alfred E. Smith, March 11, 1924, Graves Papers, box 17, folder "Donahue, John V."

7. J. B. Hayes to Loring Black, October 1, 1924, Graves Papers, box 5, folder "Black, Loring M. (Hon)."

8. "Smith Relies on His Record," *NYT*, June 23, 1924, 1–2.

9. "Davis and Smith Are Cheered in Speeches at the Night Session," *NYT*, July 10, 1924, 1, 2. Smith biographer Robert Slayton calls the speech "the worst of his career, arrogant and mean-spirited." Slayton, *Empire Statesman*, 215. Yet while the speech opens with some provincial bombast about the greatness of New York City, the lion's share is a rather formulaic outline of Smith's progressivism, not remarkably different from many of his other orations.

10. "Davis and Smith Are Cheered," 1, 2. Even David Burner, who doggedly criticized Smith's "provincialism," characterized his 1924 effort as "a serious try for the nomination"—more than just an attempt "to block McAdoo on behalf of the eastern bosses." Burner, *The Politics of Provincialism*, 112.

11. Walter Lippmann to Alfred E. Smith, July 18, 1924, Graves Papers, box 42, folder "Lippmann, Walter"; Walter Lippmann to Alfred E. Smith, telegram, July 9, 1924, Walter Lippmann Papers, Manuscripts and Archives Division, Sterling Memorial Library, Yale University, New Haven, CT (hereafter Lippmann Papers), reel 29, box 30, folder 1137.

12. Malcolm, *Red Book, 1928*, 367, 377.

13. "Debate between Governor Smith and Former Governor Miller on State Bond Issue," July 9, 1925, Smith Papers, box 28, folder 295, 38–39.

14. Quoted in Handlin, *Al Smith*, 124.

15. "Greatest Throng of Democrats Hails Smith at Chicago," *NYT*, September 28, 1925, 1, 6, quote from 1.

16. Walter Lippmann, "'Al' Smith: A Man of Destiny: A Consideration of Some of the Tragic Aspects in a Brilliant Political Career," *Vanity Fair*, December 1925, 41, 88, quote from 41. Smith informed Lippmann that he had read the article "with satisfaction." Alfred E. Smith to Walter Lippmann, December 10, 1928; Lippmann to Smith, December 11, 1928, Lippmann Papers, reel 29, box 30, folder 1137.

17. "Address of Hon. Alfred E. Smith, Governor of the State of New York," *Public Speaker Magazine*, January 1927, 7–9, 25, quote from 25, Smith Papers, box 28, folder 297; "Pennsylvania Awaits Smith's Address," *NYT*, May 3, 1926, 14.

18. Child Welfare Committee of America, Inc., "The Human Side of Government by His Excellency Alfred E. Smith Governor of New York," Smith Papers, box 2, folder 31, 9.

19. Loring Black to Alfred E. Smith, July 21, 1926, Graves Papers, box 5, folder "Black, Loring M. (Hon)"; William Cohen to Alfred E. Smith, February 7, 1927, and August 13, 1927, Graves Papers, box 12, folder "Cohen, William W"; Tampa, Fl[orid]a Fire Dept. to Alfred E. Smith, telegram, October 30, 1926, Graves Papers, box 80, folder "Campaign—1926"; Mrs. Smith Washington to Alfred E. Smith, March 8, 1928, Graves Papers, box 75, folder "WAS."

20. For example: Edward James Woodhouse, "The South Studies Governor Smith," *The Independent*, January 9, 1926, 45; "Believes Smith Reply Ends Religion Issue," *NYT*, April 22, 1927, 3; "The Governor Replies," *The Independent*, April 30, 1927, 457; "Religion in Politics," *Banker's Magazine*, June 1927, 809; "Smith Has Support of South Dakotans," *NYT*, July 26, 1927, 23; "Democrats of Ohio Widely Split over Smith's Candidacy," *Washington Post*, August 17, 1927, 2; Arnold A. M'Kay, "A Southerner Tells Why He Would Vote for Smith," *NYT*, August 21, 1927, xx16; "Smith Becomes Issue in Mississippi Primary," *Washington Post*, August 23, 1927, 4; "Smith Is Attacked at W.C.T.U. Meeting," *NYT*, September 1, 1927, 9; "Party Workers Endorse Gov. Smith at Conference of 8 Western States; Call Him 'Most Available Candidate,'" *NYT*, September 24, 1927, 1; "Western Democrats Form Association to Nominate Smith," *NYT*, September 25, 1927, 1; "Smith Men Prepare to Wage Campaign in Western States," *NYT*, September 26, 1927, 1.

21. "Heflin Assails Smith; Edge Defends Governor," *Washington Post*, March 3, 1927, 4.

22. Alfred E. Smith, "Catholic and Patriot," in Moskowitz, *Progressive Democracy*, 254–269, quote from 254. Charles C. Marshall, "An Open Letter to the Honorable Alfred E. Smith," *Atlantic Monthly*, April, 1927, 540–549.

23. Walter Lippmann to Alfred E. Smith, April 4, 1927, Graves Papers, box 42, folder "Lippmann, Walter."

24. "The Reminiscences of Joseph M. Proskauer," Oral History Research Office, Columbia University, 29–32.

25. Smith, "Catholic and Patriot," 268.

26. Smith, *Progress of Public Improvements*, 4, 6–10, 20–118.

27. Alfred E. Smith to James J. Walker, December 1, 1928, Graves Papers, box 75, folder "Walker, Hon James J."

28. Undated press release, 1926 Wagner for Senate Campaign, Wagner Papers, box 401, folder 2, no. 8, 1; Robert F. Wagner, "Acceptance Speech," October 8, 1926, Wagner Papers, box 401, folder 2, no. 10, 1; "Wagner and Smith to Stump Together," *NYT*, October 1, 1926, 2.

29. "Speech of Senator Robert F. Wagner," March 5, 1928, in *Remarks from the Congressional Record of Senator Robert F. Wagner, 70th Congress*, 4067–4075, Wagner Papers, box 106, folder, "70th Congress," quotes from 4067–4068.

30. Eisenstein and Rosenberg, *A Stripe of Tammany's Tiger*, 41.

31. "Liaison Seen between Al Smith and Wagner on Unemployment," *Syracuse Herald*, March 6, 1928; "Smith Seen Back of Wagner Move," *Brooklyn Times*, March 6, 1928; "Wagner Declares Unemployment Rife, Senate Asks Inquiry," *NYT*, March 6, 1928, 1, subheading "Move to Aid Smith Seen"; "Senate Demands Check Up of Idle on Wagner's Plea; State Labor out for Smith," *Albany Knickerbocker*, March 6, 1928; Mark Sullivan, "Democrats Putting Forth New Issue for '28 Campaign," *Troy Morning News*, March 17, 1928; Mark Sullivan, "Issue for Smith Seen in Wagner Labor Speech," *New York Herald Tribune*, March 18, 1928, clippings in Wagner Papers, box 106, folder "The Maiden Speech of Hon. Robert F. Wagner in the United States Senate." See also Huthmacher, *Senator Robert F. Wagner*, 58–61. For his part, Smith was so gladdened by the news from Washington that he cabled the senator, "because I could not wait long enough to write a letter." Alfred E. Smith to Robert F. Wagner, March 6, 1928, Wagner Papers, box 106, folder "The Maiden Speech of Hon. Robert F. Wagner."

32. Quoted in Handlin, *Al Smith*, 125.

33. Ibid., 126–127; Edward J. Flynn, *You're the Boss: The Practice of American Politics* (New York: Collier, 1962), 80; John Morton Blum, *From the Morgenthau Diaries: Years of Crisis, 1928–1938* (Boston: Houghton Mifflin, 1957), 14. On Robinson, see Cecil Edward Weller Jr., *Joe T. Robinson: Always a Loyal Democrat* (Fayetteville: University of Arkansas Press, 1998).

34. For an excellent treatment of Hoover's early career, see William E. Leuchtenburg, *Herbert Hoover* (New York: Henry Holt, 2009), 1–70, esp. 35, 47, 53, 54, 59, 71.

35. Alfred E. Smith, "Address of Acceptance, Albany," in Democratic National Committee, *Campaign Addresses* (hereafter *Campaign Addresses*), 1–26, quote from 1–2.

36. Ibid., 4.

37. Leuchtenburg, *Herbert Hoover*, 65.

38. Hoover quote, ibid., 66, 72; Mencken quote, ibid., 76.

39. Smith, "Address of Acceptance," 2–3.

40. Gilbert C. Fite, *George N. Peek and the Fight for Farm Parity* (Norman: University of Oklahoma Press, 1954), 3–20; Parrish, *Anxious Decades*, 81–88; Theodore Saloutos and John D. Hicks, *Agricultural Discontent in the Middle West, 1900–1939* (Madison: University of Wisconsin Press, 1951), 92–94.

41. Democratic National Committee, *Campaign Book of the Democratic Party: Candidates and Issues in 1928* (New York: Democratic National Committee, 1928) (hereafter *Campaign Book*), 72.

42. Kimberly K. Porter, "Embracing the Pluralist Perspective: The Iowa Farm Bureau Federation and the McNary-Haugen Movement," *Agricultural History* 74, no. 2 (Spring 2000): 381–392, esp. 383; Leuchtenburg, *The Perils of Prosperity*, 102–103; Richard M. Valelly, *Radicalism in the States: The Minnesota Farmer-Labor Party and the American Political Economy* (Chicago: University of Chicago Press, 1989), 75–77.

43. Schlesinger, *The Crisis of the Old Order*, 107–108; Roger T. Johnson, "Part-Time Leader: Senator Charles L. McNary and the McNary Haugen Bill," *Agricultural History* 54, no. 4 (October 1980): 527–541, quote from 537.

44. "The Reminiscences of Rexford G. Tugwell (1950)," Oral History Research Office, Columbia University, 1–3; Walter Lippmann, "The Sick Donkey: Democratic Prospects for 1928," *Harper's Magazine* 155 (September 1927): 415–421, quote from 419.

45. Alfred E. Smith, "Omaha," in *Campaign Addresses*, 27–42, esp. 38–39; "Full Text of Governor Smith's Speech at Omaha on the Problem of Farm Relief," *NYT*, September 18, 1928, 3.

46. "Full Text of Governor Smith's Speech at Omaha," 3.

47. Henry A. Wallace to Hon. Meyer Jacobstein, June 14, 1928, Moses Papers, box 4, folder "Campaign—National/State 1928, Feb–Aug"; Burner, *The Politics of Provincialism*, 196; Lichtman, *Prejudice and the Old Politics*, 190; James L. Sundquist, *Dynamics of the Party System: Alignment and Realignment of Political Parties in the United States* (Washington, DC: Brookings Institution, 1973), 174.

48. Joseph Proskauer to Walter Lippmann, telegram, September 20, 1928, Lippmann Papers, reel 26, box 27, folder 1005; Marion J. Pike, "Swift Smith Blows in Omaha Drive Out Foe from Trenches," *New Orleans Times-Picayune*, September 23, 1928, 21; "Crowds Greet Gov. Smith on Way through Corn Belt; Farm Speech Stirs Debate," *NYT*, September 20, 1928, 1; Paul F. Haubert, "Smith Sees McMullen in

Lincoln, Neb.," *Hartford Courant* (hereafter *HC*), September 20, 1928, 1; Malcolm O. Sillars, "Henry A. Wallace's Editorials on Agrarian Discontent, 1921–1928," *Agricultural History* 26, no. 4 (October 1952): 132–140, esp. 139.

49. "Senator Blaine in Flat Refusal to Help Hoover," *New Orleans Times-Picayune*, September 24, 1928, 1; "Norris Recites Party Peeves," *Los Angeles Times*, October 28, 1928, 13.

50. "Senator Norris Turns to Al Smith after Hoover Power Speech," *Houston Post-Dispatch*, October 25, 1928, 1. While Norris did not endorse Smith until late October, the historian Richard Lowitt notes that his "reservations slowly gave way" after a series of Smith addresses beginning with the Omaha speech. Richard Lowitt, *George W. Norris: The Persistence of a Progressive, 1913–1933* (Urbana: University of Illinois Press, 1971), 410.

51. "By the Way—," *Wall Street Journal*, November 7, 1928, 1; "Norris out for Smith" editorial, *HC*, October 26, 1928, 8.

52. N. B. Register, "Norris Indorsement Swings Disgruntled Iowa Farmers," *Washington Sunday Star*, October 28, 1928, 26; "Iowa Farmers' Union Urges Hoover Defeat," *HC*, September 21, 1928, 14; Saloutos and Hicks, *Agricultural Discontent in the Middle West*, 403; Valelly, *Radicalism in the States*, 89.

53. "Party Boot Appiled [*sic*] to 'Young Bob,'" *Los Angeles Times*, October 2, 1928, 6.

54. "Big Progressive Paper Turns Over to Smith," *Scranton Times*, October 11, 1928, 1; "Democrat Quits Senate Contest against La Follette in Wisconsin," *Boston Globe* (hereafter *BG*), October 9, 1928, 6. La Follette was also being challenged from the right by an Independent Republican.

55. "Montana Race Will Go Limit," *Los Angeles Times*, November 2, 1928, 6.

56. William Hard, "Republican Invasion of South Most Striking Phase of the Campaign," *Washington Sunday Star*, October 21, 1928, part 2, p. 2.

57. *Campaign Book*, 25.

58. Ibid., 52; "Robinson's Acceptance Speech," *Barron's* 8, no. 36 (September 3, 1928): 4; "Robinson Fires Farm Aid Blast," *Los Angeles Times*, October 23, 1928, 7; "Robinson Woos Progressives," *Los Angeles Times*, October 24, 1928, 6.

59. G. Gould Lincoln, "Shipstead Is Key in Minnesota Race but Keeps Silence," *Washington Evening Star*, October 16, 1928, 1; "Lowden Manager Bolts to Smith," *NYT*, October 26, 1928, 3; "Lowden Aide for Smith," *NYT*, November 4, 1928, 23; "Lowden Denies a Report," *NYT*, October 30, 1928, 18; "Lowden to Be Silent to End of Campaign," *NYT*, October 31, 1928, 18; "M'Mullen Relies on Hoover's Word," *NYT*, October 26, 1928, 15; "McNary Sure of Farmers," *NYT*, October 17, 1928, 13; "Smith Spurred by Brookhart," *Los Angeles Times*, October 27, 1928, 4.

60. "La Follette Hits Both Parties but Lauds Gov. Smith," *Brooklyn Daily Eagle*, October 26, 1928, 3; "La Follette's 'Agin' Everyone," *Los Angeles Times*, October 27, 1928, 4; Robert M. La Follette Jr., "Dominant Issues in the 1928 Campaign," La Follette Papers, Series C, box 555, folder "Coolidge Administration 1928 Undated," 1–3.

61. For a revisionist interpretation of Smith's campaign among western farmers, see Robert Chiles, "Courting the Farm Vote on the Northern Plains: Presidential Candidate Al Smith, Governor Walter Maddock, and the Ambivalent Politics of 1928," *North Dakota History: Journal of the Northern Plains* 81, no. 1 (Spring 2016): 16–31.

62. Felix Frankfurter to Belle Moskowitz, August 7, 1928, Felix Frankfurter Papers, Manuscript Reading Room, Library of Congress, Washington, DC, reel 105.

63. "Stenographic Report of Gov. Smith's Denver Speech on Water-Power Control," *NYT*, September 23, 1928, 2; Alfred E. Smith, "Denver," in *Campaign Addresses*, 61–76.

64. Republican platform, reprinted in *Campaign Book*, 346–364, esp. 360.

65. Smith, "Denver," 65–67; "Stenographic Report of Gov. Smith's Denver Speech on Water-Power Control," 2; "National Affairs: The Coolidge Era," *Time*, February 25, 1929.

66. Smith, "Denver," 67. This quotation appears in the published version of Smith's speech, which was based on the candidate's notes, but not in the stenographic report of the speech as published by the *New York Times*.

67. "Stenographic Report of Gov. Smith's Denver Speech on Water-Power Control," 2.

68. Ibid.

69. "Smith Challenges Hoover to Clarify His 'Evasion' Stand on Muscle Shoals," *Washington Post*, October 13, 1928, 1, 4; "Smith Challenges Hoover to State Views Clearly; Gets Tennessee Ovations," *NYT*, October 13, 1928, 1, 6; "Smith Rips Into Hoover Attitude on Water Power," *Saratoga Springs Saratogian*, October 13, 1928, 1; Smith, "Nashville," 145; Alfred E. Smith, "Nashville," in *Campaign Addresses*, 141–152, esp. 145–147.

70. Alfred E. Smith, "Chicago," in *Campaign Addresses*, 187–202, esp. 197–199; Alfred E. Smith, "Boston," in *Campaign Addresses*, 203–218, esp. 203–207; Alfred E. Smith, "Baltimore," in *Campaign Addresses*, 237–250, esp. 240–242; Alfred E. Smith, "Brooklyn," in *Campaign Addresses*, 269–286, esp. 271–73.

71. Democratic National Committee, *What Everybody Wants to Know about Alfred E. Smith*, 19.

72. "Robinson Again Attacks on Dam," *Los Angeles Times*, October 12, 1928, 10.

73. "Robinson Fears Power's Future," *Los Angeles Times*, October 16, 1928, 10.

74. "Octopus!," *Time*, November 5, 1928.

75. Quoted in Burner, *The Politics of Provincialism*, 195.

76. Morris Cooke to Alfred E. Smith, January 8, 1924, Morris L. Cooke Papers, Franklin D. Roosevelt Library, Hyde Park, NY, box 193, folder 154-159, no. 157; Cooke to Smith, January 23, 1925; Cooke to Smith, March 15, 1927, Cooke Papers, box 46, folder 433; "Amos Pinchot Tells Why He's Supporting Smith," *BG*, October 27, 1928, 13.

77. "Creeping State Ownership," *Barron's* 8, no. 1 (January 2, 1928): 1; "Governor Smith's Acceptance Speech," *Barron's* 8, no. 35 (August 27, 1928): 4; "Political Obstruction," *Barron's* 8, no. 42 (October 15, 1928): 12.

78. In response to the Denver speech, the Smith-boosting *Boston Globe* proclaimed "Smith for Control of Power by State." "Smith for Control of Power by State," *BG*, September 23, 1928, 1, 21.

79. "Norris Bases Bolt on Power Question," *NYT*, October 28, 1928, 1, 28, quote from 1.

80. Quoted in George W. Norris to Paul Y. Anderson, September 8, 1928, Norris Papers, box 4, folder 15—1928 Presidential Campaign (Smith); Robert Moses to Norris, August 20, 1928, Moses Papers, box 4, folder "Campaign—National/State 1928, Sept–Dec"; Royal Copeland to Norris, October 15, 1928, Norris Papers, box 4,

folder 15—1928 Presidential Campaign (Smith); Norris to Moses, September 8, 1928, Norris Papers, box 4, folder 15—1928 Presidential Campaign (Hoover); Burner, *The Politics of Provincialism*, 195n.

81. Norris to Paul Y. Anderson, September 8, 1928.

82. Norris to Lewis S. Gannett, September 8, 1928, Norris Papers, box 4, folder 15—1928 Presidential Campaign (Hoover), 2.

83. Norris to Anderson, September 8, 1928.

84. "Full Stenographic Report of Governor Smith's Address on Labor in Newark," *NYT*, November 1, 1928, 4. No such call appears explicitly in the Denver speech, although Smith called for government ownership and control repeatedly and remarked that the government must "keep its hands on the switch that turns on or off the power." Based on the Newark remarks, this was evidently intended as an endorsement of state operation.

85. E. Scott Miles to Norris, June 9, 1928, Norris Papers, box 4, folder 15—Hoover (1928) Campaign. Emphasis in original.

86. Donald O. Burke to Norris, September 4, 1928, Norris Papers, box 4, folder 15—1928 Presidential Campaign (Smith).

87. Henry Ware Allen to Norris, September 24, 1928, Norris Papers, box 4, folder 15—1928 Presidential Campaign (Smith).

88. Henry W. Elliott to Norris, September 24, 1928, Norris Papers, box 4, folder 15—1928 Presidential Campaign (Smith).

89. Portraits quote from "Norris Calls on Progressives to Support Smith," *Beatrice Daily Sun*, October 28, 1928, 1; Norris quoted in "Norris Bases Bolt on Power Question," 28.

90. H. A. Brubaker to Norris, October 27, 1928, Norris Papers, box 5, folder 15—Letters on Smith (condemning Senator N 1928 Campaign).

91. Norman L. Zucker, *George W. Norris: Gentle Knight of American Democracy* (Urbana: University of Illinois Press, 1966), 14; John F. Kennedy, *Profiles in Courage* (New York: Harper, 1956), 214–219.

92. Norris to Carl F. Marsh, November 27, 1928, Norris Papers, box 4, folder 15—1928 Presidential Campaign (Smith).

93. "Full Stenographic Report of Governor Smith's Address on Labor in Newark," 4.

94. "Text of Hoover's Speech on Relation of Government to Industry," *NYT*, October 23, 1928, 2.

95. "Smith Rails at Hoover," *Los Angeles Times*, October 25, 1928, 1–2, quote from 2.

96. "Alibi of Al Attacked," *Los Angeles Times*, October 27, 1928, 1.

97. Quoted in "Norris Supports Smith; Strikes at Hoover on Power," *New York World*, October 25, 1928, 1; "Declares Norris Will Shift to Smith," *NYT*, October 24, 1928, 1, 14; "Norris Bases Bolt on Power Question," 28.

98. "Panken Says Smith Is Not Socialistic," *NYT*, October 24, 1928, 9; Malcolm, *Red Book, 1928*, 380.

99. Smith, "Denver," 63–64.

100. "Panken Says Smith Is Not Socialistic," 9.

101. "Wisconsin Assembly Praises Gov. Smith," *Washington Post*, January 28, 1928, 4.

102. B. Stanley to George Norris, October 29, 1928, Norris Papers, box 5, folder 15—Commending Senator for Support of Smith in 1928 Campaign.

103. "Radio Chain to Carry Smith Speech Tonight," *NYT*, October 31, 1928, 26.

104. "Thomas Asks Liberals Not to Vote for Smith," *Washington Evening Star*, October 22, 1928, 4.

105. "Robinson Gives Smith's Record," *Los Angeles Times*, October 27, 1928, 5.

106. "Stenographic Report of Smith's Boston Speech Answering Hoover on 'State Socialism,'" *NYT*, October 25, 1928, 2; Smith, "Boston," 216.

107. Handlin, *Al Smith*, 130.

108. Quoted in "Comment Is Varied on Hoover Speech," *NYT*, October 24, 1928, 12.

109. Slayton, *Empire Statesman*, 266. Slayton's conclusions are partly based on those of Elisabeth Perry, who places Belle Moskowitz, not Raskob, at the center of Smith's circle. Perry, *Belle Moskowitz*, 184–213.

110. Edmund A. Moore, *A Catholic Runs for President: The Campaign of 1928* (New York: Ronald Press, 1956), 121–122.

111. Handlin, *Al Smith*, 128–129; Perry, *Belle Moskowitz*, 184–213; Slayton, *Empire Statesman*, 266.

112. "Stenographic Report of Smith's Boston Speech," 2; Charles Michelson, "Smith Smites Hoover for Cry of 'Socialism'; Boston Wild over Him," *New York World*, October 25, 1928, 1.

113. Smith, "Boston," 215; "Stenographic Report of Smith's Boston Speech," 2.

114. Alfred E. Smith, "Newark," in *Campaign Addresses*, 251–268, quote from 257.

115. "Celebration of Labor Day on U.S. Army Reservation Signal Day for Smith Oratory," *Brooklyn Daily Eagle*, September 4, 1928, 5.

116. "Mrs. Roosevelt Stirs Audience by Smith Plea," *Elizabeth Daily Journal*, October 21, 1928, 1.

117. L. Mastriani, letter to the editor, *Newark Evening News*, October 30, 1928, 13.

118. Lichtman, *Prejudice and the Old Politics*, 14.

119. Slayton, *Empire Statesman*, 275.

120. For example: Leuchtenburg, *The Perils of Prosperity*, 234; Schlesinger, *The Crisis of the Old Order*, 128; Arthur M. Schlesinger Jr., *The Politics of Upheaval: 1935–1936*, vol. 3 of *The Age of Roosevelt* (Boston: Houghton Mifflin, 2003), 410; Parrish, *Anxious Decades*, 213; Burner, *The Politics of Provincialism*, 194–197.

121. *Campaign Book*, 72, 75, 148–149.

122. "Hurray for Smith Heckler's Parting Shot at Curtis," *HC*, September 20, 1928, 1.

123. "Sen. Curtis Lauds Record of G.O.P.," *HC*, September 25, 1928, 4.

124. *Campaign Book*, 85–86, 134.

125. Leuchtenburg, *The Perils of Prosperity*, 8.

126. Walter Lippmann, "Hoover and Smith: An Impartial Consideration of the Candidates for the American Presidential Office," *Vanity Fair*, September 1928, 39–40, quote from 40.

127. "As Like as Two Peas," editorial, *The Nation* 127 (August 8, 1928): 122, reprinted in *Politics of the Nineteen Twenties*, ed. John L. Shover (Waltham, MA: Ginn-Blaisdell, 1970), 186–189, quote from 186.

128. "Mrs. Ross Praises Smith as Reformer," *NYT*, October 2, 1928, 2.

129. "Campaign Speech in Support of Alfred E. Smith for the Presidency," Hamden, CT, October 11, 1928, Griffin Papers, box 14, 1, 3–4, 5, 6.

130. "Robinson Flays Foe at Phoenix," *Los Angeles Times*, October 9, 1928, 5; "Robinson Flays Prosperity Cry," *Los Angeles Times*, October 11, 1928, 8; "Robinson Again Attacks on Dam," *Los Angeles Times*, October 12, 1928, 10; "Robinson Fears Power's Future," *Los Angeles Times*, October 16, 1928, 10; "Robinson Fires Farm Aid Blast," *Los Angeles Times*, October 23, 1928, 7; "Robinson Woos Progressives," *Los Angeles Times*, October 24, 1928, 6; "Robinson Gives Smith's Record," *Los Angeles Times*, October 27, 1928, 5.

131. "Robinson Pledges Labor Aid," *Charlotte Observer*, September 4, 1928, 6.

132. "Robinson Flays Prosperity Cry," 8.

133. Vaughn Davis Bornet, *Labor Politics in a Democratic Republic: Moderation, Division, and Disruption in the Presidential Election of 1928* (Washington, DC: Spartan, 1964), 139–186; Irving Bernstein, *The Lean Years: A History of the American Worker, 1920–1933* (Baltimore: Penguin, 1960), 104.

134. "John L. Lewis Delivers Radio Talk for Hoover," *Philadelphia Trades Union News*, October 25, 1928, 6; "Miners' Leader Lauds Hoover," *Los Angeles Times*, October 18, 1928, 7.

135. "Green Praises Hoover's Attitude on Immigration," *Philadelphia Trades Union News*, November 1, 1928, 2.

136. George L. Berry, "To the Officers and Members of the American Labor Movement," Smith Papers, box 22, folder 224. Fitzpatrick also served as spokesman for the Alfred E. Smith Union Labor League. "Hoover Is Accused of Being Advocate of the Open Shop," *Atlanta Constitution*, October 23, 1928, 20. "Local Labor Endorses Smith as Lewis Gives Radio Talk for Hoover," *Scranton Times*, October 18, 1928, 3.

137. *Campaign Book*, 134; Democratic National Committee, *The Labor Record of Governor Alfred E. Smith* (New York: Democratic National Committee, 1928), 13.

138. Bornet, *Labor Politics in a Democratic Republic*, 44–45; Burner, *The Politics of Provincialism*, 130.

139. Hoover for President Labor Council of the Republican National Committee, "Governor Smith WRONG on Immigration," 1928, 1, 3, 4, Smith Papers, box 9, folder 103.

140. "Full Text of Smith's Speech Accepting Party's Nomination for the Presidency," *NYT*, August 23, 1928, 2.

141. "Stenographic Report of Address by Gov. Smith at St. Paul," *NYT*, September 28, 1928, 2.

142. "Mr. Smith's 'Remedies,'" *Barron's*, 8, no. 43 (October 22, 1928), 12.

143. Mae Ngai, "The Architecture of Race in American Immigration Law: A Reexamination of the Immigration Act of 1924," *Journal of American History* 86, no. 1 (June 1999): 67–92, esp. 68. Ngai argues that Smith "opposed the quotas in the North while favoring them before southern audiences." In fact, Smith attacked the use of the 1890 quota during his acceptance speech as "designed to discriminate against certain nationalities and . . . an unwise policy," and thenceforth consistently referred audiences to that statement; yet a reading of his campaign addresses suggests that he never again enunciated this posture explicitly. "Full Text of Smith's Speech Accepting Party's Nomination for the Presidency," 2. Walter Lippmann to Belle Moskowitz, October 4, 1928; Lippmann to Moskowitz, October 9, 1928, Lippmann Papers, reel 20,

box 21, folder 844; Felix Frankfurter to Lippmann, Lippmann Papers, reel 10, box 10, folder 429; (Illegible) to Henry Moskowitz, October 17, 1928, Smith Papers, box 9, folder 104; Calvert Magruder, "Memorandum for Governor Smith," Smith Papers, box 9, folder 104.

144. "Stenographic Report of Gov. Smith's Speech to Louisville Democrats Last Night," *NYT*, October 14, 1928, 25.

145. *Campaign Book*, 100–125, quote from 102; Colin B. Goodykoontz, "Edward P. Costigan and the Tariff Commission, 1917–1928," *Pacific Historical Review* 16, no. 4 (November 1947): 410–419, esp. 410.

146. Robert M. La Follette Jr., untitled address (1), La Follette Papers, Series C, box 555, folder "Coolidge Administration 1928 Undated," 10. The same criticism was leveled against the Interstate Commerce Commission, the Federal Trade Commission, and the Shipping Board.

147. Goodykoontz, "Edward P. Costigan and the Tariff Commission," 417.

148. Lichtman, "Critical Election Theory and the Reality of American Presidential Politics," 340.

149. Lippmann, "The Sick Donkey," 419.

150. "Local Labor Endorses Smith," 3; "John Mitchell's Son Supporting Smith Candidacy," *Scranton Times*, October 23, 1928, 2.

151. "Full Stenographic Report of Governor Smith's Address on Labor in Newark," 4.

152. *Campaign Book*, 130, 133.

153. For example, the NAACP's Walter White was told frankly that Smith "planned, if elected, to extend to the nation the benefits of the social legislation New York state enjoyed." Walter White, *A Man Called White: The Autobiography of Walter White* (New York: Viking, 1948), 99–100.

154. For example, Smith, "Address of Acceptance," 24; Smith, "Oklahoma City," in *Campaign Addresses*, 43–60, 44–50; Smith, "St. Paul," in *Campaign Addresses*, 89–104, 89; Smith, "Brooklyn," 269–286; Smith, "Radio Address at Carnegie Hall," in *Campaign Addresses*, 309–316, 315.

155. Ware, *Partner and I*, 150–151; "Plan for Organizing Women Voters," Eleanor Roosevelt Papers, Franklin D. Roosevelt Library, Hyde Park, NY (hereafter Eleanor Roosevelt Papers), box 6, folder 5; "Report on Office of Organizing Women, 9/11/28," Eleanor Roosevelt Papers, box 6, folder 5.

156. Molly Dewson, "What Campaign Issues Mean to Women," Dewson Papers, box 4, folder "Smith, Alfred E. and 1928 Campaign, Corres. Re."

157. Frances Perkins, "Notes for Campaign Speech to Social Workers in Boston, Sept 1928," Perkins Papers, box 43.

158. Frances Perkins, "Notes for Campaign Speech for Al Smith (radio) NY, 9/24/28," Perkins Papers, box 43, 1.

159. Lillian Wald to Mary McDonald, September 27, 1928, 1, Wald Papers, reel 3.

160. Frances Perkins, "Speech, Boston, 10/2/28," Perkins Papers, box 43, 1.

161. Frances Perkins, "Campaign Speech by Miss Perkins for Al Smith, Oct. 1928," Perkins Papers, box 43, 1.

162. Perkins, "Speech, Boston, 10/2/28," 1–2.

163. Ibid., 2.

164. Perkins Oral History, book 2, 628, 635. Emphasis added.

165. Lillian Wald to Judge Julian W. Mack, October 4, 1928, Wald Papers, reel 3.

166. For example: Lillian Wald to June Hamilton Rhodes, September 4, 1928; Wald to G. E. Sehlbrade, September 14, 1928, Wald Papers, reel 3.

167. Wald to Rhodes, September 4, 1928.

168. Wald to McDonald, September 27, 1928, 2, 3, Wald Papers, reel 3.

169. "An Open Letter to Social Workers," Wald Papers, reel 33; see also Marjorie N. Feld, *Lillian Wald: A Biography* (Chapel Hill: University of North Carolina Press, 2008), 138–141.

170. Perry, *Belle Moskowitz*, 189, 194–195.

171. Slayton, *Empire Statesman*, 266. Emphasis in original.

172. Perry, *Belle Moskowitz*, 196–200.

173. Slayton, *Empire Statesman*, 268.

174. Perry, *Belle Moskowitz*, 196.

175. Rexford G. Tugwell, *The Democratic Roosevelt* (Garden City, NY: Doubleday, 1957), 172. It should be noted that Tugwell used the phrase, however apt, as part of a particularly disparaging diatribe against Moskowitz.

176. Perry, *Belle Moskowitz*, 196.

177. Public Health Workers for Smith, "To Public Health Workers," October 19, 1928, Wald Papers, reel 33.

178. Lillian Wald to Graham Taylor, October 25, 1928, Wald Papers, reel 3.

179. Nancy F. Cott, *The Grounding of Modern Feminism* (New Haven, CT: Yale University Press, 1987), 8.

180. Smith, "Newark," 261; "Women to Open Fight on Smith," *Los Angeles Times*, October 1, 1928, 4; "Hoover in Council with the President on the Campaign," *NYT*, September 13, 1928, 1, 3, quote from 1.

181. Walter Lippmann to Alfred E. Smith, September 17, 1928, Lippmann Papers, reel 29, box 30, folder 1137.

182. "The 'Equal Rights' Issue," editorial, *Fall River Globe*, September 25, 1928, 10.

183. "Full Stenographic Report of Governor Smith's Address on Labor in Newark," 12.

184. "Jane Addams Lauds Hoover as 'Best Bet,'" *Christian Science Monitor*, October 17, 1928, 3.

185. Joana C. Colcord to Lillian Wald, October 4, 1928, Wald Papers, reel 11. For an excellent, balanced consideration of Hoover's allure for progressives, see Leuchtenburg, *Herbert Hoover*, 74.

186. Irving Fisher to Lillian Wald, October 3, 1928, Wald Papers, reel 11.

187. C. W. Gilfillan to Lillian Wald, October 17, 1928, Wald Papers, reel 11.

188. Henry W. Farnam to Lillian Wald, October 13, 1928, Wald Papers, reel 11.

189. Anonymous to Mrs. Franklin D. Roosevelt, 1928, Eleanor Roosevelt Papers, box 6, folder 4.

190. Hastings H. Hart to Lillian Wald, October 2, 1928, Wald Papers, reel 11.

191. "'Al' Smith's Grammar," *NYT*, April 21, 1915, 1; Caro, *The Power Broker*, 88.

192. Mildred B. Duncan to Lillian Wald and John L. Elliott, October 22, 1928, Wald Papers, reel 11.

193. Mabel A. Strong to Lillian Wald, October 2, 1928, Wald Papers, reel 12.

194. Owen Stuart to Lillian Wald, October 5, 1928 Wald Papers, reel 12; Sarah E. Jenkins to Lillian Wald, October 29, 1928, Mary Van Kleeck Papers, Sophia Smith Collection, Smith College, Northampton, MA (hereafter Van Kleeck Papers), box 30, folder 4.

195. "Smith Paints Dry Law as G.O.P. Pork Barrel in Milwaukee Address," *Brooklyn Daily Eagle*, September 30, 1928, 1; Alfred E. Smith, "Milwaukee," in *Campaign Addresses*, 105–120. For example, Richard Bartholdt, a German immigrant and retired Republican congressman from St. Louis, supported Smith as the "liberal" candidate in 1928, asserting that the Republican "partnership with the forces of prohibition and reaction" was a "cold-blooded betrayal" of "the German-American element." Richard Bartholdt, *From Steerage to Congress: Reminiscences and Reflections* (Philadelphia: Dorrance, 1930), 422–423. On anti-German sentiment and Prohibition, see Thomas R. Pegram, *Battling Demon Rum: The Struggle for a Dry America, 1800–1933* (Chicago: Ivan R. Dee, 1998), 144–146.

196. "Full Stenographic Report of Governor Smith's Address on Labor in Newark," 4; Alfred E. Smith, "Philadelphia," in *Campaign Addresses*, 219–236; Alfred E. Smith, "Chicago," 187–202.

197. "Full Stenographic Report of Governor Smith's Address on Labor in Newark," 4.

198. "We, the Undersigned, Support for the Presidency, Governor Alfred E. Smith," Frankfurter Papers, reel 105, 1.

199. "Prohibition Not Main Issue," *NYT*, September 19, 1928, 1; Smith, "Omaha," 40.

200. Slayton, *Empire Statesman*, 196–201. See also Lisa McGirr, *The War on Alcohol: Prohibition and the Rise of the American State* (New York: Norton, 2016), 169–184.

201. Frederick Lewis Allen, *Only Yesterday: An Informal History of the 1920s* (New York: Harper Perennial, 2010), 221.

202. Walter Lippmann to Alfred E. Smith, May 9, 1928, Lippmann Papers, reel 29, box 30, folder 1137.

203. Walter Lippmann, "The Wetness of Al Smith: The Practical Consequences if He Were Elected," *Harper's Magazine* 156 (June 1928): 133–139, esp. 135.

204. Josephus Daniels, notes for "Life Begins at Seventy": "Attending Democratic National Convention," Josephus Daniels Papers, Wilson Library, University of North Carolina, Chapel Hill, NC, Series 2.2, folder 79.

205. Slayton, *Empire Statesman*, 258–259.

206. Pegram, *Battling Demon Rum*, 171–172, 180–181.

207. "W. J. Bryan League to Vote G.O.P.," *Los Angeles Times*, October 19, 1928, 1.

208. "Stenographic Report of Gov. Smith's Address to Democrats at Sedalia Last Night," *NYT*, October 17, 1928, 14.

209. *Campaign Book*, 174–175, 177.

210. Perry, *Belle Moskowitz*, 197.

211. "Review and Outlook: Fair Warning," *Wall Street Journal*, October 19, 1928, 1.

212. "Mellon Says Smith Distorted Figures," *NYT*, October 18, 1928, 1, 20.

213. Mary E. Dreier to Alfred E. Smith, January 23, 1928, Graves Papers, box 18, folder Dreier, Mary E.

214. "Rival Political Attitudes," editorial, *New Orleans Times-Picayune*, September 30, 1928, 30.

215. Will Rogers, "Will Rogers Comes Out Firmly against Notification Ceremonies," *BG*, September 6, 1928, 6. A representative Republican advertisement reminded

voters that "Herbert Hoover has promised you that he will carry on the policies of Calvin Coolidge." "Citizens of Massachusetts: Remember Four Years Ago Tonight!," *Lowell Sun*, November 5, 1928, 1.

4. The People's Verdict

1. Alfred E. Smith, "Remarks at Liberty Hall, Harlem," October 28, 1924, Smith Papers, box 27, folder 274.

2. "The Reminiscences of Robert F. Wagner, Jr.," Oral History Research Office, Columbia University, 215.

3. Smith, "Oklahoma City," in Democratic National Committee, *Campaign Addresses* 52, 55.

4. Ibid., 55, 58, 59.

5. "Vengeful," *Time*, December 6, 1926.

6. Eleanor Roosevelt, *This I Remember* (New York: Harper, 1949), 39.

7. "Heflin Assails Smith, Edge Defends Governor," *Washington Post*, March 3, 1927, 4; "Heflin Issues Defi to Party in Senate on Catholic Issue," *Washington Post*, January 24, 1928, 1, 10; "Papal Red in President Room, Heflin Charges," *Washington Post*, May 18, 1928, 5; "Heflin, Clad in Papal Hues, Stirs Smith Row in Senate," *Washington Post*, May 24, 1928, 1, 10; Burner, *The Politics of Provincialism*, 204; "Heflin Predicts Hoover Will Win by 10,000,000," *Boston Globe*, September 11, 1928, 13.

8. Amos C. Duncan to Furnifold Simmons, May 30, 1928; Simmons to Duncan, September 1, 1928; Chas S. Bryan to Simmons, October 7, 1928; John Deal to Simmons, October 8, 1928, Furnifold Simmons Papers, Duke University, Durham, NC, box 64, folders: May 29–31, September 1–3, 1928, October 6–10, 1928.

9. "After All Is Said," *Time*, November 12, 1928.

10. JHB, "Post-Election Probe of Bigotry Is Indicated; G.O.P. Is Blamed," *Baltimore Sun*, November 6, 1928, 2.

11. Thomas R. Pegram, *One Hundred Percent American: The Rebirth and Decline of the Ku Klux Klan in the 1920s* (Chicago: Ivan R. Dee, 2011), 218.

12. "M'Clean Urges State to Give Vote to Smith," *Charlotte Observer*, October 4, 1928, 1; Charles H. Brough to John J. Raskob, November 26, 1928, John J. Raskob Papers, Hagley Museum and Library, Wilmington, DE (hereafter Raskob Papers), file 602, box 1.

13. *The Present Crisis*, pamphlet, West Virginia Anti-Saloon League, 1928; Smith, "Oklahoma City," 55.

14. "Appointments Made by Gov. Al. Smith," Moses Papers, box 4, folder "National Campaign 1928."

15. For example: Arthur M. Jackson to Robert Moses, September 24, 1928; Louis Mahloch to Moses, September 6, 1927 [*sic*]; John H. Dillard to Moses, September 27, 1928; Mrs. Elmer K. Hoch to Moses, September 7, 1928; Robert Grady Johnson to Moses, July 13, 1928; James T. O'Neill to George B. Graves, July 24, 1928; L. H. McGehee to Moses, August 28, 1928; Rob't A. Shivers to Moses, September 24, 1928; John E. V. Jasper to Moses, September 20, 1928; Moses Papers, box 4, folder "National Campaign 1928." The Democratic National Committee responded to such "requests from different parts of the country for specific information" about the "political and religious affiliations" of Smith's appointments with a widely circulated pamphlet. Democratic

National Committee, *Appointments by Governor Smith to Public Offices in the State of New York* (New York: Democratic National Committee, 1928), 1.

16. The journal was *The Protestant*, according to Charles H. Joseph, "Random Thoughts," *Jewish Criterion*, March 23, 1928, 8.

17. Lippmann to Smith, March 21, 1927, Lippmann Papers, reel 29, box 30, folder 1137.

18. Louise B. Hill to Progressive League for Alfred E. Smith, November 1, 1928, Eleanor Roosevelt Papers, box 6, folder 5.

19. David Fichman to Lillian Wald, October 11, 1928, Wald Papers, reel 11.

20. Lillian Wald to Mary McDonald, September 14, 1928, Wald Papers, reel 3; Chambers, *Seedtime of Reform*, 141.

21. Frances Perkins Oral History, Book II, 628.

22. Huthmacher, "Urban Liberalism," 239.

23. "Klan Men Plotted March on Houston to Defeat Smith," *New York World* (hereafter *NYW*), October 17, 1928, 17.

24. Ernest K. Lindley, "Smith Rips Dry League and Klan in Baltimore; 90,000 Hear His Speech," *NYW*, October 30, 1928, 1, 4; "Smith Opens Fire on Intolerance in Oklahoma Speech," *Philadelphia Record* (hereafter *PR*), September 21, 1928, 1, 4; "Smith Flays Klan[,] Charging Alliance with G.O.P. Chiefs," *PR*, October 30, 1928, 1; Henry Suydam, "Smith's Denunciation of Bigots in Klan Zone Is Hailed for Courage," *Brooklyn Eagle* (hereafter *BE*), September 21, 1928, 1; "24,000 Cheer Smith's Attack on Klan and Dry League as 'Allies' of G.O.P.," *BE*, November 4, 1928, 1; "Smith Smashes Ku Klux Klan in Talk Here," *Baltimore Afro-American* (hereafter *BAA*), November 3, 1928, 1; "Governor Smith Hits Bigotry and Intolerance in Oklahoma Speech," *Negro World*, September 29, 1928, 4.

25. "Hoover Silent on Intolerance Charge by Smith," *BE*, September 21, 1928, 1; "Willebrandt Is at It Once More; 'Smith No Sport,'" *Brooklyn Citizen*, October 8, 1928, 1; "McDonald Raps Hoover as KKK and Lily White," *BAA*, August 4, 1928, 1; "Hoover Chief Now Playing with Ku Klux," *BAA*, August 11, 1928, 1; "GOP Guilty of Dastard Crime—Kelly Miller," *BAA*, October 13, 1928, 1; "Goose Neck Bill Scores Hoover," *BAA*, October 13, 1928, 2; "Think G.O.P. Has Put $100,000 in Klan Newspaper," *BAA*, October 20, 1928, 3; "To the Polls for Smith!," *Negro World*, November 3, 1928, 4.

26. Fred B. Watson, "Where They Roost," *BAA*, October 20, 1928, 1.

27. "Smash Republican Deal with the Ku Klux Klan Vote Right This Year," *Negro World*, November 3, 1928, 5.

28. "Who Asked His Religion?," *BE*, October 24, 1928, 10.

29. Huthmacher, *Massachusetts*, 166.

30. "Religious Intolerance Is Biggest Campaign Issue," *BAA*, October 6, 1928, 4.

31. John M. Allswang, *A House for All Peoples: Ethnic Politics in Chicago, 1890–1936* (Lexington: University Press of Kentucky, 1971), 133; Harold F. Gosnell, *Negro Politicians: The Rise of Negro Politics in Chicago* (Chicago: University of Chicago Press, 1935), 30.

32. Samuel O'Dell, "Blacks, the Democratic Party, and the Presidential Election of 1928: A Mild Rejoinder," *Phylon* 48, no. 1 (1st Quarter, 1987): 1–11, 7; Huthmacher, *Massachusetts*, 173.

33. Mrs. J. A. Robinson, letter to the editor, *BAA*, November 3, 1928, 6.

34. Robert Jackson, letter to the editor, *BAA*, November 3, 1928, 6.

35. "Religious and Racial Intolerance," editorial, *St. Louis Argus*, September 21, 1928, 8.

36. "Roosevelt Denies Tariff Is an Issue," *New York Times*, October 17, 1928, 19; "Rabbi Wise Fears New Civil Strife," *NYW*, October 17, 1928, 7.

37. "Fair Play and Foul Methods in American Political Life," *American Israelite* (Cincinnati), October 4, 1928, 1.

38. Allswang, *A House for All Peoples*, 136.

39. Personal interview with Oscar Handlin, Cambridge, MA, August 15, 2009.

40. "Brooklyn Observes Columbus Day with Many Celebrations," *BE*, October 13, 1928, 3.

41. "Walker and Olvany Will Address Uptown Italians," *Bronx Home News*, October 31, 1928, 7.

42. Basil Manly, "Hoover, if He Is Elected, Will Be First Millionaire to Occupy White House," *BE*, September 24, 1928, 3.

43. "Smith Is Hero to Servants of Household Staff," *PR*, October 28, 1928, 9.

44. "Smith Closest to People since Lincoln, Rooted in Soil, Says Psychologist," *PR*, November 3, 1928, 16.

45. "Marcus Garvey States Why He Is for Smith and against Hoover," *Negro World*, September 29, 1928, 4; "Every Negro with a Ballot Must Vote for Al Smith," *Negro World*, October 20, 1928, 1.

46. "Hoover Hovers Close to Home for Labor Day," *PR*, September 4, 1928, 18.

47. "They Know Different," *PR*, November 2, 1928, 8; "Where's the Smoke from the Chimneys, Mr. Hoover?," *NYW*, October 16, 1928; "Giving Him a Smell," *Baltimore Sun*, October 16, 1928, 14.

48. Henry Suydam, "Smith in Fighting Speech Charges Hoover Gave Aid to Power Propagandists," *BE*, September 23, 1928, 1; "Gov. Smith Links Hoover with Huge Waterpower Trust," *PR*, September 23, 1928, 1.

49. Basil Manley, "Smith Fight with Hoover Looms in Bold Stand by Democrat on Water Power," *BE*, August 23, 1928, 3.

50. Albert Parsons Sachs, "Smith Would Save Billions to Consumers of Electricity by His Water-Power Plan," *PR*, October 28, 1928, 7.

51. "To the Polls for Smith!," 1.

52. "Norris Supports Smith; Strikes at Hoover on Power," *NYW*, October 25, 1928, 1; "Out into the Open Air," *NYW*, October 25, 1928, 14; Jerry Doyle, "Carry On!," *PR*, October 29, 1928, 8; "Senator Norris Attacks Hoover for Silence on 'Water Power Trust,'" *NYW*, October 28, 1928, 22; Charles Michelson, "Smith Smites Hoover for Cry of 'Socialism'; Boston Wild over Him," *NYW*, October 25, 1928, 1; "Smith Sees Smoke Screen of Power Trust in Hoover's 'Socialism' Cry," *NYW*, October 25, 1928, 2; "Governor Nails Story of Socialism," *Brooklyn Citizen*, October 25, 1928, 1; "Government Ownership of Power Plants Hit by Hoover," *PR*, October 23, 1928, 1; "At Last—an Issue!," *Baltimore Sun*, October 24, 1928, 12; "Herbie, I Think WE Made a Mistake, When YOU Said Somethin' in New York," *Baltimore Sun*, October 25, 1928, 1; "A-Ha!! Another Straw Man!," *Brooklyn Citizen*, October 25, 1928, 1; "That Boogey Man Will Get You if You Don't Watch Out," *PR*, October 24, 1928, 8.

53. "Give-Work-and-Vote for Alfred E. Smith," *Jewish Exponent*, October 19, 1928, 9.

54. "Why New York Negroes Favor Alfred E. Smith," *BAA*, September 1, 1928, 10.

55. "Every Negro with a Ballot Must Vote for Alfred Smith," 1; "Misleading the People, I—Smith's Fitness and the Public Weal," *Negro World*, October 20, 1928, 4.

56. "To the Polls for Smith!," 1. See also E. David Cronon, *Black Moses: The Story of Marcus Garvey and the Universal Negro Improvement Association* (Madison: University of Wisconsin Press, 1969), 150.

57. "Marcus Garvey States Why He Is for Smith," 4.

58. "Around Town," *BAA*, October 6, 1928, 6.

59. "Thousands Mill around Hotel to Glimpse Smith," *PR*, October 28, 1928, 9.

60. "Campaign March Dedicated to 'Al' Smith Is the Latest Composition of Bronx Musician," *Bronx and Manhattan Home News*, November 4, 1928, 11.

61. "Truck Driver Gives $25 of $42 Wages for Smith," *NYW*, October 28, 1928, 23.

62. "Charcoal Sketch of Al Smith by Phila. Admirer," *PR*, September 4, 1928, 18.

63. "Camden Crowds Pack Streets to Welcome Smith," *PR*, October 28, 1928, 7.

64. "Smith Placards Save Boy in Motor Smash," *NYW*, October 21, 1928, 3.

65. "300 Voters Fight against Poll Ban against 40,000 in Jersey," *BE*, October 26, 1928, 2; "Democrats Fight Jersey Poll Laws," *NYW*, October 21, 1928, 3; "Jersey Jury Acts on Vote Blacklist," *NYW*, October 31, 1928, 3.

66. "Republicans Challenge Nuns at Registration," *NYW*, October 17, 1928, 5.

67. "26th Ward Head Fired by City for Backing Al Smith," *PR*, October 2, 1928, 1.

68. "Smith's Welcome in Omaha Rivals Col. Lindbergh's," *BE*, September 18, 1928, 1.

69. Henry Suydam, "Smith Rejoices as Enthusiasm Fires Northwest," *BE*, September 28, 1928, 2; "Children Cheer Gov. Smith over Twin City Route," *PR*, September 28, 1928, 1.

70. "Riot in Chicago to Hear Smith," *BE*, October 19, 1928, 1; Ernest K. Lindley, "Chicago Thunders Greeting to Smith," *NYW*, October 18, 1928, 1.

71. Lindley, "Smith Rips Dry League and Klan in Baltimore," *NYW*, 1; "'Hello, Al!' Solid South Greets Smith," *PR*, October 12, 1928, 1; "Virginia Recognizes Quality" (captioned photograph), *Brooklyn Citizen*, October 12, 1928, 1.

72. Henry Suydam, "Big Smith Ovation at Boston Spurs Hope of Winning East," *BE*, October 25, 1928, 1; "Unbroken Ovation Marks Smith Trip after Hub Triumph," *NYW*, October 26, 1928, 1.

73. "Boston Welcome to Smith Moves His Wife to Tears," *PR*, October 26, 1928, 5.

74. "Greatest Crowd Boston Ever Saw out to Hail Democracy's Leader; Will Philadelphia Duplicate This Welcome to Al Smith Today?" (captioned photograph), *PR*, October 27, 1928, 4.

75. "City Gives Smith Wild Welcome as He Tours Streets," *PR*, October 28, 1928, 1; "Smith in Arena Speech Rips Dry, Tariff Critics to Pieces," *PR*, October 28, 1928, 1.

76. Ernest K. Lindley, "Smith in Philadelphia, Has Greatest Political Triumph in City Annals," *NYW*, October 28, 1928, 1.

77. S. A. Hayes, "Philadelphia's Surrender to Smith," *Negro World*, November 3, 1928, 2.

78. "Gov. Smith Stirs Brooklyn Crowd of 45,000 to Frenzy; Day Parade Wild Tribute," *NYW*, November 3, 1928, 1; Ernest K. Lindley, "Smith Gets Biggest Ovation of His Campaign at Garden; Sees Victory as Fight Ends," *NYW*, November 4, 1928, 1.

79. William Weer, "2,000,000 Cheer Smith in City," *BE*, November 2, 1928, 1.

80. See Michael E. McGerr, *The Decline of Popular Politics: The American North, 1865–1928* (New York: Oxford University Press, 1986), 184–210; Richard L. McCormick, *The Party Period and Public Policy: American Politics from the Age of Jackson to the Progressive Era* (New York: Oxford University Press, 1986), 316–319.

81. Edgar Eugene Robinson, *The Presidential Vote, 1896–1932* (Stanford, CA: Stanford University Press, 1934), 46.

82. V. O. Key, *Southern Politics in State and Nation* (New York: Alfred A. Knopf, 1949), 319.

83. Robinson, *The Presidential Vote*, 46.

84. Samuel J. Eldersveld, "The Influence of Metropolitan Party Pluralities in Presidential Elections since 1920: A Study of Twelve Key Cities," *American Political Science Review* 43, no. 6 (December 1949): 1189–1206; V. O. Key Jr., "A Theory of Critical Elections," *Journal of Politics* 17, no. 1 (February 1955): 3–18; Duncan MacRae Jr. and James A. Meldrum, "Critical Elections in Illinois: 1888–1958," *American Political Science Review* 54, no. 3 (September 1960): 669–683; Gerald Pomper, "Classification of Presidential Elections," *Journal of Politics* 29, no. 3 (August 1967): 535–566; Carl N. Degler, "American Political Parties and the Rise of the City: An Interpretation," *Journal of American History* 51, no. 1 (June 1964): 41–59; Allswang, *A House for All Peoples*, 37–110; Larry M. Bartels, "Electoral Continuity and Change, 1868–1996," *Electoral Studies* 17, no. 3 (September 1998): 275–300, esp. 281.

85. Key, "A Theory of Critical Elections," 4. The political analyst Samuel Lubell similarly posited that "Smith's defeat in 1928, rather than Roosevelt's 1932 victory, marked off the arena in which today's politics are being fought." Samuel Lubell, *The Future of American Politics* (Garden City, NY: Doubleday, 1951), 36.

86. Degler, "American Political Parties and the Rise of the City," 53–55. Taking a longer view, the historian Morton Keller notes: "Smith went far to restore the urban Democratic majority of most of the nineteenth century." Morton Keller, *America's Three Regimes: A New Political History* (New York: Oxford University Press, 2007), 197.

87. Sundquist, *Dynamics of the Party System*, 175; Robinson, *The Presidential Vote*, 194, 198, 235, 237, 240, 289–290; Robert Booth Fowler, *Wisconsin Votes: An Electoral History* (Madison: University of Wisconsin Press, 2008), 137.

88. Generations of scholars have noted that while race was central to the geography of the southern vote, this was not only a case of white supremacist adherence to the party of Jim Crow: farm economics also influenced voting in these regions. Key, *Southern Politics*, 329. See also Robert Chiles, "Alfred E. Smith and Transitional Progressivism: The Revolution before the New Deal" (PhD diss., University of Maryland, 2012), 471–568. The 1928 election in the south is the subject of a separate, forthcoming study from the author.

89. On the Corn Belt response to Smith, see Chiles, "Courting the Farm Vote on the Northern Plains," 25–28.

90. Huthmacher, *Massachusetts*, 177.

91. Allswang, *A House for All Peoples*, 38, 43–53; Erie, *Rainbow's End*, 125.

92. Erie, *Rainbow's End*, 126–127; Chiles, "Alfred E. Smith and Transitional Progressivism," 626.

93. John L. Shover, "The Emergence of a Two-Party System in Republican Philadelphia, 1924–1936," *Journal of American History* 60, no. 4 (March 1974): 985–1002, esp. 991.

94. Fowler, *Wisconsin Votes*, 137.

95. Shover, "The Emergence of a Two-Party System in Republican Philadelphia," 991; Allswang, *A House for All Peoples*, 51.

96. Richard Klayman, *The First Jew: Prejudice and Politics in an American Community, 1900–1932* (Malden, MA: Old Suffolk Square Press, 1985), 84, 85, 117, 121; Slayton, *Empire Statesman*, 325; Lichtman, *Prejudice and the Old Politics*, 111.

97. Jerome M. Clubb and Howard W. Allen, "The Cities and the Election of 1928: Partisan Realignment?," *American Historical Review* 74, no. 4 (April 1969): 1205–1220; Walter Dean Burnham, *Critical Elections and the Mainsprings of American Politics* (New York: Norton, 1970), 56; Shover, "The Emergence of a Two-Party System in Republican Philadelphia"; Michael Paul Rogin and John L. Shover, *Political Change in California: Critical Elections and Social Movements, 1890–1966* (Westport, CT: Greenwood Press, 1970); David J. Alvarez and Edmond J. True, "Critical Elections and Partisan Realignment: An Urban Test-Case," *Polity* 5, no. 4 (Summer 1973): 563–576; Bernard Sternsher, "The Emergence of the New Deal Party System: A Problem in Historical Analysis of Voter Behavior," *Journal of Interdisciplinary History* 6, no. 1 (Summer 1975): 127–149, esp. 138; Marc V. Levine, "Standing Political Decisions and Partisan Realignment: The Pattern of Maryland Politics, 1872–1948," *Journal of Politics* 38, no. 2 (May 1976): 292–325; Bernard Sternsher, "The New Deal Party System: A Reappraisal," *Journal of Interdisciplinary History* 15, no. 1 (Summer 1984): 53–81; John L. Shover, "Ethnicity and Religion in Philadelphia Politics, 1924–40," *American Quarterly* 25, no. 5 (December 1973): 499–515.

98. Lichtman, *Prejudice and the Old Politics*, 201, 231, 239; Lichtman, "Critical Election Theory and the Reality of American Presidential Politics," 317–351.

99. The political scientist John Petrocik notes: "Realignment occurs when the measureable party bias of identifiable segments of the population changes in such a way that the social group profile of the parties—the party coalitions—is altered." Abandoning "the conventional assumption that electoral realignments are synonymous with a change to a new majority party," Petrocik's nuanced definition empowers historians to investigate alterations in the character of partisan coalitions and to track the significance of specific contests to those changes. John R. Petrocik, *Party Coalitions: Realignment and the Decline of the New Deal Party System* (Chicago: University of Chicago Press, 1981), 15–16.

100. See Chiles, "Alfred E. Smith and Transitional Progressivism," 356–370.

101. Those cities were, from largest to smallest: New York; Chicago; Philadelphia; Detroit; Los Angeles; Cleveland; St. Louis; Baltimore; Boston; Pittsburgh; San Francisco; Milwaukee; Buffalo; Minneapolis; New Orleans; Cincinnati; Newark; Kansas City, MO; Seattle; and Indianapolis. Washington, DC, was excluded because it had no presidential vote in the period under consideration.

5. The Revolution before the New Deal

1. Lubell, *The Future of American Politics*, 36; Huthmacher, *Massachusetts*, 150, 157–158.

2. "10,000 Hail Smith Party Going through Pittsfield," *Boston Globe* (hereafter *BG*), October 25, 1928, 21; Huthmacher, *Massachusetts*, 178; "Thousands Greet Governor

Smith at Springfield," *Holyoke Daily Transcript*, October 24, 1928, 1; "30,000 People Cheer Gov Smith as He Halts Here on Way to Boston," *Springfield Daily News*, October 24, 1928, 1; "Crowds Greet Train at All of Its Stops," *BG*, October 25, 1928, 21.

3. "150,000 Hail Smith on Boston Common," *BG*, October 25, 1928, 1, 24; "Battle of the Atlantic," *Time*, November 5, 1928; "Arena Crowd Twice Breaks Police Lines," *BG*, October 25, 1928, 1, 24; Charles Michelson, "Smith Smites Hoover for Cry of 'Socialism'; Boston Wild over Him," *New York World*, October 25, 1928, 1.

4. "Battle of the Atlantic."

5. "Throngs Roar Welcome to Al Smith on His Passage through Woonsocket," *Woonsocket Call*, October 25, 1928, 1; "Battle of the Atlantic."

6. "Al Smith Acclaimed by Thousands on Trip from Blackstone to Providence," *Providence Journal*, October 26, 1928, 1; "A Visit from Al," editorial, *Providence Journal*, October 26, 1928, 18 (second section).

7. "500,000 Folk Pay Tribute to Smith," *BG*, October 26, 1928, 1, 16; "Battle of the Atlantic."

8. "The Brown Derby Passes," editorial, *Woonsocket Call*, October 25, 1928, 15.

9. "A Visit from Al," 18; "Governor Smith's Reception," editorial, *Hartford Courant* (hereafter *HC*), October 27, 1928, 8.

10. "Battle of the Atlantic."

11. Republican Business Men, Inc., "A Chicken for Every Pot" (advertisement), October 30, 1928, Herbert Hoover Papers, National Archives, Washington, DC, ID: 187095.

12. "Stenographic Report of Smith's Boston Speech Answering Hoover on 'State Socialism,'" *New York Times* (hereafter *NYT*), October 25, 1928, 2.

13. Ibid.

14. Handlin, *Al Smith*, 130.

15. For example, Frances Perkins, "Notes for Campaign Speech to Social Workers in Boston, Sept 1928"; Perkins, "Speech, Boston, 10/2/28," both in Perkins Papers, box 43.

16. "Smith's Humane Record Is Mrs. Norton's Topic," *BG*, October 9, 1928, 10.

17. "Women Speakers to Tour for Smith," *BG*, October 27, 1928, 13; "'Smith Special' off for Tour of State," *BG*, October 28, 1928, A16; "Smith Flying Squadron Is Heard at Greenfield," *BG*, October 30, 1928, 18.

18. Maurice Francis Egan and John B. Kennedy, *The Knights of Columbus in Peace and War*, vol. 2 (New Haven, CT: Knights of Columbus, 1920), 160; "Quincy's New Mayor Sworn In on Saturday," *BG*, January 3, 1925, A8; "McGrath Discusses Finances at Quincy," *BG*, January 7, 1930, 7.

19. "Coolidge Asks Vote for Party Policies," *NYT*, September 30, 1928, 1, 27.

20. John D. Merrill, "Walsh Turns Down Debate with HYoung [*sic*]," *BG*, October 3, 1928, 25; "G.O.P. Elector Quits to Support Smith," *HC*, October 3, 1928, 5.

21. Kristi Andersen, "Generation, Partisan Shift, and Realignment: A Glance back to the New Deal," in *The Changing American Voter*, by Norman H. Nie, Sidney Verba, and John R. Petrocik (Cambridge, MA: Harvard University Press, 1976), 74–95; see also Petrocik, *Party Coalitions*, 55.

22. "17 Selfish Groups Backing Harding, Declares Gov. Cox," *NYT*, October 15, 1920, 1, 3.

23. Ibid., 3.

24. Allswang, *Bosses, Machines, and Urban Voters*, 100; Allswang, *A House for All Peoples*, 112–116; Huthmacher, *Massachusetts*, 19–23. Poles underwent a similar transformation: see Edward R. Kantowicz, *Polish-American Politics in Chicago, 1888–1940* (Chicago: University of Chicago Press, 1975), 115–119; see also John Morton Blum, *Woodrow Wilson and the Politics of Morality* (Boston: Little, Brown, 1956) 170, 179; John Milton Cooper Jr., *Pivotal Decades: The United States, 1900–1920* (New York: Norton, 1990), 372–373.

25. As Oscar Handlin summarizes: "The populists made no headway at all in districts where the newcomers were numerous, and William Jennings Bryan could not hold the loyalty of such traditionally Democratic groups as the Irish." Handlin, *The Uprooted*, 218.

26. Gary Gerstle, *Working-Class Americanism: The Politics of Labor in a Textile City, 1914–1960* (New York: Cambridge University Press, 1989), 19–60; Huthmacher, *Massachusetts*, 14–15; Sterne, *Ballots and Bibles*, 46, 51, 84; Gerald H. Gamm, *The Making of New Deal Democrats: Voting Behavior and Realignment in Boston, 1920–1940* (Chicago: University of Chicago Press, 1989), 77–80.

27. Huthmacher, *Massachusetts*, 23–28.

28. While these Democratic struggles with new-stock voters have been well documented, a number of studies have noted some precedents emerging in the 1920s for such voters' later Democratic preference. Although such cases are relevant, they did not exhibit the breadth, scale, or durability of the overwhelmingly Democratic voting of ethnic New Englanders beginning in 1928. See Huthmacher, *Massachusetts*, 117–149; Gamm, *The Making of New Deal Democrats*, 75; Buenker, *Urban Liberalism*, 224.

29. Erie, *Rainbow's End*, 17.

30. Connolly, *The Triumph of Ethnic Progressivism*, 160, 192; "Democrats Assign Roles in Campaign," *BG*, October 1, 1928, 4. Classified and calculated by the author.

31. "Committees Named for Smith Rally," *HC*, October 21, 1928, 14. Hartford was nearly 13 percent Italian and 8 percent Polish at the time. Classified and calculated by the author. U.S. Department of Commerce, Bureau of the Census, *Fifteenth Census of the United States: 1930, Population* (Washington, DC: Government Printing Office, 1931) (hereafter *1930 Census*), vol. 3, part 1, pp. 353, 360. On the other hand, by 1928, "the triumvirate that ruled the Democratic Party in Hartford were Thomas J. Spellacy, Tony Zazzaro, and Herman Kopplemann—an Irishman, an Italian, and a Jew." Herbert F. Janick Jr., *A Diverse People: Connecticut, 1914 to the Present* (Chester, CT: Pequot Press, 1975), 36.

32. "Italians Hold Rally," *Newport Mercury and Weekly News*, November 2, 1928, 2.

33. Quoted in Aaron F. DeMoranville Jr., "Ethnic Voting in Rhode Island" (master's thesis, Brown University, 1961), 107.

34. Ronald A. Petrin, *French Canadians in Massachusetts Politics, 1885–1915: Ethnicity and Political Pragmatism* (Philadelphia: Balch Institute Press, 1990), 83, 87, 106, 127, 157; Sterne, *Ballots and Bibles*, 84; DeMoranville, "Ethnic Voting in Rhode Island," 15–16.

35. DeMoranville, "Ethnic Voting in Rhode Island," 15–16.

36. During the 1920s, these partisan loyalties suffered numerous trials, including Republican passage of the Peck Act in 1922, which extended the authority of the state board of education to parochial schools and mandated English-language instruction. With community élites antagonized by this cultural harassment and working-class voters dismayed by the state's repressive response to the 1922 textile strikes in the

Pawtucket and Blackstone valleys, the French voted Democratic that fall. This had represented a rejection of Republican policies rather than an endorsement of the Democrats, and by 1924 French Canadian voters had returned to the GOP. Gerstle, *Working-Class Americanism*, 25, 28–29, 46–50; Sterne, *Ballots and Bibles*, 218–223; DeMoranville, "Ethnic Voting in Rhode Island," 59–61, 71, 76, 86, 87, 92.

37. "G.O.P. Certain of Rhode Island," *BG*, October 21, 1928, A64; DeMoranville, "Ethnic Voting in Rhode Island," 106–107; Gerstle, *Working-Class Americanism*, 50–53.

38. DeMoranville, "Ethnic Voting in Rhode Island," 112.

39. John K. White, "Alfred E. Smith's Rhode Island Revolution: The Election of 1928," *Rhode Island History* 42, no. 4 (May 1983): 56–66, 65; DeMoranville, "Ethnic Voting in Rhode Island," 92, 117, 121.

40. David Lawrence, "Surprises in New England Expected on Election Day," *North Adams Transcript*, October 22, 1928, 1–2.

41. "French Start Smith Drive," *Lowell Sun*, October 2, 1928, 1.

42. "Smith Drive at Height Here," *Lowell Sun*, October 5, 1928, 1.

43. "Cronin Writes Braden Again," *Lowell Sun*, October 8, 1928, 3.

44. "French-Americans Form Al Smith Club," *HC*, October 12, 1928, 17; "French-American Democrats to Meet," *HC*, October 22, 1928, 5; "Hold Democratic Rally," *HC*, October 24, 1928, 12; "Democrats End Campaign with Spirited Rallies," *HC*, November 5, 1928, 6.

45. "Brogna Named to Direct Smith Italian Campaign," *BG*, September 21, 1928, 16.

46. "Italian American League for Smith Extends Work," *BG*, October 2, 1928, 7.

47. "Smith Italian League Forms Women's Group," *BG*, October 9, 1928, 10; "Smith Italian League Organizes at Brockton," *BG*, October 15, 1928, 4.

48. Huthmacher, *Massachusetts*, 173.

49. Gerald P. McCarthy, "Al Smith Club Is Formed by Local Italians," *HC*, September 5, 1928, 2.

50. Connolly, *The Triumph of Ethnic Progressivism*, 192; "Italian American League for Smith Extends Work," 7; "Democrats Will Try for Italian Vote," *HC*, September 9, 1928, 6B.

51. "Democrats Will Try for Italian Vote," 6B.

52. Gerald P. McCarthy, "800 Italians Hold Smith Club Rally," *HC*, October 1, 1928, 4.

53. "Roraback's Message Hit by Spellacy," *HC*, November 5, 1928, 2.

54. M. E. Hennessy, "G.O.P. Certain of Rhode Island," *BG*, October 21, 1928, A64.

55. "Curtis Visit Surprise to Polish Body," *HC*, October 21, 1928, B6.

56. Ibid., B6.

57. "Polish Voters Close Campaign in Meriden," *HC*, November 6, 1928, 7.

58. "Belgian Native Praises Hoover at Polish Rally," *HC*, October 31, 1928, 17.

59. "Polish Citizen," letter to the editor, *Springfield Daily News*, November 5, 1928, 11.

60. "Lonergan Lectures Poles at Bridgeport Rally," *HC*, October 22, 1928, 4.

61. "Democrats End Campaign with Spirited Rallies," 6.

62. "Belgian Native Praises Hoover at Polish Rally," 17; "Curtis Visit Surprise to Polish Body," B6.

63. "Polish Voters Close Campaign in Meriden," 7.

64. "Belgian Native Praises Hoover at Polish Rally," 17.

65. Kantowicz, *Polish-American Politics in Chicago*, 127.

66. Louis M. Lyons, "Crowds in Suburbs Warmer Than Here," *BG*, October 16, 1928, 1, 16.

67. Kantowicz, *Polish-American Politics in Chicago*, 127.

68. "Poles And National Election," editorial, *Springfield Daily News*, October 10, 1928, 6.

69. "Asserts Club Favors Smith," *New Bedford Evening Standard*, September 27, 1928, 1.

70. Huthmacher, *Massachusetts*, 173.

71. "Big Smith Rally for Polish Voters Listed for Tonight," *Springfield Daily News*, November 3, 1928, 2.

72. John D. Merrill, "Democrats Add to Legislature Seats," *BG*, November 8, 1928, 1, 21.

73. Huthmacher, *Massachusetts*, 185.

74. J. White, "Alfred E. Smith's Rhode Island Revolution," 58. In Providence's heavily Italian Fourteenth District, Smith had a four-to-one margin, and in the Italian Seventeenth District, the Democrat's cushion was six to one, outpacing even the Irish Twenty-Fourth District, which went to Smith by a more modest three-to-one margin. DeMoranville, "Ethnic Voting in Rhode Island," 118. One study has suggested that Rhode Island Italians began drifting toward the Democracy with Wilson; but even that study, while challenging 1928 as a "revolution," shows that the 1928 numbers were unprecedented. Stefano Luconi, *The Italian-American Vote in Providence, Rhode Island, 1916–1948* (Cranbury, NJ: Associated University Presses, 2004), 18.

75. Huthmacher, *Massachusetts*, 184.

76. "Waterbury Gives Smith Plurality of 5,428 Votes," *HC*, November 7, 1928, 26; "New Haven County," *HC*, November 7, 1928, 3; *1930 Census*, vol. 3, part 1, p. 360. The *Hartford Courant* called this a "complete [Democratic] victory" in Waterbury; but Republican congressman James Glynn ran 187 votes ahead of even Al Smith, despite the fact that the Brass City was the home of his opponent, Edward Mascolo.

77. Huthmacher, *Massachusetts*, 183–185. The political scientist Gerald Gamm, in a nuanced analysis of ethnic voting in Boston, has also noted large Italian and Jewish votes for Smith but tempers the "Al Smith Revolution" argument by pointing to historical Italian membership in the Democratic Party and to the fact that Smith's success in Jewish Boston did not significantly affect party registration. Nonetheless, Gamm notes that Smith's candidacy did instigate a period of "tremendous mobilization of new voters on behalf of the Democratic Party," with Italian turnout in 1928 reaching "unprecedented" levels; while the Jewish vote for Smith—if not the whole Democratic ticket—"helped ease the ensuing period of realignment." Gamm, *The Making of New Deal Democrats*, 45, 60–61, 67, 75, 84, 86.

78. Indeed, this was only the second Democratic plurality of that period—Wilson had carried the county over Taft by 27 votes in 1912—an election in which Theodore Roosevelt's Progressive candidacy attracted over 8,000 Hamden County ballots. Clerk of the Senate and Clerk of the House, *A Manual for Use of the General Court of Massachusetts for 1929–1930* (Boston: Wright and Potter Printing, 1929) (hereafter *Massachusetts Manual*, various years), 401; *1930 Census*, vol. 3, part 1, pp. 1082, 1098, 1100; Robinson, *The Presidential Vote*, 227.

79. Election statistics compiled from *Massachusetts Manual, 1897–1898* (326–336); *1901–1902* (324–334), *1905–1906* (347–357), *1909–1911* (364–374), *1913–1914* (378–388),

1917–1918 (385–395), *1921–1922* (383–393), *1925–1926* (389–399), and *1929–1930* (397–407); demographic statistics from *1930 Census*, vol. 3, part 1, pp. 1085, 1098, 1100.

80. *Massachusetts Manual,1929–1930; 1930 Census*, vol. 3, part 1, pp. 1082, 1085, 1098, 1100.

81. *1930 Census*, vol. 3, part 1, pp. 352, 353, 360, 365; "New Britain Election Returns by Wards," *HC*, November 7, 1928, 7; "National and State Election, November 6, 1928," *HC*, November 7, 1928, 11; Robinson, *The Presidential Vote*, 155.

82. John S. Winialski, letter to the editor, *HC*, October 23, 1928, 8.

83. "Prohibition Called Curse of Country," *HC*, September 29, 1928, 6.

84. McCarthy, "800 Italians Hold Smith Rally," 4.

85. "Democrats End Campaign with Spirited Rallies," 6.

86. "Roraback's Message Hit by Spellacy," 2.

87. Alexander Bielski, letter to the editor, *Springfield Daily News*, November 1, 1928, 8.

88. J.J.Z., letter to the editor, *Springfield Union*, November 1, 1928, 10. One historian has noted that for many workers, Prohibition "smacked of paternalism and class exploitation. . . . It was a hypocritical and insulting attempt to control their personal habits in order to exact greater profits for their employers." James H. Timberlake, *Prohibition and the Progressive Movement, 1900–1920* (New York: Atheneum, 1970), 92–93.

89. "The Under Dog," editorial, *Westerly Sun*, September 16, 1928, 4.

90. V. Gentile, letter to the editor, *Westerly Sun*, October 7, 1928, 4.

91. "Hoover Still Evasive, Irrelevant," editorial, *Springfield Daily News*, October 20, 1928, 4.

92. John D. Merrill, "Essex Republicans Hear Tariff Issue," *BG*, October 4, 1928, 11.

93. "Young Assails Walsh on His Tariff Vote," *BG*, October 6, 1928, 12.

94. McCarthy, "800 Italians Hold Smith Club Rally," 4.

95. "Stenographic Report of Gov. Smith's Speech to Louisville Democrats Last Night," *NYT*, October 14, 1928, 25.

96. "Gov. Smith's New Tariff Policy," editorial, *Lowell Sun*, October 15, 1928, 12.

97. "Kopplemann Ridicules G.O.P. Prosperity Issue," *HC*, November 2, 1928, 18.

98. Robert D. Byrnes, "State Roars Welcome to Smith Train," *HC*, October 26, 1928, 1, 20, quote from 20.

99. "We Are All Protectionists Now," editorial, *HC*, October 20, 1928, 8.

100. "Fort Condemns Smith Program," *BG*, October 19, 1928, 1, 16.

101. "Our Tariff Distrust of Smith," editorial, *HC*, October 11, 1928, 8.

102. Business support of Smith: "Calumet Copper Head for Smith," *HC*, September 20, 1928, 13; "Filene of Boston Store Supporting Gov. Smith," *HC*, October 4, 1928, 4.

103. "Wool Trade Conducts Rally for Republicans," *BG*, October 18, 1928, 16.

104. "DeWitt Page Explains His Party Stand," *HC*, September 9, 1928, 1, 10, quote from 1.

105. "Battle of the Atlantic."

106. "Let's Keep What We've Got!" (advertisement), *Fall River Globe*, November 5, 1928, 8.

107. Horace G. Knowles, letter to the editor, *HC*, November 5, 1928, 8.

108. "General Cole Raps Hoover," *Lowell Sun*, October 17, 1928, 2.

109. "Insidious Coercion That Will Not Work," editorial, *Springfield Daily News*, October 1, 1928, 4.

110. "Mill Posters Boost Hoover," *New Bedford Evening Standard*, November 2, 1928, 14.

111. "Boomerangs," editorial, *Springfield Daily News*, October 3, 1928, 6.

112. "Tariff Bogey and Intimidation of Labor," editorial, *Lowell Sun*, November 3, 1928, 8.

113. Smith, "Newark," in Democratic National Committee, *Campaign Addresses*, 251-268, quote from 258-259. This was indeed a national phenomenon. At Andrew Mellon's New Kensington, Pennsylvania, aluminum works, management "let it be known to the employees . . . that unless Hoover is elected they may find themselves out of employment," and in some cases demanded that workers "must wear Hoover buttons if they expect to remain in the employ" of Alcoa. "Mellon Company Makes Employees Support Hoover," *New Orleans Times-Picayune*, October 23, 1928, 1.

114. "Intimidating Labor," editorial, *Lowell Sun*, November 2, 1928, 16.

115. "A Worker," letter to the editor, *HC*, September 30, 1928, A2.

116. "Luke Warm," letter to the editor, *HC*, September 30, 1928, A2.

117. "Northampton," letter to the editor, *Springfield Union*, November 5, 1928, 8.

118. "Reader," letter to the editor, *HC*, September 30, 1928, A2.

119. "Breadwinner," letter to the editor, *Springfield Daily News*, October 30, 1928, 6.

120. William H. Kelly, letter to the editor, *Springfield Daily News*, October 16, 1928, 6.

121. Anonymous (from Westfield, MA), letter to the editor, *Springfield Daily News*, October 30, 1928, 6.

122. "Enthusiastic Crowd of 3500 Attends Democratic Rally," *Lowell Sun*, October 20, 1928, 3.

123. "G.O.P. Prosperity Claims Attacked by Lonergan in Speech," *HC*, October 10, 1928, 6.

124. "Lonergan Raps Hoover's Ability at Smith Meeting," *HC*, October 27, 1928, 2.

125. "Walsh, Cole and Barry Speak at Ludlow Plant," *BG*, October 25, 1928, 6.

126. "Campaign Speech in Support of Alfred E. Smith for the Presidency," Hamden, Connecticut, October 11, 1928, Griffin Papers, box 14, 4-5.

127. Ibid., 5.

128. Daniel Georgianna, with Roberta Hazen Aaronson, *The Strike of '28* (New Bedford, MA: Spinner, 1993), 49-138.

129. "Enthusiastic Crowd of 3500 Attends Democratic Rally," 3.

130. "The G.O.P. Tariff Attacked," editorial, *Lowell Sun*, October 8, 1928, 10.

131. "G.O.P. Campaigners Make a Discovery," editorial, *Lowell Sun*, October 9, 1928, 10.

132. "Walsh Heads Guests at Marlboro Outing," *BG*, September 23, 1928, A15; "New Smith Clubs Hear Cole, Walsh," *BG*, October 4, 1928, 25.

133. "Walsh, Cole and Barry Speak at Ludlow Plant," 6.

134. *Massachusetts Manual, 1929-1930*, 401.

135. Ibid., 397-407.

136. U.S. Department of Commerce, Bureau of the Census, *Religious Bodies: 1926*, vol. 1 (Washington, DC: Government Printing Office, 1930) (hereafter *Religious Bodies*), 400, 452, 460-461, 479, 504-505, 572.

137. Calculated by the author from "Tabulated Vote of the City by Precincts," *Fall River Globe*, November 7, 1928, 4; *1930 Census*, vol. 3, part 1, p. 1110; *Religious Bodies*, 420–421.

138. "Mills in Fall River Cut Pay 10 Percent," *BG*, January 20, 1928, 10.

139. Georgianna, *The Strike of '28*, 45–46; "Fall River Doffers on Strike, Cut 50 Percent," *BG*, February 4, 1922, 5.

140. "Cotton Mills Cut Wages," *NYT*, January 18, 1922, 28; "Mill Wages Cut 20%," *NYT*, January 20, 1922, 9; "Wage Cut Effective in Cotton Mill," *HC*, January 24, 1922, 14; "Announce Cut for 2000 at Lancaster Mills, Clinton," *BG*, February 3, 1922, 15; "Big Wage Cuts in Textile Mills," *HC*, February 5, 1922, X7.

141. "Strikes Shut Down New England Mills," *NYT*, February 14, 1922, 16; "Textile Strike Ends in Lawrence," *HC*, August 31, 1922, 1; "Lawrence Spindles Hum," *NYT*, August 31, 1922, 28; "One Big Union Sends Men Back," *BG*, September 3, 1922, 18; Georgianna, *The Strike of '28*, 47.

142. "Armed Police Rout Strikers," *BG*, February 10, 1922, 9; "Troops Sent to Quell Strikers," *BG*, February 21, 1922, 1, 12; "Police Fire on Pawtucket Mob," *BG*, February 22, 1922, 1, 5.

143. "Tells of Plight of Cotton Industry," *NYT*, May 31, 1924, 19; "Textile Workers Plan to Resist Wage Cuts," *NYT*, September 22, 1924, 20.

144. "Lowell Textile Mills Cut Wages," *NYT*, December 19, 1924, 43.

145. "Other Mills to Follow Fall River Wage Cut," *NYT*, January 4, 1925, 15.

146. "Accept Textile Wage Cut," *NYT*, January 8, 1925, 29.

147. "New Bedford Mills to Reduce Wages," *HC*, January 10, 1925, 19.

148. "Textile Wage Cut," *HC*, January 23, 1925, 14; "Refuses to Arbitrate," *NYT*, April 11, 1925, E2.

149. For example: "Textile Strikers Accept Wage Cut," *NYT*, January 9, 1926, 14; "Amoskeag Cut Unsettled," *NYT*, December 15, 1927, 47.

150. "Wage Cuts in Woolen Mills," *BG*, July 18, 1925, 8; "Lawrence Plant Closes," *NYT*, July 23, 1925, 22; "More Mills Cut Wages," *NYT*, July 24, 1925, 5; "Pittsfield Mill Strikers to Return," *BG*, August 28, 1925, A12.

151. "Wage Earners in Cotton-Goods Industry, Classified According to Prevailing Hours of Labor in Factories in Which Employed, for Massachusetts and North Carolina: 1925," Van Kleeck Papers, box 62, folder 9.

152. C. Vann Woodward, *Origins of the New South, 1877–1913* (Baton Rouge: Louisiana State University Press, 1971), 299, 305, 306, 308; Margaret Terrell Parker, *Lowell: A Study of Industrial Development* (New York: Macmillan, 1940), 162.

153. For example: "Textile Mills Shut Down," *NYT*, July 3, 1926, 6; "July Employment Felt Usual Slump," *NYT*, August 13, 1926, 28; "Nashua Co. Sells Part of Lowell Plant," *NYT*, December 24, 1926, 22; "Three Mills Close, Two after Walkout," *NYT*, March 15, 1927, 27; "American Woolen Co. Closes Mill in New Hampshire," *HC*, March 15, 1927, 9; "Another Maine Mill Announces Wage Cut of 10 Per Cent," *HC*, December 14, 1927, 15; "Textile Mill to Close Temporarily," *NYT*, December 23, 1927, 34; "Mills to Close 2 Weeks," *NYT*, June 25, 1928, 39.

154. "Textile Cities Hit Hard," editorial, *Lowell Sun*, October 18, 1928, 14. Smith cited the same figures in his Boston address the following week.

155. "New England Should Support Smith," editorial, *Lowell Sun*, October 23, 1928, 10.

156. "1919: Average Number of Wage-Earners in the Cotton Goods Industry" and "1919: Average Number of Wage-Earners in Woolen and Worsted," Van Kleeck Papers, box 62, folder 9; *1930 Census*, vol. 3, part 1, pp. 361, 1102; part 2, pp. 169, 770.

157. For example, Gary Gerstle has demonstrated that for the French Canadian community in Woonsocket, *la survivance*, the project of cultural survival, top-down though it may have been, was central to working-class life into the 1920s. Gerstle, *Working-Class Americanism*, 19–53, 58. The historian Ardis Cameron similarly traced politics at the intersection of labor and the "series of practical actions and strategies, carefully calculated in the context of family, kin, and neighbors," that constituted the "process of daily life" in her work on women's labor activism in Lawrence. Ardis Cameron, *Radicals of the Worst Sort: Laboring Women in Lawrence, Massachusetts, 1860–1912* (Urbana: University of Illinois Press, 1993), 6.

158. See Gerstle, *Working-Class Americanism*, 53; Evelyn A. Sterne, "Patchwork of Protest: Social Diversity and Labor Militancy in the New Bedford Strike of 1928" (master's thesis, Duke University, 1994), 61.

159. "Jack Rubenstein, 9/2/80," New Bedford Textile Workers' Strike of 1928 Oral History, University of Massachusetts–Dartmouth, Dartmouth, MA (hereafter NBOH), box 1, folder 8, 12.

160. "Hattie Anderson, 1974," Mill Life Oral History Collection, University of Rhode Island Library Special Collections and Archives, University of Rhode Island, Kingstown, RI (hereafter RIOH), box 11, folder 70, 3, 9.

161. "Francis Dailey, 1971," RIOH, 6, 7, 20.

162. "Edward D. Hart, 1984," Mill Workers of Lowell: Mary Blewett and Martha Mayo, Project Directors, University of Massachusetts–Lowell and Lowell National Historical Park (hereafter LOH), 34. http://libweb.uml.edu/clh/OH/MWOL/OH1 .htm

163. "Eula Papandreu," NBOH, box 1, folder 16, tape 1, 2; "Joseph Figuerido, 1983," NBOH, box 1, folder 18, tape 1, side 1, 3; "May Alves," NBOH, box 1, folder 12, 2; "Theophile Brien, 1975," RIOH, box 11, folder 85, 1; "Ida Brown, 1972," RIOH, box 12, folder 92, 1; "Emil Ciallella, 1971," RIOH, box 12, folder 102, 1; "Gerard DiFiore, 1974," RIOH, box 13, folder 120, 1.

164. "Eula Papandreu," tape 1, side 2, 3; Gerstle, *Working-Class Americanism*, 34; "Joseph Figuerido, 1983," tape 1, side 1, 4–5, 8.

165. "Beatrice Pacheco" in "Descriptions of the 1928 Strike," NBOH, box 5, folder 63, 2; "Brigida Bristol, 1974," RIOH, box 11, folder 86, 3, 7; "Rose Fontaine, 1975," RIOH, box 14, folder 129, 1–2; "Lillian Melia, 1975," RIOH, box 16, folder 178, 1, 6; "Aldea LeDuc, 1977," RIOH, 5; "Martha Doherty & Blanche Graham, 1984," LOH, tape 84.04, 4; " Valentine Chartrand, 1984," LOH, tape 84.01, 2–5; tape 84.2, 34, 48–49.

166. "Martha Doherty & Blanche Graham, 1984," 9; "Brigida Bristol, 1974," 5; "Joseph Figuerido, 1983," tape 1, side 1, 12.

167. "Valentine Chartrand, 1984," tape 84.01, 19. Massachusetts law required provision of seats for women and children but exempted employers in cases where this was impractical to the production process—which was the case in most textile tasks. Commonwealth of Massachusetts, *Annual Report of the Department of Labor and Industries for the Year Ending November 30, 1926*, Public Document No. 104 (Boston: Wright and Potter, 1927), 15.

168. "Emil Ciallella, 1971," 4; "Francis Dailey, 1971," 9.

169. Mary H. Blewett, *The Last Generation: Work and Life in the Textile Mills of Lowell, Massachusetts, 1910–1960* (Amherst: University of Massachusetts Press, 1990), 10–11.

170. "Joseph Figuerido, 1983," tape 1, side 1, 2, 11–12.

171. "Valentine Chartrand, 1984," tape 84.01, 9.

172. "Lena O'Brien, 1974," RIOH, box 16, folder 196, 1, 6.

173. "Valentine Chartrand, 1984," tape 84.2, 50.

174. "Martha Doherty & Blanche Graham, 1984," tape 84.04, 37.

175. Blewett, *The Last Generation*, 20. These anecdotes are not merely impressionistic. In 1925 alone, Massachusetts manufacturing saw 7,961 accidents on industrial machinery. There were 3,497 injuries of workers under the age of eighteen, 56 of which resulted in permanent injuries—16 in textiles. Two textile children lost fingers in 1925. That year the state also investigated 254 cases of occupational diseases, including 5 fatalities. Commonwealth of Massachusetts, *Annual Report of the Department of Labor and Industries for the Year Ending November 30, 1926*, 9–17.

176. "Martha Doherty & Blanche Graham, 1984," tape 84.04, 9, 11.

177. "Joseph Figuerido, 1983," tape 1, side 1, 1, 10.

178. "Martha Doherty & Blanche Graham, 1984," tape 84.04, 11.

179. "Raoul Archambault, 1971," RIOH, box 11, folder 72, 4, 13, 16.

180. "Joseph Figuerido, 1983," tape 1, side 1, 12, 14.

181. "Valentine Chartrand, 1984," tape 84.2, 34–35.

182. "Beatrice Pacheco" in "Descriptions of the 1928 Strike," 2–3.

183. Georgianna, *The Strike of '28*, 26.

184. "Hattie Anderson, 1974," 5; "Francis Dailey, 1971," 5; "Gerard DiFiore, 1974," 8.

185. "Hattie Anderson, 1974," 7.

186. "Francis Dailey, 1971," 13.

187. "Gerard DiFiore, 1974," 8.

188. "Beatrice Pacheco" in "Descriptions of the 1928 Strike," 3.

189. "Francis Dailey, 1971," 10; "Ernest Denomme, 1971," RIOH, box 13, folder 117, 12.

190. Georgianna, *The Strike of '28*, 27.

191. Bruce Watson, *Bread and Roses: Mills, Migrants, and the Struggle for the American Dream* (New York: Viking, 2005), 9.

192. For example: "Brigida Bristol, 1974," 3; "Marie Brouillard, 1971," RIOH, box 12, folder 90, 3, 9; "Yvonne Desrochers, 1975," RIOH, box 13, folder 119, 5; "Rachel Landry, 1975," RIOH, box 14, folder 152, 1, 4.

193. "Valentine Chartrand, 1984," tape 84.02, 63.

194. "Anton Huettel, 1971," RIOH, box 14, folder 144, 13–15.

195. "Joseph Figuerido, 1983," tape 1, side 1, 11–12.

196. "Elizabeth Raitano, 1974," RIOH, box 17, folder 210, 4; "Victor Signorelli, 1974," RIOH, box 18, folder 227, 4, 7–8.

197. "Theophile Brien, 1975," 1.

198. "Joseph Figuerido, 1983," tape 1, side 1, 11–12.

199. "Victor Signorelli, 1974," 8, 10.

200. "Secondo Siniscalchi, 1971," RIOH, box 18, folder 228, 4–7.

201. "Beatrice Pacheco" in "Descriptions of the 1928 Strike," 3.

202. On New Bedford's decline, see Seymour Louis Wolfbein, *The Decline of a Cotton Textile City: A Study of New Bedford* (New York: Columbia University Press, 1944), 31.

203. See David Lee McMullen, *Strike! The Radical Insurrections of Ellen Dawson* (Gainesville: University Press of Florida, 2010), 120–131.

204. Georgianna, *The Strike of '28*, 80–84.

205. Ibid., 74, 83.

206. "Mayor Terms Child Picketing Contemptible, Refuses His Aid," *New Bedford Evening Standard*, May 5, 1928; "Mayor Raps at Radicals for Child Pickets," *New Bedford Times*, May 5, 1928, in "Charles F. Ashley Mayor of New Bedford from 1891–1936 Scrapbook of Newspaper Clippings," University of Massachusetts–Dartmouth, Dartmouth, MA (hereafter Ashley Scrapbook), reel 1; Georgianna, *The Strike of '28*, 85.

207. Georgianna, *The Strike of '28*, 89.

208. Alfred L. Botelho, letter to the editor, *New Bedford Evening Standard*, April 21, 1928, Ashley Scrapbook, reel 1.

209. In Rhode Island, this was the case for Italians; in New Bedford, it was largely the Portuguese. "Brigida Bristol, 1974," 4; "Emil Ciallella, 1971," 8–9; "Francis Dailey, 1971," 25.

210. "Joseph Figuerido, 1983," tape 1, side 1, 9.

211. "Jack Rubenstein, 8/19/80," NBOH, box 1, folder 8, 12, 29.

212. Ibid., 1, 8, 10–11. Indeed, while there was some violence and many arrests, there was no great push to overthrow traditional authority. Strikers and police coexisted on generally amicable terms: "Most of the picketers knew what our job was, they knew what their job was, so there was no hard feelings in between us, sometimes we exchanged jokes." "James Levesque, ca. 1981," NBOH, box 5, folder 65, 3.

213. Georgianna, *The Strike of '28*, 89.

214. "Joseph Figuerido, 1983," tape 1, side 2, 17.

215. "Check Comes from Thomas," *New Bedford Evening Standard*, May 5, 1928, Ashley Scrapbook, reel 1; "Sends $500 to Strike Council," *New Bedford Evening Standard*, May 10, 1928, Ashley Scrapbook, reel 1; "Thomas Praises Strikers for Fight Made Here," *New Bedford Morning Mercury*, September 4, 1928, Ashley Scrapbook, reel 2; Georgianna, *The Strike of '28*, 90.

216. *Massachusetts Manual, 1929–1930*, 399. Thomas had been closely associated with the Textile Council, which may explain some of his lack of popular support. Georgianna, *The Strike of '28*, 90; "Frank Manning, 1981," NBOH, box 1, folder 11, 133.

217. *Massachusetts Manual, 1929–1930*, 399; *1925–1926*, 391.

218. "Jack Rubenstein, 9/2/80," NBOH box 1, folder 8, 11–12; "Joseph Figuerido, 1983," NBOH, box 1, folder 18, 15.

219. Huthmacher, *Massachusetts*, 181, 184. Conditions were most acute in New England, and thus the pattern was most striking there; however, this fit with national trends. For example, a similar phenomenon occurred in Passaic, New Jersey. Throughout 1926 and into 1927, the city had endured textile strikes lasting upwards of a year. Passaic had been consistently Republican in presidential voting; but in 1928, the city granted Al Smith an unprecedented majority and from that time forward was strongly Democratic in national elections. McMullen, *Strike!*, 67–95; *1930 Census*, vol. 3, part 2,

p. 213; voting tracked using State of New Jersey, *Manual of the Legislature of New Jersey* (Trenton, NJ: Fitzgerald, 1917–1941).

220. "Ware Facing Ruin in Closing of Mills," *NYT*, November 25, 1926, 32. The *Boston Globe* estimated the workforce at closer to 2,000—or nearer 25 percent of the town's population. "Delay Action on Otis Company Closing," *BG*, December 21, 1926, 14; Edgar A. Bowers, ed., *Annual Report on the Vital Statistics of Massachusetts: Births, Marriages, Divorces and Deaths for the Year Ending December 31, 1920* (Boston: Wright and Potter, 1921), 221.

221. "Ware Facing Ruin in Closing of Mills," 32.

222. "Saving Ware Mills Declared Possible," *NYT*, December 21, 1926, 11.

223. "Ware Folk Hopeful after Postponement," *BG*, December 21, 1926, 14.

224. "Otis Company Mills to Stay," *Christian Science Monitor*, December 22, 1926, 5B; "Gov Fuller Promises His Collaboration," *BG*, December 22, 1926, A17.

225. "Fuller's Aid Sought to Lift Burden," *BG*, December 29, 1926, 5.

226. "Ware Taxes Reduced to Hold Otis Mills," *BG*, February 16, 1926, 17.

227. "Raise Rents of Otis Employes," *BG*, December 26, 1926, B30.

228. "Wage Readjustment for All Otis Mills," *BG*, January 7, 1927, 11.

229. "Mill Men Discuss Textile Troubles at Meeting Today," *HC*, February 8, 1927, 7.

230. Voting results tracked using the *Massachusetts Manual*.

231. Huthmacher, *Massachusetts*, 183.

232. Vera Shlakman, *Economic History of a Factory Town: A Study of Chicopee, Massachusetts* (New York: Octagon Books, 1969), 227–228.

233. James J. Lorence, "The Workers of Chicopee: Progressive Paternalism and the Culture of Accommodation in a Modern Mill Village," *Georgia Historical Quarterly* 91, no. 3 (Fall 2007): 292–323, esp. 293–294; Shlakman, *Economic History of a Factory Town*, 228–229.

234. Shlakman, *Economic History of a Factory Town*, 228–229.

235. In 1929, that figure was $1,500 for individuals and $3,500 for married couples. Ibid., 234, 235–237, 242.

236. Ibid., 233.

237. Bowers, *Annual Report*, 168, 172; Robert S. Leonard, *Editorial Review of the Vital Statistics of Massachusetts, 1928* (Boston: Division of Vital Statistics, 1929), 64, 68, 97–98, 170; U.S. Department of Commerce, Bureau of Foreign and Domestic Commerce, *Statistical Abstract of the United States: 1929* (Washington, DC: Government Printing Office, 1929), 88; *1930 Census*, vol. 3, part 1, pp. 1095, 1098–1101.

238. Voting results tracked using the *Massachusetts Manual*.

239. Boston Chamber of Commerce, Bureau of Commercial and Industrial Affairs Committee on New England Industries, "The Cotton Manufacturing Industry of New England" (1926), NBOH, box 5, folder 58, 21, 23.

240. Department of Labor and Industries of the Commonwealth of Massachusetts, "Report of a Special Investigation into Conditions in the Textile Industry in Massachusetts and the Southern States" (August 1923), NBOH, box 5, folder 57, 2–3.

241. "Ware Taxes Reduced to Hold Otis Mills," 17.

242. "Baillargeon Demands 10 Percent Tax Cut to Prevent Wage Slash in Cotton Mills," *New Bedford Evening Standard*, March 23, 1928, Ashley Scrapbook, reel 1.

243. "Aldermen Balk at Firing Any Job Holders," *New Bedford Times*, April 3, 1928, Ashley Scrapbook, reel 1.

244. "School Dentistry to Be Dropped by Health Board Plan," *New Bedford Evening Standard*, April 16, 1928, Ashley Scrapbook, reel 1.

245. "27 Plants to Put Scale in Force April 16," *New Bedford Evening Standard*, April 9, 1928, Ashley Scrapbook, reel 1.

246. McCartin, *Labor's Great War*, 20–23; "Walsh Sounds Smith Praises," *Fall River Herald News*, October 19, 1928, 1, 2.

247. "Cole Charges Attempt to Move Mills South," *BG*, September 28, 1928, 9.

248. "Cole Scores Methods of 'Big Business,'" *BG*, October 6, 1928, 4.

249. Georgianna, *The Strike of '28*, 50.

250. "Gov. Smith and Textile Workers," editorial, *Fall River Herald News*, November 3, 1928, 14.

251. National Committee Social Workers for Smith, "An Open Letter to Social Workers," October 12, 1928, Van Kleeck Papers, box 108, folder 11, 1–2.

252. The third was Illinois. Lemons, "The Sheppard-Towner Act," 782; Janick, *A Diverse People*, 28.

253. Perkins, "Notes for Campaign Speech to Social Workers in Boston, Sept 1928"; Perkins, "Speech, Boston, 10/2/28"; "Smith's Humane Record Is Mrs. Norton's Topic," 10; "Mrs. Roosevelt Stirs Audience by Smith Plea," *Elizabeth Daily Journal*, October 21, 1928, 1; "Former Boston Woman Directs Smith Offices in Region of St. Louis," *BG*, September 26, 1928, 24; Dewson, "What Campaign Issues Mean to Women"; "Labor for Smith and Why Not?," editorial, *Springfield Daily News*, October 10, 1928, 6; "Lavery at Al Smith Club in Bridgeport," *HC*, September 29, 1928, 12.

254. "Walsh Quotes Foe on Mill Conditions," *BG*, October 19, 1928, 29.

255. Mary Hinman, letter to the editor, *HC*, November 1, 1928, 8.

256. "McCormack Predicts Smith Victory Here," *BG*, November 4, 1928, A7.

257. "Fort Condemns Smith Program," 16.

258. "Is Governor Smith Bluffing a Bit?," *HC*, October 5, 1928, 8.

259. "N.Y. Bonding Scheme Hit by Trumbull," *HC*, October 10, 1928, 2.

260. Hinman, letter to the editor, 8.

261. "Candidates Contrasted by Bingham," *HC*, October 13, 1928, 1.

262. Voting results tracked using the *Massachusetts Manual*.

263. Katharine Cofski to Alfred E. Smith, October 28, 1928, Graves Papers, box 81, folder "Campaign Correspondence—1928," 1–9.

264. Indeed, as demonstrated throughout the preceding pages, it was not just Democratic campaigners who scanned New England's troubles and turned to the New Yorker's record for signs of hope. Smith's governorship was the subject of constant comment among rank-and-file supporters. For example: "Reader," letter to the editor, *HC*, September 27, 1928, A2; "Citizen," letter to the editor, *HC*, October 2, 1928, 8; "Voter," letter to the editor, *HC*, October 4, 1928, 8; Luther H. Treischmann, letter to the editor, *HC*, November 4, 1928, A3; J.J.Z., letter to the editor, *Springfield Union*, November 1, 1928, 10; "Central Labor Union Vehemently Appeals for the Election of Smith," *Springfield Daily News*, October 8, 1928, 1; "Labor for Smith and Why Not?," 6; "Deaf Mutes Form Club in Waterbury to Back Al Smith," *HC*, October 4, 1928, 1.

265. "Smith Contenders Win Inter-club H.P.H.S. Debate," *HC*, September 29, 1928, 6.

266. Dineen, *The Purple Shamrock*, 151–153; Connolly, *The Triumph of Ethnic Progressivism*, 174–175; Huthmacher, *Massachusetts*, 104–105.

267. Dineen, *The Purple Shamrock*, 153; *Massachusetts Manual, 1925–1926*, 442–452.

268. Moreover, his numbers were worse than those of his Democratic predecessor John F. Fitzgerald in Lowell and Lawrence (each with a strong tradition of state-level Democratic voting). *Massachusetts Manual, 1925–1926*, 442–452; *1923–1924*, 441–451.

269. Janick, *A Diverse People*, 36, 37.

270. DeMoranville, "Ethnic Voting in Rhode Island," 86–87, 117–122, 124.

271. "Victor Signorelli, 1974," 4.

272. "Smith Raps G.O.P. Prosperity," *Fall River Globe*, October 5, 1928, 1, 10.

273. "Mr. Hoover at Newark," editorial, *HC*, September 18, 1928, 8.

274. "Roosevelt Receives Roar of Greetings," *BG*, October 13, 1928, 1, 4, quote from 4.

275. "Mayor Batterson Praises Bonee for Party Loyalty," *HC*, October 27, 1928, 2.

276. "The Italian People Who Live in Hartford," *HC*, August 29, 1915, X1.

Conclusion

1. Mark Sullivan, "New Democratic Party Is Born," *Hartford Courant* (hereafter *HC*), September 9, 1928, E7.

2. Lester Ira Gordon, "John McCormack and the Roosevelt Era" (PhD diss., Boston University, 1976), 78.

3. Eldot, *Governor Alfred E. Smith*, 379, 396–397.

4. Matthew Josephson to Isador Lubin, January 3, 1966, Isador Lubin Papers, Franklin D. Roosevelt Library, Hyde Park, NY, box 76, folder "Perkins, Francis (Alfred E. Smith Book)."

5. Josephson and Josephson, *Al Smith: Hero of the Cities*, xi.

6. Maurice Carroll, "Cuomo Wants to Go beyond Workfare to the Work Ethic," *New York Times* (hereafter *NYT*), January 26, 1986, E6; Joan Walsh, "Obama, the Triangle Fire and the Real Father of the New Deal," *Salon*, March 25, 2011, http://www.salon.com/2011/03/25/obama_al_smith_and_the_triangle_fire/singleton/.

7. Leuchtenburg, *The Perils of Prosperity*, 231.

8. Schlesinger, *The Crisis of the Old Order*, 97.

9. Huthmacher, *Senator Robert F. Wagner*, 103. Emphasis added.

10. Leuchtenburg, *The Perils of Prosperity*, 237; Burner, *The Politics of Provincialism*, 179–180; Hofstadter, *The Age of Reform*, 300.

11. Leuchtenburg states that "for the most part, the Democratic party in 1928 chose to take a 'me too' position." Leuchtenburg, *The Perils of Prosperity*, 233.

12. Perkins Oral History, book 2, 629.

13. Muncy, *Creating a Female Dominion*, xi, 151–153.

14. William E. Leuchtenburg, "The Achievement of the New Deal," in *The FDR Years: On Roosevelt and His Legacy* (New York: Columbia University Press, 1995), 236–282, esp. 248–249; Paul K. Conkin, *The New Deal* (Arlington Heights, IL: Harlan Davidson, 1978), 60.

15. Leuchtenburg, "The Achievement," 256–260, 267–269; McCraw, *TVA*, 160.

16. Leuchtenburg, "The Achievement," 253.

17. Huthmacher, *Senator Robert F. Wagner*, 190–199; Conkin, *The New Deal*, 61–62; Anthony J. Badger, *The New Deal: The Depression Years, 1933–1940* (New York: Hill and Wang, 1989), 118; Leuchtenburg, "The Achievement," 250, 253; William E. Leuchtenburg, *Franklin D. Roosevelt and the New Deal: 1932–1940* (New York: Harper Collins, 1963), 150–152.

18. Leuchtenburg, *Franklin D. Roosevelt and the New Deal*, 338–339. Emphasis in original.

19. Ibid., 46–47.

20. Ibid., 50, 60; Frank Freidel, *Franklin D. Roosevelt: Launching the New Deal* (Boston: Little, Brown, 1973), 321.

21. James T. Patterson, *Congressional Conservatism and the New Deal: The Growth of the Conservative Coalition in Congress, 1933–1939* (Lexington: University Press of Kentucky, 1967), 340–343.

22. In the Senate, affairs were more complicated. Conservative northeastern Democrats like Peter Gerry (RI) and Royal Copeland (NY) aligned with southern "irreconcilables" by the mid-1930s. Ibid., 188–210, 250–324.

23. *Congressional Record* (hereafter *CR*), vol. 77, part 1, p. 766; vol. 77, part 2, p. 2129; vol. 77, part 4, p. 3600; vol. 77, part 5, p. 4373. All figures were calculated by the author based on the roll call votes (found in *CR*) of all Democratic representatives from Connecticut, Massachusetts, New Jersey, New York, and Rhode Island.

24. *CR*, vol. 79, part 5, p. 5150; vol. 79, part 6, p. 6069; vol. 81, part 8, p. 9293; vol. 83, part 7, p. 7449; vol. 84, part 10, p. 10957.

25. *CR*, vol. 78, part 8, p. 8116.

26. *CR*, vol. 79, part 13, p. 14644; vol. 80, part 10, p. 10271.

27. *CR*, vol. 79, part 10, p. 10637; vol. 79, part 13, p. 14626; Patterson, *Congressional Conservatism*, 71.

28. Leuchtenburg, *Franklin D. Roosevelt and the New Deal*, 45.

29. *CR*, vol. 77, part 1, p. 217.

30. *CR*, vol. 80, part 1, p. 976.

31. Each ultimately received 100 percent support from the region's House Democrats. *CR*, vol. 80, part 8, p. 8519; vol. 83, part 6, p. 6836.

32. *CR*, vol. 75, part 11, pp. 12283–12287.

33. For a glorious account of the "day of liberation," see Leuchtenburg, *Franklin D. Roosevelt and the New Deal*, 46–47.

34. Wagner was joined in introducing the bill by Senator Edward Costigan (D-CO). Huthmacher, *Senator Robert F. Wagner*, 238–243, quote from 242; Patterson, *Congressional Conservatism*, 156–157.

35. U.S. Government Printing Office (hereafter GPO), *Congressional Directory: 73rd Congress, First Session, June, 1933* (Washington, DC: GPO, 1933), 78; *CR*, vol. 81, part 3, p. 3547.

36. *CR*, vol. 81, part 3, p. 3549.

37. Ibid., 3558.

38. W. White, *A Man Called White*, 99–100.

39. Jordan A. Schwarz, *The New Dealers: Power Politics in the Age of Roosevelt* (New York: Alfred A. Knopf, 1993), xii.

40. Lizabeth Cohen, *Making a New Deal: Industrial Workers in Chicago, 1919–1939* (New York: Cambridge University Press, 1990), 251–289.

41. GPO, *Congressional Directory: 73rd Congress, First Session*, 16.

42. For example, *CR*, vol. 78, part 12, p. 245.

43. Emanuel Celler, *You Never Leave Brooklyn: The Autobiography of Emanuel Celler* (New York: John Day, 1953), 20–21.

44. Ibid., 21–22.

45. Huthmacher, *Senator Robert F. Wagner*, 128–129.

46. Wald quote, ibid., 129.

47. "A True Friend of the [Common Man?] Passes On," William P. Connery Papers, Lynn Museum, Lynn, MA (hereafter Connery Papers), folder MS/P10, 1.

48. Charles M. Kelley, "Chip off the Old Block," *Machinists' Monthly Journal* 152 (undated clipping), Connery Papers, folder MS/P10. The article is dated from "the end of the decade," because Kelley notes that Connery was in his fourth term—which would have been 1929–1930.

49. "A True Friend," 2.

50. Bulkley S. Griffin, "Two New Englanders and the President," undated clipping, Connery Papers, folder MS/P10. Although undated, this article is likely from 1931, because Hoover is president but the Democrats have taken control of congressional committees.

51. "Jam Colonial at Democratic Rally Held Friday Night—Smith Cheered," *Lawrence Telegram*, undated clipping, 1932, Connery Papers, folder MS/P10.

52. "A True Friend," 2.

53. Paul Jennings to Marie T. Connery Franciose, October 1, 1965, Connery Papers, folder MS/P10; "IUE President Lauds Connery at Lynn Dinner" (undated clipping), Connery Papers, folder MS/P10. Both FDR and Labor Secretary Frances Perkins were at best ambivalent toward the Wagner Act. It was only in response to the Supreme Court's nullification of the NRA in *Schechter* (after the Wagner bill had been passed by the Senate and approved by the House Labor Committee) that the timely FDR announced that the Wagner Act was a priority. Huthmacher, *Senator Robert F. Wagner*, 189–190, 192, 197–198. See also Winifred D. Wandersee, "'I'd Rather Pass a Law Than Organize a Union': Frances Perkins and the Reformist Approach to Organized Labor," *Labor History* 34, no. 1 (Winter 1993): 5–32; Leuchtenburg, *Franklin D. Roosevelt and the New Deal*, 150–152.

54. "A True Friend," 1.

55. *CR*, vol. 77, part 1, p. 216.

56. "Rep. Connery's Death Threatens Wage Bill," *Washington Daily News* (undated clipping); United Press, "Labor Committee Head to Be Buried Saturday at Home" (undated clipping), Connery Papers, folder MS/P10.

57. Mary Teresa Norton, "Madam Congressman" (unpublished memoir), Mary T. Norton Papers, Alexander Library, Rutgers University, New Brunswick, NJ, box 6, folder 8; GPO, *Congressional Directory: 73rd Congress, First Session*, 70.

58. "Smith's Humane Record Is Mrs. Norton's Topic," *Boston Globe* (hereafter *BG*), October 9, 1928, 10; "More Than 1,000 Women to Speak for Smith," *HC*, September 4, 1928, 2; "Asks if Death Is Part of 'Noble Experiment,'" *NYT*, October 10, 1928, 6; Perry, *Belle Moskowitz*, 196.

59. "Women in the Eighty-First Congress," *Social Service Review* 23, no. 4 (December 1949): 505–509.

60. *Massachusetts Manual, 1929–1930*, 443.

61. "Healey in Capital Asks Refined Sugar Tariff Rise," *BG*, March 2, 1933, 5.

62. "Pictures Benefits from Housing Act," *BG*, September 19, 1934, 5.

63. "Curley Addresses 700 at Somerville," *BG*, December 12, 1934, 3; "Low Cost Housing Service Bill Wins," *BG*, June 2, 1936, 4.

64. "Pay Compact Wins Approval in House," *BG*, January 21, 1936, 28.

65. Leuchtenburg, *Franklin D. Roosevelt and the New Deal*, 162, 242.

66. Gordon, "John McCormack and the Roosevelt Era," v–vi, 69, 76.

67. Flynn, *You're the Boss*, 165–166; Patterson, *Congressional Conservatism*, 53–57, 79, 176–177, 185–187, 191–192, 225–229, 235, 284–286; Leuchtenburg, *Franklin D. Roosevelt and the New Deal*, 268; "Roosevelt Urges Defeat of O'Connor and Tydings," *NYT*, August 17, 1938, 1, 12; "O'Connor Loses to Fay in 'Purge'; Wins G.O.P. Race," *NYT*, September 21, 1938, 1, 20.

68. "O'Connor Cites Record," *NYT*, September 17, 1938, 9; "Fay, New Deal Ally, to Fight O'Connor," *NYT*, August 12, 1938, 1; "O'Connor Sees Red Trend," *NYT*, August 12, 1938, 4; "O'Connor Charges Widespread Plot," *NYT*, September 1, 1938, 2.

69. "Meeting to Hear O'Connor and Foes," *NYT*, September 19, 1938, 14.

70. "Active Smith Drive Cheers Republicans," *NYT*, February 23, 1932, 3.

71. "Smith Speaker Hits 'Judases,'" *BG*, April 25, 1932, 1, 3.

72. It is true that Jersey City boss Frank Hague would be Smith's floor leader at the 1932 Democratic Convention in Chicago. Schlesinger, *The Crisis of the Old Order*, 298.

73. "Jam Colonial at Democratic Rally Held Friday Night."

74. Indeed, six of the eight Democrats to represent Massachusetts in the House of Representatives during the 74th and 75th Congresses were openly supportive of Smith, as were Senators Walsh and Coolidge and 1928 gubernatorial nominee Charles Cole. Representatives Connery, Douglass, Granfield, and McCormack were all Smith delegates, while future congressmen Healey and Higgins campaigned actively. "Full Smith Slate Named in Bay State," *NYT*, March 12, 1932, 3; "John F. Charges Foes Hit at Ely," *BG*, April 13, 1932, 14; "Smith Speaker Hits 'Judases,'" 3.

75. "Smith Speaker Hits 'Judases,'" 3.

76. Schlesinger, *The Crisis of the Old Order*, 293; Huthmacher, *Massachusetts*, 237; Leuchtenburg, *Franklin D. Roosevelt and the New Deal*, 7.

77. Huthmacher, *Massachusetts*, 237.

78. Walter Lippmann, "Boston Vote Tells the Story," *BG*, April 28, 1932, 16.

79. "More Smith Groups Win in Connecticut," *BG*, April 29, 1932, 18; "375 Smith Delegates 51 for Roosevelt in Democratic Caucuses," *HC*, April 29, 1932, 1.

80. "National Affairs," *Time*, June 27, 1932, 14; Lippmann, "Boston Vote Tells the Story," 16.

81. Huthmacher, *Massachusetts*, 248.

82. "Smith in Boston Asks Complete Support of Roosevelt and Garner," *HC*, October 28, 1932, 1.

83. "Lonergan Is Guest of Democrats," *HC*, November 30, 1932, 13.

84. William Leuchtenburg has noted that in 1938, when Democratic candidates again faced serious tests from the GOP, "new sources of Democratic strength" were revealed "among lower-income groups, especially union labor, and Negroes, Italians, and Poles." Irving Bernstein has tied this more explicitly to the Smith vote, arguing that by the mid-1930s, groups that had broken Democratic in 1928 "constituted the

bulk of the northern urban working class," noting that "they supported the New Deal; they voted for Roosevelt." Leuchtenburg, *Franklin D. Roosevelt and the New Deal*, 272; Irving Bernstein, *A Caring Society: The New Deal, the Worker, and the Great Depression* (Boston: Houghton Mifflin, 1985), 300. See also John M. Allswang, *The New Deal and American Politics* (New York: John Wiley and Sons, 1978), 73, 87–88.

85. On Smith's loss of New York, see Robert Chiles, "Vanquished Warrior: Reconsidering Al Smith's 1928 New York Defeat," *New York History* 98, no. 1 (Winter 2017): 90–111.

86. Flynn, *You're the Boss*, 88–89, 99; Perry, *Belle Moskowitz*, 205–207; Caro, *The Power Broker*, 293–296.

87. Lillian Wald to Alfred E. Smith, November 20, 1928, Wald Papers, reel 3.

88. Smith did accept an offer by Wald, extended in a letter of December 26, to join the board of directors of the Henry Street Settlement. Wald to Smith, December 26, 1928, Wald Papers, reel 3; Slayton, *Empire Statesman*, 331; Feld, *Lillian Wald*, 140.

89. Slayton, *Empire Statesman*, 150, 331, 332, 337, 344–345; Schlesinger, *The Crisis of the Old Order*, 283–284.

90. Slayton, *Empire Statesman*, 340, 343; Flynn, *You're the Boss*, 100.

91. Huthmacher, *Senator Robert F. Wagner*, 124.

92. Perry, *Belle Moskowitz*, 216.

93. Mencken quoted in Slayton, *Empire Statesman*, 382.

94. Schlesinger, *The Crisis of the Old Order*, 283.

95. Alfred E. Smith, "Water Power Control and Ownership Should Be in People's Hands," *Providence News Tribune*, April 2, 1932, clipping in Smith Papers, box 23, folder 231; Schlesinger, *The Crisis of the Old Order*, 284.

96. Leuchtenburg, *Franklin D. Roosevelt and the New Deal*, 5; Schlesinger, *The Crisis of the Old Order*, 282–284.

97. Schlesinger, *The Crisis of the Old Order*, 416. Roosevelt too had identified "reduction in Federal spending as one of the most important issues of this campaign." Leuchtenburg, *Franklin D. Roosevelt and the New Deal*, 11.

98. "Bonus Hope Is Dim in Next Congress," *NYT*, November 11, 1932, 3.

99. George Wolfskill, *The Revolt of the Conservatives: A History of the American Liberty League, 1934–1940* (Boston: Houghton Mifflin, 1962), 15; Arthur M. Schlesinger Jr., *The Coming of the New Deal: 1933–1935*, vol. 2 of *The Age of Roosevelt* (New York: Houghton Mifflin, 2003), 483–488; Slayton, *Empire Statesman*, 379–380.

100. Quoted in Slayton, *Empire Statesman*, 387–388.

101. Harold L. Ickes, *The First Thousand Days, 1933–1936* vol. 1 of *The Secret Diary of Harold L. Ickes* (New York: Simon and Schuster, 1953), 526–527.

102. Quoted in Christopher M. Finan, *Alfred E. Smith: The Happy Warrior* (New York: Hill and Wang, 2002), 319–320.

103. Perkins, *The Roosevelt I Knew*, 157.

104. For example: Slayton, *Empire Statesman*, 376–389; Finan, *Alfred E. Smith*, 297–328; Jordan A. Schwarz, "Al Smith in the Thirties," *New York History* 45, no. 4 (October 1964): 316–330.

105. Wolfskill, *The Revolt of the Conservatives*, 182–184.

106. Schlesinger, *The Politics of Upheaval*, 618.

107. Dick Lee, "Brown Derby to High Hat," *Sunday News*, February 23, 1936, 52–53, Wald Papers, reel 33.

BIBLIOGRAPHY

Primary Materials

Manuscripts and Archival Collections

Charles F. Ashley Scrapbook. University of Massachusetts–Dartmouth, Dartmouth, MA.

William P. Connery Papers. Lynn Museum, Lynn, MA.

Consumers' League of Massachusetts Papers. Schlesinger Library, Radcliffe College, Harvard University, Cambridge, MA.

Morris L. Cooke Papers. Franklin D. Roosevelt Library, Hyde Park, NY.

Josephus Daniels Papers. Manuscripts Department, Wilson Library, University of North Carolina, Chapel Hill, NC.

Mary W. Dewson Papers. Franklin D. Roosevelt Library, Hyde Park, NY.

Mary Dreier Papers. Schlesinger Library, Radcliffe College, Harvard University, Cambridge, MA.

Felix Frankfurter Papers. Manuscript Reading Room, Library of Congress, Washington, DC.

George Graves Papers. New York State Archives, Albany, NY.

Anthony Griffin Papers. New York Public Library, New York, NY.

Herbert Hoover Papers. National Archives, Washington, DC.

The La Follette Family Collection. Manuscript Reading Room, Library of Congress, Washington, DC.

Walter Lippmann Papers. Manuscripts and Archives Division, Sterling Memorial Library, Yale University, New Haven, CT.

Isador Lubin Papers. Franklin D. Roosevelt Library, Hyde Park, NY.

Robert Moses Papers. New York Public Library, New York, NY.

Belle L. Moskowitz Correspondences. New York State Archives, Albany, NY.

George W. Norris Papers. Manuscript Reading Room, Library of Congress, Washington, DC.

Frances Perkins Papers. Columbia University, New York, NY.

John J. Raskob Papers. Hagley Museum and Library, Wilmington, DE.

Eleanor Roosevelt Papers. Franklin D. Roosevelt Library, Hyde Park, NY.

Mary Simkhovitch Papers. Schlesinger Library, Radcliffe College, Harvard University, Cambridge, MA.

Furnifold Simmons Papers. Duke University, Durham, NC.

Alfred E. Smith Papers. New York State Library, Albany, NY.

Alfred E. Smith Subject and Correspondence Files. New York State Archives, Albany, NY.

Mary Van Kleeck Papers. Sophia Smith Collection, Smith College, Northampton, MA.
Robert F. Wagner Papers. Georgetown University, Washington, DC.
Lillian Wald Papers. New York Public Library, New York, NY.

Oral History Collections

Mill Life Oral History Collection. University of Rhode Island Library Special
     Collections and Archives, University of Rhode Island, Kingstown, RI.
Mill Workers of Lowell. Mary Blewett and Martha Mayo, Project Directors,
     University of Massachusetts–Lowell and Lowell National Historical Park,
     Lowell, MA. http://libweb.uml.edu/clh/OH/MWOL/OH1.htmm.
New Bedford Textile Workers' Strike of 1928 Oral History Collection. University of
     Massachusetts–Dartmouth, Dartmouth, MA.
Oral History Research Office, Columbia University, New York, NY.

> Robert Moses (1973)
> Frances Perkins (1951–1955)
> Charles Poletti (1978)
> Joseph M. Proskauer (1962)
> Rexford G. Tugwell (1950)
> Robert F. Wagner Jr. (1980)

Photographic Collections

Herman Kopplemann Collection, Jewish Historical Society of Greater Hartford,
     West Hartford, CT.
Library of Congress Prints and Photographs Online Catalog: http://www.loc.gov
     /pictures.

> George Grantham Bain Collection
> Harris & Ewing Collection

Museum of the City of New York Collections Portal: http://collections.mcny.org.

Newspapers

American Israelite, Cincinnati, OH.
Atlanta Constitution, Atlanta, GA.
Baltimore Afro-American, Baltimore, MD.
Baltimore Sun, Baltimore, MD.
Beatrice Daily Sun, Beatrice, NE.
Boston Globe, Boston, MA.
Bronx Home News, Bronx, NY.
Brooklyn Citizen, Brooklyn, NY.
Brooklyn Eagle, Brooklyn, NY.
Charlotte Observer, Charlotte, NC.
Christian Science Monitor, Boston, MA.
Elizabeth Daily Journal, Elizabeth, NJ.
Fall River Globe, Fall River, MA.
Fall River Herald News, Fall River, MA.

Hartford Courant, Hartford, CT.
Holyoke Daily Transcript, Holyoke, MA.
Houston Post-Dispatch, Houston, TX.
Jewish Criterion, Pittsburgh, PA.
Jewish Exponent, Philadelphia, PA.
Los Angeles Times, Los Angeles, CA.
Lowell Sun, Lowell, MA.
Negro World, New York, NY.
Newark Evening News, Newark, NJ.
New Bedford Evening Standard, New Bedford, MA.
New Bedford Morning Mercury, New Bedford, MA.
New Bedford Times, New Bedford, MA.
New Orleans Times-Picayune, New Orleans, LA.
Newport Mercury and Weekly News, Newport, RI.
New York Times, New York, NY.
New York World, New York, NY.
North Adams Transcript, North Adams, MA.
Philadelphia Record, Philadelphia, PA.
Philadelphia Trades Union News, Philadelphia, PA.
Providence Journal, Providence, RI.
Saratoga Springs Saratogian, Saratoga Springs, NY.
Scranton Times, Scranton, PA.
Springfield Daily News, Springfield, MA.
Springfield Union, Springfield, MA.
St. Louis Argus, St. Louis, MO.
Wall Street Journal, New York, NY.
Washington Post, Washington, DC.
Washington Star, Washington, DC.
Westerly Sun, Westerly, RI.
Woonsocket Call, Woonsocket, RI.

Periodicals

Atlantic Monthly
Banker's Magazine
Barron's
Harper's Magazine
The Independent
Outlook
Salon
Time
Vanity Fair

Printed Campaign Materials

Democratic National Committee. *Appointments by Governor Smith to Public Offices in the State of New York*. New York: Democratic National Committee, 1928.

——. *Campaign Addresses of Governor Alfred E. Smith, Democratic Candidate for President, 1928*. Washington, DC: Democratic National Committee, 1929.

——. *The Campaign Book of the Democratic Party: Candidates and Issues in 1928*. New York: Democratic National Committee, 1928.

——. *The Labor Record of Governor Alfred E. Smith*. New York: Democratic National Committee, 1928.

——. *What Everybody Wants to Know about Alfred E. Smith*. New York: Democratic National Committee, 1928.

West Virginia Anti-Saloon League. *The Present Crisis*. Charleston, WV: West Virginia Anti-Saloon League, 1928.

Government Documents (Federal)

Congressional Record. Vols. 77–84. Washington, DC: Government Printing Office, 1933–1939.

U.S. Department of Commerce. Bureau of Foreign and Domestic Commerce. *Statistical Abstract of the United States*. Washington, DC: Government Printing Office, 1920, 1925, 1929, 1930, 1933.

——. Bureau of the Census. *Fifteenth Census of the United States: 1930, Population*. Vol. 3, part 1 (Alabama–Missouri), and part 2 (Montana–Wyoming). Washington, DC: Government Printing Office, 1932.

——. Bureau of the Census. *Fourteenth Census of the United States, Taken in the Year 1920: Population 1920—Number and Distribution of Inhabitants*. Washington, DC: Government Printing Office, 1921.

——. Bureau of the Census. *Religious Bodies: 1926*. Vol. 1. Washington, DC: Government Printing Office, 1930.

U.S. Government Printing Office. *Congressional Directory: 73rd Congress, First Session, June, 1933*. Washington, DC: Government Printing Office, 1933.

Government Documents (State)

MASSACHUSETTS

Bowers, Edgar A., ed. *Annual Report on the Vital Statistics of Massachusetts: Births, Marriages, Divorces and Deaths for the Year Ending December 31, 1920*. Boston: Wright and Potter, 1921.

Clerk of the Senate and Clerk of the House. *A Manual for Use of the General Court of Massachusetts for 1897–1898; 1901–1902; 1905–1906; 1909–1911; 1913–1914; 1917–1918; 1919–1920; 1921–1922; 1923–1924; 1925–1926; 1927–1928; 1929–1930; 1931–1932; 1933–1934; 1935–1936; 1937–1938; 1939–1940; 1941–1942*. Boston: Wright and Potter, various years.

Commonwealth of Massachusetts. *Annual Report of the Department of Labor and Industries for the Year Ending November 30, 1926*. Public Document No. 104. Boston: Wright and Potter, 1927.

Leonard, Robert S. *Editorial Review of the Vital Statistics of Massachusetts, 1928*. Boston: Division of Vital Statistics, 1929.

New Jersey

State of New Jersey. *Manual of the Legislature of New Jersey*. Trenton, NJ: Fitzgerald,
    1917, 1921, 1925, 1929, 1933, 1937, 1941, 1945, 1949.

New York

Malcolm, James, ed. *The New York Red Book, 1928: An Illustrated Legislative Manual of
    the State*. Albany, NY: J. B. Lyon, 1928.
Moses, Robert. *Manual for the Use of the Legislature of the State of New York, 1928*.
    Albany, NY: J. B. Lyon, 1928.
New York State Legislative Record and Index. Albany, NY: Legislative Index Publishing
    Group, 1910–1928.
The New York State Red Book, 1896. Albany, NY: J. B. Lyon, 1896.
Smith, Alfred E. *Progress of Public Improvements: A Report to the People of the State of
    New York*. Albany, NY: J.B. Lyon, 1927.

Statistical Collections

Robinson, Edgar Eugene. *The Presidential Vote, 1896–1932*. Stanford, CA: Stanford
    University Press, 1934.
——. *They Voted for Roosevelt*. Stanford, CA: Stanford University Press, 1947.

Autobiographies and Memoirs

Addams, Jane. *Twenty Years at Hull-House*. Boston: Bedford / St. Martin's, 1999.
Bartholdt, Richard. *From Steerage to Congress: Reminiscences and Reflections*. Philadel-
    phia: Dorrance, 1930.
Bloom, Sol. *The Autobiography of Sol Bloom*. New York: G. P. Putnam's Sons, 1948.
Celler, Emanuel. *You Never Leave Brooklyn: The Autobiography of Emanuel Celler*. New
    York: John Day, 1953.
Eisenstein, Louis, and Elliot Rosenberg. *A Stripe of Tammany's Tiger*. New York:
    Robert Speller and Sons, 1966.
Flynn, Edward J. *You're the Boss: The Practice of American Politics*. New York: Collier,
    1962.
Hoover, Herbert. *The Memoirs of Herbert Hoover: The Cabinet and the Presidency,
    1920–1933*. New York: Macmillan, 1952.
Perkins, Frances. *The Roosevelt I Knew*. New York: Viking, 1946.
Riordan, William L., ed. *Plunkitt of Tammany Hall: A Series of Very Plain Talks on Very
    Practical Politics*. New York: Dutton, 1963.
Roosevelt, Eleanor. *This I Remember*. New York: Harper, 1949.
Smith, Alfred E. *Up to Now*. New York: Viking, 1929.
Tugwell, Rexford G. *The Democratic Roosevelt*. Garden City, NY: Doubleday, 1957.
White, Walter. *A Man Called White: The Autobiography of Walter White*. New York:
    Viking, 1948.

Other Published Primary Documents and Collections

Childs, Richard S., and William P. Burr. "Executive Leadership in a Democracy: Discussion." *Proceedings of the Academy of Political Science in the City of New York* 8, no. 1 (1918): 54–55.

Egan, Maurice Francis, and John B. Kennedy. *The Knights of Columbus in Peace and War.* 2 vols. New Haven, CT: Knights of Columbus, 1920.

Hughes, Charles Evans. *Conditions of Progress in Democratic Government.* New Haven, CT: Yale University Press, 1910.

Ickes, Harold L. *The Secret Diary of Harold L. Ickes.* 3 vols. New York: Simon and Schuster, 1953.

Mencken, Henry Louis. *A Carnival of Buncombe.* Baltimore: Johns Hopkins Press, 1956.

Moses, Robert, ed. *A Tribute to Governor Smith.* New York: Simon and Schuster, 1962.

Moskowitz, Henry, ed. *Progressive Democracy: Addresses and State Papers of Alfred E. Smith.* New York: Harcourt, Brace, 1928.

Roosevelt, Franklin D. *The Happy Warrior, Alfred E. Smith: A Study of a Public Servant.* Boston: Houghton Mifflin, 1928.

Root, Elihu. *Addresses on Government and Citizenship.* Freeport, NY: Books for Libraries Press, 1969.

Shover, John L., ed. *Politics of the Nineteen Twenties.* Waltham, MA: Ginn-Blaisdell, 1970.

Simkhovitch, Mary Kingsbury. *The City Worker's World in America.* New York: Macmillan, 1917.

Smith, Alfred E. *The Citizen and His Government.* New York: Harper, 1935.

"Women in the Eighty-First Congress." *Social Service Review* 23, no. 4 (December 1949): 505–509.

Secondary Materials

Scholarly Articles

Alvarez, David J., and Edmond J. True. "Critical Elections and Partisan Realignment: An Urban Test-Case." *Polity* 5, no. 4 (Summer 1973): 563–576.

Bartels, Larry M. "Electoral Continuity and Change, 1868–1996." *Electoral Studies* 17, no. 3 (September 1998): 275–300.

Boris, Eileen, and S. J. Kleinberg. "Mothers and Other Workers: (Re)Conceiving Labor, Maternalism, and the State." *Journal of Women's History* 15, no. 3 (Autumn 2003): 90–117.

Buenker, John D. "The Mahatma and Progressive Reform: Martin Lomasney as Lawmaker, 1911–1917." *New England Quarterly* 44, no. 3 (September 1971): 397–419.

———. "Sovereign Individuals and Organic Networks: Political Cultures in Conflict during the Progressive Era." *American Quarterly* 40, no. 2 (June 1988): 187–204.

———. "The Urban Political Machine and the Seventeenth Amendment." *Journal of American History* 56, no. 2 (September 1969): 305–322.

———. "The Urban Political Machine and Woman Suffrage: A Study in Political Adaptability." *The Historian* 33, no. 2 (February 1971): 264–279.

Chiles, Robert. "Courting the Farm Vote on the Northern Plains: Presidential Candidate Al Smith, Governor Walter Maddock, and the Ambivalent Politics of 1928." *North Dakota History: Journal of the Northern Plains* 81, no. 1 (Spring 2016): 16–31.

———. "School Reform as Progressive Statecraft: Education Policy in New York under Governor Alfred E. Smith, 1919–1928." *Journal of the Gilded Age and Progressive Era* 15, no. 4 (October 2016): 379–398.

———. "Vanquished Warrior: Reconsidering Al Smith's 1928 New York Defeat," *New York History* 98, no. 1 (Winter 2017): 90–111.

———. "Working-Class Conservationism in New York: Governor Alfred E. Smith and 'The Property of the People of the State.'" *Environmental History* 18, no. 1 (January 2013): 157–183.

Clubb, Jerome M., and Howard W. Allen. "The Cities and the Election of 1928: Partisan Realignment?" *American Historical Review* 74, no. 4 (April 1969): 1205–1220.

Colburn, David R. "Governor Alfred E. Smith and the Red Scare, 1919–20." *Political Science Quarterly* 88, no. 3 (September 1973): 423–444.

Crawford, F. C. "Legislative Notes and Reviews: New York State Reorganization." *American Political Science Review* 20, no. 1 (February 1926): 76–79.

Crawford, Finla G. "Administrative Reorganization in New York State." *American Political Science Review* 21, no. 2 (May 1927): 349–359.

Davis, Allen F. "Settlement Workers in Politics, 1890–1914." *Review of Politics* 26, no. 4 (October 1964): 505–517.

Degler, Carl N. "American Political Parties and the Rise of the City: An Interpretation." *Journal of American History* 51, no. 1 (June 1964): 41–59.

Eldersveld, Samuel J. "The Influence of Metropolitan Party Pluralities in Presidential Elections since 1920: A Study of Twelve Key Cities." *American Political Science Review* 43, no. 6 (December 1949): 1189–1206.

Filene, Peter G. "An Obituary for 'The Progressive Movement.'" *American Quarterly* 22, no. 1 (Spring 1970): 20–34.

Fite, Gilbert C. "The Agricultural Issue in the Presidential Campaign of 1928." *Mississippi Valley Historical Review* 37, no. 4 (March 1951): 653–672.

Gerstle, Gary. "The Protean Character of American Liberalism." *American Historical Review* 99, no. 4 (October 1994): 1043–1073.

Goldstein, Michael L. "Black Power and the Rise of Bureaucratic Autonomy in New York City Politics: The Case of Harlem Hospital, 1917–1931." *Phylon* 41, no. 2 (2nd Quarter 1980): 187–201.

Goodykoontz, Colin B. "Edward P. Costigan and the Tariff Commission, 1917–1928." *Pacific Historical Review* 16, no. 4 (November 1947): 410–419.

Gullett, Gayle. "Women Progressives and the Politics of Americanization in California, 1915–1920." *Pacific Historical Review* 64, no. 1 (February 1995): 71–94.

Henderson, Thomas M. "Immigrant Politician: Salvatore Cotillo, Progressive Ethnic." *International Migration Review* 13, no. 1 (Spring 1979): 81–102.

Huthmacher, J. Joseph. "Charles Evans Hughes and Charles Francis Murphy: The Metamorphosis of Progressivism." *New York History* 46, no. 1 (January 1965): 25–40.

——. "Urban Liberalism and the Age of Reform." *Mississippi Valley Historical Review* 49, no. 2 (September 1962): 231–241.

Johnson, Roger T. "Part-Time Leader: Senator Charles L. McNary and the McNary Haugen Bill." *Agricultural History* 54, no. 4 (October 1980): 527–541.

Key, V. O., Jr. "A Theory of Critical Elections." *Journal of Politics* 17, no. 1 (February 1955): 3–18.

Lemons, J. Stanley. "The Sheppard-Towner Act: Progressivism in the 1920s." *Journal of American History* 55, no. 4 (March 1969): 776–786.

Levine, Marc V. "Standing Political Decisions and Partisan Realignment: The Pattern of Maryland Politics, 1872–1948." *Journal of Politics* 38, no. 2 (May 1976): 292–325.

Lichtman, Allan J. "Critical Election Theory and the Reality of American Presidential Politics, 1916–40." *American Historical Review* 81, no. 2 (April 1976): 317–351.

Link, Arthur S. "What Happened to the Progressive Movement in the 1920's?" *American Historical Review* 64, no. 4 (July 1959): 833–851.

Lorence, James J. "The Workers of Chicopee: Progressive Paternalism and the Culture of Accommodation in a Modern Mill Village." *Georgia Historical Quarterly* 91, no. 3 (Fall 2007): 292–323.

MacRae, Duncan, Jr., and James A. Meldrum. "Critical Elections in Illinois: 1888–1958." *American Political Science Review* 54, no. 3 (September 1960): 669–683.

Mayhew, David R. "Electoral Realignments." *Annual Review of Political Science* 3 (June 2000): 449–474.

McDonald, Terrence J. "The Problem of the Political in Recent American Urban History: Liberal Pluralism and the Rise of Functionalism." *Social History* 10, no. 3 (October 1985): 323–345.

McGuire, John. "From the Courts to the State Legislatures: Social Justice Feminism, Labor Legislation, and the 1920s." *Labor History* 45, no. 2 (May 2004): 225–246.

Meier, Kenneth J. "Executive Reorganization of Government: Impact on Employment and Expenditures." *American Journal of Political Science* 24, no. 3 (August 1980): 396–412.

Monoson, S. Sara. "The Lady and the Tiger: Women's Electoral Activism in New York City before Suffrage." *Journal of Women's History* 2, no. 2 (Fall 1990): 100–135.

Ngai, Mae. "The Architecture of Race in American Immigration Law: A Reexamination of the Immigration Act of 1924." *Journal of American History* 86, no. 1 (June 1999): 67–92.

O'Dell, Samuel. "Blacks, the Democratic Party, and the Presidential Election of 1928: A Mild Rejoinder." *Phylon* 48, no. 1 (1st Quarter 1987): 1–11.

Platt, Harold. "Jane Addams and the Ward Boss Revisited: Class, Politics, and Public Health in Chicago, 1890–1930." *Environmental History* 5, no. 2 (April 2000): 194–222.

Pomper, Gerald. "Classification of Presidential Elections." *Journal of Politics* 29, no. 33 (August 1967): 535–566.

Porter, Kimberly K. "Embracing the Pluralist Perspective: The Iowa Farm Bureau Federation and the McNary-Haugen Movement." *Agricultural History* 74, no. 2 (Spring 2000): 381–392.

Rodgers, Daniel T. "In Search of Progressivism." *Reviews in American History* 10, no. 4 (December 1982): 113–132.

Schwarz, Jordan A. "Al Smith in the Thirties." *New York History* 45, no. 4 (October 1964): 316–330.

Sherman, Richard B. "The Status Revolution and Massachusetts Progressive Leadership." *Political Science Quarterly* 78, no. 1 (March 1963): 59–65.

Shover, John L. "The Emergence of a Two-Party System in Republican Philadelphia, 1924–1936." *Journal of American History* 60, no. 4 (March 1974): 985–1002.

———. "Ethnicity and Religion in Philadelphia Politics, 1924–40." *American Quarterly* 25, no. 5 (December 1973): 499–515.

Sillars, Malcolm O. "Henry A. Wallace's Editorials on Agrarian Discontent, 1921–1928." *Agricultural History* 26, no. 4 (October 1952): 132–140.

Stave, Bruce M., John M. Allswang, Terrence J. McDonald, and Jon C. Teaford. "A Reassessment of the Urban Political Boss: An Exchange of Views." *History Teacher* 21, no. 3 (May 1988): 293–312.

Sternsher, Bernard. "The Emergence of the New Deal Party System: A Problem in Historical Analysis of Voter Behavior." *Journal of Interdisciplinary History* 6, no. 1 (Summer 1975): 127–149.

———. "The New Deal Party System: A Reappraisal." *Journal of Interdisciplinary History* 15, no. 1 (Summer 1984): 53–81.

Terris, Milton. "National Health Insurance in the United States: A Drama in Too Many Acts." *Journal of Public Health Policy* 20, no. 1 (1999): 13–35.

Voskuil, Walter H. "Water-Power Situation in the United States." *Journal of Land and Public Utility Economics* 1, no. 1 (January 1925): 89–101.

Wandersee, Winifred D. "'I'd Rather Pass a Law Than Organize a Union': Frances Perkins and the Reformist Approach to Organized Labor." *Labor History* 34, no. 1 (Winter 1993): 5–32.

White, John K. "Alfred E. Smith's Rhode Island Revolution: The Election of 1928." *Rhode Island History* 42, no. 4 (May 1983): 56–66.

Wilkinson, Patrick. "The Selfless and the Helpless: Maternalist Origins of the U.S. Welfare State." *Feminist Studies* 25, no. 3 (Autumn 1999): 571–597.

Books

Allen, Frederick Lewis. *Only Yesterday: An Informal History of the 1920s*. New York: Harper Perennial, 2010.

Allswang, John M. *Bosses, Machines, and Urban Voters*. Baltimore: Johns Hopkins University Press, 1977.

———. *A House for All Peoples: Ethnic Politics in Chicago, 1890–1936*. Lexington: University Press of Kentucky, 1971.

———. *The New Deal and American Politics*. New York: John Wiley and Sons, 1978.

Badger, Anthony J. *The New Deal: The Depression Years, 1933–1940*. New York: Hill and Wang, 1989.

Bernstein, Irving. *A Caring Society: The New Deal, the Worker, and the Great Depression*. Boston: Houghton Mifflin, 1985.

———. *The Lean Years: A History of the American Worker, 1920–1933*. Baltimore: Penguin, 1960.

Blewett, Mary H. *The Last Generation: Work and Life in the Textile Mills of Lowell, Massachusetts, 1910–1960.* Amherst: University of Massachusetts Press, 1990.

Blum, John Morton. *From the Morgenthau Diaries: Years of Crisis, 1928–1938.* Boston: Houghton Mifflin, 1957.

——. *The Republican Roosevelt.* New York: Atheneum, 1967.

——. *Woodrow Wilson and the Politics of Morality.* Boston: Little, Brown, 1956.

Bornet, Vaughn Davis. *Labor Politics in a Democratic Republic: Moderation, Division, and Disruption in the Presidential Election of 1928.* Washington, DC: Spartan, 1964.

Buenker, John D. *The History of Wisconsin.* Vol. 4, *The Progressive Era, 1893–1914.* Madison: State Historical Society of Wisconsin, 1998.

——. *Urban Liberalism and Progressive Reform.* New York: Norton, 1973.

Burner, David. *The Politics of Provincialism: The Democratic Party in Transition, 1918–1932.* New York: Alfred A. Knopf, 1968.

Burnham, Walter Dean. *Critical Elections and the Mainsprings of American Politics.* New York: Norton, 1970.

Cameron, Ardis. *Radicals of the Worst Sort: Laboring Women in Lawrence, Massachusetts, 1860–1912.* Urbana: University of Illinois Press, 1993.

Caro, Robert A. *The Power Broker: Robert Moses and the Fall of New York.* New York: Vintage, 1975.

Chambers, Clarke A. *Seedtime of Reform: American Social Service and Social Action, 1918–1933.* Minneapolis: University of Minnesota Press, 1963.

Cohen, Lizabeth. *Making a New Deal: Industrial Workers in Chicago, 1919–1939.* New York: Cambridge University Press, 1990.

Conkin, Paul K. *The New Deal.* Arlington Heights, IL: Harlan Davidson, 1978.

Connolly, James J. *An Elusive Unity: Urban Democracy and Machine Politics in Industrializing America.* Ithaca, NY: Cornell University Press, 2010.

——. *The Triumph of Ethnic Progressivism: Urban Political Culture in Boston, 1900–1925.* Cambridge, MA: Harvard University Press, 1998.

Cooper, John Milton, Jr. *Pivotal Decades: The United States, 1900–1920.* New York: Norton, 1990.

Cott, Nancy F. *The Grounding of Modern Feminism.* New Haven, CT: Yale University Press, 1987.

Cronon, E. David. *Black Moses: The Story of Marcus Garvey and the Universal Negro Improvement Association.* Madison: University of Wisconsin Press, 1969.

Davies, Gareth and Julian E. Zelizer. *America at the Ballot Box: Elections and Political History.* Philadelphia: University of Pennsylvania Press, 2015.

Dinneen, Joseph F. *The Purple Shamrock: The Hon. James Michael Curley of Boston.* New York: Norton, 1949.

Downey, Kirstin. *The Woman behind the New Deal: The Life of Frances Perkins, FDR's Labor Secretary and His Social Conscience.* New York: Nan A. Talese, 2009.

Edwards, Rebecca. *Angels in the Machinery: Gender in American Party Politics from the Civil War to the Progressive Era.* New York: Oxford University Press, 1997.

Eldot, Paula. *Governor Alfred E. Smith: The Politician as Reformer.* New York: Garland, 1983.

Erie, Steven P. *Rainbow's End: Irish-Americans and the Dilemmas of Urban Machine Politics, 1840–1985.* Berkeley: University of California Press, 1988.

Feld, Marjorie N. *Lillian Wald: A Biography.* Chapel Hill: University of North Carolina Press, 2008.

Ferber, Nat J. *A New American: From the Life Story of Salvatore A. Cotillo, Supreme Court Justice, State of New York.* New York: Farrar and Rinehart, 1938.

Finan, Christopher M. *Alfred E. Smith: The Happy Warrior.* New York: Hill and Wang, 2002.

Fite, Gilbert C. *George N. Peek and the Fight for Farm Parity.* Norman: University of Oklahoma Press, 1954.

Fowler, Robert Booth. *Wisconsin Votes: An Electoral History.* Madison: University of Wisconsin Press, 2008.

Freidel, Frank. *Franklin D. Roosevelt: Launching the New Deal.* Boston: Little, Brown, 1973.

Gamm, Gerald H. *The Making of New Deal Democrats: Voting Behavior and Realignment in Boston, 1920–1940.* Chicago: University of Chicago Press, 1989.

Georgianna, Daniel, with Roberta Hazen Aaronson. *The Strike of '28.* New Bedford, MA: Spinner, 1993.

Gerstle, Gary. *Working-Class Americanism: The Politics of Labor in a Textile City, 1914–1960.* New York: Cambridge University Press, 1989.

Golway, Terry. *Machine Made: Tammany Hall and the Creation of Modern American Politics.* New York: Liveright, 2014.

Goodwin, Joanne L. *Gender and the Politics of Welfare Reform: Mothers' Pensions in Chicago, 1911–1929.* Chicago: University of Chicago Press, 1997.

Gordon, Linda. *Heroes of Their Own Lives: The Politics and History of Family Violence.* New York: Penguin, 1988.

———. *Pitied but Not Entitled: Single Mothers and the History of Welfare.* Cambridge, MA: Harvard University Press, 1994.

Gosnell, Harold F. *Negro Politicians: The Rise of Negro Politics in Chicago.* Chicago: University of Chicago Press, 1935.

Graham, Otis, Jr. *An Encore for Reform: The Old Progressives and the New Deal.* New York: Oxford University Press, 1967.

Greene, Julie. *Pure and Simple Politics: The American Federation of Labor and Political Activism, 1881–1917.* New York: Cambridge University Press, 1998.

Handlin, Oscar. *Al Smith and His America.* Boston: Little, Brown, 1958.

———. *The Uprooted: The Epic Story of the Great Migrations That Made the American People.* Boston: Little, Brown, 1952.

Hapgood, Norman, and Henry Moskowitz. *Up from the City Streets: Alfred E. Smith.* New York: Grosset and Dunlap, 1927.

Hays, Samuel P. *Conservation and the Gospel of Efficiency: The Progressive Conservation Movement, 1890–1920.* Cambridge, MA: Harvard University Press, 1959.

Henderson, Thomas M. *Tammany Hall and the New Immigrants: The Progressive Years.* New York: Arno, 1976.

Higham, John. *Strangers in the Land: Patterns of American Nativism, 1860–1925.* New York: Atheneum, 1973.

Hoffman, Beatrix. *The Wages of Sickness: The Politics of Health Insurance in Progressive America.* Chapel Hill: University of North Carolina Press, 2001.

Hofstadter, Richard. *The Age of Reform: From Bryan to F.D.R.* New York: Vintage, 1955.

Huthmacher, J. Joseph. *Massachusetts People and Politics, 1919–1933: The Transition from Republican to Democratic Dominance and Its Implications*. New York: Atheneum, 1973.

——. *Senator Robert F. Wagner and the Rise of Urban Liberalism*. New York: Atheneum, 1968.

Jackson, Kenneth T. *The Ku Klux Klan in the City, 1915–1930*. New York: Oxford, 1967.

Janick, Herbert F., Jr. *A Diverse People: Connecticut, 1914 to the Present*. Chester, CT: Pequot Press, 1975.

Josephson, Matthew, and Hannah Josephson. *Al Smith: Hero of the Cities: A Political Portrait Drawing on the Papers of Frances Perkins*. Boston: Houghton Mifflin, 1969.

Kantowicz, Edward R. *Polish-American Politics in Chicago, 1888–1940*. Chicago: University of Chicago Press, 1975.

Keller, Morton. *America's Three Regimes: A New Political History*. New York: Oxford University Press, 2007.

Kennedy, John F. *Profiles in Courage*. New York: Harper, 1956.

Key, V. O. *Southern Politics in State and Nation*. New York: Alfred A. Knopf, 1949.

Klayman, Richard. *The First Jew: Prejudice and Politics in an American Community, 1900–1932*. Malden, MA: Old Suffolk Square Press, 1985.

Kloppenberg, James T. *Uncertain Victory: Social Democracy and Progressivism in European and American Thought, 1870–1920*. New York: Oxford University Press, 1986.

Koven, Seth, and Sonya Michel, eds. *Mothers of a New World: Maternalist Politics and the Origins of Welfare States*. New York: Routledge, 1993.

Ladd-Taylor, Molly. *Mother-Work: Women, Child Welfare, and the State, 1890–1930*. Urbana: University of Illinois Press, 1994.

Leuchtenburg, William E. *The FDR Years: On Roosevelt and His Legacy*. New York: Columbia University Press, 1995.

——. *Franklin D. Roosevelt and the New Deal: 1932–1940*. New York: Harper Collins, 1963.

——. *Herbert Hoover*. New York: Henry Holt, 2009.

——. *The Perils of Prosperity: 1914–32*. Chicago: University of Chicago Press, 1958.

Lichtman, Allan J. *Prejudice and the Old Politics: The Presidential Election of 1928*. Chapel Hill: University of North Carolina Press, 1979.

Link, Arthur S. *Woodrow Wilson: A Brief Biography*. Chicago: Quadrangle Books, 1972.

Link, Arthur S., and Richard L. McCormick. *Progressivism*. Wheeling, IL: Harlan Davidson, 1983.

Lowitt, Richard. *George W. Norris: The Persistence of a Progressive, 1913–1933*. Urbana: University of Illinois Press, 1971.

Lubell, Samuel. *The Future of American Politics*. Garden City, NY: Doubleday, 1951.

Luconi, Stefano. *The Italian-American Vote in Providence, Rhode Island, 1916–1948*. Cranbury, NJ: Associated University Presses, 2004.

Mann, Arthur. *La Guardia Comes to Power 1933*. Chicago: University of Chicago Press, 1965.

Martin, George. *Madam Secretary: Frances Perkins*. Boston: Houghton Mifflin, 1976.

McCartin, Joseph A. *Labor's Great War: The Struggle for Industrial Democracy and the Origins of Modern American Labor Relations, 1912–1921*. Chapel Hill: University of North Carolina Press, 1997.

McCormick, Richard L. *The Party Period and Public Policy: American Politics from the Age of Jackson to the Progressive Era*. New York: Oxford University Press, 1986.

McCoy, Donald R. *Coming of Age: The United States during the 1920's and 1930's*. New York: Penguin, 1973.

McCraw, Thomas K. *TVA and the Power Fight, 1933–1939*. Philadelphia: J. B. Lippincott, 1971.

McDonald, Terrence J. *The Parameters of Urban Fiscal Policy: Socioeconomic Change and Political Culture in San Francisco, 1860–1906*. Berkeley: University of California Press, 1986.

McGerr, Michael E. *The Decline of Popular Politics: The American North, 1865–1928*. New York: Oxford University Press, 1986.

———. *A Fierce Discontent: The Rise and Fall of the Progressive Movement in America, 1870–1920*. New York: Free Press, 2003.

McGirr, Lisa. *The War on Alcohol: Prohibition and the Rise of the American State*. New York: Norton, 2016.

McMullen, David Lee. *Strike! The Radical Insurrections of Ellen Dawson*. Gainesville: University Press of Florida, 2010.

Merton, Robert King. *Social Theory and Social Structure*. Glencoe, IL: Free Press, 1963.

Mink, Gwendolyn. *The Wages of Motherhood: Inequality and the Welfare State, 1917–1942*. Ithaca, NY: Cornell University Press, 1995.

Moore, Edmund A. *A Catholic Runs for President: The Campaign of 1928*. New York: Ronald Press, 1956.

Muncy, Robyn. *Creating a Female Dominion in American Reform: 1890–1935*. New York: Oxford University Press, 1991.

Nie, Norman H., Sidney Verba, and John R. Petrocik. *The Changing American Voter*. Cambridge, MA: Harvard University Press, 1976.

Olson, Keith W. *Biography of a Progressive: Franklin K. Lane, 1864–1921*. Westport, CT: Greenwood Press, 1979.

Orleck, Annelise. *Common Sense and a Little Fire: Women and Working-Class Politics in the United States, 1900–1965*. Chapel Hill: University of North Carolina Press, 1995.

Parker, Margaret Terrell. *Lowell: A Study of Industrial Development*. New York: Macmillan, 1940.

Parrish, Michael E. *Anxious Decades: America in Prosperity and Depression, 1920–1941*. New York: Norton, 1992.

Patterson, James T. *Congressional Conservatism and the New Deal: The Growth of the Conservative Coalition in Congress, 1933–1939*. Lexington: University Press of Kentucky, 1967.

Pegram, Thomas R. *Battling Demon Rum: The Struggle for a Dry America, 1800–1933*. Chicago: Ivan R. Dee, 1998.

———. *One Hundred Percent American: The Rebirth and Decline of the Ku Klux Klan in the 1920s*. Chicago: Ivan R. Dee, 2011.

——. *Partisans and Progressives: Private Interest and Public Policy in Illinois, 1870–1922.* Urbana: University of Illinois Press, 1992.

Perry, Elisabeth Israels. *Belle Moskowitz: Feminine Politics and the Exercise of Power in the Age of Alfred E. Smith.* Boston: Northeastern University Press, 1992.

Petrin, Ronald A. *French Canadians in Massachusetts Politics, 1885–1915: Ethnicity and Political Pragmatism.* Philadelphia: Balch Institute Press, 1990.

Petrocik, John R. *Party Coalitions: Realignment and the Decline of the New Deal Party System.* Chicago: University of Chicago Press, 1981.

Phillips, Kevin P. *The Emerging Republican Majority.* Garden City, NY: Anchor Books, 1969.

Pringle, Henry F. *Alfred E. Smith: A Critical Study.* New York: Macy-Masius, 1927.

Pusey, Merlo J. *Charles Evans Hughes.* New York: Macmillan, 1951.

Rodgers, Daniel T. *Atlantic Crossings: Social Politics in a Progressive Age.* Cambridge, MA: Belknap Press of Harvard University Press, 1998.

Rogin, Michael Paul, and John L. Shover. *Political Change in California: Critical Elections and Social Movements, 1890–1966.* Westport, CT: Greenwood Press, 1970.

Saloutos, Theodore. *The American Farmer and the New Deal.* Ames: Iowa State University Press, 1982.

Saloutos, Theodore, and John D. Hicks. *Agricultural Discontent in the Middle West, 1900–1939.* Madison: University of Wisconsin Press, 1951.

Schlesinger, Arthur M., Jr. *The Coming of the New Deal: 1933–1935.* Vol. 2 of *The Age of Roosevelt.* Boston: Houghton Mifflin, 2003.

——. *The Crisis of the Old Order: 1919–1933.* Vol. 1 of *The Age of Roosevelt.* Boston: Houghton Mifflin, 2002.

——. *The Politics of Upheaval: 1935–1936.* Vol. 3 of *The Age of Roosevelt.* Boston: Houghton Mifflin, 2003.

Schneirov, Richard. *Labor and Urban Politics: Class Conflict and the Origins of Modern Liberalism in Chicago, 1864–97.* Urbana: University of Illinois Press, 1998.

Schwarz, Jordan A. *The New Dealers: Power Politics in the Age of Roosevelt.* New York: Alfred A. Knopf, 1993.

Shlakman, Vera. *Economic History of a Factory Town: A Study of Chicopee, Massachusetts.* New York: Octagon Books, 1969.

Sitkoff, Harvard. *A New Deal for Blacks: The Emergence of Civil Rights as a National Issue: The Depression Decade.* New York: Oxford University Press, 1978.

Sklar, Kathryn Kish. *Florence Kelley and the Nation's Work: The Rise of Women's Political Culture, 1830–1900.* New Haven, CT: Yale University Press, 1995.

Skocpol, Theda. *Protecting Soldiers and Mothers: The Political Origins of Social Policy in the United States.* Cambridge, MA: Belknap Press of Harvard University Press, 1992.

Slayton, Robert A. *Empire Statesman: The Rise and Redemption of Al Smith.* New York: Free Press, 2001.

Sobel, Robert. *Coolidge: An American Enigma.* Washington, DC: Regency, 1998.

Stave, Bruce M., ed. *Urban Bosses, Machines, and Progressive Reformers.* Lexington, MA: D. C. Heath, 1972.

Sterne, Evelyn Savidge. *Ballots and Bibles: Ethnic Politics and the Catholic Church in Providence.* Ithaca, NY: Cornell University Press, 2004.

Stradling, David. *The Nature of New York: An Environmental History of the Empire State.* Ithaca, NY: Cornell University Press, 2010.

Stromquist, Shelton. *Re-inventing "the People": The Progressive Movement, the Class Problem, and the Origins of Modern Liberalism.* Urbana: University of Illinois Press, 2006.

Sundquist, James L. *Dynamics of the Party System: Alignment and Realignment of Political Parties in the United States.* Washington, DC: Brookings Institution, 1973.

Timberlake, James H. *Prohibition and the Progressive Movement, 1900–1920.* New York: Atheneum, 1970.

Valelly, Richard M. *Radicalism in the States: The Minnesota Farmer-Labor Party and the American Political Economy.* Chicago: University of Chicago Press, 1989.

Ware, Susan. *Partner and I: Molly Dewson, Feminism, and New Deal Politics.* New Haven, CT: Yale University Press, 1987.

Warner, Emily Smith, with Hawthorne Daniel. *The Happy Warrior: The Story of My Father, Alfred E. Smith.* Garden City, NY: Doubleday, 1956.

Watson, Bruce. *Bread and Roses: Mills, Migrants, and the Struggle for the American Dream.* New York: Viking, 2005.

Welch, Richard F. *King of the Bowery: Big Tim Sullivan, Tammany Hall, and New York City from the Gilded Age to the Progressive Era.* Albany: State University of New York Press, 2008.

Weller, Cecil Edward, Jr. *Joe T. Robinson: Always a Loyal Democrat.* Fayetteville: University of Arkansas Press, 1998.

Wellock, Thomas R. *Preserving the Nation: The Conservation and Environmental Movements, 1870–2000.* Wheeling, IL: Harlan Davidson, 2007.

Wesser, Robert F. *Charles Evans Hughes: Politics and Reform in New York, 1905–1910.* Ithaca, NY: Cornell University Press, 1967.

———. *A Response to Progressivism: The Democratic Party and New York Politics, 1902–1918.* New York: New York University Press, 1986.

Wiebe, Robert H. *The Search for Order, 1877–1920.* New York: Hill and Wang, 1967.

Wilson, Joan Hoff. *Herbert Hoover: Forgotten Progressive.* Boston: Little, Brown, 1975.

Winkler, Allan M. *Franklin D. Roosevelt and the Making of Modern America.* New York: Pearson, 2006.

Wolfbein, Seymour Louis. *The Decline of a Cotton Textile City: A Study of New Bedford.* New York: Columbia University Press, 1944.

Wolfskill, George. *The Revolt of the Conservatives: A History of the American Liberty League, 1934–1940.* Boston: Houghton Mifflin, 1962.

Woodward, C. Vann. *Origins of the New South, 1877–1913.* Baton Rouge: Louisiana State University Press, 1971.

Yearley, C. K. *The Money Machines: The Breakdown and Reform of Governmental and Party Finance in the North, 1860–1920.* Albany: State University of New York Press, 1970.

Zelizer, Julian E. *Governing America: The Revival of Political History.* Princeton, Princeton University Press, 2012.

Zucker, Norman L. *George W. Norris: Gentle Knight of American Democracy.* Urbana: University of Illinois Press, 1966.

Unpublished Theses and Dissertations

Chiles, Robert. "Alfred E. Smith and Transitional Progressivism: The Revolution before the New Deal." PhD diss., University of Maryland, 2012.

DeMoranville, Aaron F., Jr. "Ethnic Voting in Rhode Island." Master's thesis, Brown University, 1961.

Gordon, Lester Ira. "John McCormack and the Roosevelt Era." PhD diss., Boston University, 1976.

Sterne, Evelyn A. "Patchwork of Protest: Social Diversity and Labor Militancy in the New Bedford Strike of 1928." Master's thesis, Duke University, 1994.

Index

CPSIA information can be obtained
at www.ICGtesting.com
Printed in the USA
LVOW03*2300050318

568779LV00002B/4/P

9 781501 705502